*The UN and
Global Political Economy*

United Nations Intellectual History Project

Ahead of the Curve? UN Ideas and Global Challenges
  Louis Emmerij, Richard Jolly, and Thomas G. Weiss

Unity and Diversity in Development Ideas: Perspectives from the
UN Regional Commissions
  Edited by Yves Berthelot

Quantifying the World: UN Ideas and Statistics
  Michael Ward

UN Contributions to Development Thinking and Practice
  Richard Jolly, Louis Emmerij, Dharam Ghai, and Frédéric Lapeyre

The UN and Global Political Economy

Trade, Finance, and Development

John Toye and Richard Toye

Indiana University Press

Bloomington and Indianapolis

This book is a publication of

Indiana University Press
601 North Morton Street
Bloomington, Indiana 47404-3797 USA

http://iupress.indiana.edu

Telephone orders   800-842-6796
Fax orders   812-855-7931
Orders by e-mail   iuporder@indiana.edu

The paper used in this publication meets the minimum requirements
of American National Standard for Information Sciences—Permanence
of Paper for Printed Library Materials, ANSI Z39.48-1984.

Manufactured in the United States of America

Library of Congress Cataloging-in-Publication Data

Toye, J. F. J.
The UN and global political economy : trade, finance, and development / John Toye and
Richard Toye.
    p.   cm. — (United Nations intellectual history project)
Includes index.
    ISBN 0-253-34411-5 (cloth : alk. paper) — ISBN 0-253-21686-9 (pbk. : alk. paper)
    1. United Nations—History. 2. International economic relations—History—20th
century. I. Toye, Richard, date II. Title. III. Series.
    JZ4972.T69 2004
    337—dc22   2003025353

1 2 3 4 5 09 08 07 06 05 04

Contents

Foreword

It is surprising that there is no comprehensive history of the United Nations family of organizations. True, a few of the UN funds and specialized agencies have written or are in the process of writing their institutional histories. But this is mostly a recent endeavor and, indeed, it is no more than what should be expected of all public organizations, especially internationally accountable ones, along with enhanced efforts to organize their archives. We are all aware that institutions tend to put forward the best parts of their stories, but independent researchers should also document and analyze dispassionately institutional shortcomings as well as achievements. All this is an essential part of the record of international governance during the last half-century.

Faced with this major omission—which has substantial implications for the academic and policy literatures—we decided to undertake the task of beginning to write an *intellectual* history, that is, a history of the ideas launched or nurtured by the United Nations. Observers should not be put off by what may strike them as a puffed-up billing. The working assumption behind this effort is straightforward: ideas and concepts are a main driving force in human progress, and they arguably have been one of the most important contributions of the world organization.

The United Nations Intellectual History Project (UNIHP) was launched in 1999 as an independent research effort based in the Ralph Bunche Institute for International Studies at The Graduate Center of The City University of New York. The project also maintains a liaison office in Geneva. We are grateful for the enthusiastic backing from the Secretary-General and other staff and governments within the UN system. Generous financial support from five foundations and eight governments ensures total intellectual and financial independence. Details of this and other aspects of the project can be found at our web site: www.unhistory.org.

The work of the UN can be divided into two broad categories: economic and social development, on the one hand, and peace and security, on the other.

The UNIHP is committed to produce fourteen volumes on major themes in the first arena and a further three volumes if sufficient resources can be mobilized for the latter. All these volumes will be published in a series by Indiana University Press. In addition, the Project has also completed an oral history collection of some seventy-five lengthy interviews of persons who have played major roles in launching and nurturing UN ideas—and sometimes in hindering them! Extracts from these interviews will be published in 2004 in *UN Ideas: Voices from the Trenches and Turrets.* Authors of the Project's various volumes, including this one, have drawn on these interviews to highlight substantive points made in their texts. Full transcripts of the oral histories will be disseminated in electronic form at the end of the Project to facilitate work by other researchers and interested persons worldwide.

There is no single way to organize research and certainly not for such an ambitious project as this one. The way that we have structured this history is to select topics—ranging from trade and finance to human rights, from transnational corporations to development assistance, from gender to sustainability—to tease out the history of ideas under each of these topical headings. We have selected world-class experts for each topic, but each has been given freedom and responsibility to organize their own digging, analysis, and presentation. Guidance from ourselves as the project directors as well as from peer review groups is provided to ensure accuracy and fairness in depicting where the ideas came from, what happened to them within the UN system, and what happened afterward.

The present volume is a crucial input in understanding how trade, finance, and development have been a main arena for the North-South encounter. This volume is written by John Toye and Richard Toye—a well-known development economist with a passion for history and a bona fide economic historian, respectively, who happen to be father and son. And how clearly this professional history background that runs through the Toye family comes out in the following pages! The authors have searched through UN archives in Geneva, New York, and Santiago de Chile. They have scoured personal files of UN officials—alive and dead—in Oxford, Washington, and other places.

A large part of the study is woven around seven creative personalities who have put their stamp on the topic under consideration during the first quarter-century of the UN, thus dramatizing and personalizing the world organization's story. In many places the book reads like a passage from Sir Arthur Conan Doyle in which Sherlock Holmes and Dr. Watson are in search of who is responsible for certain ideas, good or bad, within the UN and who was the first to put them on the international agenda. This is particularly striking in connection with the famous terms-of-trade debate and the Prebisch-Singer thesis of deteriorating terms of trade for developing countries. Anxious readers may wish to flip immediately to Chapter 5 to satisfy their curiosity and learn the answer.

The study highlights the subtlety of Prebisch's import-substitution approach, correcting the crude criticism of those who have not read the work of this extraordinary personality carefully enough. But above all, the authors show how difficult it is to come up with unorthodox ideas within the context of intergovernmental organizations *and* to stand up for them in the face of internal bureaucratic politicking and external pressures.

The historical sweep is impressive—the UN's antecedents in the League of Nations are systematically reviewed, while the final chapter contains important forward-looking suggestions for changes in the Bretton Woods international financial institutions and in the World Trade Organization. Finally, and perhaps most important, trade and finance are situated within the comprehensive setting of development policies. This approach means that it is possible for readers to make interesting comparisons with other volumes in the UNIHP series—those four others already published and listed at the outset of the volume as well as those to come.

We are convinced that the UN story must be documented if it is to be better understood and appreciated.[1] As UN Secretary-General Kofi Annan kindly wrote in the "Foreword" to *Ahead of the Curve? UN Ideas and Global Challenges*: "With the publication of this first volume in the United Nations Intellectual History Project, a significant lacuna in twentieth-century scholarship and international relations begins to be filled."[2] John and Richard Toye have filled a huge gap in the historical record.

We hope that readers will enjoy this journey through time.

Louis Emmerij, Richard Jolly, and Thomas G. Weiss
New York, June 2003

Acknowledgments

During the process of researching and writing this book, we have received invaluable help from many different people and organizations. We would like to thank the directors of United Nations Intellectual History Project, Louis Emmerij, Richard Jolly, and Tom Weiss, not only for commissioning the volume, but also for much valuable help throughout the different stages of our work. We would like to offer our special thanks to Louis Emmerij, who was appointed as the "guardian angel" of our volume and who fulfilled this role most admirably—encouraging, guiding, and offering us support. The UNIHP team in New York was a great help, particularly Tatiana Carayannis, who was invariably knowledgeable and efficient, and Effie MacLachlan, who finalized the manuscript. Thanks are also due to the members of the project's International Advisory Council, who provided useful and stimulating feedback on our manuscript.

Professor Gerry Helleiner and Professor Stephany Griffith-Jones provided extensive written comments on the first eight chapters, for which we are very grateful, even though we have not invariably adopted their suggestions. Participants at the Uppsala workshop, June 2002, who reviewed those same chapters, had much to say that was useful to us. Yves Berthelot gave us valuable written criticisms at that point, some of which we have be able to address. S. Cape Kasahara of UNCTAD read carefully through draft versions of Chapters 8 to 11 and provided valuable detailed comments that saved us from many inaccuracies. Comments were also gratefully received from Dame Margaret Anstee, Mr. R. Krishnamurthi, and the late David Pollock.

We received vital assistance from many librarians and archivists. They are too numerous to mention each individually, but special thanks go to Jean-Marie Philippe and Marc Fichéra for facilitating access to the UNCTAD archive in Geneva. We are indebted to José Antonio Ocampo and the staff of ECLAC for all the assistance they rendered us during our visit to Santiago. We are, moreover, profoundly grateful to Sra. Adela Prebisch for granting us access to the papers of Dr. Raúl Prebisch, her late husband, and for her kind hospitality; and to Professor Sir Hans Singer, not only for granting us access to his papers but for generously sharing his memories with us and answering patiently our persistent questions. John Shaw, Hans Singer's biographer, and Edgar Dosman, Prebisch's biographer, both kindly sent us valuable material that is acknowledged in the endnotes.

Despite all of this input from others, some errors of fact and interpretation will no doubt remain, and for these the authors bear full responsibility. Translations of foreign-language material into English are the authors' own.

In preparing the manuscript for publication, we were greatly assisted by the meticulous copyediting of Kate Babbitt of Indiana University Press, and we wish to thank her for making this a better book.

Abbreviations

ADs	Anti-dumping duties
ASG	Assistant Secretary-General
CANEX	*Documents on Canadian External Relations*
CCF	Compensatory Financing Facility
CDF	Comprehensive Development Framework
CENIS	Center for International Studies
CEPAL	Spanish acronym for ECLA
CIAP	Inter-American Committee on the Alliance for Progress
CICT	Commission on International Commodity Trade
CIEC	Conference on International Economic Cooperation
CIFT	Committee on Invisibles and Finance Related to Trade
COMECON	Council for Mutual Economic Cooperation
CVDs	countervailing duties
DDRS	Declassified Documents Reference System
DEA	Department of Economic Affairs
DESA	Department of Economic and Social Affairs
DSM	Dispute Settlement Mechanism
ECAFE	Economic Commission for Asia and the Far East
ECE	Economic Commission for Europe
ECLA(C)	Economic Commission for Latin America (and the Caribbean)
ECOSOC	Economic and Social Council
EEC	European Economic Community

EFTA	European Free Trade Area
EIS	League of Nations Economic Intelligence Service
EPTA	Expanded Program of Technical Assistance
ESAF	Extended Structural Adjustment Facility
FAO	Food and Agriculture Organization
FBI	Federal Bureau of Investigation
FRUS	*Foreign Relations of the United States*
G10	Group of Ten
G77	Group of 77
GA	General Assembly
GAOR	*General Assembly Official Records*
GATT	General Agreement on Tariffs and Trade
GSP	Generalized System of Preferences
HUAC	House Un-American Activities Committee
IADB	Inter-American Development Bank
IA-ECOSOC	Inter-American Economic and Social Council
IBRD	International Bank for Reconstruction and Development
ICAs	international commodity agreements
ICC	International Chamber of Commerce
ICCICA	Interim Coordinating Committee for International Commodity Arrangements
IDA	International Development Association
IDD	International Development Decade
IDY	International Development Year
ILO	International Labour Organization
ILPES	Latin American Institute for Economic and Social Planning
IMF	International Monetary Fund
ISA	import-substituting agriculture
ISI	import-substituting industrialization
ITC	International Trade Commission

ITF	International Trade Files
ITO	International Trade Organization
LDCs	Less Developed Countries
LSE	London School of Economics
MFN	most favored nation
MIT	Massachusetts Institute of Technology
NARA	National Archives & Records Administration (U.S.)
NGOs	nongovernmental organizations
NIEO	New International Economic Order
NIFE	*National and International Measures for Full Employment*
OECD	Organization for Economic Cooperation and Development
OEEC	Organization for European Economic Cooperation
OPEC	Organization of Petroleum Exporting Countries
PEP	Political and Economic Planning
PRO	Public Record Office (UK)
QRs	quantitative restrictions
RG	Record Group
RIIA	Royal Institute for International Affairs
SAF	Structural Adjustment Facility
SDR	Special Drawing Right
SG	Secretary-General
SSRC	Social Sciences Research Council
SUNFED	Special United Nations Fund for Economic Development
UNCTAD	United Nations Conference on Trade and Development
UNDP	United Nations Development Programme
UNRRA	United Nations Relief and Rehabilitation Administration
UNRISD	UN Research Institute for Social Development
WER	*World Economic Report*
WIDER	World Institute for Development Economics Research
WTO	World Trade Organization

The UN and
Global Political Economy

Introduction

- **The North-South Encounter and the United Nations**
- **The Paradox of Protectionism in the UN Secretariat**
- **International Public Organizations as Intellectual Actors**
- **The North-South Encounter in Outline**
- **The Contribution of This Volume**
- **Methodology and Sources**

The North-South Encounter and the United Nations

After the Second World War, the new United Nations organization was the bearer of extravagant, even utopian, hopes for the development and maintenance of an international order that would safeguard the peoples of the world from the recurrence of the extraordinary destruction that they had just suffered. In the founding vision of faith and optimism, economic and social security was accorded an importance at least as great as, if not greater than, political and military security. The rationale for this was the acute collective consciousness of the economic disaster of the Great Depression of the 1930s and the political opportunity that it provided for the forces of fascism and militarism to gain control over large populations in Europe and Asia.

As long as this consciousness remained strong, so did the will of the member nations to cooperate in the reconstruction of the international economic order inside the framework the UN provided. This order was intended to encompass and benefit both the developed industrial countries and what were then referred to as the underdeveloped countries. However, this early period was cut short. As relations between the United States and the Soviet Union deteriorated and each marked out the boundaries of their respective spheres of influence, Cold War attitudes suffused the whole international diplomatic climate. The solidarity of the great powers who were to lead the UN organization very quickly evaporated.

Meanwhile, the intended parity of esteem within the UN between economic and military security concerns swiftly eroded. Diplomatic and military crises that potentially could have had nuclear consequences took center stage. The Security Council became the UN organ on which world attention focused, while the new Economic and Social Council became a cipher. Both councils were paralyzed by distrust and dispute and delivered little but stalemate, stagnation, and disappointment. The UN Secretary-General became wholly absorbed in the unenviable task of trying to mediate between two inflexible superpowers and was not able even to protect his own staff from the repercussions of that conflict.

Between 1947 and 1955, the United States was able to maintain overall political control of the UN through the steady two-thirds majority it could command in the General Assembly.[1] As the geopolitical situation stabilized after the death of Stalin in 1953, circumstances began to enhance the authority and legitimacy of the UN as a genuine world forum. The accelerating process of decolonization played a critical part in this. The number of countries that were members of the UN swelled as more and more underdeveloped countries, free from the restraints of colonialism, joined the organization. The UN thus developed from a Western-dominated agency into a more truly global entity.

For the United States, the accession of ex-colonial underdeveloped countries to the world body meant a gradual dilution of its ability to control and manage the organization. After 1960, the U.S. could no longer rely on being able to muster a simple majority. The newly admitted countries, which refused to align themselves with either of the two superpowers, came to hold the balance of power in the General Assembly. For these recent ex-colonies, membership in the UN was both a symbol of and a guarantee for their newfound independence. They looked to the Secretary-General to support their rights and liberties through the UN, thereby enhancing his political role and making him less purely dependent on American guidance. Dag Hammarskjöld's intervention in the Congo in 1959–1961 was the major manifestation of this new UN politics.

After Hammarskjöld's death in 1961, a typical Cold War struggle ensued between the U.S. and the Soviet Union over his successor, ending with the appointment of the first non-European UN Secretary General. U Thant was a Buddhist and socialist from Burma who had experienced colonialism at first hand and who saw the major division of the world as that between rich and poor countries rather than between capitalism and communism. He embodied a new "Third World" perspective that identified economic development as a central concern of the UN system. The term "Third World," popular in

the 1960s as a collective phrase for underdeveloped countries, linked the state
of underdevelopment negatively with the East-West Cold War conflict. Underdeveloped countries were seen as belonging neither to the capitalist nor to
the socialist system; they were not only poor but also alienated from these
two rival political economies of development.

In practice, during his ten years of office, U Thant's energies were largely
absorbed in mediating the international political and military crises of the 1960s
in Congo, Cuba, India and Pakistan, the Dominican Republic, the Middle East,
and Vietnam. Nevertheless, he gave much sympathy and moral support to the
campaigns that the new "Third World" member countries fought in the UN to
highlight what they regarded as historical injustices, to appeal for greater international solidarity, and to canvass proposals to restructure the international
economic order in their favor. These campaigns helped to revive the original
view of the founders of the UN Charter that the organization should through
its economic and social work contribute to a more peaceful world—with the
crucial difference that this objective was now being pursued on a much more
extensive scale and in much more intractable conditions.

U.S. president John F. Kennedy responded to the loss of American control
of the UN by assuming a role of moral leadership, including proposing that
the 1960s be designated a "development decade" by the UN. This raised the
prestige of the UN, even though, in terms of substantial achievements, the
decade fell short of what were always optimistic targets and exaggerated expectations. The UN had other successes to its credit, as its specialized agencies proliferated (with the setting up of the World Food Programme, the United
Nations Development Programme, the United Nations Industrial Development Organization, the United Nations University, the International Telecom-
munication Union, the International Civil Aviation Organization, the World
Maritime Organization, and so on). In the field of trade, finance, and development, the hopes of the Third World rode on the new UN Conference on
Trade and Development (UNCTAD). It provided a forum for the intergovernmental discussion and negotiation of this nexus of issues, one in which
the developing countries—now forming a political bloc and euphemistically
renamed—hoped to gain economic concessions from the West.

By the end of the 1960s, the moral leadership of the U.S. had faltered, most
obviously because of its war in Vietnam. When the Bretton Woods system
finally broke down, no new system replaced it. Within the developing countries, the producers of oil flexed their market muscle, which had unantici-
pated disruptive effects on international lending and indebtedness, accelerating
inflation and decelerating economic growth. It was in these unpropitious conditions that the developing countries as a bloc, now increasingly referred to as

"the South," renewed their campaign to persuade "the North" (the Organization for Economic Cooperation and Development [OECD] countries) to set up a New International Economic Order (NIEO) that would be more supportive of their development ambitions. They had made only piecemeal progress in this direction in the 1960s, despite the creation of UNCTAD. Focusing on the issue of better terms of trade for primary commodity producers, grandiose claims were made in the 1970s, but in the end the North-South negotiating encounter produced very little.

The North-South dialogue was effectively dead by 1981, when the Cancún summit meeting took place. The global political and ideological climate, partly in reaction to the South's demands for a NIEO but partly as a result of the Latin American debt crisis, underwent a major transformation thereafter. New conservative governments in the OECD countries were determined to restore their own economic positions regardless of the repercussions on the countries of the South. The OECD countries chose to operate through those multilateral institutions over which they could exercise effective control, such as the International Monetary Fund (IMF), the World Bank, and the new World Trade Organization (WTO). The UN therefore became more marginal than ever in the trade and development field, and the U.S. and some other developed countries used the tactic of withdrawal and withholding of contributions as a means to force cutbacks on UN functions and budgets.

The evolving phases of the UN's journey from high aspirations to a more just world order to its present reluctant acceptance of ancillary status in the field of trade, finance, and development provides the basic structure of our narrative. It is one that is well enough known, and we do not claim to have made any major revisions to it. Rather, the novelty of our contribution lies in our examination, against this broad background, of the UN as an intellectual actor in this field in order to show why its positive achievements (which were not negligible) proved insufficient to arrest the decline. To this end, we explore the problems inherent in bureaucracies' attempts to produce original research, highlighting the likely tensions between the higher management's aims and the tendency of talented intellectuals in their employ to produce truths that their managers find uncomfortable. In so doing, we look closely at the intellectual contributions to the trade and development debate made, in particular, by seven famous economists while they worked in the UN.

The Paradox of Protectionism in the UN Secretariat

During the two decades from 1945 to 1964, a small number of economists working as officials of the United Nations engineered a major shift in ideas about how international trade and finance affect economic development. In 1945, the near-unanimous view of the international community was that a return to freer trade and payments on a multilateral and nondiscriminatory basis should be the chief long-term objective of international economic policy, provided that adequate safeguards against mass unemployment were built in to the international economic arrangements. Such a course would act as a permanent antidote to war, since shared prosperity would be a reliable guarantor of peace.[2] By 1964, a powerful challenge to this orthodoxy had been mounted by economists operating within the UN Secretariat, although it had been established to implement the orthodox view. These few economists, who were almost all radicals of some shape or form, had deployed arguments suggesting the existence of systematic economic forces that diminished the benefits that underdeveloped countries gained from trade and from foreign investment. They had also designed a package of interventionist measures that constituted "a new trade policy for development" and rallied support for a new international organization to put them into effect.[3] This book examines the causes and the consequences of this historic shift in economic and political opinion.

The paradox of a twenty-year revolt against free trade orthodoxy by economists inside the United Nations is partially explained by two remarkable changes in the global landscape of political power that occurred during the two decades after the Second World War. One was the start of the "Cold War" between the United States and its allies and the Soviet Union and its allies, while the other was the decision of European countries to grant independent statehood to their former colonies, partly as a consequence of U.S. pressure. These two profound currents were mediated by the UN system's rule of majority voting.[4] They created a momentum in favor of paying much more attention in international forums to the aspirations of the new leaders of poor, less-developed countries than had ever previously been paid. At the same time, the hopes placed by these leaders in the postwar international economic settlement were being severely disappointed. The generosity of U.S. Marshall Plan aid was to be confined to Europe. The laboriously negotiated International Trade Organization (ITO), whose constitution reflected at least some of the trade and development concerns of the underdeveloped countries, never came into being. The General Agreement on Tariffs and Trade (GATT)—a transitional entity that came to substitute partially for the ITO—concentrated its efforts throughout the 1950s on reducing tariffs on industrial goods, an issue of limited importance to the many underdeveloped countries that had yet to industrialize.

It would be too simple, however, to say that the growth of neoprotectionism in the UN Secretariat merely reflected great geopolitical upheavals taking place elsewhere or the limited horizons of U.S. government trade policies. That would be to separate illegitimately events from the matrix of ideas in which they are formed (as if events could occur mindlessly) and to decree arbitrarily that the line of causation can run only from events to ideas. The truth is more complex. It is not just that the new protectionist arguments were a product of the Cold War, decolonization, and the narrow front on which freer trade was advancing. It is equally true that these ideas modified the terms of super-power competition with respect to economic development, influenced the attitudes of postcolonial regimes, and widened the scope of international trade and finance policies. This volume is the story of how radical economists in the UN created the intellectual manifestations of contemporary global politi-cal changes. It is also about how they collectively, within the UN Secretariat, animated the UN member states to take up new positions by setting agendas and mediating interest-group alliances and thereby helped to shape the ways in which future events unfolded.[5]

The interdependence of international trade, finance, and development is the subject matter of the intellectual history with which we shall be concerned. The focus of the story will therefore not be on the entire UN system but on those parts of it that have responsibilities in our field of interest and even then only on those parts of the organization in which the economic radicals made the most significant intellectual contributions. So we do not deal with most of the UN's specialized agencies, funds, and other UN organizations but only with the economic and social departments of the UN Secretariat, espe-cially, but not only, in its relations with the IMF and the World Bank. The spotlight will be on the Department of Economic Affairs (DEA) (later re-named the Department for Economic and Social Affairs [DESA]) in New York and, after 1964, on UNCTAD in Geneva. Among the UN regional commis-sions, the Economic Commission for Latin America (later, and the Carib-bean) (ECLA/ECLAC)[6] in Santiago de Chile will occupy center stage.

International Public Organizations as Intellectual Actors

That international public organizations aspire to be intellectual actors is startling. The role of an international bureaucracy may extend to the collec-tion and dissemination of available knowledge if this helps it in the discharge of its functional responsibilities. That the production of novel ideas should be one of its functions would come to most people as a surprise. It could well be interpreted as going into competition with universities, institutes, think tanks, and consultancy firms but doing so without having the necessary ad-vantages of human and physical infrastructure or, perhaps more important, in terms of the structure of institutional incentives. "Universities and think-tanks can out-perform the UN in research," according to Michael Edwards, because they are "without the combination of high costs and low levels of innovation that characterises organisations lacking both market discipline and social pressures to reform."[7]

Admittedly, knowledge is a public good, and the market, if left to itself, will tend to supply too little of it to achieve maximum welfare. The force of this argument is to justify public intervention to boost investment in new knowledge. However, it does not entail that the new knowledge must be produced in a public-sector institution. Underinvestment by individuals in health and education is not a sufficient justification for setting up state schools and hospitals, because a better outcome might result from giving private schools and private hospitals a public subsidy. Similarly, if knowledge is undersupplied, it might be better for public-sector institutions to subsidize its private production rather than to produce it themselves.

Some international public institutions have, nevertheless, wanted to be intellectual actors rather than just investors in the production of knowledge. In the field of economic and social development, perhaps the foremost current example of this ambition is that of the World Bank. It is the rise of the World Bank to its current position of contested intellectual dominance in the development field that has provoked renewed interest in exploring the intellectual contribution that was made by the United Nations. This way of putting the comparison acknowledges the de facto separation of the bank and the fund from the UN, which took place in 1946–1947, although the bank's pursuit of intellectual dominance has developed only during the last twenty-five years. The economic justification advanced for it is that only by producing knowledge in house can its benefits for the bank's functional operations—such as its loan projects—be secured.[8] Partly, it is argued, this is a matter of the bank's being able to ensure that outside researchers undertake the research agenda that the bank wants them to undertake. Partly it is that, in the absence of in-house champions of specific pieces of research, potentially useful research will not get noticed and will not in fact be used. While there is doubtless merit in these arguments, they look only to the advantages of doing research in house, and these advantages always need to be balanced against the potential difficulties.

What then are the drawbacks? For the answer to this, one must turn from the economics of public goods to the sociology of bureaucracy. Weber argued that modern bureaucratic organizations would increasingly replace patrimonial ones. He claimed that they are formally the most rational means of exercising control over human beings, because their goals are set by their sponsors and are implemented by bureaucrats who remain politically neutral. In making this claim for the efficiency of modern bureaucracy, Weber simply assumed that bureaucrats' assigned formal roles are always congruent with their actual motives and orientations. However, this is not necessarily so: officials may don their organizational masks, but they do not easily or frequently become them.[9] Weber's ideal type needs to be modified to take account of the fact that people inside bureaucracies can rebel against the machine-like expectations of formal rationality.[10] Experience forces us to confront the fact that "defiant bureaucrats" exist, who "engage in behavior that is from the perspective of organizational goals and procedures irrational and dysfunctional."[11]

A modified Weberian theory of bureaucracy asserts that inside all public organizations, authority stands in potential tension with power. Authority is hierarchical and is formally delegated from the pinnacle of the executive secretary (or other like role) downward in a very precise manner. Power—the ability to make others do as one requires—may be distributed differently. It will be exercised from above only to the extent that those in authority at the top have the resources of power—personal leadership skills, access to information, incentives, and sanctions—with which to motivate, control, and appropriate the efforts of those below them in the hierarchy. This potential tension sets the scene for the outbreak of power struggles between superiors and subordinates, as the former seek to conjure up from the latter the activity that will support the goals of the organization (that is, those of its sponsors) and as from time to time they meet resistance.[12] Maintaining the congruence of power with authority is a quite onerous task that heads of bureaucracies often fail to perform.

This is especially so in international bureaucracies. Here control by sponsors is weaker because the conflicting interests of the multitude of sponsors permanently dilute it. This is partly a matter of a lesser ability to determine clear and consistent objectives. It is also because divergent interests of sponsors can reduce the resources of power available to those in high authority in international organizations; requirements of geographical balance in recruitment or the diplomatic consequences of disciplining officials of particular nationalities deplete the normal armory of sanctions for officials engaging in dysfunctional behavior.

Within an international bureaucracy, the in-house research function presents a special case. Intellectual originality and creativity are achievements that, almost by definition, cannot be commanded, sometimes not even by their authors. Original research, when produced, also has the potential to be dissonant with the objectives that a bureaucracy and its sponsors are seeking to fulfill. Therefore its authors, because of the peculiar nature of their specialized expertise, run a particularly large risk of becoming "defiant" bureaucrats in the course of defending their research procedures and results. The political neutrality required of a Weberian bureaucrat is at odds with the intellectual disinterestedness that must discipline the good researcher. Researchers need to be disinterested in their results—not uninterested, but disinterested. Ideally, they should have no personal stake in the results of their enquiries. It should not matter to them whether trade liberalization does or does not stimulate economic growth or whether commodity prices are set to rise or fall.[13] When the organization that employs researchers aims to persuade external agents of the truth of certain propositions, this threatens to damage the integrity and quality of their work. Thus in-house intellectual activity will be constantly in danger of being to some degree distorted by managers' success in imposing their organizational goals.

Even if to a lesser degree than national bureaucracies, international bureaucracies still wield some incentives and sanctions. Officials who are researchers resemble their colleagues in that all are wholly dependent on their organization's managers for their material rewards, so they may face disincentives to coming up with results that top managers find unhelpful to their goals even if the results that they produce are intellectually sound. Similarly, they may face incentives to certify propositions as valid knowledge, even if they are not, when their top managers find it helpful to their goals that that be done. The independence that is the only safeguard for intellectual honesty will be lacking when the internal power struggle favors the top management.

The significance of this drawback is amplified as we recognize that international public institutions do indeed at times identify with and defend certain doctrines. They are often required to do so by the governments that are their members and their main financial sponsors. The World Bank, for example, began by merely defending the doctrine of sound finance and had little use for its few economists.[14] Even this limited engagement with doctrine required some editorial control. An early example of the urge to control occurred in 1955, when the bank held up the publication of Jan Tinbergen's *The Design of Development* for three years because the Bank's president at the time objected to Tinbergen's support for a mixed private and public economy.[15] In the 1980s, however, the bank formulated a stronger and more elaborated doctrinal stance at the behest of the U.S., Germany, and Britain, whose governments favored the spread of economic policies that became characterized as the "Washington Consensus."[16] This consensus set up the doctrinal boundaries that had to be defended by the bank.

The defense of an organization's core doctrines can be managed in several different ways. One is to design the research agenda in a way likely to support the consensus—for example, by not devoting resources to researching topics that are regarded as marginal or potentially antagonistic to it. Another is for top managers to vet carefully high-profile research output and to edit out unwanted messages.[17] Another is the self-censorship of the researchers, who can usually guess where the limits of acceptability lie. Even when top managers try to avoid shooting the messengers that bear bad, but accurate, tidings, not every staff member will venture to put that restraint to the test.

In these circumstances, it is not surprising that when the World Bank's role as an intellectual actor was evaluated, little evidence was found for the originality of the ideas emanating from it. Even in the area of economics that concerns its own operations most closely, namely the economic appraisal of projects, the bank did not pioneer new methods.[18] However, despite failure to originate key ideas or methods in development economics, the bank's power to propagate ideas is well attested in the media and in university graduate-level syllabi. The bank has also become "the single most important external source of ideas and advice to developing-country policymakers."[19] The example of the World Bank seems to show that international public organizations can become powerful propagators of ideas if they invest sufficiently in the mechanisms of intellectual propagation. Yet it is almost impossible for them, especially when those in high authority in the organization can command the resources of power, also to operate successfully as creative intellectual actors.

The North-South Encounter in Outline

In Chapter 1, we chart the first intellectual stirrings of the North-South encounter. These can be found as early as the 1940s, particularly during the course of the series of international conferences that paved the way to the agreement for an International Trade Organization. In these debates, the representatives of the underdeveloped countries expressed the view that freeing the forces of the market would not bring about the economic changes to which they aspired. The problem they sought to define was not merely one of market failure in the economist's usual sense of that term. Rather, they believed in the existence of economic forces that, by reinforcing the existing division of labor between their countries and the industrial world, would condemn them to a permanently inferior economic status.[20]

As member governments debated this issue, the UN Secretariat was establishing its program of economic research. In Chapter 2, we introduce the seven economists whose contributions while in UN service provided the main intellectual substance of the South's point of view. They are Michal Kalecki, Nicholas Kaldor, Sidney Dell, Hans Singer, Raúl Prebisch, Celso Furtado, and Juan Vazquez Noyola. Their previous careers and their motives for joining the UN are examined. Drawing on the modified Weberian theory of bureaucracy discussed in the previous section, we then explore the particular difficulties in managing in-house economic research in the UN Secretariat, contrasting its experience with that of the League of Nations.

The difficulties of UN research management are then illustrated in Chapter 3 by the sobering tale of Michal Kalecki's UN career. Kalecki is often presented as a victim of Senator McCarthy's anti-communist crusade and its targeting of the UN. The reality turns out to be more complicated. Although Kalecki was adversely affected by the stress of working through that poisonous and demoralizing period, his resignation has to be seen as a response to top officials' efforts to improve the coherence and usefulness of a key UN research publication, the *World Economic Report*. Apart from this editorial power struggle, Kalecki was involved in various other assertions of his independence, as a result of which he promoted unorthodox ideas. He was very much the typical defiant bureaucrat of the revised Weberian theory.

Chapter 4 continues the theme of management efforts to control contentious researchers. In the early years, UN Secretariat proposals were aimed at the maintenance of full employment, but the new national and international measures proposed by Nicholas Kaldor for this purpose never commanded American support. After 1953, Dag Hammarskjöld, the new Secretary-General, sought to steer the UN away from what was referred to as "extreme Keynesianism." By the mid-1950s, the less-contentious goal of "economic development" had emerged as a central focus of UN interest and efforts. This shift of focus brought with it new instruments of technical assistance, pre-investment planning, and food aid as novel forms of multilateral endeavor. Even with these additional types of international assistance, however, what the UN could do to accelerate economic development within the resources at its disposal was extremely limited. The problem, as perceived by the underdeveloped countries, of the legitimacy of existing multilateral arrangements in a world of unequal development therefore persisted.

The fear that underdeveloped countries would be condemned to a permanently inferior economic status was reinforced by Hans Singer's thesis of secular decline in the terms of trade for primary commodities, examined in Chapter 5. Again, we show how senior UN officials tried to distance the organization from this radical message after Raúl Prebisch repeated it *con brio* in Latin America. Prebisch, however, was less radical than the other six economists whose contributions we consider. Although Latin American countries invested much hope in inducing economic development by means of import-substituting industrialization (ISI), Prebisch tried to educate them about its limitations. This depiction of Prebisch, which runs contrary to conventional wisdom, will be explained and justified in Chapter 6, which also contrasts his orthodox view of inflation with the structuralist theory of Juan Vazquez Noyola.

In the early 1960s, the election of President Kennedy precipitated a new series of American-led global initiatives, which are analyzed in Chapter 7. They took their ideological inspiration from the anti-communist modernization theory of Walt W. Rostow. Their culmination, however, was a campaign by a surprisingly united developing world that the U.S. proved unable to resist. The campaign was for a major addition to the machinery of international economic cooperation, which came into being in the form of UNCTAD. UNCTAD was intended to pioneer specific new policies of international cooperation in the field of trade and development, policies that were firmly based on an acknowledgment of the economic and political inequality of nations. The story of its inception is told in Chapter 8.

The first two-thirds of our narrative, then, is in effect a pre-history of UNCTAD, taking the story from the abortive negotiations for an International Trade Organization forward to the first UNCTAD conference in 1964. The final third of the book is devoted to the intellectual consequences of the decision to set up a UN institution to act on behalf of the developing countries. Under the leadership of Prebisch (1964–1968) and Manuel Pérez-Guerrero (1969–1974), the UNCTAD Secretariat had to preach a doctrine that supported a series of demands by developing countries—for international commodity agreements, a generalized system of trade preferences, and a world monetary order that improved financial assistance for development. In this context the generation of new ideas faltered, and the Group of 77 developing countries failed to set up its own think tank on similar lines to the OECD. During Gamani Corea's campaign for a Common Fund for commodity stabilization schemes, the intellectual impoverishment of UNCTAD was cruelly exposed. Our account of these developments is in Chapters 9 and 10.

The final two chapters of the book bring the story up to date and then look to the future. Chapter 11 explains how the Latin American debt crisis of the 1980s gave the conservative governments of leading industrial nations the opportunity to pressure developing countries to adopt what they called sensible economic policies and how those policies came to be defined. It also tells how UNCTAD was maneuvered into an ancillary role to the World Trade Organization in the 1990s. The lessons that we draw for the future are set out in Chapter 12. In brief, they are that for the time being the developing countries must make the best of a twin-track approach to global governance in which responsibility for implementation rests not with the UN but with the multilateral agencies that the main providers of funds are willing to trust. At the same time, these agencies need to be reformed in a multitude of ways to meet the evolving needs of developed and developing countries alike.

The Contribution of This Volume

We hope that we have succeeded in doing two important things. The first of these is corrective in intent. The American mania for recording allows us to recover U.S. trade negotiators' arrogant attitudes toward, and casual dismissal of, the developing countries' views on trade policy during the early years of the GATT.[21] The bias is absolutely explicit there, but it permeates more subtly much other writing on international economic relations. For our part, we have tried to redress this bias by treating seriously the developing countries' view that differences in the level of economic development are relevant to the obligations that countries should be asked to assume in international trade and financial relations. In principle, this is a perfectly respectable argument, although how to apply it in practice is inevitably contestable. Those who promoted it in the 1940s and 1950s made a genuine creative contribution to economic thinking that needs to be recovered and celebrated.

Our second objective has been constructive in intent. In our attempt to elucidate the conditions for intellectual creativity in the field of economics within the UN, we have found it helpful to regard the UN in comparative perspective as one case among several of the general phenomenon of international public bureaucracy. By seeing bureaucracy as an arena in which authority and power potentially conflict, we are able to uncover the internal tensions that inhibit the flourishing of good in-house research and critical thinking in all such agencies, including the UN. These tensions are expressed through struggles over recruitment of researchers, editorial control, and rules of publication, struggles that those in the highest authority do not necessarily win.

This understanding has helped us to explain why the UN, like the World Bank, has usually acted as a disseminator, or transmission belt, rather than a creator of ideas. It illuminates why the seven economists who were creative contributors of ideas were so often seen as mavericks inside the UN as well as outside it. It has allowed us to resolve the paradox of "UN economists" being renowned for their protectionist sympathies. The UN, we argue, like all international bureaucracies, has two aspects that do not always, or perhaps even usually, overlap—its official face expresses what its sponsors wish it to express, and its actual face, which is much more variegated, shows the somewhat chaotic interaction of those who participate in it.

An awareness of this double nature of a bureaucracy is useful in clarifying the conditions in which the interests of the developing countries could be articulated successfully in the UN. It highlights particularly the increasing difficulties that the South faced over time. One was associated with the transition after the first UNCTAD conference from relying on research findings independently generated to "preaching a doctrine" that was institutionally determined. Another was the shift in the locus of activity from the periphery to the center, from regional to global, from ECLA to UNCTAD—in short, from less to greater international political visibility.

In the end, we hope that we have raised the debate about the intellectual contribution of the UN beyond the level of "for and against." For those deeply imbued with the original idealism of the founders of the United Nations, it is tempting to assume that the UN has acted as a fertile source of new economic and social ideas. However, those with a more cynical turn of mind, which is often described by them as realism, will be tempted to assume the opposite— that economic and social ideas emerging from the UN will come to nothing unless they are in conformity with the interests of the U.S. government or of the governments of the main industrial countries, which will determine what actually comes to pass in the contemporary world. We assert that neither of these alternative hypotheses is sophisticated enough to do justice to reality. Our historical work, guided by the modified Weberian view of bureaucracy, has demonstrated that the UN, because it is not a monolithic entity, cannot sensibly be embraced wholeheartedly or dismissed out of hand. Like all such institutions, it has to be appraised in a multitude of different dimensions.

Methodology and Sources

This is a work of intellectual history. Intellectual history is like any other history in that it constructs from relics of the past a chronological narrative of change. It is different from any other history in that its subject matter is the evolution of ideas. Intellectual history is concerned in the first instance with intellectual actors—that is, individuals or groups of people who express their beliefs in text form—and with the meaning of those texts both for the authors themselves and for their contemporaries. Intellectual historians for many years treated famous texts—ancient and modern—as a timeless, universal corpus of "works of genius." In reaction against this neglect of time and space, it was then argued that to recover the meaning of beliefs from historical texts, the linguistic conventions of the time of writing must first be established.[22]

The view that intellectual history is about nothing more than reinterpreting classic texts is far too narrow to encompass the intellectual history of a modern international organization such as the UN.[23] When the objects of intellectual history are widened downward and outward beyond the stratospheric few, and as we move closer to modern times, this narrow view has to be modified and expanded. Some of the economic and social ideas generated within the United Nations, scattered in UN reports, regular publications, and so on, have become minor classics of international economics, development economics, and international political economy. Part of our task is to offer an interpretation of them and to say what we think they meant to their authors and their contemporaries.[24]

Yet in many ways, the elucidation of their meanings is the least demanding part of our task. The conventions of discourse have changed little in the last fifty years, so that meanings in our documentary evidence remain highly transparent. This transparency does not imply that authors have been correctly interpreted, only that misinterpretation when it has arisen has derived principally from failure to pay sufficient attention to the text. In our work, seeking to understand and explain the organizational context of documents has been a more central and challenging preoccupation than seeking to understand their linguistic or ideological conventions.

It is for this reason, then, that we have placed a good deal of reliance on archival material. This has been preserved (and catalogued) inconsistently across the UN system. For example, in the central UN archive in New York, the decision was taken to preserve only selected types of records—interoffice letters and memoranda—but these are catalogued and readily accessible. In contrast, UNCTAD in Geneva has kept quantities of material so large that the ongoing cataloguing process looks set to be long and drawn out. This naturally presents a problem for researchers—yet it is certainly not one of shortage of archival sources, except in the case of ECLA, where no records before 1970 have survived. However, to develop a full picture of the UN's activities, these sources need to be complemented by the records of national governments and collections of private papers.

Yet here we encounter a deep structural bias. Preserving historical material consumes current resources. Developed countries can afford better facilities for generating and preserving documentation. Developed countries also have much larger historical communities than do the underdeveloped; they produce far more academic books, they have better archive services, and they are far more likely to produce published series of historical documents such as *Foreign Relations of the United States* (*FRUS*). Their national records and private papers can therefore be drawn on more abundantly. Readers will note that with key exceptions such as the Raúl Prebisch papers, our non-UN archival sources are mainly from the U.S. and the UK.

What are the effects of this? On the one hand, the discreditable secrets of these countries are likely to be preserved for posterity alongside the records of their more creditable actions. On the other hand, our unavoidable dependence on developed-country sources may have the insidious effect of reinforcing the worldview of the developed countries at the expense of that of the

developing countries. Fortunately, this tendency can be counteracted to some
degree through the use of oral history. As is well established—and as some
interviewees attest—this is not a method that can be relied upon to establish
the minutiae of distant events with any sure degree of accuracy.[25] Nevertheless, if treated with the necessary caution, the evidence gathered can be valuable, allowing us to recover the perspective of individuals who may have been
marginalized in the archival record and thus in mainstream historiography. It
establishes indispensable biographical detail on the background and motivation of those who served the UN in a whole range of different capacities.

Oral history also taps in to a great reservoir of informed opinion on the
origins and impacts of ideas that animated the UN's debates on trade, finance,
and development. Moreover, taken cumulatively, these testimonies create a
picture of the interaction between leading figures in the evolution of ideas
cultivated within the UN and of their different relationships with the organizational framework that encouraged or constrained them. The story to which
they contribute, although by no means one of unqualified success for the UN,
forms a salutary reminder of the continuing importance of the values of international economic order and justice for which they strove.[26]

1

The UN Trade and Development Debates of the 1940s

- **The Pursuit of Multilateralism**
- **The Lessons of the Interwar Years**
- **Planning for the United Nations**
- **An International Commercial Union**
- **A UN Economic and Social Council**
- **The Idea of Underdevelopment**
- **Initial Dissent by Developing Countries**
- **Emerging Issues of Trade and Employment**
- **G. C. S. Corea on Protection**
- **Continuing Controversy on the Right to Protect**
- **Prebisch's Later View of the 1940s Debate**
- **Conclusion**

The Pursuit of Multilateralism

In June 1942, U.S. vice president Henry A. Wallace sat next to Soviet foreign minister Vyacheslav Molotov at a reception at the Soviet embassy in Washington. The conversation turned to postwar problems. Molotov, Wallace recorded, "realizes that Russia cannot have the enduring peace which she requires to develop her territory unless there is economic justice elsewhere in the world." Wallace, for his part, "thought one of the great problems of the postwar world was to bring about a rapid industrialization and improvement in nutrition in India, China, Siberia and Latin America." Molotov "agreed completely and felt that there was a 50- or a 100-year job in developing these areas and that the job should be done by the United Nations together. No one nation could do it by itself. . . . He was very enthusiastic about the way in which the United Nations could cooperate to develop the so-called backward areas of the world which have not yet been industrialized."[1] Although it is possible to question Molotov's sincerity, and Wallace's realism, this talk was illustrative of some conceptions which were widely held at the time—that the establishment of economic order and justice was a precondition of peace and that the United Nations could help achieve this by promoting economic development. These conceptions in due course had a vital impact upon the form of the UN Charter, which was agreed upon at the San Francisco conference in 1945.[2] What, then, were the intellectual bases for these suppositions? How did they influence the creation of the UN and its specialized agencies? And what consequences did they have for the UN's approaches to trade, finance, and development questions in the first crucial years of its existence?

The economic aspects of the UN system as it was designed were, with important caveats, broadly based on an American blueprint (albeit with significant British input). The central principle behind this blueprint was that just as collective action was necessary to maintain security in the military sphere, so nations needed to work together to solve the international economic, social, and humanitarian problems which themselves tended to undermine world peace.[3] The fundamental causes of these problems, it was believed, could be eradicated by the creation of a world economy based on multilateral nondiscriminatory trade and payments regimes. This in turn would facilitate a high degree of international economic specialization, unleashing forces that would help develop "backward" countries, thus increasing the prosperity both of the world as a whole and of all its constituent national parts.[4] However, American postwar planners' concomitant belief in *procedural* multilateralism—that is, that the form and purposes of multilateral institutions should be arrived at by international negotiation between prospective member countries—also had the potential to undermine the implementation of these principles. In other words, the processes of negotiation might force the United States into compromises, which subverted the purposes for which she had entered negotiations in the first place.[5]

This chapter will suggest that such compromises did in fact take place. First, it will examine the thinking that lay behind American and Allied planning for the United Nations and the extent to which this thinking was reflected (and/or modified) in the eventual UN Charter. Second, it will investigate the ways in which, in the immediate postwar years, these precepts were, to differing degrees, perpetuated and challenged within UN fora, in particular during the trade negotiations conducted at Geneva and Havana in 1947–1948. In so doing, it will address the question of whether or not the proposed moves toward freer trade on a nondiscriminatory basis were consistent with the aspirations of poor agricultural countries to economic development. It will be argued that procedural multilateralism under UN auspices did permit under-developed countries to challenge, with a degree of success, the dominant affirmative response to this question. This was a harbinger of further intellec-tual challenges to economic orthodoxy that would subsequently emerge from UN bodies, most notably ECLA, UNCTAD, and the UN Department of Eco-nomic Affairs (DEA). Accordingly, the chapter will conclude by examining the interpretation Raúl Prebisch placed upon these immediate postwar develop-ments in his report to the first UNCTAD conference. For the rejection of the economic universalism he and others perceived as inherent in the postwar in-ternational settlement provided an intellectual basis for the radical develop-ments of the 1960s and 1970s and this explicit critique of the postwar "system" helped stimulate aspirations toward a "New International Economic Order."

The Lessons of the Interwar Years

The Japanese attack on Pearl Harbor on 7 December 1941 facilitated the end of U.S. isolationism in economic relations as well as in foreign policy. The alternative universalist policy of international economic cooperation, which consequently gained such a boost, was predicated on an analysis of the per-ceived failures of isolationism in the interwar years. America had erred, not only through nonparticipation in the League of Nations, the UN's predeces-sor, but through "economic nationalism," manifested through its high tariff policy. This had contributed, in the words of Edward Stettinius (U.S. secre-tary of state from November 1944 to July 1945), to a vicious circle of isolation-ism and economic depression, culminating in war. U.S. participation in the economic and social activities of a new world organization would create an opportunity to break this cycle "once and for all."[6] Although such an analysis required there to be a national psychological shock such as Pearl Harbor be-fore it could become the dominant discourse, its roots were significantly older, dating back at least until the First World War.

That war was, of course, highly disruptive of the established patterns of world trade. On 8 July 1916, Democratic congressman Cordell Hull argued in the House of Representatives that the president of the United States should call an inter-national trade conference, to be held in Washington at the close of the war, for the purposes of establishing "a permanent international trade congress." (Later, in 1925, he used the term "International Trade Organization.") As he recalled in his memoirs, Hull had come to the conclusion that "unhampered trade dove-tailed with peace; high tariffs, trade barriers, and unfair economic competition, with war." The proposed trade congress, he told the House, should therefore consider "all international trade methods, practices, and policies which in their effects are calculated to create destructive commercial controversies or bitter economic wars, and to formulate agreements with respect thereto, designed to eliminate and avoid the injurious results and dangerous possibilities of economic warfare, and to promote fair and friendly trade relations among all the nations of the world." Hull appears to have influenced President Woodrow Wilson, with whom he discussed his ideas.[7] Wilson's Fourteen Points, the president's agenda for a peace settlement, included, third on the list, "the removal, so far as possible, of all economic barriers and the establishment of an equality of trade conditions among all the nations consenting to the peace and associating themselves for its maintenance."[8] The clear implication here was that freer trade was a precondition of the maintenance of peace, and this would later be an underlying assumption in American planning for the United Nations.

The eventual World War I peace settlement did not live up to the idealism that the Fourteen Points expressed. The Paris Peace Conference did not deal with economic questions except insofar as the victorious powers aimed at extracting reparations from Germany. The perception of the harshness of the terms was crystallized in the public mind by John Maynard Keynes's *The Economic Consequences of the Peace* (1919). Keynes wrote his book chiefly with an English and American audience in mind. He argued that by aiming at the economic subjection of Germany and making no provision for economic reconstruction, the Treaty of Versailles ignored the need for social and economic peace and would "sow the decay of the whole civilised life of Europe." Moreover, one of the positive remedies that he advanced to help "repair the mischief" was the establishment of a "free trade union" under the auspices of the League of Nations. Countries adhering to it would undertake "to impose no protectionist tariffs whatever against the produce of other members of the union."[9] (Arguably, like Hull's proposed trade congress/organization, this idea was a precursor of the International Trade Organization proposed in the 1940s, although Keynes's own ideas on trade did not remain consistent over the decades.) Whether or not U.S. policymakers during World War II were directly influenced by Keynes's ideas, there was certainly a tendency to endorse the tenor of his arguments. As Vice President Wallace argued, "The seeds of the present world upheaval were sown in the faulty economic decisions that followed the war of a generation ago. The vast sums of reparations imposed on Germany . . . were an indigestible lump in Europe's financial stomach."[10]

Another perceived post–World War I error was the U.S. Congress's refusal to allow American participation in the League of Nations. Nevertheless, in spite of this refusal, the United States did, in the interwar years, gradually come to associate itself with many of the League's economic activities (which included attempts to reduce trade restrictions).[11] These activities, considered as a whole, were perceived by British and American contemporaries as a success, at least by comparison with the League's political failures. The International Labour Organization (ILO) in particular was singled out for praise (even though the U.S. had a poor record of ratifying ILO conventions).[12] Although financed from the League's budget, the ILO had in practice won for itself almost total independence, and the USA had joined, although it was not a member of the League. The ILO's raison d'être was to promote better labor standards throughout the world, and, by so doing, to prevent nations and employers from competing unfairly by imposing poor conditions of work.[13] Preparations for the ILO's inception had been well advanced before 1914—that is to say, there was a "felt need" for it independent of the post–World War I peacemaking process—and it continued to exist when the League itself became defunct. As Evan Luard has argued, it to some extent became a model for the future. Its success within its field encouraged the notion of establishing similar specialized agencies in other fields; and the benefits that were believed to have derived from its de facto independence encouraged the idea that such agencies, if created, should similarly be allowed a wide measure of autonomy.[14] Intellectual beliefs about the failures and successes of the interwar period were thus reflected in Allied planning for postwar reconstruction.[15]

Planning for the United Nations

That planning process began in earnest in America in the aftermath of Pearl Harbor. Moreover, on 1 January 1942, the "Declaration by United Nations" was issued, signed by twenty-six countries pledged to defeat Nazism. The countries also subscribed to the principles laid down in the Anglo-American "Atlantic Charter" of 14 August 1941, which included the aim of "the fullest collaboration between all nations in the economic field with the object of assuring, for all, improved labour standards, economic development and social security."[16] (Churchill was quick to stress, though, that the Charter did not apply to India.[17]) For the next three years, the term "United Nations" would have a double meaning, denoting both the countries participating in the existing military alliance and a putative international organization with the purpose of establishing economic, as well as military, collective security. But how was such security to be achieved? One key proposal was initiated by Keynes, now an advisor to the British Treasury.

Under Article VII of the Anglo-American Mutual Aid Agreement, which was signed in February 1942, the United States was entitled to "consideration" from Britain in return for lend-lease aid. This took the form of a commitment to "the elimination of all forms of discriminatory treatment in international commerce, and to the reduction of tariffs and other trade barriers."[18] In order to make progress toward meeting this obligation, the British Treasury adopted Keynes's plan for an international clearing union, which he had first mooted (in the form of an "international currency union") in September 1941. The plan went through many drafts before emerging as a government white paper in April 1943.[19] Its purpose was to create balance-of-payments equilibrium between all nations without poorer countries having to undertake internal deflationary policies in order to achieve this.

An important aspect of Keynes's scheme was that it could, he hoped, be used to finance an international buffer-stock scheme to stabilize the prices of important primary commodities. His aim was to reduce short-term price fluctuations without disturbing longer-term price trends while maintaining a roughly constant reserve.[20] In 1938, when he had first addressed this question, he had argued in favor of short-period stabilization of commodity prices, as "assuredly nothing can be more inefficient than the present system by which the price is always too high or too low and there are frequent meaningless fluctuations in the plant and labour force employed." Yet he felt that "attempts at the long-period stabilisation of individual prices" should be viewed with suspicion.[21] As he put it in 1942, the purpose of the scheme was "to ensure that the necessary changes in the scale and distribution of output should take place steadily and slowly in response to the steady and slow evolution of the underlying trends."[22] Keynes's proposal was not adopted by the British government, owing to opposition from the Bank of England.[23] U.S. proposals for an International Commodity Stabilization Corporation also fell by the wayside during Anglo-American wartime negotiations.[24] However, the question of primary-commodity price stabilization was revived postwar in the charter for the proposed International Trade Organization and later still in the creation of the UNCTAD Common Fund.[25]

The American counterpart to the clearing union plan was Harry Dexter White's scheme for a United Nations Stabilization Fund, and, in addition, an International Bank for Reconstruction and Development (which would finance White's proposed commodity corporation, mentioned above). White was assistant secretary to the U.S. Treasury; his plan was made public at the same time as Keynes's, and it was, broadly speaking, White's ideas that became the basis for Anglo-American agreement.[26] As White explained in the scheme's first draft, the United Nations Stabilization Fund was "to provide an instrument with the means and the procedure to stabilize foreign exchange rates and strengthen the monetary systems of the United Nations." Its resources, subscribed to by member countries in accordance with quotas determined by a complex formula, would be available to countries in temporary balance-of-payments difficulties. In return, member nations' rights to maintain exchange controls and to vary exchange rates would be limited and domestic policy would be subject to fund supervision, based on a four-fifths majority decision (which, given the proposed size of its quota, would give the U.S. an effective veto). The corollary of monetary stability, in White's eyes, was the adoption of liberal trade policies by the fund's members. His vision for the proposed international bank was that it should be "an agency with resources and powers adequate to provide capital for economic reconstruction . . . to provide relief for stricken people . . . to increase foreign trade, and permanently increase the productivity of the United Nations."[27]

An indication of the close link envisaged by the Americans between the UN and economic reconstruction is the fact that White, unlike Keynes, specifically related his ideas to a United Nations framework. In due course, the International Monetary Fund and the World Bank, to which they gave rise, became UN specialized agencies. However, both he and Treasury Secretary Henry Morgenthau were allegedly "determined that the United Nations was never going to tell the World Bank or the International Monetary Fund what to do."[28] This tension between the formal UN status and the de facto operational independence of the IMF and the World Bank has been a constant feature of the international scene ever since.

In all this, there was no apparent recognition that the interests of countries participating in the proposed multilateral regime might differ—there were no special concessions to countries with less-developed economies. Furthermore, close cooperation between the British and American delegations to the July 1944 United Nations Monetary and Financial Conference at Bretton Woods (which set up the World Bank and IMF) helped ensure that the voices of developing countries were drowned out. Indeed, Keynes and White were casually disparaging of such countries, the former referring to the conference as a "monkey-house" and the latter commenting that the role of the Cuban delegation was merely to provide the cigars.[29] As Gerald M. Meier has noted, several Latin American countries put forward proposals for stabilizing the prices of, and increasing world markets for, primary commodities, yet these came to naught.[30] The postwar United Nations Conference on Trade and Employment would, however, see a significant shift in these power relations, enabling the primary commodity–producing countries to put their case on such questions to much greater effect.

An International Commercial Union

That conference, in turn, had its intellectual origin in a proposal put forward by James Meade of the Economic Section of the British Cabinet secretariat. Meade was an avowed disciple of Keynes and in July 1942 put forward the idea of an international commercial union as a complement to the clear-ing union scheme. Meade argued that Britain, whose trade in the past had been largely of a multilateral character, would benefit from a general reduc-tion of barriers and restrictions in international markets and from the re-moval of those discriminations and rigidly bilateral bargains that removed the opportunities for multilateral trading. Multilateralism and the removal of trade restrictions "do not, however, imply *laissez-faire,* and are in no way in-compatible with a system of state trading." Membership of the proposed union would bring the obligation not to extend preferences or other price advan-tages to any other member country without extending it to all countries. Dis-crimination of any kind would be allowed against nations that had not joined the union and were therefore themselves not pledged not to discriminate in turn. Also, "discrimination of a defined and moderate degree in favour of a recognised political or geographical grouping of states" would be permitted, which "would thus permit the continuation of a moderate degree of Imperial Preference." Equally, countries with severe balance-of-payments difficulties would be allowed to impose certain protective devices until such point as those difficulties were cured.[31]

This last point was particularly important, as it was a forerunner of the various special exemptions that the developing countries would later, with some success, attempt to claim for themselves during the UN's attempt to create an ITO. But Meade does not seem to have had such countries in mind when he drew up this stipulation; although he was not indifferent to unindustrialized countries' legitimate aspirations for development, he was in this instance thinking, surely, of Britain's own likely postwar economic prob-lems.[32] Similarly, the provisions on state trading and imperial preference showed an acute awareness of the political sensibilities of both main British political parties. This skillful drafting helped ensure that Meade's proposal became the basis of Anglo-American discussion. Much of the impetus from the American side came from Cordell Hull, who, as secretary of state from 1933 to 1944, formed "a personal link between the dream of Woodrow Wilson and the present."[33] However, the Americans were allergic to the suggestion that preferences might continue in any degree or form.[34] They were also wary of state trading, although they were not openly hostile, for they did not wish to preclude Soviet participation in the proposed new international arrange-ments. J. G. Winant (U.S. ambassador to London and later U.S. representative on the United Nations Economic and Social Council) felt that the widespread support for state trading in British political circles represented a "failure to grasp the importance of reconciling planning with an advantageous territo-rial division of labor."[35] In the immediate postwar years, differences between the British and the Americans over commercial policy would become yet more acute, with crucial implications for the outcome of the UN-sponsored ITO negotiations.

A UN Economic and Social Council

More immediately, however, the negotiations to establish the United Nations organization itself involved important debates about that body's own proper economic role. These emerged at the Dumbarton Oaks conference (August–October 1944), where the great powers discussed their respective preliminary plans for the new world body. The key American proposal was that it should have an economic and social council to initiate studies and work with individual governments with a view to promoting full and effective use of the world's economic resources.[36] This was in line with the recommendations made by the League of Nations' Bruce Committee on the eve of war. As Thomas M. Campbell has noted, this was a major American contribution to the eventual shape of the UN—neither the British nor the Russians made such proposals—and reflected the belief that the new organization should not concern itself solely with military security.[37] Rather, the American vision was of a "one tent" organization covering international relations generally, with autonomous functional agencies.[38]

The Soviets, for their part, were highly skeptical, Molotov's previously quoted burst of enthusiasm for a wide-ranging UN economic role notwithstanding. The Russians "earnestly and exhaustively argued that the League's experience demonstrates that an intermingling in the same organization of responsibilities for both the maintenance of peace and for economic and social matters will work out to the detriment of security." Rather, they felt that there should be a separate economic organization.[39] Insofar as can be determined, it seems likely that the Soviets were eager to join the UN in recognition of their great-power status but were only interested in international economic bodies insofar as keeping open the option of joining them facilitated their own political game-playing. Linking economic and military security in one body would complicate this strategy. (Subsequent Soviet actions over membership of the IMF and GATT tend to bear this analysis out.) Roosevelt, however, was adamant that the new organization's assembly "should have adequate functions with respect to economic and social problems," although he conceded that "the actual provisions written into the proposals might be in general terms."[40] The British gave general backing to the U.S. line—even though Churchill himself would remain doubtful about the wisdom of the UN "getting into social or economic things."[41] The Soviets backed down, and in the agreed-upon Dumbarton Oaks proposals, it was stated that one purpose of the UN was "to achieve international cooperation in the solution of international economic, social and other humanitarian problems." An economic and social council should be established to help achieve this.[42]

To some extent, however, this victory rebounded on the United States at the San Francisco conference (April–June 1945) that finalized the UN charter. In this document, the Dumbarton Oaks proposals were expanded. Thus, "the United Nations shall promote . . . higher standards of living, full employment, and conditions of economic and social progress and development."[43] The American delegation opposed the term "full employment," preferring the phrase "high and stable levels of employment" or, in the case of some delegates, no reference to the question at all. These delegates alleged in private that "full employment" smacked of communism and collectivism. Moreover, as one of them, Republican senator Arthur Vandenberg, asked, "How . . . would it be possible to get Communists and capitalists to collaborate to promote full employment?"[44] Isolated, the Americans gave way. This would have vital repercussions during the postwar trade negotiations. The full employment provision would help certain countries, particularly less-developed ones, resist trade-liberalization measures that they claimed were incompatible with that aspiration. As will be seen, this was a factor that helped unite the newly emergent underdeveloped bloc.

But at the point when the UN organization was being designed, there was no such self-aware, self-defining group of countries. (Nonetheless, at San Francisco, the smaller states did succeed in upgrading the status of the proposed economic and social council to a "principal organ" of the UN.[45]) There was little recognition of the special economic needs of such countries in the UN Charter itself or in the intergovernmental discussions which gave rise to it and to its specialized agencies.[46] To be sure, there were references to "economic development"—that is to say, there was a keen awareness that some countries were very poor and that something should be done about this. But the prescribed recipe for prosperity was the same for these nations as it was for the richer ones. (One State Department economist later recalled of the immediate postwar period that "most of us . . . felt that economic problems are economic problems wherever they happen to be. You wanted to know the facts of a particular country and situation, of course, but detailed knowledge of a particular country wouldn't make much difference as to exchange rate policy or the investment situation or trade regulations and so on."[47]) In April 1944, a Canadian government memorandum on "Post-War International Economic Policy" summed this recipe up. The broad objectives of the United Nations, it noted, were those expressed in the Atlantic Charter and the Mutual Aid Agreements of 1942—that is, international economic cooperation based on the principle of nondiscrimination. These broad objectives might be given practical effect "from the standpoint of a broad international approach; one in which all the United Nations could participate in the formulation and control of arrangements . . . and assume obligations on a multilateral basis in contrast to the alternative of bilateral agreements or exclusive undertakings within regional or special groupings."[48] Again, in this overall vision, there was no conception that such obligations press harder on poor countries than on rich ones.

The Idea of Underdevelopment

If the founders of the UN overlooked such issues, they did not do so in the face of well-elaborated and recognized theories of economic underdevelopment. In the interwar period, it is remarkable how little mainstream Western economists had to say about the development of countries outside Europe, except those of European settlement. This issue was very rarely on their intellectual agenda.[49] Indeed, in this respect, Soviet thinkers were ahead of them.[50] Notably, the economic research undertaken by the League of Nations centered on the problems of its (predominantly industrialized) member countries. (One main strand of this research focused on trade issues and, linked with this, exchange-rate regulations, the other on business-cycle analysis.)[51] Even when, during the Second World War, economic development began to be of increasing interest to governments and public opinion, the pioneering work of P. N. Rosenstein-Rodan and Kurt Mandelbaum was done in relation to Southeastern and Eastern Europe.[52]

The term "development" was certainly in use by this time, but it usually carried one of two different senses. It had often been used in a colonial context to denote the exploitation of natural resources of land and minerals without carrying any connotation of thereby promoting native welfare. (Used in this sense, it clearly enjoyed a certain measure of popular currency, being referred to ironically, for example, in Joseph Conrad's 1915 novel *Victory*.[53]) It had also been used to indicate the way in which national economies and societies evolved, implying that development was progressive. Heinz Arndt argues that Marx was "the first to aim explicitly at a theory of economic development."[54] For the Marx of *The Communist Manifesto*, however, the economic development of backward areas would come through the expansion of Western capitalism. He believed that they would progress through a capitalist phase before arriving at socialism and that their industrialization would follow the European pattern. Arndt suggests that it was the Chinese nationalist leader Sun Yat-sen who was the first, in his book *The International Develop-ment of China* (written in English in 1918 and published in 1922), to advocate economic development in something like the modern sense of the term.[55]

What was new in the 1940s was the gradual emergence of the term "under-developed," which blended the reverse of the two different senses of "develop-ment" to imply that all countries had the potential to progress economically by a more intensive use of their resources.[56] This implication was drawn out in the work of Eugene Staley for the ILO, first published in the monograph *World Economic Development* in 1944. As early as 1939, Staley had proposed a "world development program."[57] He now examined the likely effects of the economic development of new areas of the world on existing industrial areas. He saw the key to such development as "vastly increased production." He de-fined economic development (which he saw as a broader term than "industri-alization") as

> a combination of methods by which the capacity of a people to produce (and hence to consume) may be increased. It means introduction of better tech-niques; installing more and better capital equipment; raising the general level of education and the particular skills of labour and management; and expand-ing internal and external commerce in a manner to take better advantage of opportunities for specialisation.

Staley's central conclusion was that the advantages to industrial areas from development elsewhere, as a result of international investment, would far outweigh the dangers and disadvantages. He proposed an international de-velopment authority of a "multilateral, supra-national character" in order to achieve the greatest mutual benefit. Its proposed functions included raising capital that would be advanced for approved development projects, coordi-nating technical assistance, and conducting a survey of world resources. In the second edition, published in 1945, Staley suggested that the World Bank would be an appropriate organization to undertake some of these functions. He also argued that the bank should construe its mandate broadly and think "in developmental rather than mere money-lending terms," although he none-theless put strong emphasis on sound finance that would produce a return to the lender.[58]

Staley's emphasis on growth through specialization, on multilateral institu-tions, on sound finance, and on reduced trade barriers as a precondition of international development placed him in the mainstream of economic thought. He implicitly ruled out more radical development solutions such as import-substituting industrialization or Soviet-style planning. The real significance of his work was in the explicitness of his attempt to define economic development and his early use of terms such as "less developed areas" that would shortly become common currency, not least within the United Nations.[59]

Initial Dissent by Developing Countries

The tendency to use such terms showed itself particularly in the early discussions of the Economic and Social Council (ECOSOC). This body, in its first sessions, was dogged by organizational quibbling as the council attempted to define the composition and functions of its commissions. The effort to provide on paper for all possible contingencies led one of the Canadian delegates to remark privately that "one of the most depressing characteristics of the Council was its apparent conviction that its commissions would be composed of morons who had to have everything spelled out for them."[60] There were also important debates about development strategy, however, arising in the first instance from the proposal to convene a UN conference on trade and employment. A draft resolution to this effect was introduced by J. G. Winant, the American representative on the council, in February 1946. Moreover, in the belief that previous international conferences in the commercial field had failed because they had been confined to abstract discussions, the U.S. had invited fourteen other governments to negotiate reductions in specific trade barriers and discriminations in advance of this general conference.[61] ECOSOC's blessing was considered important for this latter enterprise, for if it would agree to designate these countries as the preparatory committee for the conference, this would remove possible objections to the preliminary negotiations on the grounds that they were exclusive.[62] Yet also, of course, this gave other countries a chance to influence the committee's terms of reference.

Winant introduced the U.S. proposal with rhetoric of the kind that had become standard in American circles during the Second World War. The "economic anarchy" prevalent after 1918, he argued, was the consequence of "blindly nationalistic and selfish trade policies" which had "eventually retarded all free exchange of goods across frontiers." An international organization to deal with trade and employment was the major piece of machinery still needed to make world cooperation in the economic field effective.[63] (Given the American attitude at San Francisco, it seems clear that the reference to employment was simply intended as a sop for countries such as Australia that had earlier pressed for a separate conference on the issue.[64]) During the ensuing debate, the Colombian representative, Carlos Lleras Restrepo, launched an attack upon the American analysis.[65] Claiming that Colombia supported the tendency toward greater freedom in international commerce, he nonetheless argued that just as a certain freedom of trade is considered necessary for the maintenance of high standards of employment and of economic stability, so, too, it should be accepted, from the outset, that the diversification of production and progressive industrial growth in underdeveloped countries are also essential conditions for achieving full employment and a high standard of living.

Moreover, "free trade means free competition. And free competition means the elimination of those who find themselves in less favourable conditions." It would also imply an international distribution of labor "as conceived by the early classical writers." But this could only be achieved "after painful and vast upheavals" and would place the underdeveloped countries at a permanent disadvantage:

> Certain nations, Colombia among them, would be confined to one or two fields of production, for which nature has given us special facilities. And the great industrial countries which, as the result of various historical circumstances, surpassed the others in the sphere of manufacturing industry, often with the aid of a rigid policy of protection, would establish for themselves a privileged situation indefinitely.

Arguments of this kind were later to figure in structuralist analyses of development, particularly those produced by the Economic Commission for Latin America. Restrepo went on to consider the question of full employment:

> For the United States, full employment is to be achieved by the expansion of world trade within a system of economic freedom.
>
> For us, the words "full employment" have a special and quite different meaning. What, indeed, can it mean to us that all our workers are employed, so long as they work in the least productive branches of economic life for wages ten times lower than those of other nations? And how can we ensure stability in this "full employment" if we are limited to producing a commodity which is exposed, as coffee is, to such violent fluctuations of price and volume of consumption on the international market?

Therefore, he argued, full employment in reasonable conditions was inseparable from the attainment of two fundamental objectives: variety of production and an increase in manufacturing industries which, through their ability to command higher wages than those normally obtained in extracting industries, could raise the general standard of living "and shape a mentally and morally superior working class." Thus, he argued, "The Council should ask itself if such an evolution can be assured by depriving young industries of all protection, and if it is not more natural that a policy of trade freedom should be developed in harmony with the peculiar conditions prevailing in industrially backward countries."[66] Accordingly, the Americans agreed on a version of an amendment to the resolution put forward by the Colombians (which also received particular backing from Peru). The Preparatory Committee would be instructed to study, when preparing the agenda for the conference, the special conditions prevailing in countries whose manufacturing industry was still in its initial stage of development and the question of commodities "subject to special problems of adjustment in the international markets."[67]

These questions continued to be a matter for controversy within ECOSOC itself. In June 1946, Philip Noel-Baker, the British representative, in the course of a debate on employment, argued that although "no undue restrictions should be placed on the industrialization efforts of poor and less developed areas," it was necessary to ensure that any industrial goods produced were of real use to the peoples of the countries producing them, that they reached the people who needed them, and that they were not produced at prohibitive cost. Indeed, "a rising standard of living would mean not a lesser, but a greater, international division of labour." The Soviet representative, Nikolai Feonov, repudiated these remarks. He argued, on the contrary, that the UN should help industrialize underdeveloped areas, "starting, for example, with the heavy industries which were the basis of all economic production and development." Noel-Baker quickly backtracked, saying that he had not meant that the development of the underindustrialized areas should be restricted: "He had simply endeavoured to stress the danger of unwise tariff policies to protect national industries. . . . He was convinced that an increase in the international division of labour . . . would mean not less, but more and more diversified industrialization throughout the world."[68] This realization by the Western powers that it might be unwise to be seen as opposing the industrialization of the poorer countries, plus those countries' own increased articulateness, had important results during the preparations for the conference on trade and employment.[69] Moreover, these preparations, and the conference itself, were significant not only as an attempt to deal with these problems within a UN forum but also as a key part of the postwar international settlement in relation to which subsequent intellectual actors within the UN defined their own positions on trade and development.

Emerging Issues of Trade and Employment

The preparatory committee to the conference met for the first time on 15 October 1946 at Church House, Dean's Yard, Westminster. This was where the British Parliament had met during the bombing raids of 1941 and the 1944–1945 flying bomb attacks. The Soviets, although invited, were absent. They had supported the ECOSOC resolution that established the conference; this implied support for, or at least not radical dissent from, the long-established U.S. trade strategy whereby trade concessions made to one country were extended to *all* countries granted "most favored nation" (MFN) status, as the planned trade negotiations were to proceed on a similar basis. However, at the Paris Peace Conference (July–October 1946), Molotov denounced the "most favoured nation policy" of the U.S. as "a device of the devil to ensnare and enslave small countries."[70] The Soviets gave transparent excuses for nonattendance in London, ranging from lack of personnel to preoccupation with security.[71] Even without a potentially disruptive Russian presence, it quickly became apparent that opinion at the London meeting would divide between the highly industrialized countries and those aspiring to rapid industrialization. A Canadian government report later recorded that this latter group became known as "the under-developed countries," the term clearly still being something of a novelty. Indeed, it seems not to have been used quite in the modern sense, for Australia, a major primary commodity–producing nation, identified itself with the group and even assumed de facto leadership of it.[72]

The matter under discussion was the draft charter for an international trade organization put forward by the United States. This was an elaboration of the joint Anglo-American proposals agreed upon in December 1945 at the time of the U.S. loan to Britain. These committed the British to enter into negotiations for the substantial reduction of tariffs and the elimination of tariff preferences as its contribution to a "mutually advantageous" reduction in world trade barriers.[73] (It should be emphasized, however, that the U.S. administration was pressing not for complete free trade but only for *freer* trade.[74]) There was a clear suspicion among the underdeveloped countries that Britain had been coerced into agreement on this as the price of the loan. And although the proposals emphasized that membership in the ITO would expand opportunities not only for trade but for economic development, these were attacked for being negative and for consisting merely of a series of prohibitions concerning what nations should not do in the way of maintaining barriers to trade rather than of positive measures to expand it.[75] Moreover, as R. K. Nehru, leader of the Indian delegation (and a cousin of Pandit Nehru), put it, "We deplored the fact that so little understanding was shown to the problems and needs of the undeveloped countries."[76]

Much emphasis was placed on the need for "full employment." This was really a way of expressing concern about the stability of international demand. Stress was laid, particularly by Australia and Britain, on the need for expansionist policies. In the words of the previously quoted Canadian report, "This clearly reflected the new economic ideas associated with the name of Lord

Keynes." It was maintained that the level of employment in major economies had more influence on world trade than the raising or lowering of trade barriers.[77] There was a fear, triggered by memories of the interwar depression, that in a liberalized world economy, damaging trends in the U.S. could have rapidly contagious negative consequences elsewhere. In particular, it was widely believed that the underdeveloped countries' ability to maintain markets for their primary products hinged on U.S. willingness to keep up her demand for them.[78] But as Clair Wilcox, head of the American delegation, reported, although this appeared, superficially, to be a point of vital importance, "Actually no delegation proposed any positive international measures to expand or maintain employment." The proponents of the employment issue were satisfied with recognition of the fact that a persistent U.S. export surplus or a sudden sharp decline in American demand for imports would put other countries in balance-of-payments difficulties and with a provision giving countries in such difficulties greater freedom than initially envisaged to use quantitative import restrictions to protect their monetary reserves.[79] However, the concern with employment would later find expression in the work done on this issue within the UN's Department of Economic Affairs, which in turn dominated ECOSOC's discussions in 1950.

Another key issue was the industrialization of undeveloped areas. The Australians, with the support of the Indians, Chinese, Lebanese, Brazilians, and Chileans, urged that affirmative provision be made for this. Wilcox reported that the real purpose of this drive was to obtain freedom to promote industrialization by using import quotas and noted that initially this appeared to be the most difficult problem before the Preparatory Committee.[80] It was resolved, however, when the U.S. delegation drafted and introduced into the draft charter a new chapter on economic development. Under this chapter, members of the ITO would "recognize that the industrial and general economic development of all countries and in particular of those countries whose resources are as yet relatively undeveloped will improve opportunities for employment, enhance the productivity of labour, increase the demand for goods and services, contribute to economic stability, expand international trade and raise levels of real income, thus strengthening the ties of international understanding and accord." Members would undertake to promote "the continuing industrial and general economic development" of their respective countries. They would also pledge to cooperate "within the limits of their power to do so" with international organizations to promote development. The possibility was also raised that the ITO itself would provide technical assistance to members, a provision that was ultimately included in the final charter in spite of doubts about whether this was consistent with a proper division of responsibilities between international agencies. And, critically, members would "recognize that special governmental assistance may be required in order to promote the establishment or reconstruction of particular industries and that such assistance may take the form of protective measures." They would, however, also recognize that "an unwise use of such protection would impose undue burdens on their own economies and unwarranted restrictions on international trade." The ITO itself would be responsible for judging countries' applications to be allowed to take such measures.[81]

William L. Clayton, the American under-secretary of state for economic affairs, later justified the chapter during Senate hearings on the ITO: "In those cases in which there is a sound basis for developing an industry in an under-developed country, it seems to me to be in our own interest that steps of one kind or another be taken to facilitate such development. . . . To the extent that the resources of any country are developed, wealth is created in which we and all other countries are bound to share through the processes of trade." New industries should, however, be "natural" ones, capable of competing, in time, without heavy protection.[82] This, in essence, was the argument previously put forward by Eugene Staley. The U.S. line represented by the new chapter may thus not have been especially radical, but the underdeveloped countries were somewhat mollified, not least by the mere recognition of the development issue. At the close of the London session, R. K. Nehru admitted that "some of us who were a bit sceptical as to the outcome of this Conference, are now inclined to take a somewhat different view. . . . We recognize . . . there is some change in the attitude of the more advanced countries." However, he asked, "Have we gone far enough?" Even if allowed to use protective tariffs and export subsidies, developing countries might not find it possible to give up "more direct methods" of trade regulation, "which may be vitally necessary for the execution of . . . development plans."[83] This, presumably, was a plea for freedom to make greater use of quantitative restrictions than the balance-of-payments provision would allow. Thomas Zeiler may therefore be right to suggest that although this first preparatory meeting looked, superficially, like an overall success for the U.S., the effect of the concessions made was not to buy off the opposition but to embolden the dissenters, leading them to press for more concessions later.[84]

G. C. S. Corea on Protection

Further doubts about the proposed charter were revealed in 1947 during the British Commonwealth talks during the early stages of the preparatory committee's second session. Australia, New Zealand, Southern Rhodesia, Burma, and Ceylon all expressed trepidation; only Canada, Britain, and South Africa expressed enthusiasm (in varying degrees). H. C. Coombs of Australia noted that the provisions on full employment and the maintenance of demand were not "policeable." U Nyun of Burma doubted the value of the charter to the underdeveloped countries. For Ceylon, G. C. S. (Claude) Corea attacked "the biased nature of the Charter" as well as "its rigidity and lack of realism."[85]

Corea had previously been his country's minister for labor, industry, and commerce and was now the Ceylon government's representative in the UK.[86] (He was also second cousin of Gamani Corea, the future secretary-general of UNCTAD.[87]) Prior to the meeting in question, he had outlined his objections to the proposed charter in a short memorandum. First, he believed that the process via which underdeveloped countries would apply to the ITO for prior approval to employ protective measures was too cumbersome. Second, the general prohibition on the use of quantitative restrictions would force developing countries to have recourse to a mechanism for receiving prior approval if they wanted to use this "essential" device, with potentially damaging consequences. The need to use quantitative restrictions would arise quickly in response to difficult situations, but "there can be no doubt that it will be months, to say the least, before a decision can be obtained from the Organisation and even if it were ultimately favourable it might be useless as the industry which it was sought to protect would have been killed by competition in the meantime."[88] Corea developed these views further during the course of the Commonwealth talks. The impression had grown on him, he said, that the effect, if not the purpose, of the articles in question would be "to preserve the trade of manufacturing countries at the expense of under-developed countries." Moreover, he claimed, the development of backward countries would help increase world prosperity: "The older countries, including the U.S.A, had used protective quotas for development purposes. Ceylon would not be imposing quotas to restrict world trade, but in such a way as to increase production and therefore to increase the market for the products of the older manufacturing countries."[89]

Corea, in his hint that the developed countries were hypocritically seeking to deny other countries the use of methods that had contributed to their own economic success, was echoing older arguments.[90] Most notably, Friedrich List (1789–1846), architect of the German *Zollverein,* had argued that suitable countries at a certain stage in their development should employ temporary protection for infant manufacturing industries in order to shelter them against competition from other countries, notably Britain, which had developed earlier. List may have been influenced by the ideas of Alexander Hamilton (1755–1804) and was certainly impressed by what he saw of "the great American system" that Hamilton helped to create. Hamilton believed that the benefits from free trade were more imaginary than real, as foreign countries would place barriers in the way of U.S. exports.[91] Many American protectionists subsequently put forward variants on this argument. Calvin Colton, for example, argued in 1853 that Great Britain had developed a successful manufacturing sector through 150 years of protection and adopted free trade principles only late in its history: "It is never true that the strong want protection against the weak; but it is always true that the weak want protection against the strong. . . . The manufacturing [country] will be in favour of free trade, because, in that way, it can make other [countries] dependent for those fine things, which will be wanted as soon as they are seen, but which can not be produced at home."[92]

Corea's comments had a great deal in common with such sentiments. Although his remarks were not quite so explicit as Colton's, he was certainly understood by the British to be making a dramatic and damaging claim of double standards, which they attempted to refute. James Helmore of the Board of Trade thus argued that "Mr. Corea was incorrect in thinking that the highly industrialised powers wished to use the Charter in order to maintain a privileged position in world trade. . . . Better than any general permission to use quantitative restriction (which would certainly lead to an unnecessary expansion of that device), would be a general undertaking not to use it except in certain exceptional circumstances."[93]

Continuing Controversy on the Right to Protect

The second session of the preparatory committee met in Geneva from April to August 1947. Tariff negotiations, resulting in the General Agreement on Tariffs and Trade (GATT), were conducted simultaneously with the continuing discussions on the draft International Trade Organization charter.[94] These discussions showed that in spite of the apparent accord reached at London, the concerns that emerged during the Commonwealth talks were also held by the developing countries more widely. India, rather than Australia, now took the unofficial leadership of the underdeveloped countries, but she showed no signs of exercising the moderating influence that Australia had previously shown. These countries, as Dana Wilgress of Canada later noted, "continued their efforts to secure more latitude for themselves in using for their rapid economic development measures inconsistent with the basic principles of multilateral trade." These efforts concentrated on freedom to use protective devices such as quantitative restrictions, differential internal taxation, mixing regulations, and preferences between neighboring states for the purposes of development.[95] Another issue was the treatment of private foreign capital invested in underdeveloped countries; there was a general unwillingness to give guarantees as to its security and, in some cases, a feeling that such capital in itself was suspect and a likely tool of foreign exploitation.

I. I. Chundrigar, of the Indian delegation, declared himself dissatisfied at "the grudging and apologetic way" in which the draft charter recognized and conceded the right to protection. He suggested that the whole spirit of the charter was "still that of free trade, modified only to suit particular industries. ... [T]hat kind of philosophy has no bearing on present day conditions in a large part of the world." Quantitative restrictions should not, he argued, be seen as inherently bad and inadmissible. P. S. Lokanathan, also of India, claimed that "protection should be regarded not as a mere concession to weakness, but as a legitimate instrument for development."[96] In his closing speech to the conference, Harold Wilson, parliamentary secretary to the British Board of Trade, sought to damp down such sentiments, particularly insofar as they related to the desire for rapid industrialization: "We sympathise with the aspirations of those of our friends who have made the position of the underdeveloped countries a key point in the discussions here." However, "We do feel it is possible to over-stress the distinction between developed and underdeveloped countries. No country's economy is static: each must undergo a constant process of readaptation." Moreover,

> a country which is at present mainly or wholly agricultural will undoubtedly benefit both its own economy and the world economy by sound measures to increase its productivity. This does not mean that such development should necessarily involve too wide a range of new manufacturing industries. We must not overlook the very real advances which can be made in the field of primary production, which can be achieved by irrigation, power and transport projects and by the use of modern methods and scientific discoveries.

Wilson saw the UN Food and Agriculture Organization as a key resource to help bring about the necessary "revolutionary advances in productivity."[97] Nonetheless, in spite of this attempt to soft-pedal the industrialization issue, the British, in line with the developing countries' desires, had themselves been eager to amend the draft charter so that prior ITO approval would not be needed to use quantitative restrictions in the case of balance-of-payments difficulties.[98] The reason for this, naturally enough, was Britain's own dire balance-of-payments situation, the urgency of which was compounded by the massive run on her dollar reserves during the summer's convertibility crisis. In fact, "prior approval" was retained in the charter—although such approval would be automatic if it were found that quantitative restrictions were unlikely to be more restrictive of trade than other reasonable or practicable alternatives.[99] However, it seems reasonable to suggest that Britain's increasingly evident doubts about the ITO may well have encouraged the underdeveloped countries in the increased militancy they showed at the Havana conference.

As Clair Wilcox subsequently noted, "The most violent controversies at the [Havana] conference and the most protracted ones were those evoked by issues raised in the name of economic development." He also noted that the leadership of the underdeveloped countries had shifted once more, this time to the Latin American states, and attacked those countries' "extreme" views:

> Wealth and income, they argued, should be redistributed between the richer and the poor states. Upon the rich, obligations should be imposed; upon the poor, privileges should be conferred. The former should recognize it as their duty to export capital for the development of the backward areas; the latter should not be expected to commit themselves to insure the security of such capital, once it was obtained. The former should reduce barriers to imports; the latter should be left free to increase them. The former should sell manufactured goods below price ceilings; the latter should sell raw materials and foodstuffs above price floors. Immediate requirements should be given precedence over long-run policies, development over reconstruction, and the interests of regionalism over the world economy.... The voluntary acceptance, by all states, of equal obligations with respect to commercial policy must be rejected as an impairment of sovereignty and a means by which the strong would dominate the weak.[100]

Wilcox could have been assured that the congressional audience at whom his book was chiefly aimed would have found such views inherently ridiculous, as it seems clear he did himself. Wilgress, the Canadian delegate, was scathing too. He claimed privately that the Latin American countries were disturbed about the implications for them of the Marshall Plan: "They felt the fairy godmother of the North was deserting them in favour of Europe.... Some of them even went so far as to deny the right of richer countries to assist in the reconstruction of European countries because these countries had once enjoyed prosperity at the expense of the under-developed countries."[101] The division of opinion was summed up effectively by Ricardo Jiménez Castillo, the delegate of El Salvador: "The industrialized countries' concept of equilibrium was very formal, while the underdeveloped countries felt that there should be a basic criterion—unequal treatment for unequally developed countries." (Jiménez himself felt that a compromise needed to be found between these two points of view.[102]) This request for unequal treatment was conceded later: from 1955, special treatment was granted to developing countries under GATT rules, allowing them to protect particular industries and to plead balance-of-payments reasons for adding to quantitative restrictions on trade.[103] But this message was unwelcome to the developed countries at Havana, largely because of its content but also because of the sometimes extreme manner of its expression. Indeed some countries, notably Argentina, do seem to have been out to deliberately wreck the conference.[104]

Another concern of the underdeveloped countries, again interesting in the light of future developments, rested on the belief that primary commodity–producing nations were at a particular disadvantage in relation to industrialized countries. The Chilean representative justified his country's use of exchange controls and import quotas by arguing that "the discrepancy between prices paid for the export of basic goods and the import of industrial merchandise was the cause of a serious disequilibrium in the Chilean balance of payments," which necessitated these methods.[105] Another approach to the problem was the idea of intergovernmental commodity agreements in order to stabilize the prices of primary products. The draft charter recognized that the difficulties surrounding primary products might at times necessitate such agreements and laid down rules governing their use. Agreements were to be limited in duration and subject to periodic review and were to afford consuming and producing countries an equal voice.[106] From the American point of view, commodity agreements were fundamentally inconsistent with the other provisions of the charter; but, believing that primary commodity–producing countries would inevitably enter into them, they thought that it was desirable to lay down "rules of the road" and thus eliminate some of the worst characteristics of such agreements as had been seen in the past.[107]

The commodity provisions, which tended, overall, to reflect this lack of enthusiasm, were thus attacked at Havana from the underdeveloped side. Corea, head of the Ceylon delegation, was the key critic. He claimed that the charter showed "a complete lack of realism" on the subject. He argued that "a very unhealthy situation arises when the prices of manufactured goods are allowed to soar to unprecedented heights, while the prices of primary products are kept down to uneconomic levels." In order to protect primary producers, commodity agreements should be encouraged and should be confined to producers only. Corea recommended a simpler and more efficient procedure for conducting them than that laid down in the draft charter.[108] These objections were to no avail; Corea himself (believed by the Canadians to reflect the "extreme-left" views of his government) does not appear to have carried much weight at the conference.[109] The charter as finally agreed did, in fact, recognize "that the conditions under which some primary commodities are produced, exchanged and consumed are such that the international trade in these commodities may be affected by special difficulties such as the tendency towards persistent disequilibrium between production and consumption, the accumulation of burdensome stocks and pronounced fluctuations in prices."[110] Despite such apparent concessions to the case for market failure, Prebisch later argued that "the predominant idea that ultimately emerges is that basic market trends should not be impeded."[111]

In all, then, the underdeveloped countries achieved a mixed success at Havana. Demands for complete freedom to employ quantitative restrictions for development purposes were faced down by Wilcox, who said that if agreement on the lines proposed by the U.S. could not be reached, America herself might reluctantly employ such restrictions in the future, thus damaging the welfare of other countries.[112] Nevertheless, much more liberty to employ protection in this way would be allowed under the charter than had ever been envisaged in the original Anglo-American proposals—to the fury of the British, who believed that their own interests would be damaged.[113] In addition to the exceptions already granted at Geneva, the ITO would be expected to give automatic approval to quantitative restrictions on commodities not covered by trade agreements if any of a number of conditions were fulfilled. Among these conditions was that the industry was started between 1939 and 1948; this was intended to cover the case of uneconomic industries started during the war or immediate postwar periods. Moreover, the ITO would be expected to give approval to new regional preference agreements if they conformed to certain agreed standards.[114]

Arguably, then, the fact that the United States pursued its trade goals in a multilateral United Nations forum had played a key role in watering down its initial proposals. But did the inclusion of newly independent underdeveloped nations in the negotiations result in real concessions to their point of view or merely in the payment of lip service to the question of development? Wilcox noted toward the end of the conference that "the undeveloped countries, which at first were expected to have an articulate and effective bloc, have no effective bloc because their interests are too divergent to keep them together even on developmental matters," and this naturally placed limits on the concessions they could extract.[115] Moreover, it is possible that had an international trade organization come into being, the developing countries would have been unable to make full use of the charter's exceptions in their favor. As British Foreign Office officials noted during the Havana talks: "The interpretation of many of the articles of the Charter will inevitably depend on the economic strength of the parties debating them. We can therefore hope, as we regain strength, to be able to get an increasingly favourable interpretation of the Development and non-discrimination articles, provided that we remain on good terms with the U.S.A."[116] In other words, the industrialized powers had good hopes of being able to gerrymander the system.

Nonetheless, if the value of what had been obtained by the developing countries was not immense, neither was it entirely trivial. The concessions were, if nothing else, highly significant from the point of view of U.S. domestic politics. Together with the failure to bring to an end the British imperial preference system, they fueled hostility to the ITO. This was because free trade purists, objecting to the weakening, as they saw it, of the charter, were pushed into an "unholy alliance" with protectionists. In this latter camp, one Republican congressman noted that measures that received the negative label "protectionism" at home received the positive one "development" abroad.[117]

Diverse arguments were also employed in favor of the ITO. Jacob Viner, an ardent advocate of freer trade, argued that, if adopted, the charter would "bring some, though by no means all, of the degree and type of order in the international trade field which our country needs. . . . There are no alternatives."[118] Hans Singer, by contrast, later recalled that the provisions in the charter for "positive discrimination" in favor of the developing countries were what, to him, justified the attempt to create an ITO.[119] That attempt did not succeed, as the United States failed to ratify the charter. Sensing the strength of opposition, the Truman administration (the attention of which was now increasingly diverted toward Marshall Plan aid and other Cold War issues) delayed putting the proposal before Congress. Hearings did not begin until April 1950, when the administration witnesses were pushed onto the defensive—the new Democratic majority notwithstanding. The main American business organizations had come out against the charter, and, as Richard N. Gardner has pointed out, given that the members of these were supposed to be key beneficiaries of the project, this stand greatly diminished the chances of congressional approval. The emergency of the Korean War, which broke out in June 1950, further distracted the administration's attention from the ITO; that December, it was quietly announced that the charter would not be resubmitted to Congress.[120]

Prebisch's Later View of the 1940s Debate

This meant that world trade continued to be regulated by GATT, which had only ever been envisaged as an interim measure prior to the establishment of the ITO. Each contracting party to GATT had one vote, which meant that in theory developing countries could have a significant influence on decisions. However, as T. N. Srinivasan has argued, they tended to see GATT as promoting the interests of the developed countries, and many did not participate effectively until the Tokyo Round.[121] After 1964, UNCTAD was seen as an alternative forum for discussing trade issues, and in his report to its first conference Prebisch advanced a detailed critique of the Havana Charter and of the GATT system as it had developed in practice.[122] Here, many of the ideas that had circulated at London, Geneva, and Havana in embryonic form were developed with greater clarity and force. As Prebisch put it, "We can now see clearly things which were still confused and vague in the Havana days."

> The absolute necessity of industrialization for the peripheral countries had not been recognized or realized nor had the need to intensify this process as advanced techniques permeated into agriculture. Another thing that was not properly understood was the persistent trend towards external imbalance, which was attributed more to the inflationary policy of Governments than to the nature of the growth phenomenon.

He went on to ask why GATT had not been as effective from the point of view of the developing countries as it had for industrialized countries. He suggested that this was because, first, it was based on the "classic concept that the free play of international economic forces by itself leads to the optimum expansion of trade and the most efficient utilization of the world's productive resources."[123] Moreover, "the free play concept is admissible in relations between countries that are structurally similar, but not between those whose structures are altogether different as are those of the industrially advanced and the developing countries."[124]

Prebisch argued that these structural differences resulted in a deterioration for primary producers in the terms of trade and disparities in international demand. He suggested that these points were not given the importance they deserved in the Havana Charter: "Thus, in seeking to lower or eliminate tariffs and restrictions with a view to promoting trade, neither the Charter nor the [GATT] Agreement draws any distinction between developed and developing countries. And since there is an initial assumption of homogeneity, such reductions have to be equivalent everywhere." There was thus, he claimed, a failure to take into account the fact that those equivalent concessions would intensify the trend toward trade imbalance inherent in the disparity of international demand instead of helping to correct it: "Herein lies the concept of the symmetry of a situation that was not symmetrical. . . . A clear distinction must be made . . . between this conventional and real reciprocity."[125]

Second, the industrialized countries had, when it suited them, ignored the principle to which they claimed to adhere—that freer trade on a nondiscriminatory basis was universally beneficial—even if they stuck to the letter of the GATT rules. He made particular reference to agricultural protection by industrial countries aiming at agricultural self-sufficiency (GATT did not cover agricultural products). He suggested that, in practice, whenever industrial countries had needed to safeguard their domestic production, whether in agriculture or in mining, they had found direct or indirect means of doing so.[126]

Prebisch thus presented and defined his own positive views on trade and development in explicit contrast to the international settlement that U.S. planners and others, during and immediately after the Second World War, had sought to make the economic basis of the UN system. His was certainly not the most violent attack ever made on the postwar international economic settlement, but it was without doubt one of the most cogent.[127] Prebisch's central criticism—that the Bretton Woods/GATT system was based on a failure to recognize the fundamental differences between the industrial centers and the periphery of the world economy and thus sought to apply common principles to what was fundamentally different—was largely correct.[128] He did, however, underestimate the significance of some of the concessions extracted by the underdeveloped countries at London, Geneva, and Havana.

Yet it was hardly surprising that the orthodoxy that he decried had ended up predominating. For not only were many of the underdeveloped countries inexperienced in international negotiation in the immediate postwar years, but they were also unclear about what was distinctive about their state of underdevelopment. For example, at Havana, the Uruguayan representative defined an underdeveloped country as one that exported foodstuffs and raw materials. Dana Wilgress was able to point out that this was a definition that fitted his own country very well. Moreover, Canada "also disposed of more undeveloped square miles than any other country at the Conference with the possible exception of Brazil." Yet Canada did not see any need for the kind of restrictions that the underdeveloped countries were demanding: "It was not too much to ask everybody to accept the same rights and obligations."[129] Thus, until countries were able to articulate their needs and concerns more clearly, their mere participation in a United Nations forum would be of limited value to them—for it was one thing to extract concessions and another to change the overall worldview on which agreement was based. This was what Prebisch and others would later set out to achieve.

Conclusion

The postwar international order was Anglo-American in conception. Keynes and Meade were every bit as creative in contributing to its design as their U.S. counterparts. However, Britain's serious economic exhaustion at the end of the war both weakened its bargaining position in Anglo-American negotiations and eroded its commitment to a wholly nondiscriminatory multilateralism. Consequently, the institutions of the international economic order were shaped by American desires to a great degree. In particular, these institutions were nested within the UN, albeit with a semi-detached status for the IMF and World Bank. Procedural multilateralism was thereby established as the modus operandi of the new order.

Having created the institutions that it wanted, however, the U.S. was less than wholly successful in reproducing within those institutions its own values and its own analysis of the logic of the international economic situation. On the contrary, the fora had now been created in which divergent values and analysis could make their appearance—and, crucially, the supporters of such attitudes now had an institutional framework within which they could canvass for support. As a result, and somewhat ironically, the United States quickly became the target of accusations of imperialism and colonialism. In fact, the U.S. record on this score was mixed. It included both the granting of independence to the Philippines and the negligent acceptance of renewed French colonial rule in Vietnam. Moreover, there was strong U.S. sentiment against British imperialism in particular, which was an important component of American hostility to the imperial preference system. Nevertheless, the U.S. was soon seen as the leader not only of the industrialized countries but also of the imperialist powers. This had already happened by the time the Truman Doctrine ushered in the geopolitics of bipolarity and the crusade in defense of free peoples became the defense of all anti-communist governments.

Henceforth, the increasing debate on what seemed to be purely economic questions—the nature of "underdevelopment" and the existence or otherwise of asymmetric economic structures—was never able to divorce itself from issues of unequal political power and the political ambitions of the two superpowers. At the same time, it was characteristic of these debates to attempt to do exactly that—to treat the issues as if they could exist in an entirely apolitical context. Global bipolarity and the convenient pretense that the world could be understood in purely economic terms became the strange bedfellows of the 1950s. The next chapter will examine the costs and benefits of the UN's search for "objectivity" in its economic research and the processes by which economists were recruited to carry that work out. This will provide the background for an examination of the tensions that emerged from the attempt to sustain this ideal during the first years of the Cold War, and of the UN ideas on trade, finance, and development that emerged and sometimes proved fruitful, even in spite of these problems.

2

The UN Recruits Economists

- **The Costs and Benefits of Objectivity in UN Research**
- **Gauging Intellectual Creativity**
- **The Changing Discipline of Economics**
- **Recruiting the Dramatis Personae: New York and Geneva**
- **Recruiting the Dramatis Personae: Santiago de Chile**
- **UN Economists: Forces of Demand and Supply**

The Costs and Benefits of Objectivity in UN Research

People often offer strong opinions about the United Nations—its success, its failure, its force for good, its utter hopelessness. The term "United Nations," however, has a number of different meanings that we must distinguish if we are to succeed in avoiding opacity and muddle as we chart its intellectual history. First of all, one can think of the United Nations as the collection of countries that are members of the UN and are represented by their governments. This sense we will signal by using the term "UN member governments." Second, one can think of the political organs of the UN: the General Assembly and its two councils—the Security Council and the Economic and Social Council. These are the collective bodies by which member governments act within the UN. Third, one can think of the organizations set up to carry out the mandates that have been decided on by the political organs of the UN. These consist of the UN Secretariat (the corps of officials who operate as an executive arm under the direction of the Secretary-General), including the UN specialized agencies and funds (the International Labour Organization, the Food and Agriculture Organization, the World Health Organization, the United Nations Development Programme, the United Nations Children's Fund, the United Nations High Commission on Refugees, and so on) and the five UN regional commissions. The term "the UN system" will be used to refer to this entire constellation of executive entities.[1]

The story of the global North-South encounter is, at the fundamental level, an account of the disunity between groups of UN member governments on matters of trade, finance, and development. These disagreements began to emerge very early in the life of the organization, as has been chronicled in the previous chapter. Against this high-level background of the opposing viewpoints and positions of its members, the UN Secretariat, the civil service supporting the work of the political organs, was recruited and put to work. It had to define in practice the functions that it would perform and the ways that it would do so. If the member governments, operating through the political organs of the UN, were engaged in a mixture of diplomacy and international politics, the Secretariat was engaged in a mixture of diplomatic and bureaucratic tasks.

Each autumn the member states gathered in the General Assembly and participated in its various committees, and these bodies determined what administrative work they wanted to be done and which of the executive organizations were to contribute to it. Among these organizations there was some jockeying for mandates, both because of the prestige involved and the hope that the number of mandates received would be duly reflected in the Budget Committee's final decisions on annual budgetary allocations. To a degree— and this is a much-noted feature of public bureaucracies—the work that was commissioned from the UN system was supply driven, although increasingly in recent years supplementary funding from particular donors has restored the element of member-country demand in directing the choice of work.

We are concerned above all with issues of intellectual history. We are interested in the business routines of the UN, but as a point of entry to understanding how it has operated in the intellectual realm. As indicated in the introduction, the sociological literature suggests that the model of a bureaucracy as nothing but a rational instrument of its sponsors is not tenable and is particularly problematic in relation to research. We are curious then to know what was the scope for bureaucratic behavior outside the limits set by the rational model and what it implies for the ability of international organizations to function as intellectual actors.

First let us inquire how, on a purely formal basis, the UN Secretariat discharged those of its mandates that call for research. The UN system had various modalities for the production and publication of its research. There were, and still are, various methods that can be used to this end. The most visible was that of official publications that provide information and/or analysis. Official publications come in many shapes and sizes, but some came to be regarded (such as the UN *World Economic Report*) as especially important vehicles for conveying the approved analyses to the world at large—hence the term "flagship report." Other official publications were the reports made to the political organs of the UN, and these were directed primarily to member governments. Unpublished reports and documents could also have important intellectual content and were less constrained by the need not to offend member governments. Then there were internal briefing papers that floated policy ideas and sought to persuade member governments of the desirability of proposals for action. Whether an international organization succeeded as an intellectual actor depended in part on the scale and energy with which these various instruments were used but also on the amount of genuine intellectual creativity that they could embody.

We would like to look beyond the description of the typical tools for the delivery of the results of the Secretariat's research to how they were used in practice. We want to know what sorts of opportunities they offered to the economists who had to work with them. Were they liberating or confining, and if they were both, in what circumstances did they nurture the creativity of those who used them? The answers to these questions may be sought in an exploration of the concept of "objectivity" and the benefits and costs of trying to apply it.

In the Cold War era, the traditional justification for the Secretariat itself to undertake research in house was that the research required objectivity, which could not be expected either of the UN political organs themselves or of national research institutes in member states. However, this justification brought with it very narrow limits on the type of research that the Secretariat could undertake. Any research that involved much in the way of value judgments that might be politically controversial was deemed unsuitable, and other methods of producing it—often involving outside experts taking the formal responsibility—had to be found. The research produced by the UN Secretariat thus tended to be highly factual and noncontroversial. The main problem that it faced was how to achieve meaningful international comparisons of national data. It was generally agreed throughout the first twenty years of the UN that the Secretariat should not "preach a doctrine" in its publications and should not be asked by member states to do so.[2] Doing so would have undermined the basic legitimacy of producing research in house.

However, the pursuit of objectivity carried with it a heavy disadvantage. Although many UN Secretariat research publications—precisely because they were relatively objective—were potentially useful, they were at the same time politically anodyne. They were compilations of statistical data arrayed comparably across countries and across time. Some combined such statistics with analyses of the current economic scene based on them, striving always to be objective. But once the format for a research publication of this type was designed and the methods of collecting, processing, and analyzing the data were determined, the work of its regular production became progressively more repetitive and dreary. There was consequently a serious problem of maintaining the morale of the officials who were researchers because, while they had to be creative people to do the work at all, relatively little of their creative energy was called for by their allotted task.[3]

Sagging morale quickly became a problem, and to maintain morale, UN officials in research departments were often permitted, and sometimes positively encouraged, to find other outlets for their creative talent. Many wrote signed articles in the organization's own journals or published research in outside academic publications. Even executive secretaries took this path. "[Gunnar] Myrdal retired shortly before 1960, but during the last of his stay in ECE, he already did not have much interest in ECE because things were all retrogressing or stagnant. . . . And he decided to write a book. So Myrdal wrote *International Economy,* which I think is a marvelous piece of work. This he wrote during his last couple of years."[4]

The frustration of much of the researcher's creativity by the Secretariat's pursuit of objective research often spilled over into a battle for editorial control of publications between the administrative chiefs of the organization and individual research directors. The heads of administration needed to defend themselves against complaints from UN member states, which were acutely sensitive to any perceived criticism of them, by establishing the claim that Secretariat research was objective. For this claim to succeed, however, they needed to maintain a tight central editorial control over research publications. This was something that caused internal conflict and power struggles, since it was highly unpopular with researchers. It therefore required great managerial stamina to maintain it.

Significantly, in the early years of the UN Secretariat, tight central editorial control was something more honored in the breach than in the observance. Alexander Loveday, drawing on his experience of the League, had harsh words to say in 1956 about the failure of UN administrators to exercise sufficient editorial control over their research output.

> The most glaring weakness in certain offices today is the lack of editorial courage and decision. Certain editors . . . seek a weak and flabby compromise between the divergent views of politically minded social scientists rather than scientific objectivity. As a result each document is liable to lack substance and to reflect somewhat dimly a number of preconceived views instead of views based on ascertained facts, and the whole documentation is liable to lack unity of design.[5]

Here Loveday did not disguise his disdain for the "politically minded social scientists" within the Secretariat. In evaluating their work, one therefore has to think carefully about the basis of his charge.

It is clear that Loveday was here promoting the ideal view of international organizations as politically impartial instruments of sponsoring governments. He interpreted failure of impartiality as a problem of managerial character rather than one of lack of managerial resources and power. He also saw no difficulty in reconciling "editorial decision" with "scientific objectivity." This suggests that he cultivated a somewhat arid perspective on international bureaucracy and that the appreciation expressed elsewhere in his writings of the human factor in bureaucratic life was an attempt to rehumanize an ideal that was essentially a dehumanized one. It is worth noting that earlier he had been described as "completely League-minded and completely divorced from the reality of planning."[6]

His conclusion that firm editorial control was necessary for an international organization's research group to achieve work of the highest quality is one that can be turned on its head. We are inclined to entertain the alternative possibility that the tight editorial discipline that he recommended and the imposition of a "unity of design" would have withered any originality of thought below the level of top management. If this was so, the flourishing of economic heterodoxy—and the paradoxical appearance of interesting and novel arguments for protection within the UN Secretariat—may have depended precisely on the absence of tight editorial control.[7]

What is good for organizations cannot be assumed to be good for those who work for them or for the wider society in which they operate. What is dysfunctional for them may be functional on a broader view. To achieve the compliance of participants with the goals of their organization is not necessarily an unmitigated good. Sometimes conflict within organizations may promote desirable values and legitimate interests on a grander scale. There may be more to life than the triumph of a particular bureaucracy, however elevated.[8]

Gauging Intellectual Creativity

To what extent did the institutional arrangements of the DEA, ECLA, and UNCTAD provide a fertile soil for economists studying the interdependence of trade, finance, and development? Did those who served in them as in-house researchers suffer from the difficulties and drawbacks we have just outlined, with the hypothesized cost in terms of intellectual creativity? It is not easy to test that hypothesis. If a person spent her entire professional life as a UN economist, it would be hard to decide whether her creative achievements were due to her native abilities or her work environment. The matter becomes a little easier to sort out when economists had periods of professional work inside and outside the UN. Assuming that native abilities remain constant, one can compare creative achievement in the outside and the inside periods and then attribute the difference to the effect of the respective environments. In short, one can ask whether the person was a better economist when in the UN or when out. Only in the former case would we say that the UN provided a supportive environment.

Yet that assumption with regard to native abilities is clearly unrealistic, so to infer correctly from such a straightforward comparison is not possible. If Keynes were right, for instance, that few economists have novel ideas after the age of 30, much would depend on the career stage at which the period of UN employment occurs. An economist who entered the UN for five years at 50 might be less successful at the UN compared to employment outside the UN than one who joined at 25 and left at 30. Even if, more plausibly, the period of greatest creativity varies from individual to individual, the age at which an economist joined the UN could still prove critical, albeit with less predictable effects.

In the course of our narrative, we shall find examples of economists who, even if they were at first reluctant recruits to the UN, blossomed creatively once inside the UN system and who made many different contributions while there. We shall also find instances of people of great talent whose best work was done before they joined the UN and/or after they left it. However, merely drawing up an account to see whether the former outnumber the latter would not get to the heart of the matter. The right question is this: Would there have been more creativity in total if the UN system had not existed as an employer of economists? The UN system in its early days was a great sponge for economic talent.[9] Suppose all of those talents had instead been at the disposal of national governments, universities, and private firms: Would the outcome have been superior?

There is some reason to think that it would. We suggest that many of the economists in the UN during its early years did find themselves constrained by the goals of the organization for which they worked. At this time, the limits were set not by the need to preach a particular doctrine but by a particular interpretation of what constituted objectivity. They faced the tactics of a management concerned about the political acceptability (defined as objectivity) to UN member states—and not least to the United States—of the messages that economic researchers wanted to convey. Loveday's criticism of the work of politically minded social scientists almost certainly reflected the views of the UN administrative chiefs, and their views in turn reflected those of the U.S. State Department. The economists in the Secretariat had to judge their willingness to tolerate encroachments by managers on their independence in presenting the results of their research, knowing that unwillingness to tolerate them could lead to loss of prestige or to being assigned to mundane tasks.[10] Nevertheless, when central editorial control was relaxed, as it often was in the UN, some original thinking could and did break out.

At the beginning of the 1960s, Hans Singer, who had by this time been responsible for some of this original thinking, gave a suitably cautious view of what it was possible for the UN Secretariat to do as an intellectual actor. He was sure that the UN had played an educational role, one that not only circulated ideas but also facilitated the acceptance of new policies. The UN was a forum for a vast range of international contacts between governments and between governments and technical experts. The process of repeatedly stating government viewpoints in meetings on a multifaceted economic and social agenda and then negotiating the wording of agreed-upon resolutions created a climate of shared opinion about the nature of problems and the kinds of multilateral solutions that might be feasible. To the economically literate, some of the texts agreed upon by the UN diplomats might have seemed silly or even nonsensical, but the whole process permitted proposals to be aired that seemed wild and utopian at first but often subsequently became accepted by states. In that sense, the UN was frequently to a slight extent "ahead of the curve" (although Singer did not use this term).

Singer emphasized, however, that the UN Secretariat could not produce much in the way of new ideas.

> Much as he wished to say otherwise, he did not think that the United Nations Secretariat could be called a major producer of new ideas. Creation was not a congenial job for a Secretariat; it could even be dangerous. Traditionally, the Secretariat tried not to run too far ahead of possibilities and not to bring matters up until states had more or less agreed. It wanted to avoid friction, rifts and disputes, and this pacifying role was quite a legitimate one for the Secretariat. Its job, on the whole, was to record and register changes in climates of opinion and to apply new and agreed solutions to international problems.[11]

The implication of this view was that when members of the Secretariat did produce ideas of real novelty, they should handle them very gingerly, waiting for changes in the climate of opinion to prepare the ground for their policy implications to become politically acceptable. He spoke as someone who had done just the opposite and had felt the dangers of creation at first hand. In this environment, therefore, the UN Secretariat, just as the World Bank was to do in more recent times, acted—when it was operating normally—more as a "transmission belt" than as a catalyst of new ideas.

The Changing Discipline of Economics

By the end of the nineteenth century, the intellectual discipline of economics had become a profession pursued not only in universities but also in business and in government. By 1945, this profession was on the eve of a further expansion. The new macroeconomic theory, taught by John Maynard

Keynes and his growing band of followers, required an empirical analogue in order to become operational. This it found in the long-established practice of estimating national income. Its still-rudimentary methods were quickly refined into a complex system of national accounting that articulated the formal relationships between the aggregate numbers of the national economy—output, income, expenditure, consumption, savings, investment, exports, imports, the balance of payments, and so on. National income accounting, the joint endeavor of economists and statisticians, had proved extraordinarily useful in managing the economic exigencies of the war, which had required the reallocation of resources on a grand scale—from peaceful uses to military ones and then back again. National governments in Europe and North America needed little persuading of the value of retaining and expanding their cadres of economists and statisticians. The U.S. established the President's Council of Economic Advisers in 1946, the French Commissariat Général du Plan was created in the same year, and the British created the Central Economic Planning Staff the year after.

The new postwar international organizations followed suit. Interestingly, while the IMF staffed up with economists, the World Bank was a laggard, being dominated by bankers and engineers and having some initial difficulty in defining its role. Its first big intake of economists did not occur until the second half of the 1960s. The UN, by contrast, copied the prewar League of Nations and the ILO and employed economists on an expanded scale from the start. As other new international organizations were established—for example GATT (1947–1948) and the OEEC/OECD (1948/1960)—they too recruited their complement of economists. Taken together, their demand helped to expand the profession, even if their influence on their organizations was not always commensurate with their numbers.[12]

As the discipline of economics was expanding, it was also changing. Before the war in Europe, schools of economics had tended to follow national boundaries. Each had a quite distinct intellectual identity—the Swedish school of Gunnar Myrdal, Bertil Ohlin, Erik Lundberg, and Erik Lindahl; the Cambridge and London School of Economics (LSE) economists in England; and the Austrian school of Ludwig von Mises and Friedrich von Hayek. By contrast, America had been the home of a range of different intellectual approaches, spanning the institutionalism of Thorstein Veblen and John R. Commons and the neoclassical economics of J. B. Clark and Irving Fisher. The substantial migration of European economists to North America, from Russia in the 1920s, and then from Germany in the 1930s as that country and Eastern Europe fell under the control of the Nazis began a process of blurring these national lines of demarcation. After the war, the economics profession became more international in its typical career paths, affiliations, and publication practices.

As far as the U.S. was concerned, it gained a massive injection of talent, indicated by the disproportionate share of citations and professional prizes that the immigrant economists achieved.[13] This windfall greatly strengthened the mathematical basis of U.S. economics and improved graduate training in the subject, but at the same time it encouraged a much less pluralist intellectual approach. A powerful new economic orthodoxy was rapidly taking shape in North America. In economic thinking, as in the economic reality, opening up to international influences meant increasingly coming into contact with the dominant influence of North America.

In Latin America before 1945, most of its leading economists—Eugénio Gudin is a good example—were self-taught, while those who did study economics in universities were taught in faculties of law or engineering. In a few countries such as Argentina, Mexico, and Brazil, central banks and other government agencies were starting, from the end of the 1920s, to establish journals to publish economics research and were founding national institutes to encourage and promote it. The subject of economics was still quite narrowly conceived as money and finance, the business cycle, and the construction of trade and financial indices. Latin America also benefited to a degree from an influx of European refugee social scientists, especially in Mexico, where President Lázaro Cárdenas welcomed Republican exiles from Franco's Spain.

After the war, academic economics in Latin America was increasingly separated from the tutelage of law and engineering departments. It broadened its agenda to encompass agricultural economics, development economics, and planning. Governments became increasingly willing to finance doctoral studies abroad in economics for their top-level officials. The cultural tradition of the interdisciplinary thinker lived on, however, and controversy remained around how useful such studies were for economists working in Latin American conditions. Gudin's Instituto Brasileiro de Economia sponsored North American economists to lecture in Rio de Janeiro after 1947, and this provided the basis for some crucial debates in this area. The new foundations and institutes and the new opportunities for foreign study provided the academic formation of several economists who were recruited into UN service.[14]

Recruiting the Dramatis Personae: New York and Geneva

Why were so many talented economists attracted to employment in the UN? There is perhaps an antecedent question to this: Were they indeed attracted, or did some economists come into UN employment despite their having failed to find it attractive? One of the strong attractions of working in the UN lay in the great scope that the renewal of world peace in 1945 seemed to bring for reconstruction in a world of improved international cooperation. In the extent of its membership, the United Nations organization both represented a higher level of global interdependence than previously achieved and provided an opportunity for advance to still higher levels. The major objectives of policy—the maintenance of peace and respect for treaty obligations—remained unaltered, but now there was a new emphasis on the deliberate promotion of economic and social progress by collective measures. Hope was renewed, and in the aftermath of the great disaster of World War II many people wanted to dedicate themselves to the renewed pursuit of the highest ideals of humankind.

In the international economic field, the issues were technically complex but the benefits of finding the right solutions seemed almost limitless. The broad plans of the postwar international economic system had been agreed upon, but it was still in the formative phase of its construction. The aim was to reconcile justice and order in the international economy. Justice was sought in the norms of multilateralism: the sharing of both the burdens and benefits of cross-border economic activity. Order was sought in the specification of the rules of the international trade and finance game. Moreover, economic security was seen as in turn a guarantee of continued peace. This vision— which proved a powerful magnet for a certain type of economist—required technical expertise for its fulfillment. For if an organization is to be an intellectual actor, it must have intellectuals in its service.[15]

In the years immediately after its creation, some of the brightest economic lights of the day were brought into the UN. Here we explore the routes by which seven economists who are the key figures in our history entered the organization. All but one belonged on the left wing of the political spectrum. The most illustrious as well as one of the earliest of the new recruits in New York was Michal Kalecki (1899–1970). At the time of his recruitment, he was 47. A decade earlier, he had left Poland on a Rockefeller Award and had arrived in Cambridge, England, by way of Stockholm (where he met Gunnar Myrdal) and London. While in London, he encountered the young Nicholas Kaldor at Lionel Robbins's seminar at the London School of Economics. Kaldor recalled that "at the outset, he gave the impression of a little man with a loud and creaking voice, who spoke English completely unintelligibly. . . . [But] gradually it emerged more clearly what he said, and his contributions were always relevant."[16]

During his subsequent stay in Cambridge, he had resigned from the Polish research institute where he had worked because two of his closest associates were discharged in response to government pressure.[17] John Kenneth Galbraith, who happened to be a visitor to Cambridge at the same time as Kalecki, later recalled their time together:

> An enduring reward from my year at Cambridge was friendship with Michal Kalecki, then in self-imposed exile from Poland. A small, often irritable, independent, intense man, Kalecki was the most innovative figure in economics that I have ever known, not excluding Keynes. His speciality was to bring the obvious into view and cause one to wonder why it had not been noticed before.[18]

During this period Kalecki was welcomed by the junior members of Keynes's circle and found a particularly like-minded interlocutor in Joan Robinson.

In early 1940, he had moved to the Institute of Statistics at Oxford University. There he had built up a research group, largely of European refugees from Nazism who were in sympathy with the left of the political spectrum, to work on aspects of the British war economy. During the war, while still at the institute, Kalecki made contacts with the government of Free France, for whom he went to work as an economic advisor in January 1945. His motives for joining the UN remain relatively obscure. In mid-March 1945, he resigned from his Oxford post and went to work for the International Labour Organization (ILO), which was then based in Montreal. Kaldor offers this explanation.

> After the war, Kalecki joined the United Nations, which were looking for people from countries like Poland, who could speak English like Englishmen and Americans, and who could understand economics as [if] they were English or American economists. So Kalecki immediately got a job with the United Nations, where I came across him quite a lot.[19]

This sounds quite plausible, but we have no corroborating evidence that the UN sought out Kalecki rather than vice versa.

In any case, the move to the ILO does not seem to have gone well. Mrs. Kalecki later suggested that her husband was not happy with his ILO superiors' "interference" with his drafts. Between July and October 1946, he returned to his native Poland on a mission to advise the government. On 7 November 1946, David Owen, who was the first head of the UN Department of Economic Affairs, reported an approach by the Polish government, which suggested that Kalecki should be found a senior post in the Department of Economic Affairs. A reasonable inference is that Kalecki used his time in Poland in part to get his government to lobby for a more independent position for him within the UN. Owen was prepared to find him "a senior post as an economic adviser somewhat detached from general administration and political work of my Department." Kalecki thought that he had been promised the post of director of the Division of Economic Stability and Development, but after the Kaleckis had moved from Montreal to New York, it turned out that he was appointed as a special advisor to the director with the rank of assistant director.[20]

Bringing Kalecki to Lake Success was less a normal recruitment than a response to his previous difficulties in the ILO and one that sowed its own seeds of indignation and resentment. The considerable reputation that he brought with him was mainly derived from appreciation of his studies of the British war economy made while he was at Oxford.[21] He had made little impact in his brief stay at the ILO in Montreal from March 1945 to December 1946. Moreover, in 1946 it was still not generally understood that he had anticipated the leading idea of the Keynesian revolution. He had done so in an article written in Polish in 1933.[22] Austin Robinson gave the first hint of this in the Anglo-Saxon literature when he said in his obituary of Keynes that "Michal Kalecki was independently approaching the same goal" as Keynes. The more recent and reliable view is that Kalecki actually got there first.[23] The psychological problem of dealing with other people's inadequate recognition of his outstanding achievement as an economist dogged much of his career, including his service with the UN.

Nicholas Kaldor (1908–1986) had left his native Hungary in the 1920s for Britain, where he became a student and then a successful young lecturer at the London School of Economics. He agreed to join the UN Economic Commission for Europe (ECE) in Geneva when invited to do so by Gunnar Myrdal, very soon after the latter's appointment as its executive secretary in early 1947. Myrdal was very well known as an economist, succeeding Gustav Cassel as professor at Stockholm University in 1933. He had a reputation for being the most unorthodox and imaginative of the Swedish school of economists.[24] His ideas had a powerful influence on his colleagues in the UN, encouraging them to go beyond the boundaries of economic orthodoxy. Myrdal was also a politician, and he became the Swedish minister of commerce after the war. He sought advice on potential recruits to the ECE from Rosenstein-Rodan, who recommended Kaldor.

Although Kaldor had previously arranged to take a job at the IMF, he chose instead to go to ECE as head of the Research and Planning Division.[25] Thus, even before Myrdal's offer came, Kaldor was primed for a change of professional direction and was actively seeking new pastures. He recalled in 1980:

> My later years at L.S.E. in the 1930s were not altogether happy. Though the place never lacked intellectual stimulus . . . I felt out on a limb as an early and enthusiastic supporter of Keynes, and out of sympathy with the rigid neoclassicism of Robbins, Hayek and most of the senior members of the economics department.[26]

The UN post offered him a significant role in creating the informational infrastructure for Europe-wide efforts of collaborative reconstruction, working under a political economist who, while skeptical of the novelty of some of Keynes's ideas, was nevertheless wholly supportive of them. Kaldor's tenure at

the ECE was exhilarating but brief. Myrdal believed that Kaldor's work immediately established the ECE as a practical research institution, one that could
easily stand comparison with academic and government economists who studied Europe.[27] However, the Cold War quickly arrived and the role of the ECE
began to diminish when the Organization for European Economic Cooperation (OEEC) was set up in 1948 to administer the Marshall Plan. Myrdal's original vision of economic planning in Eastern Europe assisting the adoption of
anti-cyclical policy in Western Europe faded. His ambitions of liberalizing trade
between West and East were increasingly frustrated. Nevertheless, Kaldor never
regretted his time as a UN official in Geneva. Although he returned to academic
life, moving to Cambridge in the autumn of 1949, he remained engaged with
the UN as a consultant and advisor for many years afterward, continuing to
work in very close collaboration with Sidney Dell.

Sidney Samuel Dell (1918–1990) had grown up in Britain during the depression, then studied philosophy, politics, and economics at Oxford at the
time of the Spanish Civil War and graduated with the Senior Webb-Medley
Prize just before the outbreak of war. During the war he served in the Fleet
Air Arm with distinction, including a spell in Naval Operations Research with
Professor P. M. S. Blackett. Blackett recommended Dell to David Owen, who
recruited him to the Secretariat in early 1947. Dell's motives in joining derived
from his moral and political commitments to removing poverty and oppres-
sion. As their junior, he took much intellectually from the strong Keynesian
approach of Kalecki and Kaldor. Unlike them, he remained in the UN throughout his career and has been called "the economic analyst and strategist of the
most enduring importance in the UN."[28]

Hans Wolfgang Singer (1910–) was born in the German Rhineland in 1910
and studied under Joseph Schumpeter in his Bonn period. After the Nazi sei-
zure of power in 1933, Schumpeter used his connections with Keynes to place
Singer in a scholarship in Cambridge. There he undertook a Ph.D. on secular
trends in land values under the supervision of Colin Clark. During the war,
his knowledge of the economics of urban land led to wartime employment in
the Ministry of Town and Country Planning. He also published reviews of
the state of the German economy in the *Economic Journal*. He was not a neo-
Marxist, but he supported the British Labour Party and was a sufficient irri-
tant to the Nazis that his name was put on the list of those to be arrested in
the event of a successful invasion of Britain.[29] He decided to return to British
university life once the war was over.

Singer had worked with David Owen shortly before the war on a study of
the social effects of unemployment. In 1946, Owen invited Singer to join the
United Nations. Singer had already been offered a lectureship at Glasgow
University. Owen sent a formal request to the university's principal for the

secondment to the UN either of Singer or of his friend and colleague Alec Cairncross. When Cairncross successfully declined, Singer quite reluctantly agreed to go to New York on a two-year leave of absence. This ultimately turned into a 22-year period of UN service.[30] Singer has more than once said that his employment as a development economist in the UN had a quite fortuitous beginning. Singer had worked in a ministry of "country planning" in the UK, but this term has two very different meanings in British and American usage. To the British it means location planning of rural areas; to the Americans it means national economic planning.[31]

Recruiting the Dramatis Personae: Santiago de Chile

By the mid-1940s, Raúl Prebisch (1901–1986) was a very senior and well-established figure in Latin America, having been appointed undersecretary of finance in Argentina when he was 29. He designed and then became general manager of the Central Bank of Argentina in 1935 but had since fallen on hard times. He was forced to resign this post in 1943 as a result of a Perónist stratagem. For the next five years, he retired to the University of Buenos Aires, working as an isolated intellectual to write a book, entitled *Money and the Rhythm of Economic Activity,* that was never completed or published.[32] He turned down a number of offers of foreign employment during this period, including teaching at Harvard and joining the Bank of Mexico. In February 1948, he was offered the new post of executive secretary to ECLA by Benjamin Cohen on behalf of UN Secretary-General Trygve Lie.[33] He later recalled that he "emphatically refused," saying that his motives were that he did not want to give up his university post and also that he thought that working in an international organization on development issues would be a waste of time.[34] Later in 1948, the Argentine government barred Prebisch from teaching.[35] He definitively resigned his university post in November and began to consider working outside the country.[36]

Managing Director Camille Gutt of the IMF and his deputy, Edward M. Bernstein, visited Buenos Aires in November 1948 and offered Prebisch a senior post in the fund. This followed up an offer of a short-term assignment in Washington, which had first been made the previous January. When in late December 1948 Gutt cabled that the terms of the offer would have to be changed, Prebisch replied that he was "quite willing to join the Fund on the basis proposed." However, the IMF Executive Board decided not to proceed. The U.S. government had reversed its position on the appointment because it wanted to improve relations with Perón, and Brazil also voted against him.[37] On 11 March 1949, Maurice L. Parsons, director of operations at the IMF, wrote an extremely apologetic letter to Prebisch, expressing his personal regret at the fund's short-sightedness in failing to secure Prebisch's services.[38]

Simultaneously with Gutt's approach, Eugenio Castillo, the deputy executive secretary of ECLA, asked Prebisch for help in preparing the first economic survey of Latin America. Prebisch was originally unwilling to commit himself because he much preferred to accept the IMF offer.[39] However, as the fund procrastinated, he agreed on 10 January 1949 to work for ECLA as a consultant on a short-term contract.[40] So having declined the leading role in the organization, he had to agree to sign on as a hired hand. This irony tells us something of Prebisch's political disposition. He was a scion of the old class in Argentina, and his instincts were very much those of a central banker. He firmly rejected the economics of laissez-faire and embraced government economic intervention, but he was not a socialist or a neo-Marxist.[41] He was a Latin American nationalist rather than an internationalist.[42]

Celso Furtado (1920–) also became a star in the Latin American intellectual firmament. He was one of the first Brazilians to benefit from their government's willingness to fund doctoral training abroad. He gained his Ph.D. at the University of Paris, writing a thesis on the colonial economy of Brazil in the sixteenth and seventeenth centuries.[43] Returning to Brazil in late 1948 after a stay in postwar France, he took up an editorial position with *Conjunctura Económica,* an organ of the Getúlio Vargas Foundation. The director of this financial and economic review, Richard Lewinsohn, worked in the Brazilian Ministry of Finance, and the review had its office there. One day in January 1949, Furtado heard that the head of the Economic and Financial Studies Division, Dr. Octavio Bulhoes, was trying to find an economist to work in the newly established ECLA. Lewinsohn, however, spoke to him disparagingly of the UN's prospects of survival in the newly arrived era of the Cold War and the Marshall Plan. José de Campos Mello, an economist on the UN staff in New York, was less doubtful about the survival of the UN but was certainly far from confident of ECLA's chances of survival, given American opposition to making its temporary status permanent.

When Furtado approached Dr. Bulhoes, he too was at first discouraging but then disclosed that Dr. Gustavo Martínez Cabañas, the executive secretary of ECLA, would shortly arrive in Brazil and suggested that Furtado meet him. When he did, Martínez Cabañas formally invited him to join ECLA. Furtado only discovered once he had arrived in Santiago that Deputy Executive Secretary Eugenio Castillo had opposed his appointment on the ground that, as an economic historian, he was not a serious economist. (According to the British embassy in Chile, Castillo's preference was for "Latin Americans with Anglo-Saxon training."[44]) Furtado was aware of his own ambivalence about the type of economic research he really wanted to do. He was attracted by the university-like conditions of work that ECLA seemed to promise but at the same time not convinced of the utility of pure economic research. In the end, his spirit of adventure overcame his inner doubts about what he would actually do in ECLA and he set off anyway.

The most powerful motive in Furtado's recruitment to the UN was his need to escape from what he later recalled as the suffocating atmosphere of his native land at that time. In late 1948, the Brazilian economy was showing serious signs of economic mismanagement, an overvalued exchange rate was threatening to provoke a debt crisis, and the prospects for real economic development looked very dim. Meanwhile, the government responded to social unrest with violent repression carried out under the flag of anti-communism. He was a left-wing intellectual, and, as such, he felt strong pressures to get out of Brazil for a while.[45]

Juan Noyola Vazquez (1922–1962) grew up and was educated in Mexico City at the Escuela Nacional de Economía. He was a beneficiary of one the new institutions for economics training that were being built in Mexico at this time. El Colégio de México had been established in 1939 with the aim of creating a Mexican intellectual elite. Its chief administrator, Daniel Cosio Villegas, collaborated with the Spanish sociologist José Medina Echeverría to found the Centro de Studios Sociales within the Colegio in 1943. Cosio Villegas then recruited eight students from the Escuela National, one of whom was Noyola Vazquez.[46] He was an exceptionally talented student who made a brilliant academic career. In November 1949, he defended his thesis on "Fundamental Disequilibrium and Economic Growth in Mexico" before a distinguished jury, who approved it unanimously.

About this time he went to Washington to work at the IMF, but—unlike for Prebisch—it held no great attraction for him. In October 1950, he became a consultant to ECLA in its Mexican office, then moved to Santiago as an ECLA official and became in May 1959 the director of its office in Cuba. Dag Hammarskjöld decided that this office should be closed in the autumn of 1960, as Castro showed increasing signs of alignment with the Soviet bloc. It is an indication of his radical politics that Noyola Vazquez, for his part, regarded the Cuban revolution as a continuation and fulfillment of the policy program of ECLA. He sent Prebisch a letter of resignation.[47] He then joined Fidel Castro's revolution and met a tragic early death in 1962 in an air crash while traveling to an FAO conference in Rio de Janeiro as a member of a Cuban official delegation.[48]

UN Economists: Forces of Demand and Supply

There can be little doubt about the intellectual quality of the first generation of recruits to the UN Secretariat. One of the first Yugoslav delegates to the UN, Janez Stanovnik, recalled his deep respect for them and for those who had recruited them:

> I had the greatest admiration for the secretariat during the first decade. They were the people of brain and heart. Particularly, from the beginning. I don't know who was the recruiting officer. It certainly was not Trygve Lie himself, but whoever it was really recruited the best people from the point of view of human character and the point of professional competence. If I were to go on enumerating how many, practically I would say that there was no one single great name in economic writings in the period of 1945 to 1955, that was not in one way or the other associated with the United Nations.[49]

In the recruitment of these UN economists, the end result came from the ways in which the UN selected individuals as suitable recruits, in combination with the motivations of those so identified to allow themselves to be recruited. In short, there was joint determination from both the demand side and the supply side. A striking example of mutual courtship was the recruitment of Antony Gilpin. David Owen approached Gilpin, whom he knew from his days in the British think tank Political and Economic Planning (PEP), and PEP obligingly seconded Gilpin to the 1946 Preparatory Conference on Trade and Employment. It was a temporary assignment, but Gilpin's appetite for UN work was decisively whetted. He recorded that once back at PEP, "I discreetly kept my name before David and in due course, received an offer of a post of Economic Affairs Officer."[50]

The top managers of the new organization were not operating in a vacuum. They inherited some personnel from the old League of Nations. They were also besieged with requests and recommendations, so many that they struggled to acknowledge and deal with them all.[51] How was it best to select from the abundant supply? The U.S. delegation from the beginning pressed strenuously for the UN to adopt professional methods of recruitment on merit, suitable to an impersonal modern Weberian bureaucracy. This pressure had a paradoxical result. While the modern human resources systems were being designed, agreed upon, and put in place, those responsible for recruiting began to turn to their existing networks of professional connections to identify suitable people to approach. As we have seen, David Owen, who played a major role in recruiting the economists, certainly relied heavily on his past professional network of contacts. Their recruitment was thus mainly of the patrimonial rather than the modern bureaucratic variety.

Connections among economists had by no means been dissolved by the recent war, and indeed the need to keep in touch with others may possibly have intensified them. It was in those days a veritable "old boy network" in which only a very few female economists played any part. This reliance on personal networks was, however, fully in line with the practice of the League of Nations in recruiting economists. Alexander Loveday, who had supervised the economic work of the League of Nations and who in the postwar years served on the UN Economic and Employment Commission, derived one conclusion from his League experience. "The one positive lesson is that the most successful appointments are generally of persons about whose work some member or members of the existing staff has a personal knowledge."[52] What kind of personal knowledge was relevant? Primarily, Loveday thought, the recruiter needed to know about the personality and character of the person concerned.

> In the long run the success of an international Secretariat will depend more on the personality of its officials, on their ethical outlook, and their instinctive behaviour than on their intellectual attainments. . . . It is futile to look first for brains and then sift for personality.[53]

Some among the economists whom the UN courted were noticeably reluctant to get involved. Because international work was still experimental and its institutions still dependent for their continuation on shifting political relationships, there was a basic insecurity inherent in it that did not apply to those who joined national civil services.[54] Moreover, the United Nations was then a new and unknown international organization and people were not sure in what ways it would differ from the old and, in the popular mind, discredited League of Nations. In the case of ECLA, the political conditions in which it was created made it seem a particularly risky and fragile enterprise. For some of those that the UN approached, a return to academic life or a position in the new Washington-based Bretton Woods institutions seemed more attractive postwar career options. Prebisch and Singer were of this mind and came reluctantly. This was, however, notably not true of the younger and more idealistic minds of Kaldor, Dell, and Noyola Vazquez. The revival of the spirit of internationalism immediately after the war made the UN attractive to exiles, or self-exiles, seeking a congenial intellectual home, and perhaps Kalecki and Furtado fitted this latter description most closely.

Thus, by the late 1940s, these key individual actors were assembled on their respective stages in New York, Geneva, and Santiago de Chile. Kalecki had arrived very much on his own initiative and Furtado had made good his escape from the spiritual suffocation of Vargas's Brazil. Kaldor, Dell, and Noyola Vazquez had come eagerly when invited. Singer had felt the touch of the press gang. Prebisch had declined the star part in ECLA only to be forced by a U.S. political betrayal to become the bought-in scriptwriter. And so they made their entrances. The play could now begin.

3

Michal Kalecki, the *World Economic Report,* and McCarthyism

- **The Political and Economic Context**
- **The DEA and Michal Kalecki**
- **The *World Economic Reports*: The Lack of an Architect**
- **Kalecki, GNP Decomposition, and the Analysis of Inflation**
- **Kalecki on the Problem of Financing Development**
- **The Shadow of Senator McCarthy**
- **The Harassment and Resignation of David Weintraub**
- **Reorganization of the DEA and Kalecki's Resignation in 1954**
- **Conclusion: The Weintraub and Kalecki Exits Compared**

The Political and Economic Context

The Truman Doctrine is generally seen, following the earlier buildup of tensions between the USSR and the West, as marking the start in earnest of the Cold War. In a panicky reaction to Britain's decision to withdraw military aid from Greece and Turkey, both of which were believed to be under threat from Soviet expansionism, President Harry S. Truman stated on 12 March 1947:

> I believe that it must be the policy of the United States to support free peoples who are resisting attempted subjugation by armed minorities or by outside pressures. . . . I believe that our help should be primarily through economic and financial aid which is essential to economic stability and orderly political processes.[1]

The global conflict that was thereby unleashed had major consequences for the UN's economic activities. The United Nations became the divided nations. The development of global cooperative initiatives was paralyzed.

The UN's founders had envisaged that the new organization—through its Economic and Social Council, supported at the Secretariat level by the Department of Economic Affairs—would help the world avoid the major economic dislocations that threatened peace. ECOSOC would act politically on the information and analysis provided by the essentially technical DEA.

Shared world economic goals, on the existence of which such activities were predicated, became virtually impossible, as the world was divided into spheres that operated under radically different economic systems. Moreover, the divergent interests of the great powers added further to the endemic weakness of ECOSOC. At the most mundane level, it would be very difficult, if not impossible, for example, for the DEA to draw up a meaningful UN *World Economic Report* when countries were manipulating their economic statistics for the purposes of political propaganda. How, then, and with what success, did the DEA adjust to this great geopolitical rupture, and to what extent could it still make good use of the substantial intellectual talent that was already at its disposal?

These questions must be answered with reference to the different types of Cold War pressures, direct and indirect, that had an impact on the DEA in its formative period. At the geopolitical level, the Truman Doctrine signaled the start of a "bidding war" between the U.S. and the USSR, whereby foreign aid would be used to attract or shore up political support in countries whose loyalties were malleable. The UN was the obvious forum for political grandstanding to this end.[2] At the institutional level, because of its physical location in New York, idealistic and internationally minded UN staff members were vulnerable to the spillover of U.S. domestic anticommunism. In fact, key UN personnel, including some important figures in the DEA, did become victims of the anti-communist excesses of the early 1950s. Meanwhile, the poisonous political atmosphere paradoxically enhanced the tendency to discuss economic issues as if they existed in an entirely apolitical context.

The 1947–1951 period was, in global terms, perhaps the most politically explosive of the Cold War, seeing the breakaway of Yugoslavia from the Soviet bloc (1948), the Berlin Blockade (1948–1949), the communist takeover of China (1949), the Soviet acquisition of the atom bomb (1949), and the outbreak of the Korean War (1950). Only in April 1951, once Truman had dismissed the overambitious General Douglas MacArthur from command of U.S. forces in Korea, did it become clear that neither superpower was prepared to contemplate outright world war.[3] The extreme political turbulence of these years was reflected within the UN.

As Robert G. Wesson has argued, in the first years after 1945, its reliable majority in the General Assembly (45 or 50 to 5 or 6 in East-West disputes) prompted the United States to see the UN as a court to resolve differences that could not be resolved by direct negotiations.[4] Understandably, the Soviets were displeased by the successful U.S. attempts to orchestrate pressure against them and enraged by the Truman Doctrine. Therefore, although the

Soviets supported the UN in a few cases where it contributed to the decrease in Western influence—for example, in hastening the withdrawal of British and French forces from Syria and Lebanon—their general view of the UN soon became extremely negative and remained so until the death of Stalin in 1953.[5] The Americans, in turn, increasingly reacted to this obstructionism by bypassing the UN, economically as well as politically. After the Russians rejected the Marshall Plan, the U.S. became reluctant to extend economic aid in a UN framework that was subject to Soviet blocking tactics.[6] By the opening of the second session of the General Assembly in the autumn of 1947, the UN was being widely denounced in the British, Soviet, and American press, variously as a "mere debating society," as an "American-dominated mechanism for deceiving the world's peoples," and as a "platform for communist propaganda."[7] Thus, if the UN was the child of the idealism of the U.S. wartime planners, in the immediate postwar years it quickly found itself orphaned. This was true for its economic as well as its political functions.

This was to some degree ironic, in that the Bretton Woods institutions and GATT, which were set up under UN auspices, made a significant contribution to the postwar prosperity of the West. Facilitating currency convertibility and thus the growth of world trade, these organizations are generally credited with success in supporting high levels of employment and sustained growth in the 1945–1973 era—even though they were slow in starting to live up fully to the high ambitions of their founders. GATT, the IMF, and the World Bank quickly established their operational independence of the main UN system.[8] This fact may have contributed to their relative success, for within the UN itself America played an obstructive role on economic questions. At the same time, it weakened the UN, as these institutions provided a ready-made means for the United States to pursue its international economic goals through agencies that were effectively outside the UN system. As W. Arthur Lewis noted in 1957, in economic (but not in social) matters in ECOSOC, the U.S. played the stonewalling role that the USSR played in the Security Council and the UK (still a major colonial power) played in the Trusteeship Council:

> This is because the other members of ECOSOC are usually asking the U.S.A. to undertake some obligation which it is unwilling to accept, such as to give money toward a special U.N. fund for economic development or to create a fund to prevent the international transmission of depressions or to participate in a scheme for stabilizing the price of rubber. The division between East and West which racks the Security Council is of little importance in the economic debates of ECOSOC . . . the division is between rich and poor countries, with Latin American, Middle Eastern and Asian countries on the one side, and the U.S., Britain and France on the other.[9]

The DEA and Michal Kalecki

The resultant "lameness" of ECOSOC weakened the DEA that was designed to serve it, in particular at the expense of the UN's regional economic commissions (established from 1947 onward).[10] As long as ECOSOC's deliberations were in effect stalemated, the DEA struggled to find a role. The DEA took over the League of Nations conception that there were such things as global economic problems—albeit in the Keynesian era and at a time when discussion of those problems was being broadened to include underdeveloped countries. There was no attempt to take account of the new realities of the Cold War that made pursuit of a global vision impossible. Personal tensions and bureaucratic problems in the DEA increased the weight of these impediments to making intelligent analyses and advocating sensible policies. In these early years, the department thus was threatened by intellectual sterility, the presence of brilliant individuals within it notwithstanding.

This chapter will explore these issues with reference to the key activities undertaken by the DEA in the first decade of its existence. These included the *World Economic Reports/Surveys,* which were published annually from 1948 onward. The awkward role of Michal Kalecki, the department's intellectual star player, will be considered in depth, as will the circumstances in which he left the DEA in 1954. We argue that the loss of Kalecki was more a result of the difficulties faced by the UN in managing world-class economic experts than it was of anti-communist witch-hunting. While Kalecki excelled at formulating economic arguments, he disdained the political compromises necessary to put them into effect. Meanwhile, the politicking of his bosses caused his considerable but maverick talents to be lost to the UN.

The DEA, like other parts of the UN, operated through two modalities. Its staff members handled certain tasks, while others were contracted out to outside consultants and experts. The regular work of the in-house staff is the focus of this chapter, while the reports that were prepared by expert groups, supported by the DEA, are considered in Chapter 4. The DEA got off to an unfortunate start. Initially, it seems to have been disorganized, if not chaotic.[11] It also lacked resources for some of its key tasks. For example, the preparatory meeting to discuss the ITO Charter in 1946 was almost postponed because the UN could not obtain adequate support staff; the Americans stepped in to provide the necessary assistance.[12] This symbolized the UN's broader financial dependence on the U.S., which, in due course, would inevitably have political consequences. The DEA was not without its early intellectual successes—Hans Singer's work on the terms of trade was a notable example (and will be examined in Chapter 5). Moreover, there were many other talented staff members, such as Folke Hilgerdt and his colleagues on the foreign trade side, Wright, Chudson, and Judd. However, the catch that seemed to promise the greatest things was made in December 1946, when David Owen brought into the department from the ILO no less a figure than the renowned economist Michal Kalecki.

His presence in the department was a magnet for younger talent, and during his eight years at the DEA he worked with a talented group of collaborators, some of whom, such as Dudley Seers, Jacob Mosak, and T. C. Chang, actively sought to work under his direction. Apart from these, his junior colleagues in the period 1946–1954 included Stanislaw Braun, Éprime Eshag, Sidney Glassman, Borje Kragh, S. Krestovsky, Samuel Luric, Surendra Patel, H. F. De la Peña, Lawrence Reed, Stein Rossen, Marjorie Tucker, and S. Ting. However, as Singer recalled:

> Kalecki temperamentally was a brilliant economist, full of new analytical ideas and analytical skills but utterly incapable by his personality of translating these into political practice within the UN system. He didn't suffer fools gladly, which was one of the necessary conditions to getting on in the UN! He didn't negotiate with delegations, he didn't want to get involved in this. He wanted to pursue his brilliant ideas. [13]

The *World Economic Reports*: The Lack of an Architect

The first of the world economic reports prepared within the division of the DEA of which Kalecki was assistant director[14] appeared in January 1948. Entitled *Economic Report: Salient Features of the World Economic Situation 1945–7*, it was a large volume of some 300 pages, with sections on world supply of goods, international trade and credits, major obstacles to the expansion of world production, and sources of inflationary pressure.[15] Its introduction sounded what would have been recognized as a Keynesian fanfare: "In order to create conditions of stability, maintain full employment and promote social progress and development, there may be required drastic governmental action of a kind that in some countries has heretofore not been regarded as appropriate during peace-time." It also included a separate chapter on "Progress of Economic Development." This was mainly a review of what individual governments in developing countries said they were doing or intending to do. There was an editorial emphasis on "the need for deliberate, organized efforts" and on "developmental planning" "from a national viewpoint"; a withholding of judgment on the merits of state or private enterprise; and a recapitulation of an ECOSOC resolution recommending international action to provide for the short-term needs—food, finance, and equipment—of underdeveloped countries.[16] This report paid homage to the new political themes of full employment and economic development but did not offer anything of substance to their analysis.

The *World Economic Report* for 1948 was a very similar production, but it had the misfortune to be reviewed by Austin Robinson in the *Economic Journal*. Robinson could be very forcefully outspoken when he decided that it was necessary, as he did on this occasion.[17] He did not pull his punches as he wrote:

> The United Nations *World Economic Report 1948* ... ought to be the volume in which the various regional problems, so admirably discussed in the European and Asiatic Surveys, are brought into the context of the general world situation, and focused in relation to the general world trends. The *World Economic Report* completely fails to live up to any such ideal. It is, apart from a very few sections, an arid, jejune, ill-conceived and ill-written work of scissors and paste. It neither comprehends the world's problems nor adds to our understanding of them.[18]

Robinson then rubbed salt into the wound by contrasting this report unfavorably both with the prewar world surveys of the League of Nations attributable to J. B. Condliffe and James Meade and with the regional economic survey of the UN Economic Commission for Europe edited by Nicholas Kaldor and Hal B. Lary.[19] Criticizing the lack of unity and direction of the *World Economic Report,* he commented that it appeared to lack an architect. He concluded pointedly by asking "whether such volumes as this justify the immobilisation by the United Nations of so much talent."

Robinson's verdict that the "central organization at Lake Success has completely and disastrously failed" cannot have been comfortable reading for Kalecki or his team, given the weight that Cambridge pulled in the economics universe of the time. The department reflected on the tone of the review, which they found puzzlingly sharp. The pillorying—Austin Robinson's own description of his criticisms—had come at a somewhat awkward moment, since David Owen's credit in London was at a low ebb as a result of his support for Gunnar Myrdal in the Southam affair.[20] A damage-limitation exercise was quickly mounted. Sidney Dell used his long-standing friendship with Kaldor to try to reach Robinson indirectly. He explained to Kaldor that the political danger to Owen was "a very real one" and then made his suggestion:

> If Austin felt able to review, say, "Inflationary and Deflationary Tendencies 1946–8" and the study on Terms of Trade (which will be published very shortly and sent to the E. J.—you saw it in mimeograph) it would, I feel sure, be appreciated here. . . . I'm not, of course, suggesting that you ask Austin for *favourable* reviews of our other publications. I simply feel that he may be able to give

readers of the E. J. a wider perspective on our work if he reviews some of our other publications, and I'm confident he'd be fair about it and correct any previous impression *if* he thought it necessary to do so.[21]

Dell also suggested that Kaldor and Walt Rostow both use their contacts "to give an objective appraisal of the situation at Lake Success." By stressing the constraints under which the DEA had to work—the need to please delegations "of all shapes, creeds and sizes" and its proximity to the Cold War—they "might help to dispel the idea that we're a bunch of economic nitwits."[22]

Whatever the outcome of that attempt at networking for support in the economics world, Dell had put his finger on two important factors that hampered the productive deployment of the talent that Owen had recruited. The membership of the UN was much smaller in the late 1940s than it afterward became, but diplomats representing only fifty-seven countries could still run UN officials ragged with their requests, complaints, and protests in their efforts to win credit with their foreign ministries back home. In addition, being lodged in the territory of one of the Cold War protagonists created pressures outside the normal run of these diplomatic maneuvers, pressures that in 1950 had by no means reached their peak.

The department acknowledged Robinson's criticism by reshaping the next issue of the report. In 1949–1950, the *World Economic Report* was drastically shortened to about one-third of its former size in an effort to achieve a sharper focus. This shorter publication was then split into two main sections. Part I covered major national economic changes, while Part II surveyed the state of international trade and payments. Kalecki was put in charge of Part I, while Hilgerdt was responsible for Part II. This basic division of labor was maintained until the mid-1950s. Clearly, this organizational arrangement did not meet Robinson's principal criticism, which was the absence of an architect, the lack of a single controlling editorial intelligence. It reflected the fact that Kalecki and Hilgerdt could not collaborate and that the Economic Stability Section and the Foreign Trade Section wrote their contributions virtually independently. Not surprisingly, they were sometimes inconsistent in their findings.[23]

This episode illustrates a third critical constraint on intellectual work inside the UN, in addition to pressures from delegations and the influence of the United States: the frequent inability or unwillingness of UN officials with strong personalities to find ways of working together and the consequent emergence of "intellectual baronies" that effectively frustrate the construction of a unified view. Sometimes such rivalries went to ridiculous lengths, such as the withholding of statistics from the rival section. As Donald MacDougall recalled:

> I visited New York quite often and got to know many of the UN economists
> and statisticians; and I remember, for example, two sets of indices—of export
> prices—produced by two warring sections, one of which would not allow the
> other to use its indices in its publications; but I had no difficulty getting hold
> of, or publishing, either or both.[24]

There is a legitimate place in any public organization, international or not,
for differences of opinion. Internally, disagreement and debate is healthy, but
the main formal public reports of the organization have to present a unified
view and be the product of a collective effort for which the head of the organization assumes responsibility. In such publications, inconsistencies and contradictions should have no place. In practice, however, the UN has not always
found it easy to achieve the degree of collective effort required. Even in the
new and redesigned *World Economic Reports,* it was missing.

Kalecki himself was not the right person to succeed in this kind of collective effort. His manner was confrontational: "The way that he answered his
telephone in the United Nations . . . usually took the form of a loud and clear
challenge, 'Yes?'"[25] It was not just his loud voice that was challenging. As one
of his greatest admirers, Joan Robinson, asserted: "Kalecki's views were a challenge to the authorities. . . . His unbending integrity and sharp style of argument made him something of an awkward cuss to any institution that sought
to employ him."[26] His Polish colleague, Edward Lipinski, who had known
Kalecki from the start of his professional career, referred in an obituary to his
"permanently polemical approach to everything, including even his own earlier statements." He went on:

> This seems to explain, for example, the remark made to me by a foreigner after
> a conversation with Kalecki: "What a strange fellow! The minute you start agree-
> ing with him, he stops agreeing!" A conversation with Kalecki really was an
> effort.[27]

His independence of mind was such that intellectual compromise was impossible for him, and it seems that intellectual cooperation with him would
have been difficult even on his own terms. Thus he either had to be put in
overall command of an enterprise or the result was partial incoherence. This
problem came back to haunt him before very long.

Kalecki, GNP Decomposition, and the Analysis of Inflation

After the first reorganization of the *World Economic Report,* Kalecki concentrated his energies on the area where he had been given control, namely,
on Part I dealing with "Major National Economic Changes." His chosen method

was to present for every country that was included changes during the previous year in the gross national product and each of its major components—private investment, government expenditure, consumption, and the foreign trade balance. Then the report would analyze the causes of the changes and also comment on their consequences for employment and inflation and their implications for the distribution of real income between wages and profits.

Some strong claims have been made on behalf of these exercises. Eshag claimed that most academic and governmental institutions still lacked "the rigour and precision attained by Kalecki" in the annual *World Economic Reports* some twenty-five years later.[28] This is something of an exaggeration. What Kalecki and his team achieved in Part I was to apply a Keynesian macroeconomic accounting method carefully and consistently across a range of industrial and some other countries. This provided the framework for a comparative cross-country study of the determinants of output, employment, prices, and income distribution for the year in question. He had developed a characteristic approach, which was still unusual at the time, of checking theory with statistics.[29] What he and his collaborators did at Lake Success was essentially to apply this approach to a wider range of countries, using what was still a novel classification of three types of economy—private enterprise or capitalist economies, socialist or planned economies, and developing economies. They did so in an impartial, scientific spirit, despite the pressures of delegations that wanted their own country's type of economic system to appear in a favorable light. The appropriate claim on behalf of this work was that made by Joan Robinson; namely, that Kalecki set "a standard of original analysis and attention to factual detail which was seldom attained *elsewhere in these monumental volumes.*"[30] Dell, who worked under him, confirmed that he "directed the work on each and every country studied down to the last detail."[31]

The fundamental ideas underlying these analyses had been worked out before the war, published in his *Essays in the Theory of Economic Fluctuations* of 1939, and applied in his studies of the wartime UK economy while he was at Oxford.[32] The economic scenario with which he was concerned was one in which imports of food and raw materials might be interrupted and the domestic supply of consumption goods could not be expanded but where employment and incomes were nevertheless expanding. These stylized facts corresponded to the real situation of Britain in wartime, which combined a partial blockade of an island dependent on imports of primary products with an accelerating mobilization of part of its civilian labor force for unproductive (but essential) military purposes. As Keynes had warned in November 1939, the economic danger was inflation.[33] Kalecki asked: How would inflation appear in such an economy, and what could be done about it? It was clear to him that inflationary pressure was not necessarily caused by an unbalanced budget, since higher taxation could be offset for a while by the running down of savings. It was caused by increased effective demand generated by the non–consumption-goods sectors, which pushed particular consumption-goods industries into operating on the steeply rising segment of their short-run marginal cost curves. These pressures were specific to industries or sectors, and they did not surface in price rises while stocks of the goods in question could be decumulated. Price rises could be repressed by price controls, but in that event, distribution would become random. Once consumer prices did begin to rise, workers might try to restore their real wage level by raising their nominal wages, a response that would set off a wage-price spiral. Kalecki argued, contrary to Keynes, that the best solution to this kind of inflation was a system of consumer-goods rationing.[34]

In the UN, Kalecki adapted this analysis of inflation in wartime Britain to the problems of the aftermath of war. Shipping space remained in short supply, but as a result of the demobilization of troops overseas, not of submarine warfare, and this factor prolonged the food shortages in Europe. Expenditure in the non–consumer-goods industries continued to balloon, but now for reconstruction and not for military destruction. An interesting report of 1947 focused on the inflation consequences of shortages of food as compared with other kinds of consumer goods.[35] It argued that food shortages were a stronger stimulant of inflation than shortages of nonfood consumer goods, because in the first case the extra profits of the farmers are themselves largely spent on consumption, whereas in the second case the extra profits are largely saved. The significance of this for developing countries was clearly pointed out. Whereas the poor supply of food was likely to be only temporary in Europe, in developing countries it was likely to be much more persistent, because there "the increase in food production . . . is associated with social, economic, political, and legal problems which usually take a long time to solve."[36] Here we see the emergence of the idea that economic development faces a food-supply constraint.

In his theoretical introduction to the report *Inflationary and Deflationary Tendencies, 1946–1948,* Kalecki continued to explore his wartime insights in relation to the prospects for postwar shortages and inflation. Investment for reconstruction had the same short-term impact as an increase in military expenditure (although with a very different medium-term result). The release of the pent-up demand for consumer goods was another version of dissaving that led to inflationary pressure. Unfortunately, it was not the case that the buildup of inflation necessarily brought an economy to full employment, as the Keynesian doctrine of a reversed L function of the trade-off between inflation and unemployment would suggest. Kalecki argued that "inflation is not necessarily incompatible with unemployment." The two phenomena were incompatible "only if labour is the bottleneck preventing the expansion of production. If there are bottlenecks in equipment or raw materials, then inflation may co-exist with unemployment because these bottlenecks make it impossible to employ all the available labour."[37]

Unlike the discussion of food shortages, there is no exploration of this proposition in relation to developing countries. Nevertheless, the notion of "bottlenecks" in production, like that of an agricultural or food-supply constraint, made the transition, via the UN reports of Kalecki and his team, from being a stylized fact about war-torn Europe to being one about developing countries. The economic dislocations caused by war in Britain were thus twice transposed in Kalecki's inflation analysis. Their first reappearance was as the economic dislocations of the transition from war to peace. Then, as these acute malfunctions gradually ceased to afflict the capitalist economies in the 1950s, they became metamorphosed a second time into the chronic economic difficulties of the underdeveloped countries.

Kalecki on the Problem of Financing Development

In October 1952, Kalecki was invited to give a series of lectures and to participate in a series of roundtable discussions on development economics at the Centro de Estudios Monetarios Latinamericanos in Mexico. He did so in August 1953, and the resulting paper on "The Problem of Financing Economic Development" was published in 1954.[38] Its two fundamental assumptions were at radical variance with the standard model of a competitive economy. Kalecki characterized the behavior of firms as imperfectly competitive, and assumed that firms generated all the savings in the economy out of their profits so that the aggregate saving process was governed by the way in which firms disposed of their profits. The paper showed that in a closed economy of this kind, "there are no financial limits, in the formal sense, to the volume of investment." Thus, "the real problem is whether this financing of investment does, or does not, create inflationary pressures."[39] The firms in the economy were divided into two production departments, in Marxian style, one producing investment goods and the other producing consumer goods. The existence of unutilized (and newly available) resources in the consumer-goods sector was then shown to be the condition for noninflationary growth. In the absence of such resources, consumer-goods prices rise, real wages fall, and "forced saving" occurs.

Into this basic economic setting, Kalecki introduced several refinements. First, if private entrepreneurs are too cautious, as he thought they usually were, the government may also undertake investment, and the inflationary impact will then depend on how the government finances public investment—by borrowing or by different forms of taxation. Second, rises in productivity will ease inflationary pressures, but the strength of this effect will depend on whether there is any accompanying increase in the degree of monopoly in industry. Third, improvements in the terms of trade will ease inflationary pressures when trade is balanced, but it is more realistic to expect a trade deficit financed by capital imports, and then the form in which capital is imported will affect the process of development in different ways. In brief compass, Kalecki provided a concise overview of the key elements of development finance within a model of the accumulation behavior of private businesses and the state.

His substantive message was that the primary inflationary pressures experienced in the course of economic development were "the result of basic disproportions in productive relations."[40] He was contrasting this view with others that focused on the difficulties of financial intermediation. Among these disproportions, the one that he singled out for particular emphasis was the rigidity of the supply of food. A consequent rise in food prices would have a different impact on growth depending on who were the beneficiaries of the food price rise. If it was the peasantry, their demand for nonfood consumption goods would increase and this would prevent stagflation, but if the beneficiaries were landlords, merchants, and moneylenders, they would save their gain or spend it on luxuries, so that investment for development could be accompanied by both inflation in food prices and unemployment in the nonfood consumption goods industries. The distribution of the inflationary gains affected the final outcome.

Kalecki thought that the transfer of surplus labor from the rural to the urban sector would not itself solve the problem of the food-supply constraint. Because of the underemployment of rural labor, transfer of labor from agriculture to industry would not reduce food production, but at the same time, the marketed surplus might not increase by the amount the transferred workers would have consumed before, owing to the likely increase in food consumption of those who did remain. Additionally, the per capita demand for food of the transferred labor would become that characteristic of the urban areas, which would be higher than in the rural areas.[41] A "food gap" would remain.

Thus the central policy thrust of Kalecki's paper was to stress the "paramount importance" of expanding food production in order to avoid inflation in the course of development. He proposed a range of measures with this aim in view. He recommended land reform but also proposed a range of other policies, from "cheap bank credit for peasants to improvements in the method of cultivation, small-scale irrigation and cheap fertilizers."[42] Such measures would be necessary to avoid the ill consequences of inflation—hoarding, currency speculation and capital flight, and distortion of the selection of investment projects. Nevertheless, he recognized that the central obstacle was the existing institutional arrangements in the countryside; that changing them would involve formidable administrative, legal, social, and political difficulties; and that that was bound to be a long drawn out process.

"The Problem of Financing Development" had a variety of consequences, intellectual and personal. Personally, the immediate result was a request from the Mexican permanent representative, Ambassador Rafael de Colina, to the director-general of technical assistance of the UN on 19 November 1953 for Kalecki to be seconded to Mexico for five months as an expert on the planning and financing of economic development. The senior staff of the UN Secretariat decided to reject this request. Their reasons were twofold. They felt that Kalecki's absence would cause an overload of work for other staff members, and they did not approve of Kalecki's opinions on development problems. However, they decided to decline to release him on the technical ground that countries requesting technical assistance are not permitted to designate particular experts, although it has since been doubted that this rule (sensible as it might be) existed or was enforced at this time. The internal correspondence on the Mexican request was copied to Kalecki—presumably by mistake—and he retained it in his private papers.[43]

It is a fair guess that one of the opinions that his official superiors disapproved of concerned the role of foreign capital in economic development. In "The Problem of Financing Development," he had taken a strong skeptical line about the benefits of foreign direct investment on the grounds that it could cause both economic and political distortions:

> Direct investment frequently takes place in certain branches of the economy, such as the production of raw materials for export, which may not be in line with a reasonable plan for the development of the resources of a country. It will give to that development a one-sided twist. But apart from that, the big concerns engaged in this investment will inevitably acquire considerable political influence upon the governments concerned, and the consequences of this may easily vitiate the process of economic development.[44]

It is easy to see that the U.S. government might not have felt entirely comfortable with someone holding this view advising the Mexican government on economic planning and not difficult to believe that this discomfort would have been conveyed to senior staff of the UN.

This was certainly not the first time that Kalecki's opinions on political aspects of development cooperation had irritated the UN authorities. In 1948, he had been appointed to the Advisory Council of the new International Bank for Reconstruction and Development (IBRD), which later became part of the World Bank, whose ten members included Lionel Robbins and Herbert Hoover, under the chairmanship of Sir Arthur Salter. The bank's executive directors had prepared a resolution that was placed before the Advisory Council to the effect that bank credits should be conditional on the removal of internal economic controls, the liberalization of foreign trade, and access for inflows of foreign capital. This resolution clearly prefigured the policy-conditioned lending and neoliberal agenda that the bank finally adopted in the 1980s. It provoked stout and successful opposition from Kalecki and an Indian member, Sir C. Venkata Raman.

According to the minutes of the two Advisory Council meetings in July 1948 and July 1949, Kalecki objected to the inconsistency of requiring developing countries to liberalize their economies while developed countries continued to protect their agriculture and restrict their foreign trade. He also pointed to the bias that the requirement would create in favor of capitalist countries and against the economies of Eastern Europe. Kalecki argued that the most war-devastated countries and developing countries should be the chief lending priorities, but he took the opportunity to criticize the bank for lending to "neo-colonial" projects in developing countries, such as financing labor migration or promoting foreign private investment.

After these two "contentious and inconclusive" meetings,[45] the Board of Governors of the IBRD decided to reorganize the Advisory Council, and the appointments of existing members was allowed to lapse. Kalecki was formally thanked for his service by the director-general of the IBRD in a letter of 4 October 1949. The Advisory Council was never reconstituted, and to this day has never met again, despite Article V, Section 6 of the bank's charter that requires the Advisory Council to meet at least annually.[46] According to Stanislaw Braun, the top echelon of the UN Secretariat (David Owen and others) were highly displeased with Kalecki's performance on the Advisory Council, which was the subject of much critical comment. This earlier contretemps explains the sensitivity of the UN top administrators to Kalecki's opinions on development when considering the Mexican government request for Kalecki's services. That decision, however, was linked with a much wider campaign of harassment of UN officials suspected of links with communism.

The Shadow of Senator McCarthy

The targeting and harassment of UN officials as suspected subversives must be seen in the context of the intense anti-communist hysteria of the 1950–1954

McCarthy period. Red-baiting was nothing new in American politics. The Select Committee on Un-American Activities (the so-called Dies Committee) was set up in 1938 and was replaced by the House Un-American Activities Committee (HUAC) in 1945. The list of alleged communists in the government that Senator Joseph McCarthy announced he possessed in February 1950 differed from the similar list produced by the Dies Committee ten years earlier only in that McCarthy, rather than disclose it in full, was wily enough to drip-feed names to the media a few at a time in order to keep his accusations in the public eye. What was novel—and what made McCarthy more than a nine-days' wonder—was the international context combined with the gradual crumbling of bipartisan support for Truman's foreign policy. The outbreak of the Korean War in June following the "loss" of China the previous year, not to mention the conviction of Klaus Fuchs for passing atomic secrets to the Russians, appeared to give some measure of credence to McCarthy's wild charges. A special sub-committee of the Senate Foreign Relations Committee (which became McCarthy's platform), the Senate Judiciary Committee, and various other bodies, all involved themselves in the quest to root out subversives. The Truman administration, which had launched its own, deeply flawed, loyalty program within days of the Truman Doctrine speech in 1947, was cowed, confused, and compromised by its own previously demonstrated willingness to ride roughshod over civil liberties in the same cause.[47] The UN stood to be damaged by the anti-communist tide, partly because of the proximity of its New York headquarters to U.S. political events, but not least because internationalism per se was increasingly perceived as suspicious.[48] This was especially true when it was compounded by the sin of intellectualism.[49] And the fact that Alger Hiss, the State Department official brought down by the allegations of the former communist Whittaker Chambers, had played an organizational role at the 1945 San Francisco conference doubtless helped stigmatize the UN further.

Paradoxically, it was "when the UN was most directly in conflict with Communist ambitions in Korea, that the organization was most suspect in America as a supposed hotbed of Communism."[50] The controversy surrounded U.S. nationals working for the UN; non-U.S. nationals were for the most part[51] safe from active persecution if not from whispering campaigns, although the atmosphere was oppressive and demoralizing.[52] In many ways, the situation was ludicrous. As Dean Acheson (U.S. secretary of state 1949–1953), acknowledged in his memoirs, Trygve Lie, the UN Secretary-General, "could hardly require appointments to turn upon a candidate's views in a field where the orthodoxy of one superpower became heterodoxy, or even criminality, as seen by another."[53] However, after 1949, the State Department itself had begun to offer "derogatory information" to Lie about UN employees and prospective

employees.⁵⁴ (By the end of December 1952, the department had commented
adversely on forty people, thirty-eight because they were believed to be communists or under communist discipline and two on "morals" grounds. "Morals" is possibly code for "homosexuality."⁵⁵) This, surprisingly, was at Lie's own
request. "If there was even one American Communist in the Secretariat I wished
to get rid of him," he recalled in his memoirs. The information thus provided
was unsubstantiated, and insufficient in itself, in Lie's view, to warrant action.
It was, however, enough to raise his suspicions about various individuals, and
in 1950–1952, several staff on temporary contracts "against whom I felt I had
convincing evidence of improper activity" were dismissed. The issue exploded
publicly in 1952, when the Senate Internal Security Sub-Committee and a federal grand jury in New York began to investigate U.S. nationals employed by
the UN who were suspected of subversion. During the course of these hearings, eighteen UN staff invoked the Fifth Amendment of the American constitution—that is to say, they declined to answer questions on the grounds
that to do so might lead them to incriminate themselves. (Not all of these had
earlier been the subjects of adverse State Department comment.) Lie dismissed
them on the grounds that they had breached the staff code, having "not conducted themselves as international civil servants should."⁵⁶

This was surely a further error of judgment, compounding his original
decision to try actively to vet staff for communism; and he subsequently made
more mistakes. In Lie's defense, it may be noted that, in general, he was no
mere American stooge—he had taken a firm stand, for example, in favor of
UN representation for communist China—and that he was undoubtedly under immense personal pressure. On November 10, he suddenly announced
his resignation, although no successor could immediately be found, and he
continued in office until the following spring. (Rumor had it that the timing
of the announcement was affected by his fear that members of his own en-
tourage were to be attacked.⁵⁷) Three days later, Abraham H. Feller, one of his
closest advisors who had represented him in his dealings with the investiga-
tory bodies, and who the Americans considered to have had doubtful past
associations, committed suicide.⁵⁸ Lie publicly blamed the "prolonged and
serious strain" of upholding law and justice "against indiscriminate smears
and exaggerated charges."⁵⁹ Then, in December, the New York grand jury, without bringing any indictments or naming any names, reported that there was
"infiltration into the United Nations of an overwhelmingly large group of
disloyal United States citizens" and that this constituted "a menace" to the
U.S. government.⁶⁰ On 9 January 1953, in the dying days of the Truman administration, that government issued an executive order requiring a full investigation by the Federal Bureau of Investigation (FBI) of all U.S. citizens
employed on the professional staff of the UN. Lie extended his cooperation to

this investigation to the extent of allowing FBI agents onto UN premises to conduct interviews.[61] Contrary to legend,[62] the new Secretary-General, Dag Hammarskjöld, did not order the FBI men off the premises as soon as he took up office in April but waited until November, when he found a pretext for doing so.[63] (At the same time, however, he did not reinstate those dismissed employees vindicated by the UN appeals procedure that wanted to return but elected to pay them compensation instead.) The lengthy FBI investigation rumbled on, leading to no revelations, and there was further gnashing of congressional teeth at the payment of compensation to the eleven UN employees whose appeals were upheld. But during 1954, McCarthy discredited himself terminally, and the pressure on the UN eased up.

The Harassment and Resignation of David Weintraub

In the meantime, the DEA had been scarred. One of the chief victims of these events in the DEA was David Weintraub, a former United Nations Relief and Rehabilitation Administration (UNRRA) official who in 1946 had been appointed director of the Division of Economic Stability and Development.[64] It is worth considering his case in detail as a counterpoint to the rather different way in which Kalecki was subsequently to leave the UN. Hans Singer recalled Weintraub as "a very brilliant man," a former New Dealer, and a convinced Keynesian.[65] He was the subject of a State Department adverse comment in April 1950, but at this time was counted with officials who "could be criticized for some of their past associations" but against whom it was unlikely to prove possible to sustain a case.[66] Nevertheless, during the early months of 1952 the pressure on him intensified, as he had been responsible for employing Irving Kaplan, a suspected communist, whose employment was terminated at the end of May.[67] Weintraub's appointment as director of the DEA had been mooted, but the Americans acted to block the appointment, telling Lie that he would not enjoy the confidence of the U.S. officials with whom he would have to deal. Lie curried favor by speaking of him derisively in private:

> Mr. Lie said that he was very much concerned about Weintraub. He described Weintraub as a person who constantly strove for the goodwill of the Delegations, particularly those from the underdeveloped countries. . . . In his own words "Weintraub helps everybody but me." Mr. Lie then went on to say that Weintraub had surrounded himself with Radicals and Socialists and added that he was saying this in spite of the fact that he, himself, was a Social-Democrat. . . .
>
> Lie commented that he would not appoint Weintraub unless Weintraub was recommended by the U.S. Government and that it was probable Weintraub would be looking for a job five or six months hence. [68]

The Senate Internal Security Sub-Committee questioned Weintraub in May 1952 and again between October and December of the same year, as did the grand jury.[69] He answered all questions fully, denying that he was, or had ever been, a communist.[70] Although at the end of December, the Justice Department told the Senate that there had been forty-three "derogatory" FBI reports on him—and although at some stage Whittaker Chambers, the former communist turned "supergrass" named him—no evidence against him was ever made public.[71] It is not surprising that in the atmosphere of the time, even some of his own colleagues were reportedly too scared to stand up for him.[72] He came under pressure from the higher echelons of the UN to resign. At one stage it was suggested that he might be put on leave for two years to undertake a survey for the Israeli government: "Mr. Lie said he did not care what happened as long as Weintraub was out of the Secretariat for the next couple of years."[73] Eventually, the hounding became too much and he resigned in January 1953, "to spare the United Nations embarrassment." Lie sent him a letter, which was made public, in which he stated regret at Weintraub's resignation.[74] Weintraub's friends interpreted this to mean that Lie himself did not think that the accusations were justified.[75] However, that Lie was not sincere seems to be the likelier explanation.

In April 1953, Sidney Dell reported to Kaldor:

> Morale has jumped appreciably here since the appointment of the new Secretary-General and the general talk of peace [in Korea]. Many people here have wondered whether Dave acted correctly in resigning when he did. . . . Dave himself still thinks that he would have been steadily persecuted had he stayed on, and things have moved to the point at which even the new SG couldn't have prevented that. As it is, Dave has been left completely alone since he resigned.[76]

Happily, Weintraub's friends, notably Arthur Lewis, rallied round to secure him an academic appointment in Britain.[77] At the end of June 1953, he accepted the offer of a visiting professorship at the University of Manchester.[78] Eventually, he was appointed as manager of the Industrial Development Corporation of Trinidad, where he died.[79]

Reorganization of the DEA and Kalecki's Resignation in 1954

By contrast with Weintraub, Kalecki was not a direct victim of McCarthyism but rather of his own status as a "defiant bureaucrat." Weintraub's resignation created the opportunity to try to solve a variety of problems that were perceived in the existing structure of the Division of Economic Stability and Development. It was seen as "disproportionately large," undertaking functions that were "too wide in scope." This gave rise to "complex problems" of direction and management. In particular, the principal director was overburdened with duties related to divisional organization and insufficiently connected to the substantive economic work of the division. Initial proposals centered on the creation of a new principal director's division, to be headed by a Mr. Rosenborg. In this sketch, a new and separate Division of Economic Stability would also have been created with "Kalecki as Director; no change in scope."[80]

By October 1953, no firm recommendations for change had emerged from discussions between Guillaume Georges-Picot (assistant secretary-general for the Departments of Economic and Social Affairs) and Roy Blough, the DEA principal director.[81] By November, however, Blough had circulated to Henry S. Bloch and H. E. Caustin a draft memorandum by the Secretary-General on "Reorganization of the Secretariat." The draft made the general argument that the Secretariat was overstaffed because of an excessive enthusiasm for undertaking research, sometimes following requests by delegations that the Secretariat had orchestrated. It included specific proposals for merging and splitting departments, but neither Kalecki nor Hilgerdt were to be consulted.[82] In March 1954, the Secretary-General announced that "it may prove necessary in some cases to revise the character of posts or to eliminate posts on the senior level."[83] The Secretary-General's policy was that displaced staff members should, subject to grade and qualifications, be reassigned to the maximum possible extent—in spite of the adverse impact of this on the promotion prospects of more junior staff.[84]

On 19 May 1954, Blough informed Kalecki that a reorganization of the Secretariat would result in the elimination of his post. He would, however, be allowed to continue with the rank of assistant director (grade D-1) while doing the work of a chief of section for the time being. However, it was envisaged that he would become surplus to the needs of the department in either April 1955 or April 1956, at which point he would have to be reassigned elsewhere, without any guarantee that his new responsibilities would be commensurate with his grade.[85] Kalecki interpreted this as a "drastic demotion," while he believed his eight years of service made it appropriate to promote him.

Concomitantly with the abolition of Kalecki's post, a special Board of Directors was to be formed to assume editorial control over the *World Economic Reports*. At the end of May, Hammarskjöld contacted Sir Dennis Robertson, the prominent British anti-Keynesian economist, and invited him to serve on an informal committee. The committee's purpose was to advise the Secretary-General with respect to the economic program of the United Nations, especially the *World Economic Report*. Hammarskjöld told Robertson that he expected "to lean heavily on the group for advice leading to the improvement of the *World Economic Report*."[86] The informal committee was not convened until December 1954, but the Secretary-General had already by late September decided that "a high-ranking economist would be brought in for a one-year assignment to get out the *World Economic Report*" and that "each year's report would be got out under the direction of a different man."[87]

Having indicated his dissatisfaction to Blough and received no response, Kalecki submitted his resignation to Hammarskjöld on 1 October 1954.[88] Blough drafted a reply for Hammarskjöld accepting Kalecki's resignation with regret. He said in his covering note: "I had the impression that he [Kalecki] would withdraw his resignation if certain assurances regarding his status and functions were given, but as that would seem to upset your plans for the future of the work I have not included an alternative draft along such lines."[89]

Hammarskjöld dispatched Blough's draft, which recapitulated the decision to prepare the *World Economic Report* in a different manner from the past and added that any reorganization might cause highly qualified people not to find a place that was acceptable to them. Thus, at the start of 1955, Kalecki found himself heading back to Poland, with his friends in some trepidation about how the government there would treat a man who, however communist he might be feared to be in America, the Polish authorities regarded as a "bourgeois economist."[90]

It was at this point that Hammarskjöld convened his advisory group, consisting of Robertson, John H. Williams (Harvard), Richard M. Bissell Jr., and Ingvar Svennilson.[91] The timing is significant. Hammarskjöld explained it by saying that the meeting should be at the time "when the Report is at the right stage for the group to make its most effective contribution."[92] It was after Kalecki's departure, not before. The group gathered in New York in late January 1955 and gave their advice in a four-page letter to Hammarskjöld. It began by saying that it would be wise to change the "scope and character" of the report, which should in future "address itself to a major economic problem or complex of related problems or should, at least, be constructed around a central unifying theme." This was recognition that all was not well in the division, and the problem identified by Austin Robinson—the lack of an architect for the *World Economic Reports*—had never been solved. How to solve it? The group recommended securing "each year an economist of outstanding ability who could be attached to the staff of the Secretary-General and whose main responsibility would be the preparation of the Report." The group was in fact concurring with what Hammarskjöld had already decided to do.

The informal committee was better at implying what the faults were in the existing arrangement than at suggesting a feasible alternative. In plain cipher, the existing format was too much of a straitjacket, did not produce overall consistency, and yet, paradoxically, managed to entrench "a single set approach to world economic problems"—they did not say so, but the Keynes-Kalecki view of the way that economies work was surely intended here. The proposed remedy was radical. Part II, on international trade and payments, described as "well conceived and valuable," should be spun off as a separate publication to include, in due course, commodity problems and international capital movements. Part I, the Kalecki team's analysis of individual country national accounts, should be "handled, we believe, in the three regional reports and the special supplements on Africa and the Near East." The informal committee did not, astonishingly, consider as a "serious" omission the fact that their proposal would remove all analysis of the U.S., Canadian, Australian, and New Zealand national accounts from UN publications.[93]

Clearly, Kalecki was not just a chance victim of a normal economy drive.[94] Within the overall context of genuine attempt at organizational reform, there was a determined attempt by Hammarskjöld and his top officials not just to remove Kalecki's editorial control of Part 1 of the *World Economic Report* but either to disperse or to discontinue that entire line of work. Was he therefore the victim of a deeply cynical ploy to oust him from the UN? This is what Eshag suggested when he described the reorganization as a long-awaited "opportunity for pushing Kalecki out of the UN."[95] He inferred that the reorganization was concocted in bad faith from the fact that "once Kalecki was safely out of the way, the *WERs* continued to be written as before by UN staff; not a single issue was written by outside experts."[96]

It seems quite improbable that the plan was trumped up in bad faith or that it was intended to provoke Kalecki's resignation from the UN. It is clear that both Sidney Dell and Dudley Seers believed at the time that Hammarskjöld fully intended to appoint a distinguished outsider to take charge of the *World Economic Reports*. Dell entered into intensive correspondence with Kaldor between autumn 1954 and the spring of 1955 to persuade Kaldor to take on the task in 1956. Kaldor was blackballed (probably because of U.S. opposition) in April 1955, and then Hammarskjöld wrote to Gunnar Myrdal asking him to undertake the job, although he was still head of the ECE and therefore not an outsider in the sense that the informal committee had intended. The two Swedes had very different economic perspectives, and the Secretary-General probably soon thought better of his offer.[97] The Secretary-General may also have tried to secure Dennis Robertson, but if so, no letter survives in his papers.[98] When Dell had told Kaldor that "the ideal man would be Dennis Robertson," he added "but that's not very likely."[99]

The new regime for the *World Economic Survey* emerged "after many ups and downs and much toing and froing" in October 1955, a full year after

Kalecki's resignation. Jacob Mosak was appointed as head of a new Economic Survey Branch, with Dell and Chudson as section chiefs responsible for developed and underdeveloped countries. It was at this point that it was decided "to leave the writing of the Survey entirely to the Secretariat, and not engage any outside help," except, that is, for a panel of consultants with whom the staff could "chat from time to time about the world economic situation and matters related thereto." This panel was, according to Dell, "to give the top brass here the feeling that we are proceeding along the right lines," and he foresaw that "it may disappear once confidence in the staff has been restored."[100] This suggests that the reorganization was designed to solve a real problem and one that went wider than simply Kalecki.[101] The absence of an outside author may have had no more significant cause than that an appropriate distinguished person could not be easily found. The new internal team was certainly expected to come up with a new, looser, and more flexible pattern for the report, experimenting as necessary.

Although both Eshag and Braun believed that the reorganization plan was made in the hope that Kalecki would not accept it and resign, Sidney Dell did not think so at the time. His interpretation, as relayed to Kaldor, was quite different:

> As a matter of fact, Frank Green [the executive officer of the department] told me that the people at the top believed that Kalecki would have to try and stay on at the UN no matter how much humiliation was poured on him, and consequently that they did not believe he would resign. One of the things that irked Kalecki, in fact, was that the top people had this crazy notion that he could not afford to leave. Whether he left on the right issue is, I agree, open to some doubt. But he had got very sick of life here—the filthy goings on of the last two or three years have aged him tremendously, surprisingly enough.[102]

The four previous years had been a deeply undermining experience for many UN officials. They had seen their colleagues dismissed for undeniably political reasons. Apart from Weintraub, Joel Gordon (the chief of the current trade analysis section of the Division of Economic Stability and Development, DEA) was one of those who invoked the Fifth Amendment[103] and was subsequently dismissed.[104] They had been subject to interrogation if they were U.S. or Latin American citizens or surveillance if they were not.[105] Kalecki had been under constant pressure to alter his approach to Part 1 of the *World Economic Report*, for example over his decision to include material on China.[106] Although he was not a communist, his defense of his independence of judgment left him wide open, in the oppressive atmosphere of those years, to the accusation of being one or of being a communist sympathizer. The anxiety of his situation had had a physical effect on him, and in the end he decided that he had had enough and chose the timing and manner of his departure. However, his resignation from the UN by no means marked the end of his intellectual influence there. Rather the reverse was true, because the ideas that he had set out in "The Problem of Financing Economic Development" would soon bear fruit in ECLA and elsewhere.

Conclusion: The Weintraub and Kalecki Exits Compared

The ways in which the UN careers of David Weintraub and Michal Kalecki were ended differ in three key respects. First, David Weintraub suffered at the hands of Trygve Lie at the height of the McCarthy madness. By late 1954, when Kalecki resigned, the worst excesses of McCarthyism in the UN were over. Hammarskjöld had belatedly removed FBI agents from the supposedly diplomatically immune UN headquarters, and this had raised somewhat the morale of UN staff. Second, Weintraub's life was clearly made an absolute misery, and he really was hounded out of the UN. By contrast, the reorganization that occasioned Kalecki's resignation from the UN has been given too Machiavellian an explanation. It was a genuine effort at reorganization, linked to problems of research management, and not an ad hominem maneuver to force Kalecki out. Kalecki was not affected by the early plans of 1953, although this seems to have changed in late 1953, when neither Kalecki nor Hilgerdt was consulted. Had Kalecki been able to stomach the considerable humiliation handed out to him (though a far less public one than Weintraub's), he would have been able to keep his UN employment.

Third, Weintraub was a U.S. citizen, and hence he was vulnerable to very direct pressure from the U.S. administration. Although many potentially relevant documents remain security classified, there does not appear to be any evidence that the U.S. had particular concerns about Kalecki or that they ever pressured the UN to get rid of him. The U.S. government did recognize that there were UN employees who were "out of sympathy with the Communist regimes now in control of their home countries" and saw "the importance of maintaining a distinction as between these persons, who are on the United Nations secretariat in considerable number, and secretariat employees and delegation personnel who are communists."[107] If there was no U.S. pressure, it is difficult to see why Hammarskjöld should have chosen to rid himself of Kalecki on political grounds. Other Poles with "awkward" (but noncommunist) opinions, such as Wladek Malinowski, were not forced out. Hammarskjöld was far more circumspect about these matters than Lie had been. He was concerned, to put it at its lowest, not to *appear* to be dismissing or transferring staff because they were suspected of communism, for fear that he would provoke staff troubles.[108] Nevertheless, although Kalecki was not victimized for "communism," he was treated shabbily, and the awkwardness of his (real) views played a part in bringing this about. If Weintraub was victimized for communist beliefs that he did not hold, Kalecki suffered for noncommunist beliefs about economic development that he did indeed hold—too strongly for the comfort of his senior UN colleagues.

Kalecki's experience at the UN fits well with the modified Weberian model of bureaucracy discussed in the introduction. The official requirement of objectivity, even though he tried to serve this goal most meticulously, was constraining to his creativity. His most valuable intellectual work—on the financing of economic development—was done in response to a nonofficial lecture invitation. In his official work, he pursued a strongly independent line, as exemplified particularly by his membership of the IBRD Advisory Council. Clearly Kalecki was a defiant bureaucrat, and his superiors must have regretted that his hiring had not accorded with Loveday's maxim on recruitment—select for personality first and for intellect second. It might be objected that Kalecki would have been, in Joan Robinson's words, an awkward cuss in any situation, so that his case tells us little about international bureaucracies. Kalecki, however, was not the only example of the breed of defiant bureaucrat in the UN. We have seen that Hammarskjöld's arrival brought a stronger and more active management of UN economic research. In the next chapter we show how he guided the DEA away from what the Americans called the "extreme Keynesianism" of Nicholas Kaldor and toward the more politically consensual concept of "economic development."

4

From Full Employment to Economic Development

- **The Mantle of the League**
- **The Political Economy of Full-Employment Policies in the U.S.**
- **The International Dimension of Full-Employment Policies**
- **Full-Employment Measures: The Geneva ECOSOC Meeting**
- **Evaluation and Aftermath**
- **The Retreat from "Extreme Keynesianism"**
- **From Underemployment to Economic Development**
- **The Pursuit of Economic Development: A Move to Safer Ground?**

The Mantle of the League

By 1947, the new United Nations organization was perceived to be "carrying on largely in the League [of Nations] tradition and by League methods."[1] This might seem odd, given that cooperation in economic and social matters was a fundamental objective of the UN, whereas it had never been one of the formally stated purposes of the League. The difference was, however, more one of theory than of practice. The scope and importance of economic and social tasks had grown greatly in the lifetime of the League, so that by 1939 a new Central Committee of the League was under consideration to ensure its proper coordination.[2] Thus, ECOSOC was clearly foreshadowed by the earlier institution, and there was a wealth of precedent and practical experience of promoting economic and social cooperation for the new UN to draw upon.

That the UN's Department of Economic Affairs should follow the tradition of the League of Nations and produce an annual *World Economic Report*, which in the mid-1950s even reverted to the old title, *World Economic Survey,* was therefore predictable. The DEA was the institutional successor of the League of Nations Economic Intelligence Service (EIS). Continuity of personnel, which was considerable, implied continuity in modes of operation. Folke Hilgerdt had come to the department from the EIS, where he had worked on the *Network of Foreign Trade* (1942). Another transferee was Ragnar Nurkse, who had been the editor of the wartime editions of the League's *World Economic Survey* and author of substantial parts thereof.

The DEA also inherited an intellectual perspective from the days of the League. With the financial assistance of the Rockefeller Foundation after 1933, the EIS had devoted much of its effort to analyzing the phenomenon of the business cycle and especially to the problem of the international transmission of depressions. Its director, Dr. Alexander Loveday, had seen it as his and the service's mission to elucidate the mechanisms by which the contagion of economic depression was spread and thereby to educate nations into more cooperative behavior in the international economic sphere. Even so, it was clear by 1939 that rational persuasion alone would not be sufficient to achieve this.[3]

This focus on the spread of depression was a mixed inheritance for the DEA. On the positive side, the League had been able to attract economists of much creativity, such as Gottfried Haberler, Jan Tinbergen, J. J. Polak, and Tjalling Koopmans. Their work on transmission mechanisms of depression was done at a high technical and professional standard. Under the auspices of the League, they had produced pioneering publications in this field.[4] Their work was marked by a strong quantitative basis in statistics, including innovative efforts in econometrics. They used these methods to construct numerical models of the economic interdependence of nations. In particular, they demonstrated how depressions originating in the U.S. were transmitted to the smaller and more passive European economies. The lesson that the DEA carried into the post-1945 world was the imperative need for nations to coordinate their economic policies rather than to act independently by following short-run national interest.

However, on the negative side, the League's prewar business-cycle research was deficient in two important ways to meet the emerging needs of the postwar international economic scene. First, it had stood somewhat apart from the new macroeconomics of Keynes's *General Theory* (1936). The League's senior external advisor on its business-cycle work had been Dennis Robertson, who was a strong critic and persistent opponent both of the *General Theory* and of the work of Keynes's disciples.[5] Admittedly, Robertson's supervision of the research was superficial, as he willingly admitted.[6] Nevertheless, it was clear that Keynes's advice was to be avoided.[7] The distance was exaggerated by Keynes's highly critical review of the first volume of Tinbergen's 1939 study for the League, pointing out numerous sources of bias in the novel econometric methods that it applied—although not all of these criticisms were well founded.[8] Yet Keynes's conclusion that mass involuntary unemployment was avoidable by state action brought a wholly new dimension to the idea of international economic policy coordination.

UN economic thinking combined a belief in global economic interdependence with an expectation of imminent negative economic shocks in the immediate aftermath of the Second World War. The Allied victory having established the political conditions for greater international cooperation, the UN Secretariat believed that such cooperation would be needed very soon in order to combat the spread of depression. The economists who had joined the ECE, for example, were strongly of this view. Kaldor had written of the tendency toward depression and unemployment in an appendix that he wrote to William Beveridge's *Full Employment in a Free Society*. Gunnar Myrdal, also writing in 1944, forecast a deflationary crisis within three years of the end of the war in his *Varning fo fredsoptimism* (*Warning against Peace Optimism*).[9] What had changed since the days of the League was that Keynes's policy ideas now suggested that there were ways in which negative shocks could be neutralized in their country of origin by appropriate government fiscal measures. This suggested two major—and intimately linked—areas for future international action. One was that the national measures taken by each country to counter a decline in the domestic level of effective demand should be coordinated in the international arena. The other was that appropriate trade and payments measures to allow national governments to maintain internal demand in the event of an external economic shock needed to be negotiated. Then, if each country were to take appropriate measures to maintain full employment and the international trade and payments regime was such as to permit this policy response, the international transmission of depressions could be made a thing of the past.

The second important limitation of the League's business-cycle research was that it had mostly concerned itself with the U.S. and Europe. As late as 1938, the *World Economic Survey* that James Meade edited on "world business activity" paid virtually no attention to what were by the 1940s called the underdeveloped countries.[10] Many of these in Latin America and Asia were now looking to play a different role in the world economic system than they had previously, an aspiration that would gather strength as decolonization proceeded. The early thinking of Prebisch was driven by a wish to understand the impact of the U.S. business cycle on Latin America and to use that understanding to propose a new international division of labor. The DEA would have to find ways of relating its work to these aspirations of the underdeveloped countries at a time when it was not at all clear how Keynes's theory could throw light on the problem of economic development, as opposed to that of economic stability.

These two themes, developing out of the prewar work of the League, heavily occupied the first decade of the DEA. The modality of the work shifted, however. Instead of employing distinguished economists to produce heavy research tomes, as the League had done, the DEA made much use of the device of the expert group.[11] An expert group would be constituted of a small number of well-known economists from different parts of the world. It would meet a few times and its report would be drafted by one of the members and after amendment approved by the others. This had the advantage of including representative figures from different regions and countries, thereby building up more support for the report's recommendations. Yet this approach to informing and influencing policymaking was potentially more superficial. Gottfried Haberler, for example, seems to have thought so. He preferred the League's approach to research and paid tribute to "that remarkable group of economists at Geneva," who

> supported by a very small budget (compared with the sums at the disposal of international agencies in the post-war period) . . . produced a most impressive collection of analytical and statistical documents dealing with the many problems of international trade, economic development, commercial, financial and monetary policies, while at the same time advising many governments on their economic problems.[12]

The Political Economy of Full-Employment Policies in the U.S.

In his presidential address to the American Economic Association in Detroit on 28 December 1938, Alvin Hansen declared that while the business cycle had been the problem of the nineteenth century, "the main problem of our times, and particularly in the United States, is the problem of full employment." It posed a dilemma in that to ignore rising unemployment threatened political dangers in a democratic society but so did trying to remove it.

> Continued unemployment on a vast scale . . . could be expected to lead straight into an all-round regimented economy. But so also, by an indirect route and a slower process, might a greatly extended program of public expenditures. And from the standpoint of economic workability the question needs to be raised how far such a program might be carried out in a democratic society without raising the cost structure to a level that prevents full employment. Thus a challenge is presented to all those countries which have not as yet submitted to the yoke of political dictatorship.[13]

Hansen's indirect route to a regimented economy was inflation, which he thought could spiral out of control as the tap of public expenditure was turned on to raise the level of employment.

During the Second World War, the United States itself had briefly become an all-round regimented economy, as the Office of Price Administration carried out a program of price control, of which John Kenneth Galbraith was the principal architect. This had been highly unpopular, and a pledge to end rationing and price control was a factor in the Republican congressional victory of 1946. At the same time, the Employment Act of 1946 was passed, but with the words "full employment" omitted, replaced by the ambiguous phrase "maximum employment, production and purchasing power." This legislative attempt to counterbalance the employment objective with an anti-inflation objective was an obvious intellectual fudge. However, it accurately reflected the divided state of opinion both between the political parties and within the U.S. economics profession.

Broadly speaking, there were three attitudes, both among American economists and politicians, toward the policy of full employment, and they endured for at least the next twenty years. As far as the economists are concerned, some, such as Henry Simons of Chicago University, held that inflation was an inevitable result of a budget deficit and that "we should set ourselves resolutely against using inflation as a means of enlarging employment."[14] This was also the standard Republican attitude. On the Democratic side, some, such as Paul Samuelson and Robert Solow, believed that the pursuit of full employment was possible without inflation getting out of hand but that wage and price controls in peacetime would be unacceptable to Americans.[15] Others, such as J. K. Galbraith, Lawrence Klein, and Walt Rostow, were in favor of guaranteeing full employment and using wage and/or price controls, if they proved necessary, to halt any inflationary consequences of doing so.[16] In the light of the wartime experience of controls, however, this left-Keynesian position was unpalatable to many American voters.

Thus, as the UN prepared to address the issue of full employment, there was no Keynesian consensus in the U.S. This is true both in the sense that full employment remained a partisan issue in national politics and in the sense that among its supporters and advocates crucial cleavages of opinion existed about how it should be brought about and sustained. There was much genuine uncertainty about what this pursuit of full employment by governments implied in practice and where it might land the world's largest capitalist democracy. Michal Kalecki had captured this public mood in his 1943 article on the political aspects of full employment:

> The necessity that "something must be done in the slump" is agreed; but the fight continues, firstly, as to *what* should be done in the slump (i.e. what should be the direction of government intervention) and secondly, that it should be done *only* in the slump (i.e. merely to alleviate slumps rather than to secure permanent full employment).[17]

Kalecki also astutely foresaw that a government commitment to a policy of permanent full employment would be a significant threat to business interests and would be resisted in the political arena. In late-1940s America, such resistance was beginning to crystallize, driven by antipathy both to inflation and to "big government."

The International Dimension of Full-Employment Policies

In its first five years, ECOSOC was very active in considering international measures to promote full employment. In 1957, however, Arthur Lewis reported that ECOSOC's "interest in employment policies has waned in recent years."[18] He attributed that to the low level of cyclical unemployment in industrial countries, but that was just one of several contributory causes. Not the least important among these was the strong differences of view on this subject between the governments of the United States and those of other industrial countries, notably the UK, where the Keynesian consensus was stronger. Another important influence was the economic perspective of Dag Hammarskjöld, who succeeded Trygve Lie as UN Secretary-General in 1953.

Divergent attitudes to full employment between the UK and the U.S. were evident by the end of the Second World War. In May 1945, James Meade noted in his diary

> a very dangerous trend of thought in the USA, of which Will Clayton in the State Department may be taken as the symbol, that the way to cure unemployment is to have stable exchange rates and free trade rather than (what is much nearer the truth) that the only way to achieve the conditions in which one can establish freer trade and more stable exchange rates is for countries to adopt suitable domestic policies for maintaining employment.[19]

The anxiety about the balance-of-payments consequences of trying to maintain full employment at home in the face of any decline in foreign demand for their exports was not uniquely British. Most other developed countries shared it at the time. Because of its uniquely strong position as a creditor nation, the United States was the only nation that was free of this fear during this period. Furthermore, the new Bretton Woods agencies were far from confident of their ability to prevent a depressive spiral should it begin. The IMF acknowledged in the Sub-Commission on Employment and Economic Stability of the UN Economic and Employment Commission the limitations on its capacity to deal with international economic fluctuations.[20]

The different credit positions of the U.S. and the European countries, particularly Britain, in the world economy put them at loggerheads, quite apart from the differences between them in the degree of national consensus around Keynesian policies. The Labour government of Clement Attlee was keen to use the UN as a forum to entrench Meade's view of the matter as the international orthodoxy as a shield against American pressure to liberalize trade and move toward currency convertibility.[21] When economic activity in the U.S. slackened in the spring of 1949, it initiated the resolution in ECOSOC of 11 August 1949 to establish a group of experts to examine the question and report.[22] Nicholas Kaldor, the research director of the Economic Commission for Europe, was one of the appointed experts.[23] The others were E. Ronald Walker (Australia, chairman), J. M. Clark (U.S.), Arthur Smithies (U.S.), and Pierre Uri (France).[24] Kaldor carried the main responsibility for drafting the report during seven weeks at the end of 1949.[25]

The report proposed a set of measures to maintain domestic full employment, which was essentially a codification of existing Keynesian policy practices and ideas. What was novel was the addition of a call for governments to adopt prespecified employment targets and to announce "automatic countermeasures" in the event either of rising unemployment or (interestingly, to modern eyes) of rising inflation. More dramatic and unconventional were the report's further proposals for international coordinated action. The report recommended that countries that permitted their imports to fall below a "normal" level (that is, a level consistent with full employment) should be obliged to deposit with the IMF an amount of their currency equivalent to the deflationary impulse thereby propagated. This would constitute a pool of foreign currencies available to be bought with the currencies of countries whose exports had been adversely affected by the deflation. In this way, the report filled out the idea of "appropriate full employment policies" that Meade had appealed to and gave them the international dimension that had previously been missing. "Without the restoration of over-all equilibrium in balances of payment, it will be impossible to achieve the kind of stable international framework within which [domestic] full employment policies can succeed."[26] Stable exchange rates and free trade alone would not restore balance-of-payments equilibrium in a world of scarce dollars, and "any premature attempt" to liberalize world trade before creating the conditions to maintain international demand "would consequently be doomed to failure."[27] This can be read as a coded reply to the U.S. position.

To emphasize the supportive external environment that national full-employment policies would require, the report made two more proposals that were effectively stepping-stones to greater international planning of trade and investment. They were that ECOSOC should convene a "world trade-adjustment conference . . . in which governments would examine each other's future trade plans and adjust their own plans in the light of what was thus revealed." Apart from this, the experts believed that "the problem of full employment cannot be solved except in the context of an expanding world economy of which the economic development of the underdeveloped countries would form the most important single element."[28] This required a new system of pre-planned and stable long-term international capital movements from the industrial to the underdeveloped countries. These capital transfers should be on a government-to-government basis, channeled through the IBRD. They should no longer be in the form of loans for specific projects but should rather be program loans for general development purposes.

The British watched the progress of the report through the Fifth Committee and the General Assembly and in U.S. and UK political forums and media with keen interest and not a little hope.[29] In the British press, *The Observer* was very favorable to the report. On the other hand, according to Kaldor, "*The Times* carried a fairly long report this morning on the speech of Sidney Caine in the Council. Though Robert Hall [head of the Economic Section of the Cabinet Secretariat] assured me that he had strict instructions to give warm support of the report as a whole, *The Times* account of his speech sounded highly critical."[30] On 21 January, Sidney Dell, whom Owen had recruited in 1947 and who had known Kaldor since before the war,[31] complained to Kaldor that the discussion of the report in the UN had "been on a pitifully low level. We were particularly annoyed with [the] U.S. and Canada who protest violently that they love the report, but who nevertheless seem to be doing their best to damn it."[32] Also, there was "disappointingly little editorial comment in the United States."[33] From London, Kaldor reflected back the Labour government's genuine enthusiasm. "With regard to the fate of the Report at this end, I gather H. M. G.'s attitude will be rather good since [Sir Stafford] Cripps [the Chancellor of the Exchequer] is very keen on it."[34] In Whitehall, Robert Hall was "trying hard to get it a favourable welcome. . . . So it will go forward quite strongly pushed and I think that Ministers will be even warmer."[35] The British plan was to get it referred to governments for the next ECOSOC in order to give time for reflection. Pragmatically, Hall thought "that the UK is stuck with Full Employment anyway so we *can't* lose by it and if [the] U.S. would accept it, it would be a great step forward."[36] The report was referred to the next ECOSOC meeting in Geneva in July 1950.

Full-Employment Measures: The Geneva ECOSOC Meeting

For the eleventh ECOSOC meeting in Geneva, Cripps urged UK representation at the ministerial level by Hugh Gaitskell, his minister of state at the

Treasury. Hall noted that both ministers "wanted us to be much more enthusiastic, to press for follow-up action, and to try hard to get the U.S. and other countries not only to accept the objectives but to report fairly soon on what they could do."[37] They were "thinking of introducing a Full Employment Bill for political reasons! and hence that it might be useful to have more obligations than we might otherwise have done."[38] The main problem for Britain was that it could hardly promise credibly that it would stabilize its external investment regardless of all else.

In the preliminary general discussion of the eleventh session, the report ran into opposition from both the IMF and the IBRD. The fund representative held that full employment was not a more important objective than a freely operating multilateral trading system, that there were technical and administrative deficiencies in the experts' plan, and that, if its resources were inadequate (which it had stated publicly previously), there were better ways of increasing them than by the mechanism proposed. The fund clearly feared that the effect of the experts' currency-deposit and -purchase scheme would be used to delay adjustment to a new international trade equilibrium rather than to facilitate it. Very lamely, the fund spokesman offered to examine the proposal as an alternative to the "scarce currency" clause in its articles—which was, and was to remain, a dead letter.[39]

The representatives of the bank were critical of the proposals for an expanded system of program loans through the IBRD. Kaldor wanted to address the council, but there was an attempt by the U.S. to prevent him from doing so on the ground that the expert group had by this time been dissolved. He was nevertheless invited to speak in his personal capacity.[40] He used the opportunity to indicate the scale of lending that he thought would be satisfactory both to accelerate economic development and to ease the international balance-of-payments problems sufficiently to return to general convertibility—some $2,000 million per year, net, of the repayment and amortization of current loans. He said that if the IBRD loaned at this rate, it would exhaust its resources in a little more than one year. According to him, the fundamental principle on which all the experts were agreed was "the need for greatly expanding the flow of capital to under-developed areas," and he was sure that the best technical method of doing it could be worked out. He ended by urging the bank to set its own lending target and indicate the resources that it would need to meet it.[41]

On 17 July, Gaitskell told ECOSOC that the danger of a U.S. economic downturn had been averted but "that was no reason for neglecting to make preparations" for a future occurrence.[42] The UK wholly agreed with the experts on the desirable domestic measures, but that was "the easiest part of the problem."[43] The problem was dealing with the balance-of-payments consequences of domestic demand management when "there was still an acute scarcity of dollars."[44] International discussions to map out a path toward a new equilibrium in world trade were highly desirable, but this would contain implications for what countries could do in terms of the export of capital. He also supported the proposal that countries in depression should make financial assistance available to the rest of the world; although that was second best to maintaining their normal level of imports through stockpiling, tariff cuts, or fiscal action. In sum, he called for other governments to join the UK to make the report "a blueprint for vital international economic cooperation."[45]

The U.S. delegate (Dr. Isador Lubin) did much as Dell had foreseen. He concurred with the report's recommendations for national unemployment targets and for the preparation of domestic countermeasures while rejecting the idea of their automatic application. On the international dimension, he agreed with the report's analysis that a new equilibrium in world trade was desirable and offered U.S. participation in consultations and further studies to that end. However, he rejected the proposals for pre-announced and stable levels of long-term export of capital and for an IMF-based scheme for currency deposit during depression. He argued that the first was not necessarily conducive to the formulation of sound investment projects, thereby sidestepping the experts' plea for program lending, and that the latter was unnecessary under existing IMF arrangements. He pledged instead that America would seek economic growth not only for domestic reasons "but also because of the place the American economy occupied in the world economic and political structure."[46]

After the meeting was over, Gaitskell reflected realistically on the limitations of ECOSOC as a political forum:

> We were able to make quite a splash with the speech both with the press here and at Geneva. But the atmosphere there was not very encouraging. One did not really feel, as one does in Paris, that anything much was really being done. Partly I think this was due to the lower level of quality of the delegates; partly perhaps to the fact that until recently ECOSOC, like other arms of the U.N.O., had simply been a battleground of propaganda between the Russians and the rest of us. The Russians, etc. were not there this time[47] and that gave opportunities for profitable discussion, but the people concerned were scarcely prepared for it. I was the only minister present, which was perhaps an indication of the kind of attitude adopted by most Governments towards ECOSOC.[48]

This passage catches both the enduring character of ECOSOC meetings—the low level of representation and delegates' lack of preparation—and the impact of the Cold War.

Evaluation and Aftermath

Jacob Viner provided the academic critique of the report that informed the U.S. diplomatic position. His considerable hostility to the report was based partly on reading into it the dark designs of creeping socialism on a world scale but partly also on having identified astute technical questions about how these grand schemes would be made to work in practice.[49] Despite his commitment to a "free market, free trade, free enterprise world," he was sufficiently fair-minded to say of the proposals: "Even more ardent individualists than I am can salvage a substantial number of ideas useful for the building of even their kind of a better world."[50] On the domestic front, he commended the idea of automatic stabilizers and flexible taxes as anti-depression devices, if these could be designed. On the international front, he agreed that the IMF and the IBRD both needed more resources and that the requirement that the bank lend only for specific projects should be removed. However, he found much more to castigate as wrongheaded, dangerous, or just plain impractical.

Viner challenged the idea, attributed to the report, that full employment should be pursued as the single social goal despite its costs in economic efficiency, inflation, and economic freedom.[51] On the international trade proposal, his main point was the difficulty of determining how much of any import decline is attributable to a general decline in effective demand and how much to other causes and the consequent time lag between the start of any recession and the time when the deposit and purchase of currency could take place.[52] To the idea of an increased and pre-planned flow of capital to underdeveloped countries, he objected that the bank lacked not resources but appropriate projects and that the capacity of underdeveloped countries to absorb capital would vary from year to year.[53] Leaving aside his ideological anxieties about free markets, Viner raised many unanswered questions about how the proposed arrangements could work.

Viner's tone was much sharper than that of the *Economic Journal* review by Walt Rostow, who had worked alongside Kaldor in the ECE. Rostow was much less questioning of the practical detail but nonetheless thought that the proposals "would require . . . a vast series of technical and political operations, by individual governments and among governments; and they conceal important, largely unexplored, economic problems."[54] Like Viner, Rostow saw the report as a political message "addressed to the American government and the American people."[55] Both men believed that the Depression was now history and that there was not much point in preparing to refight the battles of the 1930s.[56]

Nevertheless, despite the academic criticism, Dell was pleased with the impact on governments. "I was quite amazed when I read the resolution ultimately adopted—no one last December could possibly have imagined that the FE re-port would have so rapid and direct an impact upon governmental thinking."[57] Kaldor himself believed that the final ECOSOC resolution embodied "an im-portant new principle—each country should take positive measures to offset to the extent feasible, the adverse effects of its own economic recession on the level of employment in other countries." He added that "but for the Korean events, which for the time being removed any danger of recession in the near future," it would have been recognized as a very important document.[58] Much later, Dell admitted that the significance of the 1950 full-employment resolution in ECOSOC had been "short-lived," adding that "the resolution was in fact not generally implemented."[59]

Perhaps the best indication that *National and International Measures for Full Employment (NIFE)* had been regarded as politically unacceptable is the fact that on 15 August 1950, ECOSOC resolved that a second group of experts be invited to formulate alternative practical ways of reducing the interna-tional impact of recessions.[60] In March 1951, they were further charged with advising on how to reduce fluctuations in international markets affecting pri-mary producing countries. The rather more conservative economists produced a further report entitled *Measures for International Economic Stability.*[61] This second report had three main recommendations. It proposed the negotiation of a series of international commodity agreements. It proposed the expan-sion of the IBRD's total capital and its capital available for lending and ar-gued for countercyclical lending. Finally, it recommended an increase in the fund's resources and recommended modifications of existing IMF practices to make them less restrictive in the event of a recession. It was duly discussed in ECOSOC, which urged the fund to apply its rules more flexibly, as recom-mended, and to review the adequacy of monetary reserves.[62] Despite the group's effort to be realistic, its report was no more successful than its prede-cessor.[63] Essentially, it ran up against a blank wall both at the IBRD and at the IMF. In its subsequent review, the fund again acknowledged the inadequacy of its resources in the event of a depression and took the line that "primary reliance for the avoidance and cure of depressions must be placed upon ap-propriate measures at the national level, especially in industrial countries."[64] This merely handed responsibility for maintaining international economic stability back to the United States.[65]

The IMF, however, was happy enough to have the United States in the po-sition of final arbiter of the matter. It could be relied on for the defense of sound money. Per Jacobssen, who was to become managing director of the IMF 1956–1963, confided to his diary in 1954 this speculation:

I just wonder when I read Kahn and all the others, who fear a dollar shortage and try to prove it in various ways, whether their real line of thought—perhaps half unconsciously—is the following:

They all believe in an abundant money supply being necessary for full employment—they imagine (?) that they can neutralise the effects in the balance of payments by a severe import control—but are they quite sure they will succeed in doing that? Is there not a lingering suspicion that there will be a deficit in the balance of payments and that this will have to be met by an outflow of gold and dollars?

Instead of then having to admit that this is then the result of their own "full employment" policies they like to speak of a "dollar shortage." Maybe such an explanation could induce the Americans to put up the dollars? Was not that the "try-on" of the UN Committee on the International Aspects of a Full Employment Policy?[66]

The Retreat from "Extreme Keynesianism"

In the aftermath of *National and International Measures for Full Employment,* the UN began to pay heed to the criticism that its reports were "too Keynesian." This term conveyed a number of different and partly overlapping meanings. It was by no means an attempt to overthrow the main propositions of Keynes's *General Theory.* That was never on the cards in the 1950s. In the U.S., at the level of popular political discourse, "Keynesian" policies remained suspect, partly because they derived from a fancy doctrine and partly because they were a foreign import, and these unsophisticated suspicions fed (or rather were fed) into the anti-communist paranoia that spread in America after the outbreak of the Cold War.[67] In professional economists' discourse, however, the epithet "excessively Keynesian" embodied a rather more weighty complaint. It was a criticism of reductionism in economic analysis and policymaking. It often contained the implication that Keynes himself would have disapproved of this. Viner touched on this in his comments on the *NIFE* report:

The analysis presented here . . . is "Keynesian" in the simplest and most mechanical sense of that adjective. It is, I have no doubt, more Keynesian than was at least the final Keynes himself, especially in its confidence in forecasts and targets and in formulae, and in its unqualified pursuit of a single social goal.[68]

The Keynesian approach was faulted for being exclusively concerned with aggregative methods and for treating the "purely formal" summary concepts of investment, saving, consumption, and employment as if they were "the core of the analysis itself."[69] This pushed out of sight a host of microeconomic factors—price-cost relations, monopolistic practices, local technical changes—that were relevant to determining the level of employment.[70] In this aggregative approach, it was alleged, unemployment was attributed almost entirely to the lack of effective demand. The policy result of this, it was further claimed, was that very ambitious targets for "full" employment were then set, with automatic devices put in place to achieve them, while the danger of inflation was not treated symmetrically and was either ignored or proposed to be suppressed by direct controls.

The full indictment was not merely that many theoretical economic complexities had been washed out by the aggregation and that unemployment in industrial countries was attributed solely to lack of effective demand. There was an additional charge that there was a political dimension to the simplification, by which the economy was assumed to respond in an unproblematic way to regulation by the political authorities. There was more than a little truth in this. Because the Keynesian revolution had been to many economists counterintuitive, its ideas once grasped were often treated as a kind of economic hydraulics. For some economists, there was no employment problem that Keynesian hydraulics, used with enough political determination, could not solve. This was a manifestation not of idealism but of Icarus's urge to fly to the sun on wings bonded with glue. Even Kalecki, whose staff had assisted the experts who produced the *NIFE* report, had been skeptical of the realism of some of the proposals for international action, particularly the recommendation that governments should maintain external disbursements on current account in the face of a downturn in internal demand.[71]

"Extreme Keynesianism" was the term used by Charles P. Kindleberger in 1955 to criticize the *NIFE* report. To him, it represented "a fairly extreme Keynesian solution . . . offered to a problem to which the underlying analysis was not clearly appropriate and presented to a world which was not prepared to accept extreme Keynesian solutions (even though Keynesian analysis has been widely adopted)."[72] According to him, this was "the high-water mark of academic naivety" in the UN. He thought that it was this that had made the report ineffective, claiming that it had received little attention "save from the reviewers of the professional economics journals."[73] If criticism had been confined to the pages of academic journals, the proponents of international full-employment policies need not have been very concerned, but that was not the case.

An unexpected ally for the critics of "extreme Keynesianism" was the new Secretary-General, Dag Hammarskjöld. He no doubt would have been sensitive to both the professional and the populist resonance of Keynesian analysis and policy. As part of his education, he had studied economics under Keynes in 1927. Keynes had found him highly intelligent but not an original or creative economist.[74] This was not a wholly well-judged comment, since Hammarskjöld's dissertation of 1933 on the propagation of business cycles did include a more sophisticated analysis than Keynes's own of the determination of the price level of consumer goods.[75] What is true is that this work was not very influential and that Hammarskjöld subsequently published very little in the economics field. Before becoming Secretary-General, he had been a national public official concerned with financial and economic affairs in Sweden. During this time he was described by his fellow countryman Per Jacobssen as "conservative, of bureaucratic origin," having "a certain inclination to patriarchism." In Jacobssen's view, Hammarskjöld was "really a 'tory' and as such able to let the state's guardianship go quite far before he reacts."[76]

As an international civil servant, however, Hammarskjöld did react to his inheritance of staff with strong Keynesian commitments in the economic offices of the UN. His manner of doing so was to interpret the ideal of objectivity as maintaining a pragmatic and nondoctrinaire approach to economics. This attitude was illustrated by his remarks on the occasion of Gunnar Myrdal's departure from the ECE in 1957:

> I think it is our duty collectively to reflect as well as we can not this or that trend in political thinking in economics, but certainly the development of economic thinking at its best. It is eclectic; it is pragmatic, if you want.[77]

Temperamentally, he was inclined to isolate himself and to avoid getting entangled in debates about particular schools of economic thought, and his arrival at the UN left those who did identify themselves as Keynesians feeling more than a little exposed.

In fact, some interpreted Hammarskjöld's public statements of pragmatism as covert anti-Keynesianism. We have seen that Kaldor, as the main proponent of Keynesian "naivety," had already become a bête noir to the Americans.[78] Kaldor suspected that Hammarskjöld was taking their anti-Keynesian line. He recounted how "Gunnar [Myrdal] was rather surprised about what I told him about H's general views—he rather thought he was an economic planner and rather Left Wing and not an anti-Keynesian."[79] Dell responded by expressing his exasperation with the new anti-Keynesian feeling.

> I'm damned if I can see what all this prejudice is about—it's really sheer ignorance and nothing else. You'd be amazed at the level of discussion on these issues. We are told from on high, for example, that to discuss economic trends in aggregative terms is "too Keynesian." (Sometimes the thing has its funny side, in a horrible sort of way.)[80]

One of Hammarskjöld's actions to reassert management control over the Secretariat was to shut down its informal interaction with the delegations.

His compatriot Sune Carlsson, who was a director of the Economic Department, had set up a small free-form discussion group of officials and delegation members that discussed a circulated paper on a current ECOSOC issue in a nonofficial and nonpartisan atmosphere. This useful innovation did not last long. Janez Stanovnik recalled:

> Unfortunately, the secretary-general—at that time it was Hammarskjöld, I must say—had forbidden that to his own people from the secretariat. Namely, complaints were coming from certain delegations that this was a kind of influence of the secretariat on the delegations. Therefore, they had to discontinue this thing that I think was extremely useful. In a completely friendly, disinterested way, we [in the delegations] were able to see the gist of the matter.[81]

Hammarskjöld was evidently unhappy that the Secretariat staff were spreading controversial, and to the Americans, unacceptable views.

In a more positive mode, the Secretary-General's speech on the "World Economic Situation" to the July 1955 meeting of ECOSOC in Geneva marked a major switch of policy emphasis, away from the problem of managing effective demand in the industrial countries and toward the problem of underdevelopment. He put his case thus:

> We have now gained considerable insight into the problem of bridging a gap which may emerge between effective demand and the capacity to produce in developed countries. We have yet to acquire adequate experience and wisdom, however, in the matter of closing the large divide between productive capacity and human requirements in underdeveloped countries. This is the major long-term problem facing our generation, the greatest economic challenge to nations, both individually and collectively. . . . [I]t defines the major task of the UN.[82]

On the same occasion in 1956, he remarked that "unfortunately, the achievement in stabilizing the national economies of the developed countries finds no parallel in the stabilization of the national economies of the underdeveloped countries" and spoke of the "need to intensify our efforts, both national and international, to speed the process of economic development."[83] In these speeches, he was clearly drawing a line under the early Keynesian schemes of international measures to maintain full employment. At the same time, he was preparing the UN to address the coming decolonization of Africa.

From Underemployment to Economic Development

At the tenth session of ECOSOC, Brazil, Chile, India, Pakistan, and Peru had complained that resolution 308 (IV) of the General Assembly had stressed the need for action to overcome unemployment and underemployment in underdeveloped countries but that the *NIFE* report had thought that this was outside their terms of reference.[84] At the eleventh ECOSOC meeting in July 1950, the U.S. delegate, Isador Lubin, had concluded his speech by proposing that "the Secretary-General should be requested to appoint a group of experts to prepare a report on under-employment, particularly in the underdeveloped areas. Such action would, in his Government's view, be the logical development of activities already initiated in the United Nations."[85]

This U.S. proposal was acted on by resolution 290 (XI). A new expert group was appointed "to prepare, in the light of the current world situation and of the requirements of economic development, a report on unemployment and under-employment in under-developed countries, and the national and international measures required to reduce" them. George Hakim (Lebanon) chaired this expert group, and its other members were Alberto Baltra Cortéz (Chile), D. R. Gadgil (India), T. W. Schultz (U.S.), and W. Arthur Lewis, originally from the Caribbean but then a professor at Manchester University in England. In this expert group, the work of drafting the report seems to have been heavily influenced by the thinking of Arthur Lewis.

In fact, the report, published in 1951, had remarkably little to say specifically about unemployment and underemployment. It simply finessed the whole debate on these topics. The strategy adopted by the group was to put their emphasis on specifying "the requirements of economic development" and then argue that employment problems would be resolved once rapid economic development had got going.[86] Hence, they entitled their report *Measures for the Economic Development of Under-developed Countries*.[87] One widespread criticism was that the report never spelled out what it meant by the terms "economic development" or "economic progress," which were used interchangeably. That was assumed to be self-evident.

On the other hand, it did have much to say that was in tune with the very broad scope of the idea of development that became widely accepted by the end of the twentieth century. It stressed that a country's institutions must be conducive to development, not only its economic institutions, but also its social, legal, and political institutions (paragraph 23). It stressed that the political leadership of a country must be committed to a strategy for development rather than the entrenchment of its own privileges (paragraphs 37–38). It stressed that governments must do more than provide basic services and that they must be able to regulate economic activity, whether in the public or the private sector (paragraph 39). However, having laid out these fundamental political and social preconditions for successful economic development, the report tended to assume that they are, or easily can be, fulfilled in underdeveloped countries. It then proceeded to elaborate a much narrower model of strictly economic development. Between the sociopolitical preconditions and the working through of the economic model, there was an enormous leap of faith, a leap hardly avoidable given the unwritten diplomatic conventions of the Cold War.

This report, and the subsequent writings of Arthur Lewis, established a powerful paradigm of the process of economic development. Three optimistic economic assumptions followed up the underlying leap of faith about the soundness of the sociopolitical foundations for development. The first was that underdeveloped countries could draw on an ever-increasing stock of technologies, which had made each latecomer country's period of catching up shorter than its predecessor's.[88] The second was that the marginal productivity of capital must be higher in underdeveloped countries because of its scarcity there relative to labor. The third was that, because of gross underemployment of labor in the agricultural sector, labor was available at very low real cost and that this could be put to work with additional capital to produce labor-intensive manufactures for export.[89]

These assumptions gave credence to Lewis's basic model of economic development as a process of capitalist accumulation, one that gradually transferred into industrial employment, at a fixed real wage and without any shrinkage of agricultural production, of surplus labor from the agricultural sector. Once initiated, the transfer of labor would generate steady growth of the industrial sector because capitalists—whether private or public—saved and then reinvested their profits. Industry thus became ever larger in the structure of national output, and savings and investment became an increasing proportion of a growing national income.[90] It was this model, or rather this grand design for development based on previous economic history, which stood behind the 1951 report, even though it was not finally published until 1954. This kind of thinking legitimized the near-identification of economic development with industrialization. It then led perfectly naturally to the calculations in the expert group report of required rates of capital accumulation for industrial growth (paragraphs 239–241), the savings gap (paragraphs 246–248), and targets of capital exports from developed countries (paragraph 268).

The link between supplies of capital and economic growth was simple and mechanical, a number called the "capital/output ratio." Somewhere inside this capacious portmanteau of a statistic lay the problem of the lack of labor skills. T. W. Schultz, who was a member of the expert group, had at this point not started to develop the idea of human capital as a complementary factor to physical capital, or its corollary, the need for an appropriate balance between investment in physical and in human capital.[91] This did not happen until 1956.

The expert group, while acknowledging a skill shortage in underdeveloped countries, thought that the remedy was large-scale technical assistance.[92]

Anxieties about the international transmission of recession, and "Keynesian" schemes to prevent it, are here left behind. Lewis thought that, in that regard, future prospects were good. He had written in 1949:

> The U. S. A., whose fluctuations dominate the world economy, has learnt much since 1929. Agricultural prices can no longer topple catastrophically, because the parity formula puts a floor to them, and nearly all responsible Americans now seem to agree that it is the duty of their government to pursue a budgetary policy that will minimize industrial fluctuations. The world will yet see many slumps: but it is unlikely to repeat the horrors of the 1930s.[93]

Accordingly, the process of economic development could be analyzed in the classical framework of long-term structural change. Short-run problems that had occupied the Keynesians could be ignored. That meant that economic development was dealt with in a virtually closed economy model, any emerging savings or foreign exchange gaps being neutralized by offsetting external capital flows.

It was not this feature but that of a stagnant agriculture that raised most eyebrows. Peter Bauer was moved to protest:

> Especially in the early stages of economic development (but not only then), when agriculture and its ancillary activities account for most of the national income, and more particularly at the stage when an exchange economy is spreading but has not yet become dominant, there is often much activity in the extension and improvement of the cultivable area. . . . They are often an essential factor in economic growth at the early stages of the exchange economy. Their disregard vitiates much current discussion on underdeveloped countries.[94]

Partly, Lewis simply took over the assumption of stagnant agriculture from classical economic thought, which regarded the prospects of agricultural improvement as slight in "old" or "settled" countries. Partly, however, its use was validated in the 1950s because agricultural improvement in underdeveloped countries was understood as the mechanization of agriculture, which would necessarily displace rural labor. This point was made repeatedly in the ECOSOC debates.[95] Indeed, the terms of reference of the expert group had asked them to make recommendations on social security measures for agricultural workers who became unemployed because of technological progress. Thus, it was regarded as better to begin with industrialization that would absorb labor than with agricultural improvement that would, it was then thought, necessarily displace it.

Apart from generating a concept of economic development that made a profound impact on professional economic opinion, the report was important because it also popularized the practice of development planning. It recommended that developing-country governments should establish a central economic unit to carry out national economic surveys, make development programs, advise on policy measures for implementing them, and report on the outcomes. It specifically called for the drawing up of a national capital budget, showing how much new investment can be financed from domestic and how much from foreign sources.[96]

This emphasis on "planning" was picked on by economists of free market persuasion as evidence that the UN was promoting a technocratic, if not an autocratic, approach to development.[97] Such criticism was absolutely wrongheaded and misleading. The development planning of the report was distinctly different from Soviet-style physical planning, with its array of quantitative production targets for individual commodities. Lewis had previously distinguished this kind of "planning by direction" from "planning through the market," which was the method that he favored.[98] Development planning, far from replacing market forces, assumes that they operate actively and then checks in a systematic fashion whether politically given growth targets are economically feasible. Feasibility depends on the prior identification of the constraints on growth. Constraints that were seen as particularly important at this time were the two constraints that Kalecki had identified—rising inflation and the limited ability to increase rapidly the supply of food. These constraints would bind precisely because markets would be operating freely.

When used properly, development planning is still a diagnostic tool for governments that are serious about economic development, and it directs their attention toward the policy changes that they need to make if they are to realize their growth ambitions. In this way, it is still used by the World Bank under the label that they prefer to use, that of "macroeconomic programming." It can, needless to add, also be used by governments that are less serious about development as a technical window-dressing for policy inactivity and as a mandatory enclosure in letters seeking foreign aid. The spread of both of these practices was much influenced by the UN's report on *Measures for the Economic Development of Under-Developed Countries*.[99]

The Pursuit of Economic Development:
A Move to Safer Ground?

Despite the accusations of naiveté and extremism and the cogent criticisms of many aspects of its practical proposals, the *NIFE* report was an important and pioneering study. It went beyond the closed-economy framework of Keynes's thinking and showed how the international economy was integral to the problem of maintaining the level of employment. As one of its critics acknowledged, "The report renders great service in stressing that in a true world economy, full employment, like peace, is indivisible."[100] Sidney Dell, its junior author, pointed to the start that was then made on the practical measures that this global interdependence by implication required. The *NIFE* report "led to a path-breaking ECOSOC resolution in 1950 that set in motion the process of monitoring the progress of the world economy and the extent to which countries were implementing their employment commitments."[101] Unfortunately, in 1950, an integrated world economy was a long way off. Among the industrial countries, there were clear divisions of national interest. The report's proposals would have had the effect of requiring the United States both to adopt domestic policies for which there was no domestic political or professional consensus and to assume by far the greatest part of the international responsibility for the maintenance of full employment. Kaldor and his co-experts had tried to put the U.S. government on the spot and at the same time to get the Western European countries (notably Britain) off the hook of having to relax their controls on trade and payments before their industries could stand the inevitable competition. This was no better than the cunning plan of the mice to put a bell around the neck of the cat. Nevertheless, it raised issues that the United States would have to deal with in one way or another.

As it happened, the Cold War was heating up in Korea. If the U.S. was to assume international responsibilities, it preferred to do so by waging war on communism under the flag of the United Nations. To underpin at the same time the international effort to maintain full employment seemed to many Americans a costly diversion, to the extent that it might detract from realizing the nation's maximum economic potential. In the event, rearmament and the prosecution of the war provided all the stimulus to effective demand that was needed to keep employment at levels much higher than had previously been believed to be possible. Rising commodity prices at the same time brought balance-of-payments relief to hard-pressed underdeveloped countries.

In leading the retreat from "extreme Keynesianism," Hammarskjöld steered the UN on to the less-divisive ground of economic development. Here, greater consensus came to exist among the industrial countries about what needed to be done. During the 1950s, their experiences in Vietnam, Malaya, Suez, and Algeria (to list some of the more important) led the European colonial powers reluctantly to conform to the U.S. view that their empires were no longer tenable. In the transition from empire, a new common purpose among Western nations could be fashioned in relation to the future of the former colonies.

Development was also an area where there was more of a consensus between the West and the Soviet Union and China.[102] This was undoubtedly assisted by the way in which the Lewis model avoided raising awkward questions about the meaning of "economic development" or "economic progress." The idea that economic development was a matter of increasing "output" was one that could be accepted both in the West and in the socialist countries without discomfort, provided that no questions were raised about the definition of "output." In fact, statisticians in the two blocs used different definitions about what counted as output and different conventions to attribute value to the different categories of production that were so counted. These differences were aligned with their different economic philosophies of the respective roles of the market and the state and of the relative desirability of consumption and investment goods production. Given silence on these issues, however, which Lewis duly observed, "economic development" could act as a unifying concept.[103]

Thus, the UN's early attempt to analyze and respond to the fact of global interdependence petered out in the middle of the 1950s as member governments became increasingly preoccupied with the problem of development. As Sidney Dell later commented:

> In retrospect, it seems unfortunate that this was the outcome but it is important to note that the shift from global to development objectives was not the result of any particular failure of the UN. It reflected rather the sense of priorities at the time—based on the fact that while the world economy was, on the whole, doing well, the Third World was being left behind.[104]

As has been argued here, however, it was unrealistic to try to establish monitoring of country performance in an area where the divergence both of understanding and of interest between the U.S. and the UK was so sharp. It was the Secretary-General himself who warned the economists in the secretariat against "extreme Keynesianism" and prevented them from informally educating delegations. He saw the need to establish less-contentious priorities within the UN Secretariat, sensing the surprisingly little disagreement between member countries about the appropriate means of promoting economic development despite the different content given by the two sides of the Cold War to the term "planning." When it came to the modality of external intervention, the Cold War was actually a unifying factor, as the utility of foreign aid—bilateral and multilateral—in the great game of geopolitical influence was lost neither on the Soviet Union nor on the West.

Thus, the UN followed what Dell called the sense of priorities at the time, moving from research on the business cycle to proposals for full employment and then to planning for economic development. In the next two chapters, we examine the ideas of Raúl Prebisch and Hans Singer; they also made the transition away from the Keynesian thinking of the 1940s to the new field of development economics. However, they did not tread the conservative and consensual path that Hammarskjöld had in mind. In returning to the challenging theme that successful economic development was vitally related to the particular opportunities that countries faced in terms of their engagement in trade and their access to international finance, they opened up a new and radical structuralist perspective on economic development.

5

The Early Terms-of-Trade Controversy

- **Introduction**
- **Prebisch's Intellectual Formation**
- **Singer Starts Work on the Terms of Trade**
- **How Prebisch Made Use of the Singer Study**
- **Anonymity of Authorship in the UN**
- **Prebisch's Contribution: The Economic Mechanics of Secular Decline**
- **Channels of Dissemination**
- **The North American Critical Onslaught of the 1950s**
- **The End of the Early Controversy**

Introduction

By the late 1940s, one of the main political results of the Second World War had become apparent: an increasing differentiation of the power relations of the countries of the world. Europe was now divided, and Western Europe needed massive foreign aid for reconstruction. The Marshall Plan, followed by the establishment of NATO, "began in earnest an era of American military, political and economic dominance over Europe."[1] The revelation in September 1949 that the Soviets had succeeded in exploding an atomic bomb confirmed the USSR as the second "superpower." Japan, defeated, was only just beginning to switch its energies from military to economic efforts. The other countries of the world, in the rest of Asia, in Latin America, and in what was still colonial Africa[2] were for the most part wretchedly poor and at best were regional powers. The new UN forum had allowed them to find their voice in international economic affairs and to begin to articulate a view of their own situation. This modest progress was, however, far outdistanced by the great leap in the exercise of worldwide power made by the United States. In this broader context of growing imbalance in the power of nations, it is possible to discern in the controversy over the trend in the terms of trade not only a lively academic debate but also the emergence of a contest around the ideology of economic nationalism in poorer countries in response to these changing political realities.

Despite the increasing global differentiation in the political power of nations, the UN still represented the idealism of its wartime origins and was indeed the most advanced institutional embodiment of mankind's aspiration to unity. As Hans Singer later recalled, "the UN was the home of mankind.... [I]t was then at the center of the international organisations, [while] the Bank and the Fund were very much on the periphery in those days."[3] In the years before the advent of McCarthyism in early 1950, the UN Secretariat still had the self-confidence to raise issues and concerns about forces that might undermine the path toward unity. Moreover, the faster-flowing currents of nationalism outside North America and Europe affected the choice of topic of the economic research undertaken by the UN, while the UN network then provided the means for wide dissemination of the results.[4] These were powerful ways of spreading unorthodox economic ideas that suited well the new nationalist mood of nonindustrial countries. This was not always what the highest ranks in the UN intended, however, as we shall see later in this chapter. The self-appointed defenders of economic orthodoxy were, for their part, not slow to respond, producing a vigorous, multifaceted but inconclusive controversy around the trend in the terms of trade of primary producers. It revived some years after its early efflorescence in the 1950s. It is continuing still, though now in a new and much more sophisticated form.

The "Prebisch-Singer thesis" is generally taken to be the proposition that the net barter terms of trade between primary products and manufactures have been subject to a long-run downward trend. The publication dates of the first two works in English that expounded the thesis were nearly simultaneous. In May 1950, the English version of *The Economic Development of Latin America and Its Principal Problems,* by Raúl Prebisch, appeared under the UN's imprint. In the same month, Hans Singer published an article on the consequences of foreign direct investment, "The Distribution of Gains between Investing and Borrowing Countries," in the *American Economic Review.* The continuing significance of the "Prebisch-Singer thesis" is that it implies that, barring major changes in the structure of the world economy, the gains from trade will continue to be distributed unequally (and, some would add, unfairly) between nations exporting mainly primary products and those exporting mainly manufactures. Further, inequality of per capita income between these two types of countries will be increased by the growth of trade rather than reduced. This could be, and has been, taken as an indicator of the need for both industrialization and tariff protection.

Prebisch and Singer identified two types of negative effects on primary producers' terms of trade. One effect occurs because of systematically different institutional features of product and factor markets, such as cost-plus pricing and the unionization of labor in industry. Another negative influence is that of technical progress, both from the asymmetric distribution of its fruits and from its asymmetric impact on future demand, that is favorable to that of industry while unfavorable to that of agriculture. The empirical significance of the thesis has been much disputed and continues to be controversial after more than fifty years. One recent investigation has claimed that these two effects have operated strongly in the forty years after the Second World War and that they have indeed outweighed the positive influences on primary producers' terms of trade arising from capital accumulation and the growth of industrial production. This particular study suggested that the economic mechanisms that disfavor primary product producers, which were specified by Prebisch and Singer, have had significant impacts. Although the *net* secular decline of primary producers' net barter terms of trade has been found to be relatively small, at around 1 percent a year, this has a significant cumulative impact.[5]

The "Prebisch-Singer thesis" contradicted a long tradition of contrary belief among economists. The nineteenth-century English political economists believed that the terms of trade of industrial manufactures relative to agricultural produce would tend to decline. This belief underpinned their pessimism about the sustainability of rapid population growth. That manufactures' terms of trade would decline and that rapid population growth was therefore unsustainable were two propositions that caused political economy to be dubbed "the dismal science." This basic framework of ideas remained remarkably stable throughout the entire century and a half from Robert Malthus to the early works of Maynard Keynes. Although by the late 1940s this proposition was rarely stated explicitly, when Prebisch and Singer came to reverse the classical expectation of declining terms of trade for manufactures, their conclusions were immediately controversial and are still so regarded by some today.[6]

At the time Prebisch and Singer made their respective contributions, both were working for the United Nations. Prebisch was working for the ECLA in Santiago de Chile and Singer was in the DEA at UN headquarters in New York. It might seem odd that the United Nations, whose role it was to find solutions to world economic problems in order to promote peace, should be the cradle of such a controversial doctrine, one that lent itself so readily both to the economic nationalism of the underdeveloped countries and to the polemics of the Cold War. Here we tell exactly how this came about; we focus on events surrounding the preparations for, and the aftermath of, the ECLA conference in Havana in May 1949 and the subsequent controversy.

Prebisch is frequently credited with being the first of the two to formulate the declining-terms-of-trade thesis. Joseph Love claimed: "Prebisch clearly seems to have reached his position earlier than Singer."[7] Other authors have held that Singer discovered the thesis independently and simultaneously. Cristobal Kay wrote that "Singer . . . reached his conclusions independently from Prebisch and around the same time [so that] the thesis on the deterioration in the terms of trade is known in the economic literature as the 'Prebisch-Singer thesis.'" This second view was indeed that held by Singer himself.[8] Our account of the events surrounding the Havana conference reveals that Prebisch did not independently discover that the terms of trade of primary products were secularly declining but relied wholly on the previous work of Singer. The false impression that he had made the discovery (either first or simultaneously) was the consequence of political tensions between the developed and the underdeveloped countries that had welled up at Havana and the way in which those at the top of the UN Secretariat responded to those tensions.

They had long been brewing. By the time of the Second World War, the belief had already begun to gain ground that agricultural countries had better reasons than industrial ones to be pessimistic about their economic prospects. The experience of the interwar years had appeared to demonstrate this. As the Swedish economist Gustav Cassel noted in a League of Nations study in 1927, "From 1913, a very serious dislocation of relative prices has taken place in the exchange of goods between Europe and the colonial world."[9] The world crisis of 1929 drew further attention to such questions, particularly in Latin America. As Sanford A. Mosk noted in 1944, when reviewing trends in the continent's economic thought: "The relatively unfavourable price position for raw materials and foodstuffs that prevailed in the interwar period, and especially during the depression of the 1930s, profoundly affected the outlook of Latin Americans."[10] This perception had already led to the claim, which had become increasingly commonplace in the region, that primary-product exporters were at a disadvantage in international trade compared to exporters of industrial products.[11]

Primary commodity–exporting countries such as Brazil and Argentina were starting to see their future economic security in terms of promoting industrialization. The war years intensified such resolve and also raised confidence that an industrialization drive, particularly if organized by the government, could succeed.[12] Charles Kindleberger bolstered this conviction by suggesting as early as 1943 that industrialization was the path of the future, invoking Engel's law of demand against the classical orthodoxy on the terms of trade. In that year he wrote that "inexorably . . . the terms of trade move against agricultural and raw material countries as the world's standard of living increases (except in time of

war) and as Engel's law of consumption operates."[13] (In his memoirs, Kindleberger referred to this as a "youthful indiscretion."[14]) It is well established that
another of Kindleberger's articles with a similar pro-industrialization message,
based both on the differing elasticities of demand for primary and manufactured products and on the special "institutional organisation of production in
industry," was read by Prebisch.[15]

Although many North American neoclassical trade theorists reacted very
critically to the "Prebisch-Singer thesis" in the 1950s, others among them were
not immune from this emerging current of opinion. Paul Samuelson has been
frequently caricatured as the high priest of an overabstract and ideological neoclassical orthodoxy.[16] Yet, remarkably, in 1948 he himself asserted the tendency
of the terms of trade of primary producers to decline. He wrote at the end of his
famous article on the equalization of factor prices as a result of trade: "[Now]
the terms of trade are abnormally favourable to agricultural production. Without venturing on rash prophecy, one can venture scepticism that *this abnormal
trend of the terms of trade, counter to historical drift,* will continue."[17] Up to this
time, however, anticipation of the "Prebisch-Singer thesis" remained in the cat-
egory of remarks made en passant or obiter dicta made during the course of the
demonstration of other, quite distinct, propositions. It is nevertheless surprising that one of these stray anticipatory remarks was from the pen of Samuelson,
the economist who was later set up as the archenemy of structuralism, and that
this fact has been hitherto generally overlooked.

Prebisch's Intellectual Formation

It was only on 10 January 1949 that Prebisch agreed to work for ECLA as a
consultant on a short-term contract.[18] His allotted tasks were to coordinate
and pull together in final form the commission's planned *Economic Survey of
Latin America,* which was to be presented to the ECLA conference in Havana
in May 1949. Gustavo Martínez Cabañas, a Mexican, had already been appointed executive secretary after Prebisch had turned the post down, but he
did not take up his post until January 1949. Thus Eugenio Castillo, a Cuban,
who was his deputy, was in effect running the commission at the time that
Prebisch became a consultant.

Up to this point, Prebisch had made only one contribution on the terms-
of-trade issue that needs to be noted. The Depression of the 1930s had created
exceptionally unfavorable terms of trade for exporters who relied on agricultural products and raw materials. By 1932, export prices had fallen in Argentina to 37 percent of what they had been in 1928, and her net barter terms of
trade were down to 68 from a 1928 value of 100, indicating a less precipitous

fall of import prices.[19] Prebisch had documented this when was he was director of Research at the National Bank of Argentina. He published an article in
1934 arguing that "it is a well-known fact that agricultural prices have fallen
more profoundly than those of manufactured articles" and that Argentina
had to export 73 percent more than before the Depression to obtain the same
quantity of manufactured imports.[20] However, Prebisch was merely noting a
fact and did not provide any theoretical analysis of it.[21] He saw it as a feature
of Depression economics; that is, as a short-run cyclical problem. He believed
that the remedy was to be found in expansionist economic policies, not, as
the "Prebisch-Singer thesis" would later imply, in major changes in the structure of the international economy.[22]

Prebisch attended the World Economic Conference in 1933, and *The Means
to Prosperity,* which Keynes published at this time, powerfully affected his hitherto orthodox thinking.[23] His views must also be seen in the context of the
emerging current of opinion in Latin America that asserted that primary
commodity–producing nations were at a particular disadvantage in relation to
industrialized countries. Before 1949, Prebisch played only a marginal role in
promoting this discourse. During his years at the University of Buenos Aires,
the focus of Prebisch's research was on the international business cycle, in the
tradition of W. C. Mitchell and Joseph Schumpeter, and on the prospects for
the use of Keynesian countercyclical policies.[24] It was in this context that he first
used the terms "cyclical center" and "periphery."[25] In his introductory class in
1945, he referred to the maintenance of full employment as the supreme responsibility of the United States, as "the monetary and economic center of the
world," although he did not use the term "periphery" in this particular lecture.[26]
In an intervention in a meeting of American central bankers in 1946, he used
both terms together to argue that the responsibilities of the "cyclical center" had
been too much emphasized and that the "countries of the periphery" themselves must resolve disequilibria with internal causes.[27] In 1948, he reverted to
his previous (1945) theme that the main responsibility for carrying out a
countercyclical investment policy rested with the cyclical centers.[28]

A glimpse of Prebisch's overall research program at this time can be found
in a letter to Eugenio Gudin:

> I believe that the cycle is the typical form of growth of the capitalist economy and
> that this is subject to certain laws of motion; very distinct from the laws of equi-
> librium. In these laws of motion the disparity between the period of the produc-
> tive process and the period of the circulation of the incomes therefrom holds a
> fundamental importance. So I have tried to introduce systematically the concept
> of time into economic theory and also that of space, which in the ultimate in-
> stance resolves itself into a problem of time. It is precisely the concept of space

that has led me to study the movement in the center and the periphery, not with the aim of establishing formal distinctions but to point out transcendent functional differences.[29]

He also believed that, more generally, economic theory required "renovation" in order to bring it nearer to reality.[30]

Love has stated, on the evidence of a transcript of lectures given by Prebisch in 1948, that "Prebisch implicitly already had his opinions about the direction of Latin America's long-range terms of trade, since he had argued in the classroom in 1948 that the benefits of technological progress were absorbed by the center." Furthermore, "Prebisch had formulated the elements of his thesis before the appearance, in 1949, of the empirical base on which the thesis rested in its first published form—the UN study, *Relative Prices.*"[31] Part of Prebisch's 1948 lectures did discuss the case where one country (call it A) experiences technical progress in some of its economic activities (manufacturing) and then trades with another country (B) that does not experience technical progress. Prebisch argued that country A can retain for itself the fruit of technical progress and specifically asserted that historically both Great Britain and the United States had done so. His argument about the conditions under which this happened was, however, confused, and in the course of it he did not actually use the terms "center" and "periphery."[32] The argument is not sufficiently well specified to permit the claim that it could have only one logical implication for the net barter terms of trade of country B. In the context, one would certainly not have been surprised if Prebisch had asserted that country B's terms of trade would continuously decline, but the crucial point is that there is no evidence that he did so.

Before he became aware of the UN data, Prebisch never explicitly stated the thesis that Latin America's terms of trade had been subject to long-term decline, as opposed to the sharp short-term decline that he noted in 1934. Nor does Love claim that he did, only that "he implicitly already had his opinions." In the final analysis, claims for priority of discovery need to be based on explicit statements. Prebisch had clearly by 1948 arrived at the idea that the fruits of technical progress could be distributed unequally, an idea that he would later refine and integrate into his explanation of the phenomenon of secular decline. Nevertheless, the phenomenon itself was one of which, it appears, he was still unaware.

Singer Starts Work on the Terms of Trade

Singer had taken up his duties with the UN in New York in April 1947, knowing there only Michal Kalecki and Sidney Dell, while Owen was absent at the international trade negotiations in Geneva. He found himself unrestricted in his choice of research subject and immediately began to work on trade problems, although his previous economic background had not specifically related to trade issues. Singer later recalled:

> A strong influence among the early colleagues in the United Nations was that of Folke Hilgerdt, the Swedish economist who had already shaped the League of Nations publications on the Network of World Trade. Working with him was Carl Major Wright, a Danish economist who was particularly interested in the relationship of primary commodity prices to trade cycles and economic growth in industrial countries. Two other staff members in the trade section were Walter Chudson (United States) and Percy Judd (Australia), the latter being very expert in the economics and details of commodity agreements. Discussions with these four must have drawn my attention quickly to problems of terms of trade.[33]

The official stimulus for this work was the report of first session of the UN Sub-Commission on Economic Development. The members of the subcommission were elected on 5 June 1947. Considering problems of economic development in underdeveloped countries, the report of its first session contained the following comment:

> The recent rise in the prices of capital goods and transport services has made the task of economic development particularly difficult in the case of the underdeveloped and the least developed countries. The Sub-Commission therefore considers it important that a careful study be made of the prices of capital goods and of the relative trends of such prices and of prices of primary products, so that it may be in a position to make appropriate recommendations concerning the problem.[34]

As a result, the UN Secretariat began to study the terms of trade. The task was to address a short-term problem. The original objective was not to discover the historical drift of the terms of trade, or what had happened over the long run. The problem was that during the war, a number of underdeveloped countries had run export surpluses that they subsequently wished to use to import capital goods for development. In the interval, the prices of capital goods had risen, so the export surpluses were worth less in terms of imports than they had been when they were earned. This provoked the question of whether underdeveloped countries' terms of trade could be expected to continue to deteriorate in this way and the implication of this for their economic development. This was the official purpose of the research on which Singer embarked.

Singer worked under the general guidance of Folke Hilgerdt, who, as director of the UN Statistical Office, provided a key link between its work and the statistical work of the former League of Nations on trade. He was the principal author of a series of studies on commerce and commercial policy, which the Economic, Financial and Transit Department of the League issued as part of its program of studies on postwar problems. The final volume, *Industrialization and Foreign Trade* (1945), included an appendix on the statistics of international trade between 1871 and 1938. Appendix Tables VII and VIII, when read in conjunction, show that between those dates the price index of manufactured articles fell significantly less than that of primary products. However, nothing was made of this in the summary of findings of the report. The statistical base for this study was available for Singer's research.[35] Moreover, Hilgerdt expressed puzzlement to Singer over the behavior of the British terms-of-trade data.[36]

In his Ph.D. dissertation, Singer had studied problems of the very long run. Unlike Hilgerdt and Wright, he was not interested in cyclical effects on the terms of trade produced by booms and slumps in industrial countries. He, being more influenced by Gunnar Myrdal, focused on structural differences between industrial and nonindustrial countries and their long-term effect on the evolution of the terms of trade between them. His overarching concern was that of distributive justice. His question was not whether gains from trade existed, which he did not doubt, but whether the distribution of those gains between the countries that traded was "fair." If there were power differences between countries—disparities in market power or in technological power— did trade, and changes in the terms on which it was conducted, become a mechanism causing diverging growth rates between nations? His interest in the commodity terms of trade was thus a derivative of the larger question of the dynamics of world income distribution. That question itself was framed by the historical context of the process of decolonization, as in the transition to an independent India in 1947. Were the colonial powers, he wondered, willing to relinquish control of their colonies only because the international economic system would now spontaneously generate the same world division of labor that had previously been enforced militarily and politically?

The results of Singer's research were presented in a UN document entitled *Post War Price Relations in Trade between Under-developed and Industrialized Countries* that appeared on 23 February 1949.[37] This was an advance version of the terms-of-trade study, subject to final checking of the data, which was made available to the Sub-Commission on Economic Development. The document was retitled *Relative Prices of Exports and Imports of Under-developed Countries* for its general circulation in late 1949, with the subtitle *A Study of Post-War Terms of Trade between Under-developed and Industrialized Countries.* It was remarkable for at least two reasons. It included an attempt to see what historical statistics indicated about the long-term trend in the agriculture versus manufactures terms of trade, although its origin lay in developing countries' concern with future relative prices as industrialization drives gathered pace. It showed that the terms of trade of underdeveloped countries had improved between 1938 and 1946–1948. This recent improvement was, however, placed in a much longer historical perspective, showing that between 1876 and 1948 they had seriously deteriorated.

The historical section contained the report's most dramatic finding. It was that "from the latter part of the nineteenth century to the eve of the Second World War, a period of well over half a century, there was a secular downward trend in the prices of primary goods relative to the prices of manufactured goods." Singer recalled that he and Hilgerdt together spotted this trend in the data.[38] The cumulative effect of secular decline was calculated to be substantial: "By 1938, the relative prices of primary goods had deteriorated by about 50 points, or one-third, since [the 1870s] and by about 40 points, somewhat less than 30 per cent, since 1913."[39] The statistical evidence for this downward trend was given in Table 5 of the report, of which a simplified version is presented in our Table 5.1.

What was the significance of this secular decline? The report was careful not to suggest that if a country's terms of trade improved, its welfare necessarily increased. It might or might not, depending on the circumstances in which the rise in export prices takes place. If the price rise was a result of a

Table 5.1. Ratios of UK Imports to Exports, 1876–1948 (1938 = 100)

Period (or Year)	Current-Year Weights	Board of Trade Index
1876–1880	163	NA
1881–1885	167	NA
1886–1890	157	NA
1891–1895	147	NA
1896–1900	142	NA
1901–1905	138	NA
1906–1910	140	NA
1913	137	143
1921	93	101
1933	98	96
1938	100	100
1946		108
1948		117

Note: NA = "not available"

Source: United Nations, *Relative Prices of Exports and Imports of Under-developed Countries* (Lake Success, N.Y.: UN Department of Economic Affairs, 1949), Table 5, p. 22.

failure of supply, it might not leave the exporting country better off. Nevertheless, in general, an improvement in terms of trade would increase the availability of resources for development. A secular decline for underdeveloped countries meant a loss of capacity to absorb foreign financing for development and thus to respond to the "added incentive towards industrialization." A further, far more controversial, implication was also drawn; that "the under-developed [countries had] helped to maintain . . . a rising standard of living in the industrialized countries, without receiving, in the price of their own products, a corresponding equivalent contribution towards their own standards of living."[40] This carried a clear message of historical injustice, and this message was, as we shall see, very shortly to be rejected by the subcommission.[41]

Singer had already announced this message in a seminar that he gave to the graduate faculty of the New School of Social Research, New York, on 23 December 1948. There he said that "Marxist analysis, in which rising standards of living for given groups and sections are somehow held to be compatible with general deterioration and impoverishment, is much truer for the international scene than it is for the domestic." He attributed the growing inequality in the distribution of world income to the change in price relations between primary materials and manufactured goods.[42]

How Prebisch Made Use of the Singer Study

One of the justifications for establishing ECLA was to provide better information about economic conditions in the region as a whole.[43] Originally, it was assumed that this could be achieved merely by collating statistics submitted by the individual Latin American governments. When most governments failed to provide the required figures, the commission realized that it would have to collect them itself for the first *Economic Survey of Latin America*, which was due to be presented to the ECLA conference in Havana in May 1949. Additionally, the first meeting of ECLA, in June 1948, had passed a resolution asking for the preparation of "a study of the movements of import and export prices, the determining factors of such movements, and the consequences thereof on the balance of payments."[44] By the autumn of 1948 it became clear that these tasks were beyond the unaided capacity of the ECLA office in Santiago.[45] The weak statistical abilities of the fledgling commission thus form an important background factor in the preparations for Havana.

Accordingly, Louis Shapiro, a statistician in the Department of Economic Affairs, was sent from the UN office in New York to Santiago for three months between December 1948 and March 1949 in order to organize these tasks. It was during this mission that he received from Hans Singer the provisional draft of his study on the terms of trade. From Santiago, Shapiro wrote Singer a letter of acknowledgment dated 5 January 1949:

> Thank you most kindly for your letter of 17th December 1948, and for the enclosed provisional draft of the General Part of your study on the Terms of Trade. I have also received via the pouch drafts of the country sections of Terms of Trade for which many thanks. I have read quite carefully the General Part and find it most admirable. Your note on the methodology and the statistical "caveats" are especially noteworthy. I have passed this on to Mr. Castillo who also agrees that this is an excellent piece of work. ECLA plans to include a substantial statistical section on the terms of trade in the forthcoming Survey of Latin America and will, with your permission and clearance, rely heavily on your data.[46]

The IMF had also promised to send ECLA a study on the terms of trade. Shapiro reported to Singer that he had not been encouraged by its progress and content when he had visited Washington but indicated that ECLA would study carefully the IMF work in conjunction with Singer's own and that Castillo was "in complete agreement with this procedure." Shapiro also asked to be sent revised drafts of the General Part and of the Latin American country sections as they were completed.[47]

A version of the IMF study was available by March 1949, although it was not published as an IMF staff paper until the following year. It dealt mainly with the period 1938 to 1946 and included no data at all from before 1925. It found (as indeed had Singer's study; see Table 5.1 above) that the terms of trade of Latin America as a whole had improved between 1938 and 1946. The IMF study made no comment, however, on the UN study's thesis of secular decline since the 1870s.[48] Nevertheless, the IMF study left a larger imprint on the *Economic Survey of Latin America* than did Singer's study. In the event, the survey's one mention of secular decline in the terms of trade of primary producers was extremely brief and was almost certainly inserted after Prebisch had completed and circulated the document that became *The Economic Development of Latin America*.[49] Thus Singer's work did not create any real impact in ECLA until it had reached the hands of Prebisch himself.

How did this happen? The second route by which the Singer study was transmitted to Latin America was via Martínez Cabañas. Before arriving at ECLA, Prebisch had gone to Mexico to deliver lectures at the Universidad Nacional Autónoma de México, arriving in mid-February.[50] In late February or early March, Francisco Coire, head of the Latin American section of the DEA in New York, sent him both the Singer study and the IMF study.[51] On 5 March, Martínez Cabañas wrote from New York to Prebisch in Mexico drawing both these works to his attention:

> Our friend Coire has informed me that he has already sent you two studies on
> questions relating to foreign trade: one drawn up by Sr. Singer which is to be
> found under the number E/CN.1/Sub3/W5 with the title *Post-war Price Rela-*
> *tions in the Trade between Undeveloped and Industrialised Countries*. . . . [T]he
> other study is from the International Fund and refers more concretely to the
> theme of Foreign Trade.

He reported that the conclusions of the Singer study had been "much debated." He pointed out to Prebisch that both studies had a bearing on a problem—that is, the terms of trade—which was "one of the most important of
those that will be treated in the general study that we are going to present at
the Havana Conference." He repeated to Prebisch that he (i.e., Prebisch) would
have the final responsibility for drawing up that report.[52] Thus it was the
Martínez Cabañas visit to New York, rather than the early version seen and
favorably commented upon by Castillo, that made the effective link from Singer
to Prebisch.

Prebisch must have arrived in Santiago soon after 9 March, when he had
received a telegram from Castillo asking him to come immediately.[53] This was
shortly after Shapiro's return to New York. It seems that before long Prebisch
turned his mind to the question of the terms of trade, as one would have
expected, given the strong urgings of Martínez Cabañas. Then, on 1 April 1949,
Prebisch sent a request, through Castillo, to Shapiro in New York for three
types of additional data—additional, that is, to the data contained in Singer's
study on *Post War Price Relations,* which it seems clear that Prebisch had now
read.[54] Castillo did not explain the reasons behind Prebisch's request, but the
wish for data starting in 1873, the year the British Great Depression began,
suggests an interest in the respective experience of the UK and the U.S. as
"cyclical centers," a problem he returned to in the *Economic Survey of Latin*
America in the following year (United Nations 1951).[55] Prebisch was also anxious to see an early draft of Kalecki's study on inflation and Coire's draft of
Part II of the survey.[56]

Celso Furtado, an ECLA staff member, later recalled how Prebisch initially
worked very much on his own, and then a month after his arrival (i.e., presumably in mid-April) circulated a first draft of an introduction to the *Eco-*
nomic Survey within ECLA. Furtado described this draft as a digest (Fr.
mouture) of the papers that Prebisch had brought with him from Buenos Aires.
The subjects covered were disequilibria in the balance of payments, the declining U.S. import coefficient, capital controls, low saving leading to domestic inflation, and the limits of industrialization. Thus, the first draft of Prebisch's
introduction did not cover the terms of trade, according to Furtado's account
of it.[57] He did employ his "center-periphery" terminology and acknowledged

the importance of industrialization. It seemed to Furtado that "[t]his text contained extremely interesting ideas, but the author placed himself on the defensive."

Furtado recalled as follows:

> We had hardly started to discuss the document, when it was suddenly discarded, without any explanation. Prebisch's new text was not circulated for discussion. I suppose that it was ready on the eve of the Havana Conference, because it was sent to us typewritten, in its final version, shortly before we left. It was a much longer text including tables and charts. The tone had changed, now it was a manifesto urging Latin American countries to launch into industrialization. One could discover there a definite taste for a polished and polemical style.[58]

This account suggests that mid-April 1949 was the decisive point in Prebisch's drafting process. At this point, however, Prebisch had not received any reply to Castillo's data requests of 1 April. The reply was not sent until 27 April, and it was the third channel of transmission of Singer's study. Shapiro scribbled the words "in Singer Paper" over Prebisch's second request, and this was the only one he could fulfill (apart from the U.S. national income figures for 1910–1929).[59] However, it is almost certain that this data arrived too late to have any influence on Prebisch's introduction. There are no traces of it in the finished product, which, as far as the terms of trade are concerned, contains only the UK part of the data in Table 5 of *Relative Prices of Exports and Imports of Under-Developed Countries,* slightly reformulated. Prebisch spliced one of the UK series down to 1913 with another of the UK series thereafter and put them on a base of 1876–1880 = 100 instead of 1938 = 100, as originally.[60]

If it was not the arrival of additional information, then, what was it that stimulated Prebisch to abandon his original draft? This remains unclear. Around this time Prebisch received Coire's draft of Part II of the *Economic Survey.* Only one chapter of this was used in the finished product and the remainder is now apparently lost, but from Coire's remarks to Prebisch it seems clear that it had a strong pro-industrialization message and had a polemical tone in places.[61] This, or perhaps further reflection on the implications of the Singer study, may have given Prebisch extra inspiration.

Prebisch dealt with the whole issue of secular decline extremely briefly in his new text. The introduction that summarizes its argument does not even mention the terms of trade. The subject is then handled in the first three pages of Chapter II. Prebisch's only comment on the terms-of-trade statistics, albeit one that was to resonate through the subsequent critical debate, was that "it is regrettable that the price indexes do not reflect the differences in quality of finished products." This short but crucial section powerfully reinforced his other main arguments—that the international division of labor was an "out-dated schema" and that "industrialization is the only means by which the Latin American countries may fully obtain the advantages of technical progress."[62]

Anonymity of Authorship in the UN

As has been seen, it is not possible to sustain the claim that Prebisch was the first to discover the phenomenon of the secular decline in the terms of trade of primary producers. On the ground that Prebisch's contribution was complete by May 1949 while Singer's paper was not presented to the American Economic Association meeting until December 1949, Love concluded that "Prebisch had reached his position earlier than Singer."[63] This was faulty reasoning, given Singer's authorship of the UN study, something of which Love does not seem to have been aware. John Spraos has commented on the general lack of awareness of Singer's authorship and correctly attributed it to the UN rule of anonymity of authorship of its publications.[64]

Anonymity is indeed the general fate of the authors of UN publications. Since the UN has employed many distinguished economists, it has become a standard task for their biographers to try to disentangle those sections of UN publications that they authored.[65] What is odd in the present case is not that Singer's authorship should have been invisible but that Prebisch's should have been visible. What was originally intended to be the introduction to the ECLA survey for 1948 eventually appeared under Prebisch's name as *The Economic Development of Latin America and Its Principal Problems.* Had the piece been retained as the introduction to the survey, its author would, like Singer, have remained anonymous. However, it appeared as a separate UN publication but with the author personally identified. The UN rule of anonymity was applied to Singer and Prebisch asymmetrically. How did that come about?

The Sub-Commission on Economic Development held its third session from 21 March to 11 April 1949. It discussed *Post-War Price Relations in Trade between Under-Developed and Industrialized Countries.* It accepted, somewhat grudgingly, the statistical evidence but rejected the lessons that had been drawn from it. Its report said:

> The Sub-Commission is constrained to point out that the study under review contains certain conclusions in regard to the price relationship between developed and underdeveloped countries which, in its opinion, do not represent a correct picture of the actual position. As a result of the discussion, the Sub-Commission agreed that while the document contained an adequate study of relative price trends of primary commodities and manufactured goods, it was necessary to broaden the scope of the study into that of the terms of trade

between underdeveloped and industrialized countries, including prices and quantities traded, and in extending it, to cover the most recent movements in these fields.[66]

The most controversial of the suggestions that Singer had made in interpreting his findings, was, of course, that underdeveloped countries were helping to maintain a rising standard of living in industrialized countries without receiving any equivalent compensation. This was potentially politically explosive. While it appealed to the underdeveloped countries, it appealed not at all to the developed.[67] It seems plausible to suggest that the sub-commission used the (acknowledged) fact that the picture presented by the study was in some ways incomplete as an excuse for disclaiming its radical conclusions.

It is probable, given the slow rate of circulation of UN documents, that Prebisch was not aware of the sub-commission's report when he wrote. Be that as it may, in the final version of his introduction, he repeated the implication to which it seems the sub-commission had objected by quoting the relevant passage from Singer's study. Worse, by using his terminology of center and periphery, he further dramatized it:

> The enormous benefits that derive from increased productivity have not reached the periphery in a measure comparable to that obtained by the peoples of the great industrial countries. Hence, the outstanding differences between the standards of living of the masses of the former and the latter and the manifest discrepancies between their respective abilities to accumulate capital.[68]

When he presented this version in Havana, it received the acclaim of the delegates of the Latin American countries.[69] However, what was music to the ears of the delegates of Latin American countries would have displeased the industrial countries, especially the United States. This fact appears to have caused some consternation among UN high officials in New York, who were anxious to distance the UN from Prebisch's introduction. Accordingly, after the Havana conference was over, it was submitted to the Secretary-General as an "essay" commissioned in the process of "fostering research."[70] It was then proposed to the UN Publications Committee that it break the rule that authors of UN publications should not be identified by name. This course of action was designed to ensure that Prebisch took "credit (and responsibility) for the report ... in order to emphasize that the views expressed ... were those of the author and not those of any UN organ." The proposal was presented "as an exceptional one, unlikely to recur but in the present circumstances very desirable."[71] Prebisch's suspicion that no international organization would feel comfortable with the viewpoint of the underdeveloped countries was thus confirmed.

The UN's tactic backfired. The Spanish original had been issued in May 1949, but, as Furtado has noted, it was some time before both this and the English translation were eventually published in New York by the United Nations, being circulated, as he put it, "with the slowness characteristic of official documents."[72] Meanwhile, however, a Portuguese translation of the Spanish original, undertaken at Furtado's own urging, was published in Brazil in September 1949. It is at this point that the history of Prebisch's enormous influence began, spreading out from Brazil eventually to become worldwide.[73] The publication of the English version of *The Economic Development of Latin America and Its Principal Problems* merely strengthened that effect in North America and Europe. In fact, this was how Singer discovered the existence of Prebisch: "I believe it was between presenting my paper to the AEA in December 1949 and its publication in the summer of 1950 that I discovered that Raul Prebisch, my colleague at the UN, had developed very similar opinions and had also put the problem of poor terms of trade for primary products into the center of thinking of the Economic Commission for Latin America."[74] The main result of identifying the author was that the polished and polemical Prebisch rapidly gained greater recognition in Europe and North America as a "UN economist" than did the more understated Singer, who had published under his own name only in academic journals.

Prebisch's Contribution: The Economic Mechanics of Secular Decline

Given the evidence outlined above, it seems clear that if the "Prebisch-Singer thesis" is defined as the statement of the phenomenon of secular decline in the terms of trade of primary products, and if anyone can be said to have anticipated Singer, it would be Kindleberger or Samuelson rather than Prebisch. After all, both of them, unlike Prebisch, enunciated it explicitly. Prebisch, however, made a contribution distinct from that made by Singer. This was to advance a cyclical-cum-structural mechanism to explain the decline, one more complicated than the purely structural interpretation of Singer.

Unlike the 1948 lectures, which singled out restrictions on labor immigration from countries not experiencing technical progress (type B), the new mechanism was based on institutional factors that permitted the retention of productivity gains by labor in countries where there was technical progress (type A). Prebisch further argued, characteristically, that "the existence of this phenomenon cannot be understood, except in relation to trade cycles and the way in which they occur in the centers and at the periphery, since the cycle is the characteristic form of growth of the capitalist economy, and increased productivity is one of the main factors of that growth." He suggested that even though in the boom primary product prices typically rise faster than industrial prices, deterioration in the commodity terms of trade of the periphery is nevertheless possible if, in the slump, primary commodity prices decline steeply enough compared with industrial prices. The explanation offered of why primary product prices declined severely in the slump compared with industrial prices was "the well-known resistance to a lowering of wages" at the center. By contrast, "the characteristic lack of organisation among the workers employed in primary production prevents them from obtaining wage increases comparable to those of the industrial countries, and from maintaining the increases to the same extent."[75]

However, instead of leaving matters there, Prebisch also made another argument that seemed inconsistent with his first explanation. He identified industrial production and primary production with groups of countries described as "center" and "periphery." He then argued that the differing strength of organized labor at the center and the periphery was not the crux of the matter, because even if workers at the periphery were able to resist wage decreases as strongly as industrial workers were, adjustment would take place by another process. The high prices of primary products would force a contraction of industrial production, which in turn would cut the demand for primary products. Pointing to the episode of the Depression, Prebisch commented that "the forced readjustment of costs of primary production during the world crisis illustrates the intensity that this movement can attain."[76] This was the germ of the idea, later taken up by dependency and world system theorists, that the "center" was able to drain resources away from the "periphery" regardless of their respective states of labor organization.

As has been seen, Prebisch had arrived at his explanation in April and May 1949. Prebisch and Singer probably arrived at their respective explanations of primary commodity terms-of-trade decline independently, though again Singer was first. Singer had presented his explanation, in embryonic form, in a paper originally presented in December 1948 and published in March 1949, then more fully in another paper to the American Economic Association conference in December 1949.[77] This further paper explored factors that had "reduced the benefits to under-developed countries of foreign trade-cum-investment based on export specialization in food and raw materials." The first of these was that the secondary and cumulative effects of foreign export enclave investment were felt in the investing country, not the country where the investment was made. The second was that countries were "diverted" into types of economic activity offering less scope for technical progress and internal and external economies. The third factor, "perhaps of even greater importance," was the movement of the terms of trade. Singer, while conceding that the statistics in *Relative Prices of Exports and Imports of Under-Developed Countries* were open to doubt and objection in detail, regarded the general story that they told as "unmistakable."[78]

Singer's proposed mechanism of secular decline was less complicated and based less on business cycles than Prebisch's. It was an asymmetric process whereby (a) the gains from technical progress in manufacturing are distributed to the producers in the form of higher incomes, while (b) the smaller gains from technical progress in primary commodity production are distributed to the consumers in the form of lower prices. On this basis, the industrialized countries have the best of both worlds, as producers of manufactures and as consumers of primary products. The underdeveloped countries have the worst of both worlds, as consumers of manufactures and as producers of primary products. Thus, the benefits of foreign trade are shared unequally, and traditional foreign investment in plantations and mines did, after all, form "part of a system of 'economic imperialism' and of 'exploitation,'" albeit not in the classical Marxist or Leninist sense.[79]

Prebisch's interpretation of the secular decline, although possessed of its own ambiguities, gave an illusion of greater concreteness than Singer's. Instead of two sets of countries defined by the types of products that they exported and imported, Prebisch's concept of center and periphery seemed to have a spatial, even geographical, reality to it. His introduction of economic cycles into the mechanism allowed the short and medium term to be integrated with the long term and countered the static quality of the purely structural approach. In general, this more complex schema opened the door to broader analyses of the economic conjuncture and policy recommendations on the issues of immediate concern to Latin American economists. Although fertile in these ways, Prebisch's interpretation itself was still very succinct, perhaps reflecting the novelty of the secular-decline thesis even to him, and it therefore remained obscure on a number of crucial questions.[80] It was also quite different from the theoretical model that Prebisch published in 1959, which resembled the standard neoclassical model of a small open economy but with the exception of a small number of special assumptions.[81] This new and different model was presumably developed as a vehicle for communication with North American economic orthodoxy.

Channels of Dissemination

ECLA had been born against the wishes of the United States. In preparing for its first major conference, it lacked the statistical infrastructure to discharge one of its primary tasks—to survey the common economic and technical prob-

lems of the region. This provided the cue for statistical help from UN headquarters in New York. During the preparations for the conference, Singer's work
was transmitted to ECLA by three different channels between December 1948
and April 1949. An early version arrived in December 1948 but does not seem to
have been followed up by Castillo. The second transfer was via Martínez Cabañas
and Coire to Prebisch before the latter arrived in Santiago, and this was the
critical route. At Martínez Cabañas's prompting, Prebisch "latched onto the terms
of trade idea," in the words of Victor Urquidi,[82] and meshed it with his own
framework of thought in April/May 1949. The additional data he requested from
New York (the third route) arrived too late to be useful. The document that
became *The Economic Development of Latin America and Its Principal Problems*
thus contained—as far as the terms of trade was concerned—merely a small
part of the original UN study data, minimally reformulated.

Thus the conventional view, that Prebisch achieved priority over Singer in
stating the thesis of secularly declining terms of trade for primary producers, is
not based on an accurate chronology of ideas. The near-simultaneity of the
dates of the first English publications of the thesis by Prebisch and Singer
cannot be relied upon as a means of dating the two men's contributions. The
key events did not take place in 1950 at all, but in 1948 and 1949 in the run-up
to and the aftermath of the ECLA conference at Havana. Prebisch's presentation to the Havana conference was a resounding success, turning him into a
champion of the interests of the underdeveloped countries. Senior UN officials
attempted to distance themselves from Prebisch by identifying him as the
author of the views to which the developed countries took exception. In so
doing, they unwittingly heightened his prestige.

The common belief that the thesis of the deterioration of the terms of
trade was first picked up from Latin America by the Anglo-Saxon world during the 1950s is therefore inaccurate.[83] What happened in the 1950s was in fact
the transmission of the thesis *back again*. The more detailed chronology of
events given here has also indicated a further unsatisfactory aspect of the conventional wisdom; namely, the general lack of precision about what constitutes "the Prebisch-Singer thesis." Is it to be understood simply as a claim
about a long-run downward trend in the terms of trade of primary producers; that is to say, the statistical phenomenon of secular decline? Or is it the
delineation of an economic mechanism that could account for a long-run
secular decline? Or is it both? If the thesis is the empirical fact of a secular
decline, it is clear that Singer had priority and Prebisch's work was wholly
derivative. If it is the specification of a theoretical mechanism to account for
a secular decline, Singer also had priority, but Prebisch's contribution was
independent, if also more convoluted.

In terms of the wider dissemination of these ideas, however, it is clear that Singer benefited from the existence of Prebisch as much as Prebisch had previously benefited from the existence of Singer. Let us ask what would have happened to the ideas of each had the other been absent. If Singer had not overcome his personal reluctance to join the UN, Prebisch may well not have integrated declining terms of trade into his text. However, if Prebisch had gone to work for the IMF and not ECLA, the impact of Singer's study in Latin America might have amounted to no more than the very faint mark that it left on the 1948 *Economic Survey*. From the viewpoint of publicity and political repercussions, therefore, it was indeed "the Prebisch-Singer thesis."

The North American Critical Onslaught of the 1950s

When the academic controversy came, it was the more piquant because Prebisch had spiced his *Economic Development of Latin America and Its Principal Problems* with a provocative footnote. It said:

> One of the most conspicuous deficiencies of general economic theory, from the point of view of the periphery, is its false sense of universality. It could hardly be expected that the economists of the great countries, absorbed by serious problems of their own, should devote preferential attention to the study to those of Latin America. The study of Latin America's economic life is primarily the concern of its own economists. . . . An intelligent knowledge of the ideas of others must not be confused with that mental subjection to them from which we are slowly learning to free ourselves.[84]

From one angle, this was a note about the need for Latin American economists to apply economic theory to the problems of their own countries, just as North American and European economists use theory to tackle their countries' problems. In other words, it was a platitude. From another angle, it was a suggestion that general economic theory makes false claims to universality, which had placed Latin Americans in a position of mental subjection and from which they needed to be liberated. In other words, it was a call for an intellectual revolution against an alien ideology.

Indeed, the words were understood in both senses. In ECLA, Latin American economists, many with North American or European economics training, came together to formulate the economic problems of their own region and seek solutions. ECLA also started a training program to augment the cadre of suitable economists. However, in addition, although Prebisch had never directly confronted classical and neoclassical trade theory, he was understood as proposing that it should be superseded. The hint that a new *methodenstreit* was looming engaged the interest of North American trade economists, who promptly waded into debate to defend neoclassical trade orthodoxy against the South American heretics.

As in any debate, there were simple muddles. Some of the critics failed to understand fully what was being asserted and what was not. Neither Singer nor Prebisch was saying that foreign trade was disadvantageous to developing countries or recommending wholesale withdrawal from it. Both recommended increased trade, but on better terms for developing countries; that is, terms that would loosen constraints on their internal capital accumulation.[85] Neither man thought that technical progress in agriculture was impossible or undesirable, rather that it was hard for developing countries to benefit from it and base their development strategy on it. Nobody ever claimed that a decline in the commodity terms of trade for primary products *necessarily* involved a welfare loss for primary commodity–exporting countries.[86] Quite a lot of ink was spilled before these points were clarified.

Muddles apart, the orthodox critics made two main types of rejoinder to Singer and Prebisch. One was to assert that the terms of trade of primary commodities had not, in fact, experienced a secular decline and that the statistics of *Relative Prices of Exports and Imports* were misleading. The other was to admit that a secular decline had taken place but to reject the interpretations that had been given to it. For good measure, some critics followed both lines of defense at the same time. Jacob Viner was the first major North American economist to deliver a broadside in lectures given at the National University of Brazil, Rio de Janeiro, in July–August 1950. Although his main attack on the views of the UN economists was directed to their support for the policy of industrialization, he also denied that there had been a secular decline in the terms of trade of primary products. "As far as the data go, no such uniform trend can be found. . . . For comparisons over long periods, moreover, the available data are largely irrelevant."[87]

Viner seized on the issue of the changing quality of commodities, claiming that the quality of manufactures had improved while the quality of primary commodities had not. The increased prices of manufactures reflected, he argued, both the incorporation of newly invented products into the index and a marked increase in the quality of the manufactures that existed when the index began.[88] This point had already been discussed in *Relative Prices,* in the appendix setting out the statistical caveats. There, however, it was noted that the quality of industrial products could go down as well as up, and there was not much empirical evidence available with which to correct the series.[89]

In *Relative Prices,* Singer had made an a fortiori argument that, given the greater technical progress in manufacturing than in agriculture, a secular movement of the terms of trade against agriculture must imply that the benefits of technical progress were not being passed on to importers of manufactures. In *Economic Development,* Prebisch had reproduced this argument.[90] This was a point that Viner failed to address. He contented himself with denying that technical progress was necessarily any faster in industry than in agriculture and with asserting that if technical progress had caused the real cost of manufactures to fall, it would have (presumably, necessarily) caused a favorable movement in the relative prices of agricultural products. That in reality it had not done so was precisely the point that Singer and Prebisch had already made. In this instance, it is hard not to sympathize with the impatience of Furtado with Viner's critique.[91]

Many of Viner's points informed the position taken by the U.S. delegation to the fifth session of ECLA in 1953. Robert E. Asher, speaking on behalf of the delegation, warned against the use of terms-of-trade indices as a measure of welfare. He instanced the difficulties of measuring quality changes in manufactured products:

> Measured in constant prices, I doubt whether a Chevrolet car today costs very much more than it did 35 years ago. Nevertheless, today's Chevrolet is quite different from the early model. With its self-starter, with tyres that are good for 40,000–50,000 kilometers, with automatic gear shifts, with heaters, windshield-wipers, and dozens of other improvements, it is really a new product.[92]

The quality-change argument was the mantra of the North American critics. In 1955, Professor P. T. Ellsworth of the University of Wisconsin found it highly convincing.[93] However, he also produced a new explanation for the statistics showing a secular decline. In the sub-period 1876–1905, the cause was attributed to "the sharp decline in railway and shipping rates."[94] Thus, "the terms of trade of primary countries, were f.o.b. prices used for their exports as well as for their imports, may well have moved in their favor." This speculation was bolstered by a long citation from the work of Carl Major Wright, who was one of Singer's UN colleagues in New York.[95] Wright had found that in the down phase of the cycle, the fall in transport costs of bulky primary commodities was often greater than the fall in their f.o.b. price, so that producer incomes could rise even as the delivered price in London fell. Ellsworth generalized this cyclical phenomenon to the whole of the final quarter of the nineteenth century and concluded that the decline during this sub-period could be set aside as spurious.

Nevertheless, Ellsworth conceded that the decline between 1913 and 1933 was real enough, while contending that it was explicable by a series of discrete causes. Overinvestment in primary production in the face of rising demand, the perverse effects of supply-restriction schemes, and the Great Depression itself had all exerted downward pressures. At the same time, he recognized that some elements of Prebisch's view were indeed relevant to this decline, such as the pricing behavior of British manufacturers in the 1920s and the effect of technological progress in the rubber and raw cotton industries in pushing down prices.[96] However, it was the introduction of the theme of falling transport costs that the later critics most recalled about his paper.

Theodore Morgan, Ellsworth's colleague at the University of Wisconsin, reiterated both the quality-change and the falling-transport-cost arguments.[97] The major claims of the paper were, first, that if the British data used in *Relative Prices* was pushed back to 1801, the whole series showed "a huge rise and fall in the terms of trade plus much instability—not a single trend." The second was that British data alone could not reveal the whole picture of the trade situation of primary producers. So he examined terms-of-trade series for six other countries—the United States, India, Japan, New Zealand, the Union of South Africa, and Brazil. He concluded: "Of these six series, two show a major relative rise for primary products, the rest, various change or ambiguity. The data do *not* show a general worsening of the price position of primary producers." Only the abstract of this paper was ever published. Morgan's data series themselves were not. His claims were thus not open to critical inspection and comparison with Singer's.

Gerald Meier, then of Wesleyan University, also joined the critics of Singer and Prebisch in 1958 in the course of a critique of Myrdal's opinions on foreign investment enclaves. Meier guessed (surely rightly) that Myrdal implicitly supported the Singer and Prebisch view and proceeded to raise doubts about it. Quality improvements in manufactures and falling transport costs reappear as two of these doubts. So does the inadequacy of looking only at British terms of trade and the point that welfare conclusions can be drawn only from the factoral terms of trade.[98] His main additional criticism was that even if there had been a long-term decline in the past, it was wrong to design policy as if it would continue into the future when the opposite case was more likely.[99] In effect, the developing countries were invited to embrace again all the forces that the classical political economists had expected to move the terms of trade against manufactures.

In his Cairo Lectures of 1959, Gottfried Haberler provided a summing up and robust restatement of these early criticisms of the thesis of secular decline. The failure of the statistics to take account of quality changes and the impact of falling transport costs were again rehearsed. So was the point, due to Kindleberger and taken up by Meier, that the British terms of trade cannot be taken as indicative of those of industrial countries as a group, and therefore their inverse cannot be read as an indicator of the terms of trade of the nonindustrial countries. Haberler's verdict was that "the theory under review is based on grossly insufficient empirical evidence [and] it has misinterpreted the facts on which it is based."[100] He also, following Meier, denounced the presumption that secular decline, if it had occurred, would continue in the future. (This was precisely the presumption that Samuelson had endorsed at the end of his 1948 article.) For Haberler, it was "irresponsible" to recommend policies on the basis of such uncertain extrapolations.

Both sides of the debate recognized that the commodity terms of trade had moved in favor of primary producers between the middle 1930s and the Korean War period, but no one knew whether this improvement would continue or go into reverse thereafter. Logically, this should not matter if, as the critics asserted, the movements in the commodity terms of trade do not have any particular welfare implications. Nevertheless, nagging doubts seemed to remain in the minds of the critics that there was a long-term tendency and that the decline of primary producers' terms of trade might resume. This accusation of undue and irresponsible pessimism had the effect of keeping the statistical debate alive, as the latest data were incorporated into new calculations to see what difference it would make to the long-term trend.

In theoretical terms, Haberler chose to travel light. In military parlance, he shortened the neoclassical front. While vigorously reasserting that trade increases welfare compared with no trade, something that neither Singer nor Prebisch had denied, he sidestepped both the abstract complexities and the ideological implications of the Samuelson theorem. While denouncing the errors of the secular-decline thesis, he avoided—unlike Meier—giving the appearance of returning to the embrace of the Cambridge doctrine of the terms of trade. "If you ask me which of the two schools is right," Haberler remarked trenchantly, "the answer is that both are wrong. . . . [L]et us not forget that the terms of trade may not change at all or may for some time go one way and then move in the opposite direction. That is what they seem actually to have done."[101] It is to his credit that he did not reserve his skepticism for the economists of the UN but distributed it equally among his neoclassical colleagues.

The End of the Early Controversy

Haberler's Cairo lectures mark the end of the first phase of the terms-of-trade controversy. This is not because the debate thereafter ceased but because all the principal criticisms of the thesis of secular decline had been aired by the late 1950s. The means to settle the points of difference were not yet to hand. During the 1950s, Singer and Prebisch had to face a two-pronged critical attack. It was said that the empirical result that they rationalized was a mere statistical artifact. At the same time, their critics denied that it had any welfare significance, even if not an artifact. Why did the North American economists who launched this double volley not have an immediate and crushing triumph in debate? For all the critics had succeeded in doing by the end of the decade was to force a draw in the intellectual contest and ensure a replay at a future date. One reason might be that Singer had handled the relevant statistics carefully and had been the first to draw attention to one of the critics' major cavils, the quality-change issue. Then the critics had to rely on the empirical research of another UN economist, C. M. Wright, to reinforce their contention about the effect on the measured terms of trade of falling transport costs. The UN clearly remained an authoritative source of trade data and research. The critics were not able to bring alternative empirical evidence to bear. To the extent that they did so, in Morgan's data sets, they never received the same degree of critical scrutiny as the original UN figures.

At the end of the 1950s, the academic debate had reached an impasse. Singer and Prebisch had done enough to establish that the fact of a secular decline was at least plausible. The critics had done enough to suggest that it was very far from proved. While the debate proceeded, the new data that was reported was irritatingly inconclusive. As Hans Singer reported in 1960:

> The terms of trade of underdeveloped countries . . . presented a rather mixed picture during the postwar period. The more pessimistic assumptions of a steady long-term deterioration in the terms of trade were not borne out; the terms of trade of underdeveloped countries throughout the postwar period have been more favourable than during the 1930s . . . [but] commodity prices did show a weakening tendency from their Korean boom level throughout the 1950s. Thus it was possible for both sides to claim some confirmation for their views.[102]

Also, one might add, it was possible for both sides privately to nurse stronger convictions for and against the secular-decline hypothesis than anything yet said in the intellectual exchanges could justify. It would only be a matter of time before one side or the other would try to settle the issue decisively. The question that had not yet been answered was whether all the objectors' points of criticism, when all of them were taken in account together, were sufficient to remove the decline from the secular trend.

Meanwhile, Prebisch personally had become quite popular within UN circles and had replaced Martínez Cabañas as the executive secretary of ECLA. The radicals within the UN then began to serve as a rallying point for those who were anxious about the intellectual and ideological consequences of the new economic and political dominance of the United States. Although its first confident vigor was gone, the UN nonetheless still provided a good platform. The faster-flowing currents of nationalism outside North America and

Europe became reflected in the choice of topics for the economic research undertaken by the UN, while the UN network provided the means for wide dissemination of the research results.[103] Moreover, Prebisch proved able to move events beyond the academic debate and toward the construction of institutional change.

By the 1960s, the thesis was already in play in the official rhetoric of the Cold War. The U.S. move in 1951 to close down ECLA (see Chapter 6) had many causes, but one was its propagation of the terms-of-trade thesis. After the U.S. failed to close down ECLA, successive U.S. administrations slowly learned that Prebisch was in fact more pragmatic than he was polemical. By 1961, President Kennedy proposed to the UN a "Development Decade" and launched the Alliance for Progress in the hope of a more constructive U.S. relationship with Latin America. Mr. M. V. Lavrichenko, deputy head of department of the USSR Ministry of Foreign Affairs, argued in the Second Committee of the General Assembly that ECOSOC "should devote more of its attention to such urgent economic problems as the prevention of the economic plundering by the imperialist Powers of the countries of Asia, Africa and Latin America." In support of this claim, he reminded his listeners that "a United Nations survey published in 1949 concluded that, in the course of almost half a century, there had been a steady drop in the prices of raw materials in comparison with those of industrial goods."[104] This demonstrated the long-lasting controversial power of the thesis that Prebisch and Singer had between them articulated and that the United Nations had attempted to bury yet had inadvertently ended up promoting, despite the barrage of scholarly criticism emanating from North America.

6

ECLA, Industrialization, and Inflation

The Creation of ECLA: "An Act of Audacity"

In spite of the McCarthyite pressure on radicals at the center of the UN system, the U.S. was markedly less successful at exerting its will on those at the system's periphery. The proliferation of UN regional commissions was in itself a snub to the original American conception of a strictly global organization; and of these, the Economic Commission for Latin America in particular proved a fertile ground for ideas on economic development, causing successive U.S. governments, not to mention the IMF and the World Bank, varying degrees of discomfort. The Eisenhower administration, most notably, felt that ECLA, by priming Latin American governments with "technical economic jargon" to back up their claims for U.S. development assistance, was helping to divert attention from the anti-communist cause. Although in the late 1950s this attitude softened, it was under the Kennedy presidency and the Alliance for Progress that U.S. leaders most clearly sought to appeal to the Latin American democratic left, among other groups in the region, in a bid to secure its support in the Cold War. A similar appeal was also extended to other under-developed regions when Kennedy—in the course of an address largely on Cold War themes—proposed in 1961 that the 1960s should be officially designated the United Nations Decade of Development.[1] The UN activities that this initiative helped stimulate—again somewhat to U.S. discomfort—were based on an intellectual agenda that had to an important degree been pioneered by ECLA and by its dominant personality, Raúl Prebisch.

The contribution of ECLA and Prebisch to the early controversy on the manufacturing–primary production terms of trade has been described in Chapter 5. We argued that it was less pioneering than is usually claimed. However, on the question of industrialization strategy for peripheral countries—crucial to understanding the agenda followed by UNCTAD in the 1960s—ECLA and Prebisch move to center stage. This was the issue that most profoundly concerned them and that they explored with relatively little assistance from other UN organs, although it was by no means their exclusive preserve. How did ECLA come into being and what role did it play in relation to the movement toward industrialization in Latin America? How was that role modified by the arrival of Prebisch at ECLA, and what precisely did he help ECLA to add to the pro-industry discourse in Latin America? What were his views on the use of inflation to stimulate investment and growth? This chapter addresses these questions, setting out the general intellectual trajectory of ECLA in the Prebisch years and examining in detail the seminal early *Economic Surveys*.

Fifty years on, the mainstream economics literature still recognizes Prebisch as an advocate, and a very powerful and important advocate, of import-substituting industrialization (or ISI) as a development strategy for Latin America.[2] He was indeed such an advocate. He did believe in ISI, and he was persuasive in arguing for it—he compared his literary style to that of George Bernard Shaw.[3] However, this advocacy was only part of his legacy to the region and perhaps not the most important part. A greater contribution, and one that should be able to be seen more clearly today, was his exploration of the limits of industrialization, of the ways in which excessive industrialization can reduce economic welfare.

Hernán Santa Cruz, the Chilean representative on ECOSOC, initiated the creation of ECLA as the result of "an act of audacity."[4] He felt that Latin America was being unjustly ignored by the great powers and conceived the idea of a commission to deal with the region's economic and social problems. Receiving no orders to the contrary from his government, he took the initiative and submitted his proposal as an item for the ECOSOC agenda.[5] On 1 August 1947, he formally introduced his resolution to a meeting of ECOSOC. He argued that the Latin American economies needed to develop economically through "both industrialization and diversification." The countries in question were predominantly agricultural, existing industries being mainly confined to the processing of primary materials, and were largely dependent on exports of agricultural products and raw materials. This made Latin America highly vulnerable to cyclical fluctuations, hence the need for diversification.

Diversification, however, needed to be aimed at "balanced development to secure equilibrium and not as a means of attaining self-sufficiency." Santa Cruz expressed clear doubts about the actual course of ISI as it had developed in Latin America during the recently concluded world war:

> The extraordinary war effort had temporarily furnished markets for domestic producers which replaced those disrupted by hostilities, but had also led to selling at export prices fixed by the buyers and brought about an economic diversification to replace interrupted imports which was largely artificial and uneconomic. Such diversification had not only delayed sound development but had squandered the resources needed to accomplish it.

Thus, a commission was needed because "the co-ordinated development of Latin America was necessary in order to avoid the establishment of artificial or uneconomic industries." The UN, which could supply the necessary technical and other services, should provide the context for the rationalization of the already ongoing process of industrialization.[6]

In the subsequent debate, Santa Cruz gained support from the representatives of Norway, China, India, Lebanon, Peru, Venezuela, and Cuba.[7] Only the USSR spoke out openly against the proposal—which, it claimed, would "confuse the structure of ECOSOC."[8] However, there was concealed opposition from the U.S., the UK, Canada, and possibly New Zealand. As Arnold C. Smith of Canada noted, "We are trying to avoid a blunt 'no,' but do not want to encourage this regional machinery at the present stage at least."[9] This was partly because it was felt to be desirable to avoid duplication of the activities of the Pan-American Union and its Inter-American Economic and Social Council; also, a regional economic approach was felt to be undesirable except for a specific purpose such as the reconstruction of areas devastated by war.[10] Indeed, as Wladek R. Malinowski—who, as chief of the Regional Commissions Section of the DEA (1959–1965), was himself a great supporter of ECLA— later pointed out, regionalism was to some degree at odds with the centralized global conception inherent in the UN Charter.[11]

Feeling unable to oppose the ECLA idea openly, the above-mentioned countries tried stalling tactics. However, Pierre Mendès-France, the French delegate, privately offered Santa Cruz his support for an ad hoc committee to study the feasibility of the proposal, provided that European countries were accepted as members of ECLA.[12] Such a committee was indeed established, and when it reported favorably in January 1948, opposition could be taken no farther. On 25 February of that year, a motion establishing the new body was passed with no votes against and four abstentions (Byelorussia, Canada, the U.S., and the USSR).[13] As Leroy Stinebower, who was present on behalf of the U.S., later recalled, "The forces of globalism were being overwhelmed—or at least over shouted—at that moment by a lot of regionalism stuff.... [E]ven in my worst dreams I didn't think that regionalism would go as far as it's gone in this world."[14]

ECLA before Prebisch

The report of the ad hoc committee which recommended the commission's creation is a useful starting point in assessing the ideas current in UN circles about Latin America during ECLA's early, pre-Prebisch period. A report written by Harold Caustin and David Weintraub on behalf of the UN Secretariat to assist the committee argued that the region's reliance on primary exports marked it out as "a semi-colonial economy." A paper was also drawn up by the representatives of four countries—Chile, Cuba, Peru, and Venezuela—which analyzed the problems facing Latin America in view of its "underdeveloped, agricultural, non-industrial economy of low living standards." The discourse, like the problems, was familiar. However, the paper made one particularly striking comment that pointed toward a new agenda: "The economies of the Latin-American countries being competitive rather than complementary are weakened by their ensuing lack of regional integration." This comment pointed to a problem that obstructed attempts to rationalize the ISI strategy.[15] It would subsequently form an important element in Prebisch's critique of the actual Latin American industrialization process.[16]

The first session of ECLA met in Santiago in June 1948. The need for industrialization was emphasized widely by the Latin American delegates. It was generally considered that it should involve the processing of indigenous raw materials—the easy, initial stage of ISI.[17] As Julio Alvarado, the representative of Bolivia, put it, "[A]ll our countries feel with perfect right—what we might call the '*need for basic national industry.*'" Alvarado argued for "the establishment of our domestic industry to satisfy our main needs" and went on to advocate ISI and import-substituting agriculture (ISA) policies (although he did not use those terms), which, he suggested, would result in the accumulation of considerable foreign exchange reserves.[18] Industrialization was not, however, the sole economic remedy promulgated at the conference. In addition, the abolition of double taxation was considered an important means to attract foreign capital to the region.[19] Mass European immigration to Latin America was also proposed.[20] Elaborate financial clearing arrangements were advocated too.[21] Nor was industrialization itself seen as a panacea. Juvenal Monge, the Peruvian delegate, pointed out some possible dangers:

> [C]ountries producing raw materials which seek to industrialize themselves run great risks if they aim at self-sufficiency, since in order to protect their infant industries they will have to resort to tariff barriers or other means of protecting their industrial products on the home market. Furthermore, abroad their products will have to be placed upon competitive markets, in which they will not be taken up, as the costs of industrialized countries using scientific production techniques cannot be competed with.

Monge warned that "Latin America should not fall into the error of chaotic industrialization" whereby substantial purchases of heavy machinery would be accompanied by "a disquieting drain on currency reserves and a consequent threat to the new industries from coming world competition."[22] The United States and Britain both reacted to ECLA's first session with some mild relief.[23] Subsequently, however, there was a distinct attempt within the U.S. State Department to move away from procedural multilateralism as a means of achieving American goals in the Latin American context.[24]

Love has implied that such stress as was placed on industrialization at the session was due, at least in part, to the familiarity of Alberto Baltra Cortés, the Chilean minister of economy, who presided over the conference, with the ideas of Prebisch.[25] This seems unlikely. Similar enthusiasm for industrialization had been expressed at Chapultepec in February 1945, at a time when Prebisch's influence would be more difficult to call on as an explanation.[26] This enthusiasm derived more from the fact that there was already within Latin America a well-established discourse of industrialization, which was taken to be a means of overcoming perceived disadvantages inherent in specialization in primary production. As we have seen, Prebisch himself had played only a very marginal role in promoting this view before 1949. What Prebisch did, in and after that year, was to reformulate this preexisting discourse, incorporating into it important new elements, including warnings on the limits to industrialization, in order to increase its intellectual coherence as a regional strategy for development.

The Preexisting Discourse on Industrialization

The Great Depression that began in 1929 was a key historical landmark by which Latin American structuralist thinkers referenced their ideas. Prebisch later recalled that it was this great world crisis that led him to throw his free trade ideas overboard.[27] The impact of the Depression must be assessed, however, in the context of a much-longer-standing process of industrial expansion in Latin America dating back to the late nineteenth century. This process was consequent on export-led growth generating substantial domestic markets and hence manufacturing sectors.[28] In Chile, which in the years before the Second World War probably industrialized more fully than any other Latin American country, an industrialists' association had appeared as early as 1883.[29] Gabriel Palma has argued that here, and perhaps elsewhere, the First World War began a phase of ISI.[30]

Nevertheless, 1929 was the great watershed. The October crash led to a dramatic fall in primary product prices for all Latin American countries and a fall in export volumes for most of them. This produced a sharp decline in the purchasing power of exports over the worst years of the Depression, while the real burden of existing debt rose and new lending halted. These circumstances, and the protectionist policies of the United States and the British empire, stimulated the growth of a strong import-competing sector. In response to the crisis, most of the Latin American republics raised their tariff rates, increasing the real cost of imports sharply. This encouraged a switch in expenditure toward domestic substitutes, not only in manufactures but also in agricultural products, which many countries had imported in substantial quantities in the 1920s.[31] The import substitution of the 1930s and 1940s has been described as a "spontaneous process" of both governments and firms responding to external shocks.[32]

The growth of the industrialization discourse of the 1930s was out of proportion to the true role of ISI in fostering recovery from the Depression.[33] This was because although industrial growth was able to satisfy much of the demand for consumer goods previously met by imports after the crisis years of 1930–1932, Latin American countries failed to reduce their import bills as the marginal propensity to import remained extremely high. These countries therefore had to wait for their traditional export markets to revive before they could stabilize their balance of payments.[34] Although recovery had derived mainly from the external sector, the Depression had been transmitted to Latin America via that sector. The obvious question was whether this external transmission mechanism could be geared down, and industrialization seemed a plausible answer. Moreover, as Santa Cruz's concern about artificial industries suggested, if the ISI of the 1930s had been undertaken more rationally, its contribution to recovery would have been greater than it was. Industrialization, in these years, was a dramatic and visible phenomenon, far more so than the moves toward "normalization" in traditional export industries. This led people to exaggerate its economic importance. Because of its easy associations with modernity and progress, industrialization was venerated with little regard to the calculus of costs and benefits of particular industrial investments. This was the case, contemporaneously, in the Soviet Union and in India.[35]

Although Latin American pro-industry enthusiasts were little influenced directly by the Soviet model of planning, the "scientific" labor rationalization process promoted by the American Frederick W. Taylor (1856–1915) was a significant influence in both cases.[36] For example, Roberto Simonsen, the foremost Brazilian industrial spokesman, argued that labor rationalization would bring social peace, as the resultant productivity increases would be reflected in lower prices for manufactured goods and increased wages for workers. He thus commended the process, particularly as he saw its political effects as acting "against the fundamental ideas of Marxism."[37] Moreover, the modernity that industrialization represented was, for many Latin Americans, a symbol of national pride and inspiration. Reliance upon exports was seen as a sign of "dependence" that industrialization could remove. Indeed, the concept of Latin American "dependence" existed in popular rhetoric long before it was formalized in "dependency theory."[38]

During the Second World War, practical considerations increasingly became the main driving force behind Latin American industrialization, which was undertaken for military purposes, in order to reduce reliance on foreign sources of weapons supply. This was notably true in Brazil, where nationalist and developmental aspirations overlapped.[39] War also changed the nature of the industrialization conundrum. Previously, ISI was undertaken as a means to liberate precious foreign exchange. Once primary products were at a premium, large foreign exchange balances accumulated quickly, so there was plenty of capital available for domestic investment. The problem became instead the physical shortage of the means necessary for industrialization.

The United States was willing to supply capital equipment and technical assistance to most countries as the price of access to primary products. She did not tend to receive credit for this, however. There was a common belief among Latin Americans that politicians and financiers in the industrial nations, and especially in the U.S., regarded the region purely as an easily exploitable source of cheap raw materials.[40] This perception resulted partly from contradictions in U.S. policy, as Merwin L. Bohan, a technical officer attached to the U.S. delegation to the 1945 Inter-American Conference on War and Peace at Chapultepec, pointed out:

> The United States has promoted the industrialization of Latin America not only as a matter of general policy, but specifically through lending capital and technical assistance. However, when the governments of Latin America take

measures to protect the industries thus created, there is a disposition to frown on all forms of protectionism.[41]

Moreover, American help was not in itself enough to overcome the region's difficulties. The new wartime industries faced major difficulties competing in conditions of peace. Nonetheless, Latin Americans were on the whole inclined to treat the burgeoning of their industries not as a temporary aberration wrought by extraordinary conditions but as a base upon which to build. They hoped that the United States would be able to help them do this, but their confidence in the export-oriented industrialization strategy was dented after the 1947–1948 Havana conference by the failure to create the ITO. Industrialization became associated not only with progress but also with some degree of anti-Americanism.

The Intellectual Trajectory of ECLA under Prebisch

If emotional economic nationalism was a key factor in public support for industrialization, and also in conditioning the way in which governments carried out ISI, there were also powerful economic arguments to be deployed in its favor, given the economic situation in which the Latin American countries found themselves at the end of the Second World War. Prebisch, reflecting later on the origins of his own ISI policy, argued convincingly that worldwide protectionism during the 1930s, the economic disruption of the Second World War, and European protectionism in the immediate postwar years successively made it impossible to think about expanding exports during this era. He was talking specifically of the export of manufactures, as he was attempting to rebut the suggestion that he should have advocated this sooner than he did. For this reason, he said, ISI was "the only possibility."[42]

Indeed, it is vital to understand the postwar Latin American economic crisis in order to appreciate properly the significance of Prebisch's writings of 1949–1950. The problems were numerous. Much of what industrial plant existed had been worn out during the war, and it needed to be replaced. Moreover, many of the industries created in wartime stood little chance of surviving without heavy protection in peacetime conditions, a situation that had been recognized in the provisions of the Havana Charter. Furthermore, during the war, the Latin American nations had accumulated large reserves of foreign currency, owing both to increased world demand for raw materials and physical shortages that limited imports. After 1945, however, dollar reserves were quickly dissipated through rising prices for imported manufactures and through increased demand for such goods (in part as a consequence of overvalued exchange rates). Sterling balances, on the other hand, were for the most part either completely blocked or were inconvertible into dollars (except for a brief period in 1947). This was another barrier to the continuation of the post–World War I "three-way" pattern of trade, whereby American purchases from Europe paid for European (dollar) purchases of Latin American raw materials, thus facilitating Latin American purchases of imports from the U.S.—a multilateral compensation system that had already started to break down in the 1930s.[43]

What was to be done? It became clear at the 1948 Inter-American conference at Bogotá that there would be no Marshall Plan for Latin America.[44] Nor did the final outcome of the 1947–1948 international trade negotiations satisfy Latin American aspirations.[45] Such factors increased receptivity to radical doctrines of change to the international economy. M. A. P. Leopoldi suggests that in the case of Brazil, ECLA merely "gave a technical gloss to the discourse of an industrial bourgeoisie indignant at the inequality of forces in the area of international trade."[46] However, beyond that, the conjunctural problems facing Latin America certainly made a break with the orthodoxy of agricultural specialization an increasingly attractive option.

In July 1948, the UN Sub-Commission on Economic Development noted its view that industrialization formed "the decisive element" in the development process.[47] This was a widely but not unanimously held view in UN circles and was the natural corollary of the perception that primary commodity–producing nations were at a special disadvantage in relation to those that exported manufactured goods, a perception that the statistical work of Singer reinforced but did not create. However, if sentiment in favor of industrialization was strong prior to the late 1940s, it did not yet have a comprehensive economic justification. The work of Prebisch and his colleagues at the Economic Commission for Latin America went some way to provide this: the reasons why peripheral countries, and specifically Latin American countries, needed to undertake a form of ISI in order to stimulate economic development was one of ECLA's strongest themes from its first years until the early 1960s.

From a technical economic point of view, as previously noted,[48] there were two major versions of the ECLA model. In the early years, the ECLA doctrine rested on neo-Ricardian assumptions, with export prices from the center being driven by technical progress and nonmarket distributional processes. In his 1959 article, Prebisch used a standard neoclassical approach but with some key assumptions altered: the demand curve for exports was downward-sloping rather than horizontal; instead of full employment of labor, there was a labor surplus because of exogenous demographic trends; and there were positive externalities from investment. With these variations of the standard open economy model, there is a perverse outcome in which the exchange rate cannot equilibrate the external imbalance and a second-best outcome can be reached only by import tariffs or export taxes.[49] The later version was an attempt to address the objection that ECLA expounded its doctrine obscurely, even in the eyes of sympathetic commentators, and that its intuitions of reality were handicapped by difficulties in articulating them.

That criticism is, however, quite distinct from the simple misunderstanding of ECLA and the ISI strategy still perpetuated by mainstream economists. ISI has repeatedly been described, quite mistakenly, as an inward-oriented development strategy, the "ultimate aim" of which was "to achieve economic self-sufficiency."[50] Moreover, it is also claimed, again wrongly, that only in the late 1950s did ECLA begin "to consider the complexities of ISI," with an agonizing reappraisal taking place in the 1960s.[51] In fact, from its first years, the commission created a body of work that emphasized not only that ISI was what modern economists call a "second-best" response to external shocks but also that it had potential practical shortcomings. To say this is not to deny that ECLA favored industrialization or import substitution as a major element in the process of economic development. Indeed, Prebisch himself later compared his own belief in industrialization to the love that one has for one's mother—something that it is not necessary to mention every moment to know that it exists.[52] However, the commission was always aware of the limitations of ISI, and it never naively or uncritically favored ISI as it was actually implemented in Latin America. This, Prebisch believed, was based on protection that often exceeded rational levels and resulted in industries incapable of doing more than supplying at exorbitant cost the national markets of the countries concerned.

It was these concerns that differentiated the ideas of Prebisch and ECLA from the intellectual heritage the League of Nations bequeathed to the UN. This already included, to some degree, a rationale for the industrialization of "backward" areas. Although the League's economists had traditionally been determined advocates of free trade, its economic section had argued in 1937 that agricultural nations should undertake a small measure of industrialization, on the ground that factor flows remained substantially blocked as a consequence of the Depression.[53] Furthermore, a 1945 League publication, mainly the work of Folke Hilgerdt, had proved more influential. It showed two rather arresting correlations. The first was between having a high percentage of the labor force engaged in agriculture and having a low average national income. The other was between having a high share of labor in agriculture and experiencing low yields of agricultural output per acre.[54] Although the League itself did not draw this inference, it was common at the time to infer from such statistics that in underdeveloped countries additional investment in industry would be more remunerative than the same amount of additional investment in projects in the agricultural sector. Moreover, if population growth were accelerating in low-income areas, as was often the case, some economists responded by recommending "a quick forward advance" in industrialization as the most promising approach toward higher real incomes.[55] The general tendency within the UN to favor industrialization extended, by the late 1940s, to the advocacy of ISI policies, which was by no means the exclusive preserve of ECLA.[56]

Prebisch's work, however, put the already-familiar industrialization issue into a new and broader context of international economic power relations. In 1949, he stated his first arguments for ISI in *The Economic Development of Latin America and Its Principal Problems.* He argued from the secular decline in the terms of trade between manufactures and primary products that the benefits of technical progress had been distributed unequally between the center and the periphery. Given that prices of manufactures did not fall in line with increases in productivity, "industrialization is the only means by which the Latin-American countries may fully obtain the advantages of technical progress."[57] He always maintained that there was "no other alternative than that of import-substitution" in the 1929–c. 1952 period.[58] Prebisch later stated that "my proposed development policy . . . sought to provide theoretical justification for the industrialization policy which was already being followed (especially by the large countries of Latin America), to encourage the others to follow it too, and to provide all of them with an orderly strategy for carrying this out."[59] In other words, there were orderly and disorderly ways of implementing an industrialization policy.

Although Prebisch's views of 1949 had provoked concern at UN headquarters, as noted in Chapter 5, his career in ECLA did not suffer for it; rather, the reverse happened. David Owen came to Havana to offer him the position of director of ECLA's research center with the same rank and salary as the executive secretary. Prebisch successfully negotiated his total independence from the executive secretary on intellectual matters, staff appointments, and travel arrangements.[60] As might have been predicted, this swiftly proved to be an unworkable arrangement, which was resolved when, after the 1950 ECLA session in Montevideo, he displaced Martínez Cabañas as executive secretary at the behest of Trygve Lie, the UN Secretary-General.[61] The rebel voice was thus swiftly incorporated into the UN top echelon but without having to agree to compromise his intellectual independence.[62] This was an extraordinary success and gave Prebisch an unprecedented position in the UN system. He used it to create an elite team of economic and social researchers drawn from across the continent, whose work he synthesized, shaped, and persuasively projected both south and north of the Panama Canal.

The *Economic Survey of Latin America 1948*

We must now assess critically the industrialization policies advocated by the commission in the Prebisch years in order to examine the validity of the criticism that it promoted excessively inward-oriented development.[63] Responsibility for the chapter of the *Economic Survey* on industrialization did not fall to Prebisch but to a small group of ECLA staff members under Milic Kybal, formerly of the U.S. Federal Reserve.[64] Celso Furtado, who was a member of the group, recalled that Kybal gave the impression of walking on eggshells. It was important to offend neither the representatives of the still-powerful import-export sector, who believed that import substitution was damaging their markets, nor Latin American governments, many of which were expressly in favor of industrialization. Despite this tension, the group did not shy away from advocating industrialization. It took as its starting point the 1945 League publication by Folke Hilgerdt.[65] Its members drew from this study the lesson that the expansion of industrial production would stimulate international trade in manufactures; by augmenting the purchasing power of the population, it would provoke a more-than-proportional growth in demand for manufactures and would thus stimulate imports. (This, of course, was potentially problematic, a point, later raised by Prebisch, that the group appears to have overlooked.) Furtado, focusing on the need to expand Latin America's supply of manufactures, set out to explore further the relationship between industrialization and foreign trade.[66] His analysis was in due course included in the *Economic Survey of Latin America 1948* in the section on manufacturing.

As published, this section set out to consider the question from two angles. First, to what extent was it possible to increase the Latin American nations' supply of manufactures by means of an increase in trade with the industrialized nations? Second, what might be the consequences for foreign trade of an increase in domestic manufacturing output? The second question was not, however, explored very thoroughly. The survey argued that "unless industrialization increases substantially in Latin America, it is difficult to realize the magnitude of the imports of manufactures that would be necessary to increase the total supply of such goods in the region to a level comparable to that prevalent among the industrialized countries [and] a completely unrealistic volume of foreign trade would have to be envisaged." Moreover,

> the expansion of Latin-American exports is limited by the low elasticity of the demand of raw materials and foodstuffs in the world markets. The structural changes in international trade which took place between 1914 and 1918, and the contraction occurring during the 1930's, rendered doubtful any possibility of achieving by means of international trade a broad economic development in the countries which are traditional exporters of primary commodities.

Australia, Canada, New Zealand, and South Africa were given as examples of countries that had enjoyed a dramatic increase in the supply of manufactures, a development that, it was argued, "was only possible to the extent to which industrialization accompanied the development of foreign trade." The report continued, "In the long run, therefore, industrialization appears to be the principal means whereby a substantial increase in the standards of living in Latin America can be achieved."

The possible impact of industrialization on the balance of payments (especially given the need to import capital goods) was not considered. Nevertheless, the survey did emphasize that industrialization, if it were the principal means to development, was not the sole one, "since this process implies the introduction of labour-saving devices in all fields of production." Balanced economic development would involve improvements in the technology of agriculture, transportation, and power and the modernization of the distribution system. Finally, this section of the survey concluded, "[I]ndustrialization is more than an economic process. It is also the cause and effect of deep changes in the political and social institutions of all the countries where it takes root."[67]

The document that was eventually published separately under Prebisch's name as *The Economic Development of Latin America and Its Principal Problems,* originally intended as the introduction to the survey, made many arguments about industrialization similar to those contained in the survey, although they were more strikingly expressed. It argued additionally that it would not be necessary to restrict the individual consumption of the bulk of the population, which Prebisch considered on the whole too low, in order to accumulate the capital required for industrialization and the technical improvement of agriculture. "An immediate increase in productivity per man could be brought about by well-directed foreign investments added to present savings." Once this had been accomplished, much of the increased production could be dedicated to capital formation rather than "inopportune consumption." Furthermore, the rise in employment that had in recent years been necessitated by industrial development had been made possible by the use of workers whom technical progress had displaced from primary production and other low-paid occupations. Hence, the industrial employment of the unemployed, or ill-employed, had meant a considerable improvement in productivity and consequently, where other factors had not intervened, a net increase in national income.[68]

For all that, Prebisch insisted that the welfare purpose of industrialization must mean that the process faced economic limits.

> If industrialization is considered to be the means of attaining an autarchic ideal in which economic considerations are of secondary importance, any industry that can produce substitutes for imports is justifiable. If, however, the aim is to

increase the measurable well-being of the masses, the limits beyond which more intensive industrialization might mean a decrease in productivity must be borne in mind.[69]

The *Economic Survey of Latin America 1949*

Prebisch's analyses were always intellectually controversial; as Celso Furtado noted, his contributions were all implied criticisms of laissez-faire.[70] The *Economic Survey of Latin America 1949*, written under his direction, justified ISI as an inevitable response to the dramatic decline in the import coefficients of both the UK and the U.S. over the previous twenty-five years, which compelled Latin America to lower its own import coefficient. The survey also tackled a related problem which had been left open in the previous year's study: the balance-of-payments problems likely to be caused by the spread of technical progress. It was argued that the fundamental economic problem of Latin America lay in increasing its real per capita income by virtue of an increase in productivity, since the possibility of raising the living standards of the masses by redistributing income was strictly limited. However, when this occurred, imports likewise tended to increase at a greater rate than the population. If exports did not follow suit, balance-of-payments disequilibrium would result.[71] Latin America was therefore caught in a scissors trap, between low external demand for its primary products and its own increased demand for imports as it tried to escape the former problem by industrializing. This trap was tightened further by the deterioration of the terms of trade.[72]

How, then, could disequilibrium be counteracted? Prebisch knew that exchange control, import quotas, currency depreciation, and tariffs were mere improvised measures that might limit existing imbalance but not remove it. He proposed not to reduce imports but to alter their composition "in such a way that the contraction of certain imports will allow the expansion of others which are indispensable to economic development."[73] What was new was not the advocacy of import substitution itself—which in this analysis was already happening spontaneously because of Latin America's declining capacity to import—but the suggestion that the process should be planned. This suggestion was made more explicit in later ECLA studies, in line with the growing influence of the ideas of Arthur Lewis, which we have discussed in Chapter 4.[74]

For Prebisch, industrialization had to be planned because the process had limits. He saw that "one of the essential conditions which must prevail in order that primary production in the Latin American countries may retain for itself the benefits of technical progress is that the surplus of active population resulting from such progress be absorbed into industry and other activities." Yet he also saw that this labor transfer, if taken too far, would become detrimental to agriculture. "Without tariff protection it would have been impossible to reach the stage of industrial progress achieved in a good many Latin American countries."[75] However, in many countries the levels of protection were already excessive and were driven more by political than by economic considerations.

ISI ought to have a regional dimension. Prebisch noted that when tariffs had been raised against goods from the industrial centers,

> not only have imports from such centers been reduced but imports of manufactured goods from other Latin American countries have been obstructed. Consequently, we are faced with industries established on either side of a frontier, each having a relatively limited market which could be expanded by a more rational distribution of the industrial efforts of the Latin American countries. Certain forms of specialization would thus be encouraged with evident advantages to be gained in productivity.

He therefore proposed that "the industrial development of the Latin American countries also requires the development of reciprocal trade in manufactured goods," in addition to trade in foodstuffs and raw materials.[76] The need for regional integration—which had been recognized at ECLA's inception, even before Prebisch's arrival—would become one of the commission's key themes in the years that followed. On this basis, it seems difficult to accept the argument that ECLA's doctrines were narrowly inward oriented.

Furtado recalled that the survey itself seemed too abstract to the great majority of readers but seemed to specialists to lack conceptual precision.[77] Perhaps predictably, the Latin American countries generally welcomed it, whereas the U.S. delegate to the 1950 ECLA conference commented skeptically that portions of it were "of a thought-provoking but highly theoretical character. . . . I rather doubt whether the many economists here present will agree with every one of the ideas set forth."[78] Although the U.S. and UK governments' initial suspicion and hostility to UN regional commissions did linger on, British and U.S. attitudes toward Prebisch and ECLA at this time were not as unremittingly hostile as Prebisch and other ECLA staff themselves believed (and as David Pollock has argued).[79] The British Foreign Office took the line that

> we should probably not wish to support the abolition of ECLA except as part of an operation involving the winding up of all the regional commissions. This is because we consider that there is some advantage in Latin America's economic problems . . . being discussed in a body of which we are members rather than in the Latin American Economic and Social Council, while ECLA has avoided both the extravagance and the political squabbles which have characterised the work of ECE and ECAFE.[80]

At its 1951 meeting in Mexico, a U.S. proposal to close the commission down was narrowly averted after Prebisch offered a stout defense of its work (and after Mexico had been persuaded to do a volte-face and President Vargas of Brazil had intervened).[81] This episode appears to have diminished American doubts about the value of the commission.[82] The U.S. delegation reported that it was "much impressed with the work of ECLA and of its Secretariat, and particularly with Dr. Prebisch himself." Significantly for the argument of this chapter, "The Delegation felt that ECLA is building up a body of Latin American thought in the fields of economic development and trade which is essentially realistic and useful. . . . [I]t was felt that Dr. Prebisch is in a position to bring home to Latin American officials economic truths which they would not accept on the basis of any statement made by U.S. representatives."[83]

Prebisch's robust style served him well. Göran Ohlin observed of him, "[I]f he was 51 per cent convinced of something, [he] went for it one hundred per cent and left it for others to argue the final points and to continue the discussion long after he had left the scene."[84] This gave colleagues, such as José Antonio Mayobre, Juan Noyola Vazquez, and Celso Furtado, an important role in refining and testing his hypotheses.[85] It is Prebisch, however, who chiefly concerns us here, given his later international role, for the ideas that he went on to develop at ECLA during the 1950s later animated UNCTAD's thinking and gained a worldwide audience.

Squeezing the Lemon: The Second Stage of ISI

By the early part of that decade, the more industrially advanced Latin American countries, such as Mexico, Brazil, and Argentina, appeared to have passed through the first "easy" stage of ISI, when imports of nondurable consumer goods such as clothing and shoes are substituted by domestic production. They therefore faced a choice between undertaking a second stage of ISI, substituting, for example, imports of cars and refrigerators, or turning to the export of manufactures. Bela Balassa has argued that Prebisch adopted the former course, favoring the expansion of manufacturing industries oriented toward domestic markets.[86] The truth is quite different. Prebisch realized that the ISI process was like squeezing a lemon; the first squeeze would yield a great deal of juice, but subsequent squeezes would yield progressively less and less. In retirement, he emphasized that "to say we had an 'import-substituting model' when we were the first to talk of reciprocal trade between the Latin American countries and of the export of manufactures to the rest of the world, is to twist, to disfigure, the thinking that we had."[87]

Indeed, he was not even sanguine about the prospects for countries in the "easy" ISI phase. In 1951, he noted that Cuba had just raised its tariffs in order to protect its infant textile industry. Following the analysis of the 1949 *Economic Survey,* he observed that the reductions in textile imports thus obtained might well be more than offset by larger imports of other goods, as had happened in other countries. He said, however, that he would "not adopt the common attitude of condemning inflation," although he was "convinced of its serious evils," as any meaningful anti-inflationary policy needed to be coupled with recommendations that permitted acceleration of the rate of investment.[88] The next year, nevertheless, he spoke of the commission's "perplexity" and "great anxiety" over the incompatibility "between the wish to intensify investments and the equally praiseworthy desire to raise the standard of living of the masses." He argued that "in order to attain these goals simultaneously, some countries have allowed inflation to reach a very dangerous stage: namely, that of cost inflation." This resulted from such countries' inability to raise productivity sufficiently to absorb higher wages and social security charges and the consequent economic dislocation tended to lower productivity in turn.[89] Prebisch, though he continued to argue that inflation was not purely a monetary phenomenon, insisted on its dangers.

In the same speech, he warned explicitly of the problems that could be associated with inward-oriented development. Speaking of Central America, he said that "with the tendency to develop inwards, through industrialization, a very serious difficulty arises . . . namely, the incompatibility between the need to develop certain forms of industrialization and the small size of the [domestic] markets." In order to overcome this, he advocated Central American regional economic integration, with particular countries specializing in particular industries and exporting manufactures to one another: "[W]e envisage the possibility of a profitable industrial trade, complemented by trade in agricultural products and raw materials among these countries."[90] He would later see the failure of Latin America as a whole to undertake such integration as the region's key developmental failure.

Programming Development

By 1953, Prebisch was riding high. Although U.S. hostility to ECLA was renewed with the advent of the Eisenhower administration, Prebisch had the unstinting support of successive UN Secretaries-General, which was enough to protect the commission from all, bar minor U.S., interference.[91] Support for the commission within Latin America itself was growing; its 1953 Rio conference was the first at which all the countries of the region were represented. Colombia, one of the few countries that had previously been rather doubtful about ECLA, offered its capital for the next meeting.[92] The commission itself was also evolving. Its early work had been of a largely theoretical character.

Prebisch now emphasized that although it had been "necessary to elaborate certain principles for practical guidance," the time for "concrete action" had arrived.[93]

This change in direction resulted in the production of sectoral studies, studies of particular industries, and country studies. There was a particular focus on the technique of development "programming." (Interestingly, this term rather than "planning" had to be used to placate the World Bank.[94]) In his memoirs, Furtado summarized the philosophy behind this kind of planning, which he distinguished from Soviet planning, Keynesian-style full-employment planning, and French-style indicative planning. The aim was to increase the transparency and rationality of the decision-making process. By forecasting rates and trends of development on the basis of varying hypotheses, countries could in effect be told, "[H]ere are your possibilities; all have a price, each that is chosen must be paid for by the renunciation of something else."[95] This process also had the advantage of allowing the commission to make implicit recommendations—via the select presentation of hypotheses and outcomes—without antagonizing either national governments or the top authorities at United Nations headquarters.

The growing flurry of reports helped bolster the commission's influence. Even the U.S. State Department, whose interest in Latin America now focused on "obtaining a ringing hemispheric declaration against encroachments of Soviet communism," was forced to acknowledge this. Its report on the tenth Inter-American conference in March 1954 noted that at no previous such conference "did the Latin American Delegations come so well prepared with statements of economic problems and aspirations of their countries."

> Delegate after delegate presented lengthy and in many cases well-prepared documents. . . . In much of this was evident the work . . . of the secretariat of the United Nations Economic Commission for Latin America, under the direction of Raul Prebisch. The various Latin American countries had available from ECLA a very considerable number of studies of their economic problems on which they could draw for material, and in many cases the delegates had picked up technical economic jargon learned from Prebisch.[96]

The commission had helped increase the sophistication of the Latin American governments' economic arguments, which went some way toward strengthening the region's political power—and its own—in relations with the United States. ECLA's influence on the Latin American countries' economic policies was, however, far more limited than its influence in the UN and in the academic world.[97] Prebisch's own later frustration with the way the industrialization process evolved is eloquent testimony to this.

The Early ECLA Theory of Inflation

In elaborating his account of the external disequilibrium caused by industrialization efforts in Latin America, Prebisch argued that although in some
countries inflation had undoubtedly exacerbated external imbalance, this was
really the result of the "much deeper and more fundamental forces."[98] As it
was put in the 1949 *Economic Survey*, "[T]he organic phenomenon of economic development must be distinguished from the circumstantial phenomenon of inflation. . . . [T]he tendency toward disequilibrium will be constant
and will inevitably have monetary consequences whether inflation is present
or not."[99] This distinction indicates that inflation was not at this time regarded
as the major cause of macroeconomic imbalance in Latin America, although
it was recognized as an aggravating factor in some countries.

In the first decade of its existence, ECLA's economists were preoccupied
with the problems of the external sector of the Latin American economies.
They treated inflation as a minor problem and one on which they needed to
say little.[100] The question that they examined in the 1949 *Economic Survey* was
whether inflation could be used as an instrument for increasing investment,
and hence economic growth, by imposing forced saving on consumers and
changing the distribution of real national income in favor of the profits share.
The ECLA conclusion was that that strategy was not sustainable. It was not
always possible to make forced saving effective except in the short run. When
Chile permitted inflation, the *Economic Survey* noted that "the mass of the
population has learned how to defend itself."[101] It also doubted the robustness
of the link between a growing profit share and a growing investment share,
pointing out that rising luxury consumption could equally result. When Brazil deliberately used inflation to redistribute income away from fixed-income
earners to profit earners and (it was hoped) investors, the ECLA response was
to warn against merely redistributing consumption toward the better off.

Not until 1953 does the *Economic Survey* devote a whole chapter to the
monetary situation. In this chapter, however, there occurs very briefly a crucial insight into the way in which domestic inflation aggravated the problem
of maintaining external equilibrium. Inflation penalized exporters, whose
incomes were fixed by the combination of world prices and a constant foreign exchange rate. If their ability to invest were to be undermined by inflation, so would be the country's future capacity to import:

> Inflation directed towards raising investments . . . often provokes a transfer of
> resources towards some activities to the detriment of others. If, as is often the
> case, the latter activities are those upon which the capacity to import is based,

a dislocation occurs which soon results in disequilibrium in the balance of payments and in supply difficulties.[102]

This was the nearest that ECLA got to stating the proposition that the use of inflation (under fixed exchange rates) to promote investment in industries that turn out to be unable to export can only worsen the external constraint on growth. The concern was reiterated in an evaluation of the Chilean economy in the following year's *Economic Survey*.[103]

In its first decade, ECLA, though not wholly consistent, expounded a largely orthodox view of the mechanisms of inflation. The level of the foreign exchange reserves plus the amount of domestic credit determined the money supply. Inflation was caused by the expansion of the money supply in excess of the demand for money. Monetary contraction would cause disinflation. This was the message of the 1953 *Economic Survey*:

> Apart from exceptional cases, there is a very close correlation in Latin America between variability in the money supply and price fluctuations, the latter usually following the former. Thus a study of variations in the money supply and their determining factors, whether of an internal or an external nature, is a first step to analysing the problem of inflation.[104]

The only deviation from strict monetarism came with the assumption that the money supply was passive or accommodating in the upswing of the economic cycle. Nevertheless, governments could and should use fiscal austerity to bring inflation under control. So in this period, ECLA was not soft on inflation, even though inflation was regarded as a relatively minor obstacle to the process of economic development. ECLA did not encourage or approve of inflation; rather the reverse, as one might expect, given Prebisch's long service as the head of a central bank and his opposition to the populist economic policies of Perón. At the same time, it seems fair to say that the ECLA economists should have brought into sharper focus at an earlier stage the significant balance-of-payments dangers of relying on inflation to fuel economic growth.

The Structural Theory of Inflation

The spur to break away from the conventional account of the forces driving inflation was the experience of inflation in Chile. This had a particular salience for the economists of ECLA, whose location was in Santiago de Chile. The 1949 *Economic Survey* had already noticed the Chilean population's ability to defend itself against the distribution consequences of inflation. The 1953 *Economic Survey* hinted at a dynamic behind Chilean inflation: "[T]he inflationary process in Chile is caused by the combined or successive forces of the upward movement in wages and the rise in public expenditure."[105] Chile had had both well-

developed class antagonisms and chronic double-digit inflation for many decades past, but these were first put together as cause and effect in the *Economic
Survey* for 1954. This novel theory of social conflict as the source of inflation
was probably inspired by the work of Henri Aujac, whose paper on the subject
had appeared in French in 1950 and in English in 1954.[106]

This paper was known to Juan Noyola Vazquez, who probably wrote the 1954
section of the *Economic Survey* on Chile's inflation and who soon thereafter
published an article that first elaborated what quickly became ECLA's structural theory of inflation.[107] The structural theory differed from the social conflict
approach. It distinguished two components of causation—basic inflationary
pressures that initiate inflation and propagation mechanisms that maintain its
momentum. In the structural theory, social conflict is a propagation mechanism and its centrality is thereby reduced relative to the theory of Aujac. At the
same time, the role of economics was restored as the source of the basic
inflationary pressures. These were a variety of "bottlenecks" on the supply side
of the economy: the three main ones were found to be in agriculture, imports,
and taxes, although some class antagonisms could also create bottlenecks. The
agricultural bottleneck was derived from Kalecki's familiar food-supply constraint in his Mexican article of 1954. Noyola Vazquez referred to this article as
"the analysis by Kalecki which stresses the importance of the rigidity of supply
and the degree of monopoly in the economic system."[108] Osvaldo Sunkel also
cited Kalecki in his 1958 Spanish article giving a structuralist analysis of Chilean
inflation.[109] Thus Kalecki's thinking lived on in the UN.[110]

Kalecki was not the only external influence on the birth of structuralism.
ECLA invited Nicholas Kaldor to visit Chile in 1956. He regarded the obstacles
in the path of Chile's accelerated improvement as "essentially political." He
thought that the agricultural bottleneck was the underlying cause of inflation
and that the difficulty in breaking it was the strength of the political opposition to land reform.[111] In this he was essentially following Kalecki's line. Hollis
Chenery was also a visitor to Santiago shortly after and published an article
on structuralist lines.[112] These external voices were an important stimulus to
the new theory of inflation and provide an intellectual link back to the analyses of the limits of the price mechanism as a resource allocation mechanism
that flourished in wartime and postwar Britain.[113]

Several of the ECLA economists took issue with Kaldor on the sufficiency of
the food constraint as the trigger of inflation, including Noyola Vazquez, Sunkel,
Pinto, and, belatedly, Prebisch. They saw Kaldor's sole or primary emphasis on
the food constraint as a way of privileging internal over external pressures in
the analysis of inflation. They pointed to the nexus of frequent terms-of-trade
shocks to commodity exports and the fiscal adjustments to them that magnified
rather than moderated their impact. This nexus was analyzed as a combination

of an import bottleneck and a tax bottleneck, which, in addition to the food constraint, created the basic inflationary pressures.[114]

What was the policy thrust of this new structural inflation theory? The theory was developed after the Chilean government had engaged a group of U.S. consultants, the Klein-Saks mission of 1955, to stabilize the economy and curb the recent acceleration of inflation. The success against inflation was limited, but in the process of achieving it, the economy contracted, hurting mainly the working class. The reasons for this were murky but include the government's failure to implement the taxation part of the recommended package of measures. The reaction of the structural inflation theorists was not, as is sometimes stated, to conclude that traditional fiscal and monetary stabilization measures cannot work in the presence of structural bottlenecks. It was to say that they could still work but that when such bottlenecks exist, the use of traditional measures would prove to be very costly in terms of welfare.

The basic point of the structural theorists was absolutely right. It was that most macroeconomic theory assumed, and indeed often still assumes, an economic structure like that of the United States, whereas that of Latin America and of other developing countries is quite different. Therefore, the economic justifications for the use of policies such as fiscal and monetary tightening and devaluation have to be rethought in the actual circumstances to which they are being applied. Insistence on this truth was progressive in the sense that it drove forward a process of rethinking in both economic theory and economic policy. In the short run, there was an impetus to more radical thinking and a cry that only political and social revolution could achieve the total transformation of "structures" that was needed. Somewhat later, it induced more careful consideration of what constitutes economic structure. Are habitual policy responses to terms-of-trade shocks part of the economic structure? Is a tax bottleneck structural or political? By the late 1970s, such questions had led mainstream economists to reflect on whether structures can be changed and whether traditional macroeconomic policies could be made more effective if they were accompanied by "structural adjustment." Among heterodox economists, the question was addressed of whether the propagation mechanisms of inflation could be interrupted decisively, and a variety of heterodox shock treatments were devised to this end in Latin America.

Prebisch's Later View of the Latin American Experience

Before any of this came to pass, however, Prebisch reflected in the 1960s on what had gone wrong with development in Latin America. He used these reflections as a guide to future development policies, not only in Latin America but also elsewhere in the world. In his 1964 report to the first UNCTAD conference, he looked back as far as the 1930s. Talking mainly about Latin America, he commented: "[I]n the developing countries which undertook to industrialize at that time, industrialization proceeded piecemeal in a large number of watertight compartments with little inter-communication, to the serious detriment of productivity." The Second World War, he argued, "gave this form of inward-looking industrialization still further impetus, and nothing happened thereafter to alter this characteristic trend." Moreover, "industrialization based on import substitution has certainly been of great assistance in raising income in those developing countries, but it has done so to a much lesser extent than would have been the case had there been a rational policy judiciously combining import substitution with industrial exports."[115]

Once more he rehearsed the theme of limits. "There are limits to import substitution in the developing countries which cannot be exceeded without a frequent and considerable waste of capital." Second, the relatively small size of national markets "has often made the cost of industries excessive and necessitated recourse to very high protective tariffs"; such tariffs encouraged the establishment of uneconomical plants, weakened incentives to modernization, and slowed down the rise in productivity. Third, industrialization had generally not taken place as the result of a planned development program but had been dictated by adverse external circumstances; this tended to lead to sub-optimal forms of import substitution. Finally, Prebisch argued, "[E]xcessive protectionism has generally insulated national markets from external competition, weakening and even destroying the incentive necessary for improving the quality of output and lowering costs under the private-enterprise system. It has thus tended to stifle the initiative of enterprises as regards both the external market and exports."[116] As he put it yet more strikingly in 1967, the Latin American experience had shown that this was "a bad type of industrialization."[117]

The distorting effects of excessive protection on economic incentives, particularly on the incentive to export, were written about extensively in the 1970s by orthodox economists such as Ian Little, Tibor Scitovsky, and Maurice Scott and Bela Balassa.[118] However, as Henry Bruton has noted, "[T]his feature of import substitution was appreciated much earlier by Prebisch." Bruton pointed out that in his 1964 report, Prebisch had criticized the actual protection practices of Latin American countries on the grounds that "the criterion by which choice [of protection measures] was determined was based not on considerations of economic expediency, but on immediate feasibility, whatever the cost of production."[119] He still believed, however, that a more rational process of import substitution, based on regional integration, could lower costs and facilitate exports to developed countries.[120] He still believed that because the agricultural sector in the developing countries was too small to provide adequate employment for the increment in the economically active population, these countries "must become industrialized, come what may."[121]

Prebisch's work at ECLA contributed to a long-established, dominant regional discourse around the belief that industrialization would be the decisive factor in escaping underdevelopment. Yet ECLA's contribution was by no means restricted to rationalizing a process of economic change that had already begun. Rather, under Prebisch's leadership, the commission's key policy insight was that unless governments took deliberate preventative action, the existing form of "spontaneous," inward-oriented industrialization would have negative welfare effects. It would exacerbate the very forms of disequilibrium that less-critical advocates of ISI confidently expected it to overcome. The remedy for this was regional integration—preferably on the basis of a uniform and moderate external tariff—aimed, to an important degree, at the export of manufactures. Indeed, as Sidney Dell later pointed out, in his criticisms of inward orientation based on excessive protectionism, Prebisch "was criticizing the Latin American countries for precisely the policies that, according to Balassa and others, he was supposed to be advocating."[122] On the inflation front, too, ECLA was accused of promoting the policies of inflationary growth when in fact it cautioned against them while pointing out the social costs of trying to curb inflation with the conventional instruments of stabilization.

Why, then, the persistent misinterpretations? Suspicion of ECLA's motives started early in the United States. In a vitriolic article in *Inter-American Economic Affairs,* the U.S.-based journal that he edited, Simon G. Hanson accused the Latin American participants at the founding session of ECLA of living in a dream world. Hanson argued that "nothing could be more unreal and ineffective, from the viewpoint of the policy maker, than the repeated effort of delegates at the Santiago session to identify century-old shortcomings of internal economic policy as the results of wartime sacrifices, with the implication that responsibility for the present situations should be assumed by the United States." ECLA was "an unnecessary institutional device," as "international activity will be of little avail until the individual nations act on the basic problems which are well within their own competence."[123] This polemic assumed that ECLA would simply collude with the anti-American dream world of unreformed Latin American governments, an accusation the falseness of which should now be clear.

What subsequent commentators have failed to realize is that ECLA's influence on Latin American governments was always quite small. As Prebisch later noted, the ideologies of Perónism, ECLAism, and Latin American developmentalism had a common denominator in the belief that it was necessary to industrialize.[124] In his opinion, while ECLA succeeded in proving that this was the theoretically correct course, this did not imply that the dominance of the industrialization idea should be attributed to ECLA.[125] Because of the surface similarities between different forms of pro-industrialization ideology, the commission has tended to be unfairly blamed for the consequences of policies of which it in fact opposed key aspects. The political influence of UN bodies, even when successful at generating and disseminating ideas, does not include the power to implement them. This always rests with national governments. Governments may appropriate those ideas for their own purposes, but they do not necessarily implement them in the way that their originators intended. In short, although Prebisch never intended to legitimize all existing practices of ISI and inflationary growth, to some degree that was what happened—to his own considerable frustration. Prebisch's later UNCTAD statement was more indicative of the intention behind his work at ECLA, both in emphasizing the necessity of industrialization and in pointing out the likely pitfalls of a chaotic industrialization process.

Prebisch's ECLA experience had more positive outcomes, too. In the commission, he built up one of the most fertile grounds in the UN system for producing new and challenging development ideas. Further, Prebisch's leadership of it helped to propel him toward even greater international prominence in the 1960s. Moreover, the ideas that ECLA helped to generate in reaction to the Latin American experience, provided the intellectual basis for Prebisch's subsequent work at UNCTAD. For he believed that the lessons that he had derived from that experience were applicable to other developing regions as well. To a major degree, he would interpret his UNCTAD role as being to help new African nations avoid the mistakes made by Latin American countries in managing their international trade and finances.[126]

These more positive outcomes were in part the result of his ability to extricate himself from the role of defiant bureaucrat. In negotiating institutional guarantees for his intellectual independence within the UN system, he performed a rare feat. Yet in rising to the top, he accepted the constraint inevitable at the highest levels of an international organization, and he moderated his advocacy in accordance with the doctrine of objectivity. In August 1949, he wrote a draft outline (in his capacity as research director) for the next economic survey. He noted that "when explaining the terms of the problem of economic development in Latin America, I think it is necessary to enter into the theoretical field but without the advocacy of any practical solution, in order to keep thoroughly the objectivity of the report. (That means that the tenor of this report has to differ greatly from my last one.)"[127] In 1955, Louis N. Swenson, a member of ECLA's executive office, confirmed that Prebisch had learned the need for "objectivity." "Prebisch has always been scrupulous to be completely objective and neutral vis-à-vis the Latin American governments even . . . to the point of opposing general recommendations in our reports."[128] His assimilation of the norms of international bureaucracy no doubt was helpful to him in enabling his next move, from regional to global eminence.

7

Competitive Coexistence and the Politics of Modernization

- **Competitive Coexistence and Enlightened Anti-Communism**
- **The U.S. and the "People Whose Goodwill and Friendship We Want"**
- **Walt Rostow and the Idea of Modernization**
- **Hans Singer and Modernization Theory**
- **Prebisch and the Alliance for Progress**
- **The UN Decade of Development**
- **Conclusion: The Limits of the Modernization Metaphor**

Competitive Coexistence and Enlightened Anti-Communism

Two great shifts in international power relations took place in the 1950s. After the death of Stalin, the Soviet leadership moved to a strategy of peaceful coexistence between social systems and competition between them. This was accompanied by a new, more cooperative Soviet strategy toward the UN's economic activities. Simultaneously, many newly created states joined the UN, raising the membership from a total of 60 to 100.[1] As a result, the relative influence of developing countries within the organization grew. Moreover, the new era of "competitive coexistence," when the two superpowers battled for the allegiance of underdeveloped countries, led also to a modification of political attitudes in the U.S. As the political fate of underdeveloped countries took on a new significance in Cold War battles, so the Western powers became increasingly sensitive to the need to be seen to be supporting these nations' legitimate economic aspirations.

The most strongly flowing intellectual current in the development discourse of the West was modernization theory. Spreading beyond the narrow confines of previous models of economic development, the exponents of the modernization perspective argued from a reading of economic history that

whole societies could be transformed to resemble the most modern then existing, including the United States, under certain social and political conditions.
This current of thought, represented in this chapter by one of its chief creators
and exponents—Walt Whitman Rostow—was highly influential in the late 1950s
and early 1960s. Its influence operated directly through Rostow's connections
first with the Eisenhower administration, then with John F. Kennedy and his
foreign policy team. However, it also operated indirectly on the views and actions of the economists in the UN Secretariat, on their response to the Kennedy
administration's international initiatives on development, and on their expectations of future reform of the international trade system.

   During the UN's first years, its practical activities in support of developing
countries took place on a small scale only and were largely restricted to the
field of technical assistance. The UN Technical Assistance Administration,
inaugurated in Paris in late 1948, did receive a certain boost as a result of
point 4 of President Truman's 1949 inaugural address, which called for "a bold
new program . . . for the improvement and growth of underdeveloped areas."[2]
In mid-1949, the Technical Assistance Administration evolved into an Expanded Program of Technical Assistance (EPTA), although its initial U.S. funding appropriation of $26.9 million was tiny.[3] Joseph D. Coppock, a member
of the American delegation to ECOSOC, recalled that this congressional reaction "was pretty much of a token response to the goodwill people, the church
people, the do-gooders, the idealists, the internationalists and such. But to
those of us who thought up the program, it was a limited, long-run program
. . . with the expectation that better economic conditions would be more conducive to democratic institutions."[4]

   The death of Stalin in March 1953—and the emergence by early 1955 of
Nikita Khrushchev ahead of his rivals for the leadership of the USSR—brought
a change in the Soviet attitude toward developing countries and toward the
UN. This in turn elicited new responses from the United States. Moving on
from Stalin's "two-camp" view of the world, in which there could be no neutral or middle ground, Khrushchev recognized the fact that at the 1955 Bandung
conference some important regional powers had declared themselves as neu-
tralists.[5] These countries would soon be referred to as the Third World—that
is, neither capitalist nor socialist. These Khrushchev began to court, to the
alarm of the West. His campaign was mainly conducted on a bilateral basis,
but in addition the UN provided a useful platform for Soviet propaganda,
not least because of its rapidly expanding membership.[6]

   There was a certain improvement in the atmosphere of UN discussions. As
early as 1953, Roy Blough (then principal director of the DEA) noted the newly
"harmonious . . . very friendly" quality of ECOSOC discussions.[7] Naturally,

the Soviets continued to press their views: that heavy industrialization was the key route to economic development, that developing countries were merely the "raw-material appendages" of the capitalist countries, and that Western aid to the Third World amounted to neocolonialism. Much of this platform was clumsily put across as newly independent countries, greatly in need of aid, tended to resent the idea that by accepting it they were accepting Western "domination," but other parts of it were potentially attractive.[8] In addition, the USSR now began to take positive initiatives within the UN, some of which had significant repercussions for the future.

One of the earliest of these UN initiatives was the surprise announcement in July 1953 that the Soviet government would contribute 4 million rubles ($1 million) to EPTA. By 1955, after some initial hesitation, neutralist countries began to take up this Soviet assistance, which coincided with Moscow's launch of a bilateral foreign aid program. In reaction, the Western countries began to expand their own aid programs. As was also the case with Soviet aid, much more of this Western effort was channeled bilaterally than went through the UN. This was in order to benefit particularly those developing countries thought to hold strategically important positions at the expense of others not similarly blessed. One Nigerian official complained that "America is more likely to help a country which is likely to fall into the Soviet orbit than a country which is completely independent and not in danger of falling into any orbit." In 1964, the specialist in Soviet affairs Alvin Z. Rubinstein quoted the following private remark of an (unnamed) member of the Indian cabinet:

> I would be less than candid if I did not admit that, as a result of the Great Power struggle, and India's central political and strategic position, India benefits greatly from the Cold War. If most Soviet and Western aid, currently distributed through bilateral channels, were given through the UN, India would lose much of its preferential treatment.[9]

Geopolitics undoubtedly detracted from the multilateral aspect of the superpowers' aid to the Third World. Nevertheless, as this chapter will explain, the strategic competition for the allegiance of India in the second half of the 1950s resulted, in the first half of the 1960s, in both an overall increase in foreign economic aid and a rise in the amount of aid channeled through multilateral institutions.

The U.S. and the "People Whose Goodwill and Friendship We Want"

By 1954, John Foster Dulles, President Eisenhower's secretary of state, had come to the view that it is going to be very difficult to stop Communism in much of the world if we cannot in some way duplicate the intensive Communist effort to raise productivity standards. They themselves are increasing their own productivity at the rate of about 6% per annum, which is about twice our rate. In many of the areas of the world such as Southeast Asia, India, Pakistan and South America, there is little, if any, increase. That is one reason why Communism has such great appeal in areas where the slogans of "liberty," "freedom" and "personal dignity" have little appeal.[10]

Although Dulles was personally convinced of the political need to help underdeveloped countries to raise their productivity levels and thought that a new U.S. public investment program there was desirable, he proved unable to move the first Eisenhower administration to embrace such a policy and was unwilling to be seen trying to do so.

Within the United States, the suspicion began to grow that the West was losing the Cold War. Nikita Khrushchev finally consolidated his control over both the Communist Party and the Soviet government in the spring of 1957. The *Sputnik* launch in October of that year was the event that triggered serious public anxiety in the U.S. and prepared the way for fresh thinking and new policy initiatives.[11] It also revived the Sino-Soviet alliance, but at the cost of papering over different understandings of "peaceful coexistence" as China deserted the spirit of Bandung for more militant support of wars of national liberation in Taiwan and South Vietnam. The external pressure continued when in 1958 Khrushchev demanded the surrender of West Berlin. At this point, the danger began to be felt much closer to the United States itself. In the Western hemisphere, the strong anti-U.S. feeling and the physical violence that Vice President Richard M. Nixon encountered when riots disrupted his visit to Lima and Caracas in May 1958 heightened public perception that the U.S. position in the world was weakening.[12] This impression was strengthened even more when Fidel Castro took over control of Cuba in early 1959, backed by the Cuban communists, and when he accepted Soviet economic assistance in 1960 while asking the United States for nothing. A public impression was fostered that Eisenhower's foreign policy, though slowly evolving from speeches into action, was still failing to meet its challenges.[13]

Under these external pressures, U.S. congressional opinion began to change with respect to the issue of long-term loans for economic development. A small Development Loan Fund was established in 1957. A Senate resolution passed in July 1958 facilitated U.S. participation in a multilateral soft-loan scheme ultimately to be placed in the World Bank. In August 1958, Eisenhower agreed to participate in a multilateral development bank for Latin America. The Organization for European Economic Cooperation began to evolve, under

U.S. guidance, into the Organization for Economic Cooperation and Development, which had a new responsibility for co-coordinating the external development assistance of its industrial country members. The Kennedy-Cooper resolution on aid to India passed the Senate in 1959.[14] Nevertheless, a larger and better-coordinated U.S. foreign economic aid policy remained out of reach in the Eisenhower years.

In the presidential election of 1960, both candidates—Nixon and his Democratic rival Senator John F. Kennedy—projected themselves as being tough on communism and laid emphasis on the need for America to bid harder for the support of underdeveloped countries in the Cold War. Nixon told the Republican convention, "[I]t may be just as essential to the national interest to build a dam in India as in California."[15] Kennedy, in a campaign press release in October launching the policy idea that would be known as the Alliance for Progress, stressed that "although the cold war will not be won in Latin America—it may well be lost there."[16]

Both candidates saw foreign aid as a tool of enlightened anti-communism, and, notably, enlightenment in both cases included an increased willingness to work through the UN. The multilateral turn was particularly clear in the case of food aid. Referring to America's mounting problems of storing her agricultural surpluses, Kennedy proclaimed in September 1960 that food could be "a helping hand to people around the world whose goodwill and friendship we want." At the same time Nixon suggested the creation of a multilateral surplus food distribution facility operated by the United Nations. Eisenhower promptly proposed this to the General Assembly, which passed a resolution requesting the director-general of the Food and Agriculture Organization (FAO) to make a study of how this might be done.

Kennedy, the election winner by a very narrow margin, maintained the rhetoric of enlightened anti-communism in his inaugural address.[17] He followed through, too, on the move toward greater multilateral engagement. He immediately set up a Food for Peace office in the White House and appointed George McGovern as the first director of the Food for Peace program. Those three words "food for peace" encapsulate as well as any the fundamental idea of development cooperation as an instrument of global strategy. However, McGovern quickly stated that he saw no conflict between his own bilateral program and an expanded multilateral approach. Governments met in Rome in April 1961 to discuss the FAO study, which did not contain any specific proposals. At this meeting, McGovern's team drafted its own proposals and then sought—through Theodore Sorensen—Kennedy's approval. It was given within twenty-four hours. The U.S. proposals became the basis of the new UN World Food Program.[18]

Walt Rostow and the Idea of Modernization

If the enlightened anti-communism of the Eisenhower and Kennedy years had a prophet, it was Walt W. Rostow.[19] After the war, in the State Department, he proposed that the U.S. should make its primary policy goal a unified Europe. This led to the creation of the ECE, where Rostow served as a UN official in 1947–1949.[20] As special assistant to the executive secretary, Gunnar Myrdal, Rostow occupied a key place in the policymaking of the commission and acted as a trusted link between Myrdal and the State Department. While Kaldor busied himself with the preparation of the ECE's *Economic Survey of Europe,* Rostow was involved in the high politics of postwar Europe.[21] Myrdal informed David Owen that "[Rostow] thinks we have a chance to make history (or at least to be involved in it) and, as a historian, he wants to be on the spot."[22] As Europe grew increasingly divided with the Soviet-backed communist takeover of Czechoslovakia and other parts of Eastern Europe, the pan-European aspirations of Myrdal, Rostow, and the ECE became ever more politically unrealistic. Rostow left Geneva in October 1949 "and left a big vacuum," but he continued to "remain a very close adviser."[23]

At the suggestion of Max Millikan, an ex-CIA man, Rostow joined the Center for International Studies (CENIS) at MIT. CENIS, funded by the Ford and Rockefeller Foundations as well as by CIA-inspired government contracts, produced studies of the USSR and communist China as well as of underdeveloped countries. Rostow drafted with C. D. Jackson, a White House staff member, a "world development plan" for U.S. support of economic development in "uncommitted areas."[24] Arising out of this, Jackson encouraged Rostow to write, with Max Millikan and Paul Rosenstein-Rodan, *A Proposal for a New Foreign Economic Policy* (1956). The authors criticized the fact that U.S. foreign aid was directed mainly to political allies for military purposes and was essentially reactive and short-term in nature. According to them, a successful U.S. foreign policy required that aid also be given for longer-term purposes of economic development to nations who were unwilling to enter into anti-communist military pacts with the U.S. It was circulated in draft to the State Department, and it aroused much interest among its officials and in the intelligence services.[25] However, Eisenhower could not override his fear of the budget consequences of a new type of foreign aid and did not proceed with it, except in a number of small policy initiatives that have already been noted.[26]

In addition, along with the Social Sciences Research Council (SSRC) Committee on Comparative Politics, CENIS/MIT was the main force behind the production of a new body of theory on the politics of underdeveloped countries—modernization theory.[27] Rostow made his chief intellectual contribution at MIT as an economic historian with a penchant for schematic think-ing. During his period at ECE in Geneva, he saw the worldwide problem of development in a distinctly Eurocentric way—in terms of the need to reduce the cost of Europe's imports of food and raw materials.[28] At MIT, however, he approached the development problem from a starting point similar to that of Arthur Lewis, aiming to understand the role of capital accumulation in the process of economic growth. To a much greater extent than in Lewis's theory, however, Rostow's account of these processes integrated social psychology and political and social change with the economic factors generating growth and development.

In the course of formulating his ideas, Rostow developed a taxonomic scheme of the so-called stages of growth.[29] He turned this taxonomy into an alternative history of capitalism to the Marxist-Leninist version. Marx's dy-namics inevitably tended toward the overthrow of capitalism and had been incorporated into the official ideology of the Soviet Union. While still a col-lege student at Yale, Rostow had already decided to "do an answer one day to Marx's theory of history."[30] It was modernization theory: a theory as holistic and historicist as Marxism, and therefore every bit as methodologically ob-jectionable, but incorporating very different dynamics and producing a com-pletely opposite and optimistic prediction of the future viability of capitalist society. Such a theory had obvious and powerful attractions for the Western politicians of the day.

Like the American critics of "extreme Keynesianism," Rostow wanted to get beyond the Keynesian economic aggregates when analyzing economic growth. He wanted to examine the role of particular sectors and industries during the growth process. He wanted to introduce more flexible and realistic assump-tions about economic motivation, recognizing that people differ in their pro-pensities to create and to accept innovations, to take risks, to value large families, and so on. Modernization theory was intended to provide a framework accord-ing to which the variety of growth experiences could be systematically arrayed. In *The Process of Economic Growth,* Rostow posed the problem of formulating an answer to Marxism, whose harshness and oversimplicity he criticized, but he did not yet claim to have found such an alternative.[31]

In a classic article in 1956, he took the next step. He argued that it was useful to think of the process of economic growth as centering on "a relatively brief time interval of two or three decades" during which the rapid transfor-mations that occur make economic growth thereafter more or less automatic. This was to put the old-fashioned and ill-defined concept of an "industrial revolution" (on the British experience of which he had written his Ph.D. dis-sertation at Yale) back as the pivot of the growth process but under the new title of the "take-off into self-sustaining growth." Like Arthur Lewis, Rostow stressed that "in the end takeoff requires that a society find a way to apply . . . the tricks of manufacture. . . . Only thus, as we have all been correctly taught, can that old demon, diminishing returns, be held at bay."[32] And like Lewis, Rostow thought that a large upward shift in the investment share of net national product was required for the takeoff.

Rostow's distinctive contribution was initially an empirical one, to identify and to date nine completed episodes of takeoff in Great Britain, France, Belgium, the United States, Germany, Sweden, Japan, Russia, and Canada. He also identified four underdeveloped countries (Argentina, Turkey, India, and China) as having begun, but not completed, the takeoff. This led him to suggest the dropping of the concept of "underdeveloped areas" and the substitution for it of a quadripartite distinction among economies: traditional, pre-takeoff, takeoff, and growing.[33] Finally, in *The Stages of Economic Growth: A Non-Communist Manifesto* (1960) he provided a way of generalizing the sweep of modern economic history as a set of five stages of growth. The stages were the traditional society, the preconditions for takeoff, the takeoff, the drive to maturity, and the age of high mass consumption. For Rostow, the motor of socioeconomic development was entrepreneurial application of technology rather than the conflict of classes around changes in the forms of labor exploitation. The social and political aspect of the economic growth process was delineated in terms of the triumphant emergence of an entrepreneurial elite. The connotations of the rise of an entrepreneurial elite were, for Rostow and his sympathizers, wholly positive because it was the very embodiment of all modern values.[34]

Rostow and other U.S. modernization theorists were implicitly claiming that an ideal of modern society remarkably similar to the actual United States could be realized if societies in undeveloped areas would give sufficient authority to the representatives of their entrepreneurs and innovators. In any underdeveloped country, once power begins to gravitate into the hands of a modernizing elite, they implied, an economic and industrial takeoff becomes possible. That elite need not be of the private sector but may be operating through government institutions. The colonial history of the country concerned is of no relevance because before the preconditions for the takeoff begin to be met, all societies are simply "traditional societies." These messages were attractive ones for many of the democratic and undemocratic governments of Latin America in the 1950s, and they ran strongly counter to the more pessimistic assessment of the prospects for economic development that were issuing from ECLA.

Rostow's bold generalizations from economic history were academically controversial from the start. They came in for some weighty criticism from Simon

Kuznets of Harvard, whose own research program on historical series of national statistics had not revealed such clear regularities in the data.[35] He rejected the notion of a distinct and commonly found takeoff stage. He found Rostow's definition of this and other stages so analytically fuzzy that "there is no solid ground upon which to discuss Professor Rostow's view of the analytical relation between the take-off stage and the preceding and succeeding stages."[36] Kuznets also warned against the appealing connotation of the term "takeoff": "[A]ppealing terms employing mechanical or biological metaphors carry the danger of misleading us into believing that the suggested connotations are relevant to observable reality."[37] Albert Fishlow of Berkeley pointed out that Rostow had failed to explain how changes in the national income aggregates were integrated with developments in the leading sectors of the economy in periods of rapid growth and with technical changes in the leading industries. The attempt to get beyond the Keynesian aggregates had, to his mind, merely produced a nonintegrated or dualistic theory. The result was the diversion of attention from interesting cases where economies entered well into the transition to modern economic growth but did not succeed. He noted that "some of the nations of Latin America seem to have been so beset."[38]

Such warnings did not deflect Rostow. Rostow was not just an intellectual actor but also an action intellectual.[39] He was committed to a paradigm of "policy science" in which knowledge creation was aimed at solving fundamental world problems. In 1958, he joined Jack Kennedy's presidential campaign.[40] The young senator had decided to advocate greater U.S. aid for India's Second Five Year Plan, which was focused on heavy industry but in danger of failing for lack of foreign exchange. Having consulted CENIS/MIT on this topic, he then employed Rostow to write campaign speeches on the economic gap between rich and poor countries and the dangers that this posed for America. Once Kennedy became president, Rostow initially served him on the White House staff. It is interesting, given the academic critique of his theory as fuzzy, that outside academia he was seen as "this verbose, theoretical man, who intended to make all of his theories work" and that this irritated some powerful figures, including Dean Rusk, Kennedy's secretary of state.[41] In December 1961, Rostow was moved to chairman of the Policy Planning Council of the State Department. In 1966, he became President Lyndon B. Johnson's special assistant for national security affairs.[42]

These roles clarified for him the political implications of the modernization doctrine when blended in with anti-communism. As he put it in 1964:

> The process of modernization involves radical change not merely in the economy of underdeveloped nations but in their social structure and political life. We live, quite literally, in a revolutionary time. We must expect over the

next decade recurrent turbulence in these areas; we must expect systematic efforts by the Communists to exploit this turbulence.[43]

This thinking would be very influential in the Kennedy administration, as it engaged with Fidel Castro's revolution in Cuba and its consequences, not just for the Latin American region but also for the entire course of the East-West conflict.[44] A lesson drawn from it was the need to try to anticipate crises in underdeveloped countries by working proactively and positively with groups who were friendly to U.S. national and international interests. A more ominous lesson, and one that the U.S. still had to learn, was that modernizing elites tend to be urban based, while turbulence can erupt in the rural areas, as was already happening in Vietnam.[45]

Hans Singer and Modernization Theory

Hans Singer was receptive to the theory and policy of modernization in a way that was not entirely surprising. Rostow rejected the modeling approach of the neoclassical economists, as did he. Like Rostow, he was not a Marxist. Moreover, the wider political implications of the modernization doctrine for international conflict were yet to unfold. Singer appreciated Rostow's attempt to rationalize long-run historical trends and welcomed his scheme of stages as a substantial improvement on what had gone before. There was more to this rapprochement than just a congruity between Rostow's ideas and his own. Both men were also pursuing a political agenda in support of foreign economic aid. Although these agendas were convergent as to their main thrust—greater Western financing for economic development—they were in conflict in their specific institutional objectives.

While Rostow and his CENIS colleagues were trying to persuade the Eisenhower administration that the U.S. and its allies should provide longer-term aid to support economic development through various mechanisms that were U.S.-controlled or subject to a predominant U.S. influence, Singer and like-minded colleagues in the UN Secretariat sought to create a soft-loan facility for economic development located within the UN itself. The original idea for this came in 1949 from V. K. R. V. Rao, who had been one of Hans Singer's fellow Ph.D. students in Cambridge.[46] It was endorsed by the 1951 report *Measures for the Economic Development of Under-Developed Countries.*[47] It was kept alive within the UN as SUNFED (Special United Nations Fund for Economic Development) by, among others, Singer.[48] His desire for a soft-aid mechanism located within the UN owed less to his dislike of the World Bank's subjection to the predominant voting power of the U.S. and more to the fact that the bank's president, Eugene R. Black, at this time disdained soft lending altogether as unsound.

The distance between the agendas of Rostow and Singer was hardly significant when compared with the gulf between Singer and elements of the extreme right wing in the U.S. They subjected Singer and others in the UN who
were closely associated with the SUNFED proposal to a campaign of character assassination in the U.S. press in mid-1956. SUNFED was described as "a
Socialist UN plan to disarm and bankrupt the United States," sure to cost $50
billion, of which 70 percent would be paid by the U.S. taxpayer. Singer's professional connections before his UN days were paraded as proof that he was
engaged in a left-wing conspiracy within the UN.[49] His colleagues within the
UN immediately rallied to his defense, and a sober explanation of the SUNFED
proposal was published under the name of Philippe de Seynes.[50]

This incident affected Singer badly, and he acknowledged his distress in a
letter to David Owen, who had written him a note of commiseration:

> But between old friends there is no need to conceal a quiver of that stiff upper
> lip—yes, I have been at times depressed and upset. It all seemed so incredibly
> wicked, and I felt defenceless, and all the time one thought of the viciousness
> behind it, the obscure reasons for all this, and one felt there was nothing from
> which such people would shrink. . . . The devil of it is, of course, that one not
> only *feels* defenceless, but *is* defenceless. Having given one's soul and 10 years to
> the UN and the problems of poor countries, there is probably little else that
> one can do now.[51]

In early 1957, he was suffering from ill health and had to withdraw from an
assignment in Thailand. He felt bad about "letting everybody down," and David
Owen wrote to C. V. Narasimhan, the executive secretary of ECAFE, to explain that "he has been through a pretty bad time, and he is still emotionally
disturbed."[52]

The battle for SUNFED, however, seemed to be on the verge of success. In
July 1955, the Russians had reversed their initial opposition to the concept of
SUNFED as part of their attempt to win support from the developing countries.[53] In 1957, at the 24th session of ECOSOC, the decision to recommend to
the General Assembly the establishment of SUNFED was taken. This vote was
an historic one, representing the first formal split in ECOSOC between the
developed and the developing countries. Canada, the UK, and the U.S. all
voted against SUNFED, while the other members of ECOSOC were unanimously in favor of it. This vote marked a new line of international political
division that was to loom larger over the next two decades.[54] However, on this
occasion a compromise was reached and the ECOSOC decision was modified
in the General Assembly. The developing countries did not use the power of
their undoubted majority.[55] They succeeded in insisting on the principle of a
UN special fund, but they accepted that its function was confined to "creating

conditions which would make [development] investments either feasible or more effective."[56]

The function of making long-term loans for development projects on soft terms was allotted to the World Bank through a new arm, the International Development Association (IDA). The U.S. motivation for favoring this option is clear enough. Richard Demuth, a senior bank official, informed his colleagues after holding conversations with U.S. officials that IDA "was not a U.S. affirmative program" but resulted from "a desire to assuage Congress" and a need "to keep off SUNFED."[57] Black confirmed this himself in 1963, calling IDA "an idea to offset the urge for SUNFED."[58] In their campaign for SUNFED, the developing countries and their supporters in the UN Secretariat had won what proved to be a Pyrrhic victory.

They tried to recover in various ways. One was to embrace modernization theory as a justification of the importance of the functions that remained with the UN Special Fund, the so-called pre-investment activities. Singer, for example, noted that "in earlier years too often 'the underdeveloped countries' were lumped together in spite of their immensely varying problems and requirements" and, by way of contrast, commended *The Stages of Economic Growth* as an attempt to establish some useful distinctions. He continued by asserting that the book had "served to illuminate the crucial importance of pre-investment since the development from one stage to another of the preconditions which govern the movement of individual countries is largely governed by pre-investment aid" in spheres such as literacy, health, and administrative improvements.[59] Singer proceeded to work out the different types of pre-investment activities that would be appropriate at each of the first four of Rostow's stages of development.[60] Evidently trying to save the UN's face after the decision to place a SUNFED-style soft-loan facility inside the World Bank, Singer used his version of Rostow's stage theory to claim that "as a result of all these developments the concentration of the United Nations on pre-investment activities is no longer felt to be a sort of slight on it or a reduction of its status."[61] The Special Fund, and later the United Nations Development Programme (UNDP) (into which it was merged in 1966), faced a problem of demarcating their functions in a way that both avoided overlap with the World Bank's role and amounted to something substantial. Singer saw the answer in "pre-investment activities," although he later conceded that he created something of a mystique around this term: "[P]erhaps I can say that I invented (we had great difficulty because the Special Fund and then the UNDP was not supposed to invest in projects—that was the business of the World Bank) the concept of pre-investment."[62]

He justified this as politically necessary and useful from the viewpoint of the UN.[63]

Prebisch and the Alliance for Progress

On 13 March 1961, within two months of taking office, President Kennedy formally launched the Alliance for Progress, a bold program of United States assistance for the development of Latin America. Although there were substantial elements of continuity with Eisenhower administration policy, such as the Social Progress Trust Fund, the Alliance for Progress, which reflected many of the key concerns of the modernization theorists, appeared revolutionary.[64] The president told his audience that North and South Americans had "to demonstrate to the entire world that man's unsatisfied aspiration for economic progress and social justice can best be achieved by free men working within a framework of democratic institutions."[65] He promised that the U.S. was ready to seek "practical methods" of dealing with the "violent changes in commodity prices."[66]

Kennedy's concern was driven by his powerful fear of creeping communism in Latin America, Fidel Castro's Cuba being seen as the agent of a Soviet conspiracy in the whole region. The choice, as Kennedy and his advisors saw it, was between peaceful modernizing revolution and violent Castro-style revolt. The public presentation of this stance, however, was given a strongly progressive emphasis. As Rostow put it, "[W]e needed a policy which would align the United States with the great forces in Latin America which seek economic development and greater social justice. To this our response was the Alliance for Progress."[67] In reality, Kennedy was addressing two different constituencies. The proposal had to be sold to Congress as an anti-communist and anti-Castro measure. Kennedy's team argued that "the way to victory" in the Cold War lay in "the build-up of [the developing countries'] economies, accompanied by measures that ensure social progress."[68] At the same time, they had to recruit the support of Latin American leaders by projecting an exciting vision of nation-building and social progress. The beauty of Rostow's modernization theory as a political ideology was that it was able to straddle both of these constituencies.

Kennedy wanted to court Prebisch in particular. On 10 December 1960, between Kennedy's election and his inauguration, his advisor Adolf Berle took the ECLA executive secretary out for breakfast, "pursuant to instructions from Senator Kennedy's office."[69] Prebisch's response to Berle's approach was unequivocal. As he put it later, "I was not the promoter of the Alliance for Progress, but I jumped on the wagon when the train was starting to move."[70] He encouraged the new rhetoric, saying that "the whole job was to give economic and social content to the idea of freedom, and that a strong statement by Kennedy along those lines would be a great deal of help to him. . . . In his view this was an historical moment and it required everyone to get on board."[71]

The common ground between the Kennedy team and ECLA was the need for economic and social reform in Latin America. Land reform was at the head of both parties' lists, followed by tax reform and education reform.[72] Prebisch later claimed that "the papers of ECLA were the basis" of the Alliance for Progress and that he had drafted the letter to Kennedy in which Latin American governments agreed to be part of it but that he never concurred with the name given by the Americans to the initiative.[73]

This initial convergence soon came under some strain. The alliance began to fail soon after its formal inception by the Charter of Punta del Este in August 1961.[74] U.S. business interests were suspicious of the emphasis on social reforms, and Latin American landowners threatened to play the nationalist card in defense of their interests.[75] The U.S. envisaged national programs of reform supported by an additional $20 billion in aid over ten years. The initial focus of the alliance on increased U.S. economic assistance to Latin America was shifted in 1962 when Dean Rusk announced that America could be only "a junior partner."[76] Latin American leaders, meeting in Sao Paulo in November 1963, set up the Inter-American Committee on the Alliance for Progress (CIAP) in order to take greater collective responsibility for directing the activities of the alliance. Prebisch declined the position of chairman, apparently because he made conditions that the U.S. government was not inclined to accept but possibly because of Argentine government opposition.[77] He did, however, help to develop a system whereby a CIAP "committee of experts" would come and work alongside national planning teams. This bore real fruit only when national governments had solid reform agendas of their own—an analysis that applied to the impact of the alliance more generally.[78]

Moreover, the original rhetoric of the promotion of democracy became somewhat tarnished. The firm anti-communist motivation of the new administration led the U.S. government to shore up repressive regimes in Latin America with foreign aid and to destabilize several democratic ones. This also played its part in derailing the alliance's admirable social and economic reform objectives. Few of its ninety-four objectives were achieved, and in particular the growth rate of 2.5 percent that was at first projected failed to materialize. Whether there were political gains for the U.S. in blunting the spread of Castro's revolution to Latin America, notwithstanding the Bay of Pigs fiasco, depends on one's view of the strength of that threat. Kennedy and his advisors may well have overestimated it.

The UN Decade of Development

Rostow encouraged Kennedy to make the 1960s the "economic development decade." Remarkably, he predicted that with U.S. assistance, Argentina,

Brazil, Colombia, Venezuela, India, the Philippines, Taiwan, Turkey, Greece—and possibly Egypt, Pakistan, Iran, and Iraq—could attain self-sustaining growth by 1970. Within a decade, he foresaw optimistically, 80 percent of Latin America's population and half the population of the developing areas would be "off the international dole." Drawing on "my ideas as an economist," Rostow was able to assure Kennedy (and Congress) that the 1960s would see the requirement for foreign aid peak and then decline.[79] In his special message to the Congress on 22 March 1961, President Kennedy referred to the 1960s as the "crucial Decade of Development."[80] By July, the managing director of the Development Loan Fund was noting, "Although Congress has not yet passed the necessary legislation and the new Agency for International Development remains to be established, we have already, for all intents and purposes, embarked on the President's program for the Decade of Development."[81]

However, this concept had not yet been crystallized into a formal proposal linked to the UN. By the end of August, the idea of an International Development Year (IDY) was circulating within the State Department. After consultation with Harlan Cleveland, the assistant secretary of state for International Organization Affairs, Under Secretary of State for Economic Affairs George W. Ball decided to recommend an International Development Decade (IDD) instead. In a memorandum of 9 September, Ball argued that "[a]n IDY proposal might be regarded by many of the underdeveloped nations as a mere gimmick," of the type "that might have been expected to emanate from the Eisenhower Administration." By contrast, a development decade "would imply a commitment by the UN and the advanced industrial nations to concentrate on the problem of economic development for a long period of time, and would permit the evolution of new functions and institutions which might be impracticable within a single year. . . . If the proposal is recast in these terms, I would also be inclined to favor having it mentioned in the President's speech at the UNGA."[82]

When on 25 September 1961 President Kennedy addressed the General Assembly, his speech included the statement that the United States "now proposes officially designating this decade of the 1960s as the United Nations Decade of Development." Within that framework, he suggested, the UN's development efforts could be expanded and coordinated.[83] On 6 October, Philip M. Klutznick, the U.S. representative in the Second Committee, outlined the U.S. proposal in more detail. The rhetoric of modernization theory was evident in his speech. "During the United Nations Decade of Development," he said, "it was necessary to capture the rich experience of the industrialized countries and devise effective means of accelerating sound industrial development in the less developed countries."[84] The U.S. proposals were embodied in resolution 1710 (XVI) and agreed unanimously on 19 December.[85]

This bold exercise of leadership by the U.S. was a new tactic adopted in response to a changed voting pattern in the UN that the 1957 ECOSOC vote on SUNFED had revealed. Foreseeing the possibility of being outvoted on unacceptably worded resolutions, the U.S. tried—quite successfully—to exercise a moderating influence by putting itself at the head of the majority and championing its expressed wishes, where this could be done without sacrifice of principle. This tactic had its dangers, though, and the U.S. was uncomfortable that it had sacrificed too much on some issues—for example, on the more equitable sharing of natural resource rents—and on reexamining the principles of international economic cooperation.[86]

As far as the UN Secretariat was concerned, Kennedy's declaration of a Decade of Development was a bolt out of the blue. According to Hans Singer:

> My recollection is that when Kennedy uttered his magic words, it came as a complete surprise to me. I can only compare this with the equally complete surprise, happy surprise, when I listened on the radio to Truman's inaugural address. . . . And my recollection is that we had no previous warning in the UN, at least I hadn't.[87]

The UN thus was required to react, and it was inconceivable that it would not do so in a spirit of positive acceptance. There was a strong tendency to share the view that a decade was long enough to get over the hump of a global development effort and thus to go along with Rostow's overoptimistic timetable. The U.S. initiative, however, posed a challenge to the UN to improve the coordination of various programs and activities in support of economic development. The initial reaction of the UN specialized agencies was defensive; they feared that the development decade would become a vehicle for increased central control of their work and that their independence and autonomy in the development field would be undermined. In preparing the documents indicating how the UN would implement the concept, Singer had to take extreme care to ensure that they reflected the agencies' existing activities and plans.[88] This limited the extent to which overall coordination within the UN could be improved.

At the same time, the UN Secretariat saw the opportunity to present the international community with a challenge by encouraging member states to move from general declarations to specific quantitative targets, both for aid and for economic growth. The Nigerian representative consulted both Prebisch and Singer over the setting of a target rate of economic growth during the development decade. They came up with the rate of 5 percent per annum, which was both the outcome of an economic calculation and a politically symbolic number:

> This was a simple back of the envelope calculation based on the Harrod-Domar formula, more or less, but assuming a capital output ratio of 3 to 1. . . . It was very primitive. But the 5 per cent also happily coincided with [preventing relative divergence, so that] the developing countries would not fall further and further back.[89]

The U.S. was opposed to the adoption of the 5 percent target for growth and the 1 percent of GNP target for financial flows to developing countries. They were adopted by the General Assembly over the objections of the U.S.[90]

Even so, the Decade of Development was as much as anything an exercise in public relations and one that responded successfully to the prevailing public mood. David Owen (then executive chairman of the Technical Assistance Board) summed it up quite soberly: "There was probably nothing very new in the Decade for Development. It was, however, a useful way of projecting an idea and giving it dramatic appeal. It set measurable targets and provided something attainable to strive towards."[91]

However, successful public relations can have unintended consequences. In this instance, the rhetoric of the development decade significantly raised the expectations of the developing countries that North America and Europe would agree to modify those parts of the international trade system that they believed were obstacles to their economic development. Hans Singer voiced "the gathering conviction that things cannot be allowed to go on as they are. It simply does not make sense to expand aid programs and help the underdeveloped countries along while at the same time they are allowed to lose on the swings of trade—which is more important to them than aid—what they gain on the roundabout of aid."[92] These heightened expectations quickly became problematic for the policymakers of the U.S. and the EEC when the developing countries were bold enough to call for fine words to be followed by fine deeds.

Conclusion: The Limits of the Modernization Metaphor

During his short assignment to the ECE, Rostow still thought about economic development as Rosenstein-Rodan had in the early 1940s—as a desirable transformation of East and Southeast Europe. The Cold War both put the prospects for pan-European economic unity on ice and, after Stalin's death, opened an escalating competition between the superpowers for influence in those parts of the world defined by negative prefixes—undeveloped and nonaligned. For them, the prize was national industrialization, and their question was which of the two blocs would provide the more supportive linkages and networks for its successful achievement. In the 1950s, the case of India, around which the Kennedy-Rostow nexus was first forged, was typical. India was a democratic country with a large private sector that was nevertheless experimenting with socialist economic planning and could possibly, like China, fall into the Soviet orbit. How could that be forestalled? India disdained client status and would not accept foreign aid that was conditional on a formal alliance. On the other hand, a formal obligation on the U.S. to defend India militarily would have been prohibitively expensive and probably less effective than the provision of foreign aid.[93] To keep such countries balanced between the competing centers of geopolitical attraction, the United States had to find ways of offering a new form of economic cooperation and legitimating its use. This was the political function that modernization theory was made to perform.

Since the beginning of the nineteenth century, the metaphor of an industrial revolution has been used in contrast to a political revolution and as the preferable option of the two.[94] Rostow reworked that old idea, suggesting to underdeveloped countries that in a period of a generation they could undergo a complex, intensive, and highly desirable process of transition, provided that they would create a political opening for their middle class. At the same time, he suggested to the already developed countries that the requirement for their support to that process would be brief, although it would be greater in the short term; the bulk of the task could be done in a decade of development.

The scholarly underpinning of such claims was always fragile. What was especially misleading was the unjustified and excessive schematization to which available historical studies of growth were subjected, particularly the identification of a central process—the famous "takeoff into self-sustaining growth"— which was everywhere the same and which could, therefore, be replicated under stated sociopolitical conditions. Kuznets specifically criticized this assertion as a mere assumption.[95] It was an illusion—possibly a pragmatic illusion, but an illusion nonetheless.[96] In the first place, actual industrial revolutions have been far from identical. In the second place, their assumed identity ruled out in advance the possibility that the early development of some countries might affect the prospects for the later development of others—either for better or for worse. These assumptions about industrial revolutions surely begged the question.

Singer embraced modernization theory despite its intellectual fragility. He shared with Rostow the need for a justification of expanded foreign aid, one that carried an optimistic message about the prospects for development. At the same time, however, he adapted it for the purposes of the UN. To advance and refine the concept of pre-investment activities was very useful for expanding the UN's remit at a time when, at the insistence of the developed countries, all forms of project investment (including those to be financed on highly concessionary terms) were placed in the province of the World Bank.

Prebisch, too, eagerly collaborated with the Alliance for Progress, which was another embodiment of the modernization perspective. He thought he saw the opportunity to put the political influence and financial muscle of the United Stated behind ECLA's ideas for socioeconomic change in Latin America. However, the moment quickly passed with the death of Kennedy, Prebisch thought. More likely, the cause was the gradual surfacing of previously submerged political hazards in both halves of the American continent, which testified to a lack of realism that had always been at the heart of the project.

When Kennedy proposed a UN development decade underpinned by modernization theory, economists within the UN Secretariat were caught off balance but welcomed his initiative with open arms. They were undoubtedly charmed by the vision of social reform and progress that Kennedy and his team expounded. Not the least of these charms was the fact that the substance of the vision was a process of industrialization brought about by means of government economic planning. This substance was derived from Kennedy's initial decision to crusade for aid to India. This choice made sense in terms of both Cold War strategy and U.S. domestic politics, given the post-1949 international and national repercussions of "losing" China to communism. Yet the choice of Nehru's India also brought with it willy-nilly a particular development objective—industrialization—and a particular organizational means—economic planning—that were then taken to be of general application, to Latin America no less than to South Asia. This end and these means were both very congenial to those whom Singer later referred to as the "wild men in the United Nations"—a group in which he was satisfied to include himself.[97]

They were also impressed by the Kennedy administration's recognition that achieving this vision would be a shared endeavor. This seemed to presage a more enlightened and less manipulative form of intervention by the U.S. in the economic affairs of underdeveloped countries than it had practiced in the previous decade. They were willing to turn a blind eye, publicly at least, to the fact that the new dispensation was associated with anti-communist attitudes as vehement as any since the time of Senator McCarthy. They used the opportunity given by Kennedy to raise the profile of the UN on the world political scene, establishing an image of UN interagency collaboration, though they could scarcely advance the reality of it. At the same time, they helped the developing countries set up targets for their economic growth and inward financial flows and looked forward to genuine action by the international community to ensure their fulfillment. They also looked forward to future changes beyond the realm of aid, in which the international trade system would be made more responsive to the special problems of countries in the process of development.

In these expectations, they were to be sustained less than fully by events. No mechanism had been created for the monitoring of the UN development decade targets, and after 1965 the enthusiasm of the U.S. and other donors for aid began to decline. The complexities of managing modernization began to reveal themselves in Vietnam. For his part, Walt Rostow had shed his enthusiasm for the UN when he joined CENIS in 1951. He thereafter saw America as the midwife of worldwide economic and political development, not the UN. He at no time wanted the idea of a development decade to be formalized within the United Nations. When it was, he increasingly turned his official energies in other directions, most notably to animating U.S. counterinsurgency activities in southeast Asia. In this role, too, he was notable for his excessive optimism.[98]

In the Kennedy years, the economic radicals in the UN Secretariat actually became fellow travelers, but they traveled the road with conservative U.S. Democrats. Clearly, Walt Rostow was a vastly more sympathetic U.S. public figure than Joe McCarthy from their perspective, and the UN economists clearly needed some links into the U.S. political scene. Yet to go along the path of Rostow's theory and practice of development involved important compromises. They were persuaded of the moral case for an international redistribution of resources, whereas Rostow saw foreign aid as a form of pump-priming in an effort to raise levels of productivity abroad. He treated them as idealistic do-gooders, a label that attracts pious sympathy but condemns its wearers either to abuse or tokenism in U.S. domestic politics.

He also disagreed with their encouragement of what he called "noisy United Nations agitation" for a soft-loan facility for economic development. He later claimed that they had only a minor impact on the decision to set up the IDA, as compared with the grindings of the U.S. political process.[99] In this claim, he seems to have been mistaken. As we have shown, internal political factors were pushing the Eisenhower administration toward a policy of expanding development assistance, but this did not necessarily imply the use of a multilateral channel. After all, from a U.S. point of view, bilateral aid was more manageable, easier to deploy strategically and to manipulate tactically for diplomatic purposes. In the establishment of the IDA, the SUNFED factor was indeed decisive:

> Among the growing UN delegations in New York in the 1950s the demand for multilateral aid in the SUNFED mode did not subside; indeed the Soviet Union was a particularly insistent supporter. Two Americans much respected by Eisenhower, Paul Hoffman and Henry Cabot Lodge, took up that cause, but Secretary [Robert] Anderson and Eugene Black rejected it, being prepared to accept an IBRD-based IDA as, at a minimum, a lesser evil.[100]

More generally, Rostow criticized a pervasive view held by supporters of the developing countries within the United Nations of what the UN could achieve:

> [F]or good or ill, the United Nations was an organization of sovereign nations, not a global government. Ultimate sovereignty was jealously guarded by all members, perhaps most jealously by the governments of developing countries, many freshly emerged from colonialism. This meant that only partnerships . . . would work: and partnerships demand consensus. Charters of rights and duties, in which all the rights are allocated to developing countries, duties to advanced industrial countries, proved in these circumstances unhelpful.[101]

This rebuke is illuminating because it indicates the limits that circumscribe the attempts of developing countries to exert influence through the UN on its most powerful member state. It expresses the reality that America's cooperation with developing countries will be only on its own terms. Even when the U.S. moved to greater multilateral engagement, as seen hesitantly under Eisenhower and boldly under Kennedy, these policies remained fundamentally unilateral in intent and execution.[102] As the following chapter will indicate, the truth of this would be driven home further when the developing countries tried to advance major changes in world trade relationships under UN auspices.

8

The Birth of UNCTAD

- **The Politics of International Trade Policy**
- **The Developing Countries Unite at Cairo**
- **Prebisch Prepares the Ground**
- **The U.S. Approach to UNCTAD**
- *Towards a New Trade Policy for Development*
- **The Conference and Its Achievements**
- **Prebisch and the Politics of Economic Ideas**

The Politics of International Trade Policy

Many contemporaries perceived the birth of UNCTAD as a historical turning point. At the close of its first conference in 1964, the seventy-seven developing countries represented declared that it marked "the beginning of a new era in the evolution of international co-operation in the field of trade and development."[1] Raúl Prebisch told the ECOSOC meeting of July 1964: "[T]he world now has a foundation to support the new policy of international cooperation, a foundation which is essential to achieve the objective . . . of accelerating the rate of growth of the developing countries."[2] Diego Cordovez, a member of the UN Secretariat, argued in 1967 that the conference had "exploded the myth that all countries are economically equal and thus established the principle that a code of rules of international trade should reflect the existence of basic differences of economic and social organization, economic development and bargaining power."[3] Thus, ideas that previously had had an effective institutional voice only through a UN regional body, ECLA, were now projected onto the global stage. Moreover, Prebisch himself had made the transition from regional to global stature, moving from ECLA to become secretary-general of the conference, which later became a permanent new body.

This did not come about because the economic worldview of the Western powers had changed substantially since the 1940s. The majority of these powers, and most important the United States, saw the new initiative as unrealistic and utopian and were still wedded to GATT as the sole instrument of international trade cooperation. Therefore, one has to ask how it was that the OECD countries were unable to prevent the creation of this new organization, which had such radical aspirations and which was potentially destabilizing of some Western economic interests.

By the early 1960s, misgivings about the international trade system were welling up in a series of international reports and recommendations for change. The Soviet Union took a hand in this. In 1954, the Soviet Union called for a world meeting of trade experts; in 1955, for the ratification of the Havana Charter; and in 1956, for a conference on international trade, all unsuccessfully.[4] Then the Treaty of Rome was signed and the European Economic Community (EEC) of France, West Germany, Italy, and the Benelux countries came into being at the start of 1958. Many developing countries, especially in Latin America, feared that as a result they would lose their traditional European markets for their exports as a result of the trade diversion effects of the new customs union. The USSR tried to play on the fears of the developing countries and at the same time to divert them from their Western orbit. At a UN General Assembly meeting in 1961, a Soviet spokesman denounced "closed Western economic groupings" as inimical to international economic cooperation.[5] On 30 May 1962, Khrushchev coupled another denunciation of the Common Market with a renewed call for an international trade conference. He claimed that the "subordination of the young sovereign states of Africa to the Common Market would signify their consent to reconciling themselves to the role of agrarian and metropolitan raw-material appendages of former metropolitan countries."[6]

This rhetorical challenge was made in the context of the consideration that dominated the international trade arena of the early 1960s; namely, the expected enlargement of the EEC to incorporate the United Kingdom. Everyone believed that this event was imminent, and few, if any, at that time suspected that de Gaulle's veto would delay British entry by another decade. The expected expansion of the EEC raised a number of problems that exercised the minds of trade ministers in both developed and developing countries. For developed countries outside the Common Market, such as the U.S., the lowering of internal tariffs made an equivalent lowering of external tariffs urgent in order to avoid the diversion of trade away from their exports and toward the exports of other Common Market members. This was a major motivation behind the decision to launch what later became the Kennedy Round of tariff-reduction negotiations in GATT, but it was also a common interest with Latin America that informed the Alliance for Progress.

For the developing countries, the key problem was how British adherence to the Common Market would affect the system of commonwealth preferences that commonwealth developing countries still enjoyed, despite their anomalous position in the philosophy of GATT.[7] This system provided privileged access to commonwealth producers of agricultural commodities to markets that were dominated by British farm-support policies. Could commonwealth preferences be made compatible with the treatment that the EEC accorded to its own Associated Overseas Territories in relation to its arrangements for protecting European farmers, the EEC Common Agricultural Policy? How could any newly forged system of preferences be accepted as compatible with the GATT principles of multilateral nondiscrimination? The U.S. government saw the construction of entirely new global arrangements for agricultural trade as one possible way around the latter problem. As George Ball suggested in a memorandum to Kennedy, "[T]hese preferential systems can be adequately disposed of only if we are in a position to cooperate in the development of global arrangements for important agricultural commodities."[8] At high levels, the Kennedy administration began to contemplate new international commodity agreements for both temperate and tropical products.

The prospects for the successful launch of a new GATT round were clouded by another difficulty. Even if new arrangements could be made for agricultural trade, the demand from developing countries that the industrial countries absorb more of their manufactured goods was increasing in strength, encouraged by the announcement of the UN Decade of Development. Additional absorption of manufactured exports was something that the governments of industrial countries were unwilling to agree to do because they were fearful of the political pressure that lobby groups of domestic industrialists could apply. The powerful effect of such lobbying had indeed already been demonstrated in the case of cotton textiles. In this case, the main developing countries that exported cotton textiles had been forced, by threats of anti-dumping actions in the GATT, to agree to so-called voluntary export restraints against a promise of a series of phased increases in the "voluntary" import quotas. Far from feeling able to absorb more manufactures from developing countries, the developed countries were very reluctant to unwind restraints that had just been imposed in defiance of the GATT principle of nondiscrimination. The governments of industrial countries were persistently anxious about entering into trade negotiations aimed at tariff reductions in years when elections were due. Until the Trade Expansion Act of 1962, the U.S. government did not have the power to compensate domestic industry or assist its structural adjustment when protective tariffs were lowered.

The Developing Countries Unite at Cairo

The developing countries were at the time engaged in forging a new and higher level of solidarity. In July 1962, a Conference on Problems of Developing Countries was held in Cairo. It was organized outside the auspices of the UN and attended by a total of thirty-six countries. This was not a vast number, but its significance lay in its composition. The participants included African, Asian, and Latin American countries. An Afro-Asian bloc had begun to operate in the tenth General Assembly after the Bandung conference, and an African caucus had started in 1958 after the Accra Conference of Independent African States.[9] The Cairo conference marked the first joint initiative of countries from all three regional groups. At the 1961 General Assembly, the Latin American countries, with the notable exception of Brazil, had remained lukewarm to the idea of a trade conference.[10] The willingness of Latin American countries to join the Afro-Asian group, notwithstanding the U.S.'s gesture of reaching out to them through the Alliance for Progress, would prove to be an event of great significance. It is noteworthy that Prebisch was the official who was appointed as the personal representative at the Cairo conference of U Thant, the new UN Secretary-General following the death of Hammarskjöld in September 1961.[11] The Cairo declaration called for an international conference on "all vital questions relating to international trade, primary commodity trade and economic relations between developing and developed countries" within the framework of the UN.[12]

The tri-continental solidarity of the Cairo conference was also evident in ECOSOC. A group of developing countries from all three regions, which had formed around India, Yugoslavia, Brazil, Ethiopia, and Senegal, now also began to take the initiative in ECOSOC. At its Geneva meeting of July and August 1962, this group prepared its own draft resolution, and the U.S. leadership role now was to find a way of combining this draft with its own preferred version. This was a very different situation from the way the General Assembly had worked in the previous year. Ultimately, a wide-ranging umbrella resolution was negotiated with a strong emphasis on improved access to world markets for developing countries and the stabilization of commodity prices.[13] The ECOSOC umbrella resolution 917 (XXXIV) of 3 August 1962 also supported the convening of a United Nations Conference on Trade and Development (UNCTAD), the first occasion on which this name was used.[14] The U.S. viewed the role of the leading developing countries in the Geneva meeting as "active and on the whole constructive."[15]

The ECOSOC resolution was sustained and amplified in the General Assembly of autumn 1962 (resolution 1785 [XVII]). The U.S. ambassador to the

UN, Adlai Stevenson, effectively reversed the previous negative stance of the U.S. toward the conference. He seems to have concluded that since the plan for a conference could not be directly blocked, it was preferable to accept it positively rather than embitter the developing countries and play into the hands of the Soviets. By doing so, the U.S. could retain the hope of exercising some influence over the conference's timing and content. Once the U.S. position switched, so did that of the other OECD and Latin American countries, and the existence of UNCTAD in some shape or form was assured.[16]

Behind the scenes, however, there was less unity among the developing countries. As Sidney Dell reported to Kaldor in October 1962:

> Although the underdeveloped countries are pressing for this [trade] confer-
> ence, and have persuaded the West to go along with it, they are so drastically
> divided among themselves that they seem incapable of coming to any signifi-
> cant degree of agreement on conference objectives.[17]

The developing countries still saw their own fate in the trade arena as closely linked with the trajectory of the EEC. They wanted to have a platform from which to state their case before the EEC's negotiations with the rival European Free Trade Area (EFTA), which included the UK, had advanced too far. Their preferred date of June 1963 for the conference was impossibly close, however, and this caused some disarray and confusion. The U.S. employed delaying tactics to postpone the conference as much as they could. By December 1962, the developing countries had accepted the inevitability of delay. General Assembly resolution 1785 (XVII) called for the trade and development conference to take place early in 1964.[18]

As Prebisch later emphasized, the proposed conference was not his idea, but at the instigation of Brazil, Argentina, and Yugoslavia, he agreed to allow his name to be put forward for the post of its secretary-general. He was accepted for the job—having won out against a strong Australian candidate, Sir John Crawford—only on the very eve of the meeting of the conference's preparatory committee in January 1963.[19] His appointment put an end to Philippe de Seynes's hopes of using the planned conference to build up the Department of Economic and Social Affairs (DESA) in New York.[20] However, Prebisch's first impressions of the preparatory committee were not good. He recalled that it was initially characterized by generally violent arguments between the Soviet and American representatives. They were, however, called to order by the Nigerian delegate: "Gentlemen, we have come here to deal with the problems of the developing countries. This is a political debate that belongs in the General Assembly and not here." After this, the quality of the discussion improved. Prebisch began to draft his report for the 1964 conference and planned a series of journeys to countries both developed and underdeveloped for the purposes of consultation.[21]

In the meantime, in an attempt to find some proposals around which the developing countries could unite, Sidney Dell had written to Lawrence S. Finkelstein, a veteran of the 1944 Dumbarton Oaks meeting who was by this point an officer of the Carnegie Endowment for International Peace. Dell sent Finkelstein a letter of request in the names of Richard Kahn and Richard Ruggles seeking Carnegie funding for a meeting of experts in advance of the UN trade and development conference.[22] This plan soon got into difficulty. Finkelstein thought that his Carnegie colleagues would be more favorable if the expert group meeting had a clear link with a high-prestige U.S. institution such as Yale.[23] Richard Kahn, who had not been told about the approach to Carnegie in his name, had to be persuaded not to withdraw from the proposed meeting of experts. Dell stressed to Kahn the importance of convening an international group as a means of warding off accusations of "extreme Keynesianism":

> I am sorry indeed if, as you say in your letter of Nov 19 received today, we are getting at cross purposes. [I]t may not be quite enough for your group to produce the answers we need: however good those answers may be, we must be able to sell them to a broad spectrum of countries in the UN, and I cannot help feeling that it might be a bit easier if an international group were convened. . . . I believe that there is now a sufficient state of uncertainty and misgiving about this even in Washington for new ideas to be studied with some care, especially if it can be shown that even respectable economists untainted by Cambridge go along with them.[24]

Ironically, part of Kahn's problem with getting involved in the proposed meeting of experts was *his* desire to avoid being tarred with the extreme Keynesian brush in the form of Kaldor's earlier proposed international measures for full employment. Dell had to assure Kahn repeatedly that he "held no particular brief for Nicky's international scheme [of 1949]."[25] Kahn had come round by January 1963, when the date of the conference had been put back in line with American wishes, so the meeting of experts was penciled in for the summer.[26] Dell then contacted Andrew Shonfield, the director of the Royal Institute for International Affairs in London (RIIA), seeking sponsorship for the meeting.[27] He explained that both he and Richard Kahn thought that there was a conspicuous lack of positive and constructive ideas and that without them the conference could end in confusion and frustration. Dell portrayed the developing countries as clear about their complaints (deteriorating terms of trade, Common Market agricultural policy, and their position in GATT) but short on feasible alternative solutions:

What is lacking in the present situation is the sort of high-level thinking ahead
and exploration of ideas that preceded the Bretton Woods and Havana Charter
conferences. While the under-developed countries know what they do *not* like
about the present situation, they have been unable to develop significant positive proposals for consideration by the conference, and do not seem likely to
do so as matters stand. The developed countries, on the other hand, are sympathetic, in a general way, to the above-mentioned problems . . . but have been
too busy with other issues . . . to devote much time or thought to these problems. Thus there is a serious lack of intellectual leadership on both sides in the
preliminary phase of preparations for the conference.

Dell explained his reasons for wanting an informal group.[28] He thought that
preparations made inside the UN would be much more inhibited by various
kinds of political limitation, but in addition he argued that the UN

is not normally a major innovator in the field of ideas: its function is rather the
adaptation of existing ideas, wherever possible, to the realities of the international environment. The present situation calls for fundamental thinking of a
type best provided by independent private expertise, selected without too much
regard to political considerations, geographic representation, etc.

The group of fifteen economic experts who attended the Bellagio meeting
from 16 to 24 September 1963 did nonetheless contain a balance between the
OECD countries (eight), the Eastern bloc (two), and the developing countries
(five).[29] Its contribution was less that of brainstorming new ideas than of assay-
ing the policy ideas on trade that were already in circulation. They produced a
summary of their discussions and a statement of policy that records the recommendations that they were all able to agree on.[30] It is interesting to note that
while they were able to agree on the need for high-income countries to open
their markets, on the desirability of greater trade among developing countries
and between them and the Eastern-bloc countries, and even on the need for a
new world trade organization, other matters were more difficult. The idea of a
general preference for developing-country industrial goods received a mixed
response, while the problem of world commodity prices uncovered "deep divisions on issues of principle," specifically "the role of independent market forces
in deciding the fate of primary producing countries."[31] These differences did
not augur well for the prospects of these two policy ideas in the conference
itself. Dell spent four days in Bellagio before rejoining Prebisch on a tour of
Eastern Europe, and he judged the conference as "very successful."[32]

In Dell's mind, there seem to have been three tasks or phases to a successful
UN innovation. The first was to identify an external source of expertise and
access its fundamental thinking. The second was to adapt the idea for UN
purposes with due regard to the possibility of "brand resistance." The third

was to "sell" the good idea to as many UN members as possible in a political and diplomatic marketing exercise. He was in charge of the first two, while Prebisch took the lead with the third.

Prebisch Prepares the Ground

When consulted by Dell, Prebisch raised no objection to the Carnegie/RIIA initiative. Dell was able to tell Finkelstein in late March that Prebisch welcomed the idea and considered that it would make a valuable contribution.[33] By June 1963, Prebisch seems to have changed his mind. He started to worry about the possibility of overlap or conflict between his own report to the conference and the report of the RIIA group.[34] He seems to have wanted both to recruit helpers and to remain his own man. His fluctuating attitude perhaps reflected his difficulty in holding the balance between recruiting sufficient support for a set of proposals and maintaining control over the proposals for which he was recruiting support.

By October, Dell was principally engaged in drafting Prebisch's report for presentation to the conference. He now had before him the statement of policy and a summary of the discussions that had emerged from the Bellagio meeting. At the same time, a number of other consultants were working either in New York or in their own countries on commissioned papers or on drafts of sections of the report. Kaldor, for example, was in New York for a fortnight "around Christmas 1963" in order to contribute a paper on the subject of international liquidity—the Kaldor-Hart-Tinbergen plan.[35] It was not clear which of all these drafts would be embodied in the report and which would be issued separately as "consultants' papers."[36]

That ambivalence was certainly evident in relation to Gamani Corea. Corea, at the time a high-level official of the Central Bank of Sri Lanka, was concerned with establishing a capacity for development planning. Prebisch invited ECAFE, as he did other UN regional commissions, to recommend participants for a pre-UNCTAD meeting in Geneva, and Corea was the chosen Sri Lankan. At the meeting, Dell asked him to come to New York as a consultant to help Prebisch to write the conference report. He agreed, but when he arrived in New York, neither Dell nor Prebisch were there, so he went to Jacob Mosak to explain why he had come. "That is interesting," said Mosak, "but Prebisch is a man who writes his own reports." So it proved. Although Corea wrote a draft report covering all the themes that ultimately appeared in *Towards a New Trade Policy for Development,* Prebisch did not use any of it but wrote his own draft in Spanish.[37] It was this document that became the main focus of discussion and the anchor of the ensuing conference.

The reason why Prebisch was so often absent from New York was his extensive round of visits to capitals for consultations in advance of the conference. He started in Europe, visiting Paris, Brussels, and London, and then moved on to Australasia, visiting Canberra, Tokyo, Bangkok, New Delhi, and Karachi. After discussions in Cairo, he went to the Eastern-bloc capitals of Moscow and Warsaw, plus the nonaligned Belgrade, and concluded his travels in Bonn and, finally, Washington. Although he did not find time to go to any African capitals (and already knew Latin America intimately), these consultations were still very wide ranging and indicated his global intentions for the forthcoming conference.[38]

In his advance consultations, Prebisch was engaged on a variety of political and diplomatic tasks. He aimed at strengthening the interregional solidarity that the developing countries had shown in Cairo while expanding the numbers of actively participating developing countries. Aware that it was the support of the Soviet bloc that had helped the developing countries to get the conference convened in the face of U.S. indifference, he wanted to be able to offer the Soviet government some political incentive to stay on board.[39] At the same time, he did not want the agenda to be dominated by the USSR's familiar topics—the economic benefits of disarmament, trade discrimination, and the creation of an ITO.[40] In the capitals of the industrial world, he tried to explain why he believed that international trade could not be left to the GATT system alone and what kind of options for change he foresaw. He was persuading certainly, but he was also listening to the concerns of his interlocutors so that his concrete proposals could be drawn up in ways that met those concerns as far as possible.

Given these strategic aims, the shape of his package of proposals began to emerge. To encourage the unity of the developing countries, Prebisch made one "fundamental point"—developing countries should be compensated for past and future terms-of-trade losses:

> Whether they relate to a surcharge arrived at through commodity agreements or to compensatory financing to offset the deterioration in the terms of trade, either method entails re-transferring all or part of the income earned by the countries which have gained by the deterioration in the terms of trade to the countries that have lost by it.[41]

The promise of compensation for terms-of-trade losses was a powerful one, particularly for those that accepted the secular decline in the terms of trade of primary products. The difficulties of designing a compensation scheme were skirted by talking about options, while it was made clear that the recipient of the "re-transfer" would not be the primary producer but the government of the developing country in support of its development plan. The language of "compensation" and "re-transfer" chimed nicely with their idea that the purpose of the conference was not so much trade promotion or giving aid as the rectification of enduring injustice.

The other main incentive for developing countries to remain united was to try to gain trade benefits for their manufactured exports. A campaign to eliminate existing special restrictions on selected products such as textiles would have been obviously too narrow and too divisive if prosecuted on its own. So this was coupled with two other demands—for a system of preferences for all manufactures exported by developing countries and for permission to be granted for developing countries to subsidize some of the marketing costs of their industrial exporters. In this way, a veneer of common interest was created, although only few developing countries could benefit directly and immediately from such preferences. Prebisch certainly thought that he could diffuse the alarm that these proposals would raise in the industrial countries by pointing out that their impact on supply would be less than 5 percent of the expected increase in consumption.[42]

In order to maintain the interest of the Soviet bloc in the conference, Prebisch spoke approvingly of state trading while holding up multilateral trading as the ultimate goal. He distinguished between the bilateral trading of the Depression years, the unavoidable outcome of economic distress, and the use of bilateralism as a means of expanding trade between the Soviet bloc and the rest of the world. He reported the satisfaction of the developing countries with the experience of long-term trade agreements with the Soviets and expressed confidence that despite disagreements about the principles of trade such as the most-favored-nation principle, "[I]t is perfectly possible to arrive at recommendations that will permit the development of trade for the benefit of both sides."[43]

In considering the institutional machinery of the world trading system, Prebisch did not seek to revive the abortive Havana Charter. This was the solution long promoted by the Soviet Union and endorsed in the meetings of the African and Latin American Preparatory Committees at Niamey and Alta Garcia. He interpreted the intentions of the negotiators of the Havana Charter (apart from its single concern of full employment) as retrogressive and as an attempt to find a system of rules that would take the world back to an earlier, pre-Depression order. He argued that what the world needed was not a set of rules of the game but a clear and agreed-upon set of policies in support of the developing countries. The existing machinery of trade cooperation—GATT—was not, in his view, adequate to the task of developing and monitoring the implementation of such policies. It was lacking in universality because the Soviet-bloc countries were absent from membership, as were many developing countries, and because its rules were primarily directed toward private-enterprise trading, not state trading. Trade issues were considered without reference to problems of development and finance, and existing GATT rules failed to take account of the structural differences between developed and developing countries. Thus his message on his travels was that the world needed new and more comprehensive machinery to implement a new trade policy for development.

A significant group in the developing-country camp would not have been satisfied with anything less than the replacement of the GATT by a new UN institution. As Janez Stanovnik, then Yugoslav ambassador to the UN later recalled:

> There were what I would call the more radical members of the G77, among whom the most influential were Ismat Kitani from Iraq. Then there was also the Burmese delegate, U Maung, and Moteiro from Brazil. They were, from the beginning, pressing for a new organization, which would substitute for GATT. Of course, this was a "red flag in front of a bullock."[44]

In the Secretariat, the great driving force behind the campaign for a new UN institution was Wladek Malinowski, who was Prebisch's advisor, close associate, and friend.[45] Malinowski was the first of Prebisch's associates to supply the organizational and tactical imagination needed to create a new UN institution.[46] The moderates among the representatives of the developing countries, such as Stanovnik, advocated an alternative institutional model, one that would have been more in the spirit of the SUNFED compromise discussed in Chapter 7. This did not win over Prebisch, who remained firmly under Malinowski's influence on the institutional question, as Stanovnik later noted:

> I was, on this matter, at a basic disagreement with Wladek Malinowski, who had great merit for many things at the early days of the United Nations and was Prebisch's right hand in the preparatory committee. But on this matter . . . we disagreed completely. He was pressing for a new organization, while I thought that it would be much more impressive to have a small "think tank" around Raúl Prebisch. The logic was to produce ideas with which we would then press in the General Assembly, the ECOSOC, and other forums, and would get results within the existing order.[47]

If Malinowski was, with Prebisch, the creator of UNCTAD, he was also the destroyer of the think tank option, which now faded from the G77 agenda. Prebisch, for his part, was determined that UNCTAD should be an activist organization—more so, indeed, than ECLA was.[48]

As yet, however, the developed countries were highly resistant to the discussion of institutional changes. The Americans had proposed a group of experts to survey existing trade organizations, identify gaps and overlaps, and make recommendations. This group set out four alternatives: a new and all-embracing ITO, a reinvigoration of existing organs, a complete revision of GATT, or a periodic conference with review responsibilities in the trade field.[49] Prebisch supported the last option, but there was still plenty of scope for conflict with the U.S. on the question of how it would relate to the GATT.

The U.S. Approach to UNCTAD

The U.S. government had several worries as the UN trade conference approached. The most serious of these concerned domestic politics. Unless the developing countries could be diverted from the demand for industrial preferences, the administration would have to address it at precisely the time when domestic pressures for protection would be strongest—at the start of an election year. A related anxiety was the international repercussions of the developing countries' demand for industrial preferences. It held considerable potential for causing disunity among the OECD countries. The UK and France, in particular, would have no difficulty with the principle of granting preferences, given their existing preferential schemes. This could leave the U.S. isolated in the face of developing-country accusations that it was actively discriminating against them through the cotton textile agreement.[50]

At the end of his diplomatic tour, Prebisch came to Washington, and George Ball, the under secretary of state for foreign affairs, met him on 1 November 1963 for discussions about the forthcoming conference. Prebisch rehearsed his case in terms of the target rate of growth of the UN development decade. He argued that the target of growth could not be met by the developing countries unless their trade gaps could be reduced. This in turn required that existing trade barriers be reduced and that "additional measures"—such as preferences for industrial exports of developing countries—be taken for a transitional period. The share of these exports in the industrial countries' increment to consumption would be small, he argued, not exceeding 5 percent, and perhaps some overall limit could be placed on the effect of the preferences in order to safeguard industrial countries' interests. As a possible alternative to a scheme of equally allocated industrial preferences, Prebisch cited Kaldor's idea of an export tax on primary commodities, the proceeds of which could be used to subsidize the exports of new manufactures.

Without asserting a U.S. position on industrial preferences, Ball pointed out the problem of adjustment of old U.S. industries and concerns about the level of employment. He repeated the claim that even small quantities of a product offered at a low price could cause "market disruption" so that even a limitation on the volume of trade receiving preferences would not be seen as an adequate safeguard. For him, an attractive suggestion was "greater use of regional arrangements among countries at the same level of development." He thought it would be a mistake for the industrial countries "to endorse ideas or say 'pious' things at UNCTAD that they could not live up to."[51]

Prebisch suggested that a compromise was emerging on the shape of the future international trade machinery. Among the developing countries, the desire to set up an entirely new world trade organization seemed to be a minority view. The proposal to transform GATT to include the state trading countries (made by Jean Royer at the Bellagio conference) was seen as a dilution and weakening of GATT. The retention of GATT as an autonomous institution reporting to another larger body was the likely compromise, with state trading, commodities, and manufactures dealt with by committees that also reported to a regularly recurring world conference serviced by its own secretariat. Ball left the meeting without discussing the machinery issue.

The weekend before he was assassinated, President Kennedy received a memorandum from Ball.[52] It was dated 12 November, and it begins by referring to Kennedy's "interest in the United Nations Trade Conference" to which "Mr. [McGeorge] Bundy has called my attention." Ball explained to the president that the forthcoming conference was the result of two forces, both of which were external to the U.S.: the discontent of the developing countries with GATT and the Soviet Union's interest in undermining GATT for its own political purposes. Ball saw the danger that "some well-intentioned people— encouraged by others less benign—can do considerable mischief." However, he thought that the damage could be limited.

The memorandum identified the USSR as having two interests. One was to get onto the conference's agenda subjects such as East-West trade and disarmament that could be used for propaganda advantage. The other was to disrupt GATT, in which practitioners of state trading had little material interest. In the first aim, Ball reported, it had decided not to press its point, and in the second it would succeed only if the U.S. could not educate the developing countries out of the most foolish of their proposals. The bulk of the rest of the memorandum indicated which of the trade proposals supported by the developing countries the U.S. found "the stickiest" and suggested the lines on which the "education and persuasion" of developing countries should proceed.

The proposal that seemed most objectionable was that the developed countries should grant special preferences to the industrial exports of the developing countries. The Herter-Clayton report of November 1961 had urged unilateral granting to groups of "contested countries," but not to industrial countries, the right to free trade on their exports of raw materials to industrial countries. It had also urged a reduction in import tariffs by the contested countries at the rate of 5 percent per annum in consideration of the industrial countries reducing their duties at the rate of 10 percent per annum.[53] Although Herter-Clayton helped to give impetus to the Kennedy administration's trade-liberalization program, the administration was to ignore these particular suggestions as firmly as those coming from Prebisch. Ball advised that it would be unwise to hold out any hope to the developing countries that the U.S. would support any form of industrial preference. The primary objection to it was political, that the administration did not want to have to defend it at the same time that it would have to resist domestic interest groups seeking trade preferences. It was safer and easier to hold the center ground of tariff reduction on a nondiscriminatory basis in both domestic and international arenas. The economic arguments were secondary, although the slogan of comparative advantage was pressed into service. If the U.S. were to take this line from the start, it would need some additional tactics to preserve its position. These should include arguing that the American record of absorbing developing countries' manufactures was good compared with the European record and calling for NATO countries to do more to remove existing measures of discrimination—as prevailed in cotton textiles, shoes, and electronics. The U.S. would also call for the formation of free trade areas for regional blocs of developing countries. These devices would be used so that the U.S. would not seem to be turning a deaf ear to the requests of developing countries.

Apart from industrial preferences, the U.S. was unhappy about the possible use of commodity agreements to transfer resources to developing countries. Kennedy had shifted policy on commodity agreements early in his administration from doctrinaire opposition to measured support for them. (Adlai Stevenson, Kennedy's ambassador to the UN, had stated that "little things, like stabilization of commodity prices, can mean more than economic assistance. The change in the price of coffee by half a cent per pound can wipe out all of the economic assistance that we [i.e., the U.S.] could hope to give . . . for a long time."[54]) Ball, however, made a firm distinction between international mechanisms that address the volatility of commodity prices and mechanisms that permanently raise them above the long-run average market price. While conceding that U.S. agricultural price support did exactly that, Ball warned against it on the international scene. He thought that participating in negotiations on that basis ran the risk of having to recommend commodity agreements that Congress would not ratify.

Finally, the developing countries' discontent with GATT had led to two different ideas for reform. One was the idea that a single encompassing trade organization that would accept the Soviet-bloc countries as members and attend to the interests of developing countries should replace GATT. The other was the idea of a new organization separate from GATT but dedicated to promoting the interests of developing countries in the international trade system. Ball wished, whatever happened, to preserve GATT. In a passage that well conveys the tone of the whole, he concluded:

> We must, of course, be concerned to preserve the GATT against efforts to transform it into a debating forum for special interests or to supplant it with a more diffuse organization. Fortunately, I think this problem is manageable. Already there are signs that the more stable leaders in the developing countries are having second thoughts on the value of the GATT, and I am confident that with a steady American policy we should have little difficulty in saving it from serious impairment.

Towards a New Trade Policy for Development

Toward the end of January 1964, the work of the Preparatory Committee of the conference was nearing completion. Donald Mallett, OECD representative in Washington, told the British that Prebisch had completed the draft of his long-awaited report. He also said that Prebisch had shown a 200-page draft to the executive directors of the UN regional commissions and that those responsible for Africa and Asia were far from pleased with it because it largely reflected Latin American views and Prebisch's own ideas on compensatory financing. He had apparently been asked by the executive directors to amend and tone down the draft and to reduce its length by approximately half. Mallett suggested that there was a growing rift between Prebisch and the representatives of the African and Asian developing countries, who tended to regard him as the champion only of the Latin Americans.[55] The UK Foreign Office understood that "as a result of criticism by other members of the United Nations Secretariat, he [Prebisch] was persuaded to withdraw this first draft and to prepare a more balanced document."[56] Prebisch acknowledged "the extensive and creative labors of the Preparatory Committee . . . in particular at its second session" but also made it clear that his report to the conference "went beyond the findings of the Preparatory Committee." This was due to "the extensive consultations that took place with officials of many governments in all parts of the world and at various sessions of the [UN] regional commissions."[57] The basic document for the conference, under the title *Towards a New Trade Policy for Development,* had thus already undergone significant modification in its successive drafts before it reached the conference table.

There seems to have been some truth in the claim that Prebisch was having some difficulty holding together the tri-continental coalition. Prebisch "felt much disquieted by indications of some African thought moving towards an area of a Euro-African preferential system, which as he saw it could only provoke a corresponding United States Latin American system, encouraging some already existing thoughts of this kind and militating against a general lessening of barriers."[58] His disquiet was shared by the U.S., which was trying to dissuade the EEC countries from offering to extend their preferences to more African countries.[59] It is ironic that the U.S. pressure to induce "sobriety and responsibility" in the attitude of its European allies also discouraged the Africans from defecting from tri-continental solidarity.

The English version of the preliminary version of Prebisch's report appeared on 13 February 1964.[60] Prebisch later described this work as a "synthesis" and recalled that much of it had derived from the work of the Preparatory Committee.[61] As presented to the conference, it was a high-profile exercise in international development targeting. This had caused some dissension in the making. Janez Stanovnik recalled:

> Jack Mosak, who was an excellent economist, was quite at odds and there were difficult hours in between Jack Mosak and Raúl Prebisch, as Prebisch insisted that he elaborated a complete econometric model on the "trade gap." Jack was arguing back that there were such loopholes in the whole concept that he said, "When I come to the mathematical expression of the ideas, the things must be rigorously correct. I cannot bridge the gaps with verbalisms." Prebisch was dissatisfied with the way Jack Mosak had been doing this. He gave it then to Sidney Dell. It was finally Sidney Dell who produced the model which was then also used by Prebisch in his report to UNCTAD.[62]

The model's point of departure was the target growth rate that had been adopted, against U.S. wishes, for the UN development decade; namely, 5 percent annual growth in GNP. Since population was still growing at 2.5 percent a year, this would permit per capita economic growth of 2.5 per head a year— the minimum that would be consistent with "development." However, the report argued, a 5 percent GNP growth rate could not be sustained unless imports to developing countries were growing at 6 percent. This contrasted with a projected growth rate of developing-country exports of only 4 percent. The divergence between required imports and projected exports was the estimated trade gap, which, using the figures just quoted, would grow to $20 billion by 1970. This calculation was simple enough to be displayed in a single box diagram and dramatic enough to attract the interest of the average newspaper reader. It was an inspired representation of the developing countries' plight and it led straight into detailed proposals for measures to close the gap.

The report gained some important favorable publicity. The *Financial Times* gave it an editorial on 17 February 1964 in which it conceded that there was some justice in the case put forward on behalf of the developing countries:

> It is no secret that many of the industrial countries would much rather that this conference was never held, and that they expect few positive results from it. But it is clear from Dr. Prebisch's report that something has to be done for the less developed countries in the southern part of the world if the gap now separating their standards of living from those of the richer northern nations is not to widen. The Kennedy Round of G.A.T.T. negotiations has been chiefly concerned with tariff cuts among industrial countries, so the less developed half of the world understandably argues that G.A.T.T. alone is not enough to solve its problems.[63]

The editorial, however, predicted that the outcome of the conference would be negligible. No agreements were in sight, it thought, and the most that could be hoped for was that the conference might be established in semi-permanent form so that negotiations on the issues could continue and the Russians be denied the opportunity to make greater trouble.

Le Monde praised the report's "tone of moderation and spirit of impartiality," which it said fully justified the title of the third section of the report—"Realism and Renewal." It noted with approval that Prebisch had incorporated some ideas that the French had produced in their submission and that in matters of policy he belonged to the *dirigiste* persuasion. It published extracts from a prior interview with Prebisch in which he had made clear that he did not lay the blame for the protectionism of the developed countries only at the door of the EEC but indicted the U.S. in equal measure.[64] This was friendly publicity, in tune with the French government line of sympathizing publicly with Prebisch's ideas.[65]

Despite the supportive press coverage, the governments of the developed countries remained unimpressed. (Prebisch later recalled that it was clear from the start that these governments took the view that the attitude taken by him and his secretariat was a clear violation of the neutrality appropriate to an international organization. This would become a running theme of his years at UNCTAD.[66]) "The economic philosophy is not expounded in any very rigorous way," was the British Board of Trade's assessment of the report. It was criticized for giving "a potted and controversial account of a very complicated field." The section on the reasons for expecting the terms of trade of developing countries to deteriorate was "at the same time the most important and least satisfactory part." Why, the skeptical official in the Board of Trade wondered, did this argument not apply equally to "peripheral" countries such as Australia and New Zealand—which, because of strong trade unions and no pressure of surplus labor in agriculture, were by contrast achieving rising export earnings and high and rising standards of living?

The British also considered that Prebisch's criticism of the Havana Charter and GATT was unfair, since neither was in fact based on absolute laissez-faire principles and both already recognized to some extent the special problems of developing countries. Prebisch was judged as "far from having proved his case or even explained it sufficiently carefully in the report to make a balanced discussion of it possible."

> Much of the approach in the Report is emotive rather than deliberative, for example, repeated references to the "new order" and a lavish use of pejorative phrases. Dr. Prebisch overstates the commitment on the part of industrial countries implied in the Development Decade as being that, having willed the end, they should will the means. In fact, the industrial countries assumed no such precise commitment.[67]

The U.S. had certainly committed itself to nothing. As the conference loomed, George Ball privately lamented that "the less developed countries have been the victims of a high-class confidence game conducted in elegant economic jargon." He feared that "when they finally open the package and find it contains old newspapers they will be mightily upset." He was confident that at the conference "chaos will result since the interests and views represented will be many and diverse" so that at the end the U.S. would be in a position to "put together all that is good and salvageable."[68]

The Conference and Its Achievements

The UN Conference on Trade and Development was held in Geneva from 23 March to 16 June 1964. It was the largest international trade conference that had ever been convened, attracting 2,000 delegates from 121 of the 123 countries that were eligible to participate.[69] Everyone present was acutely conscious of the fact that of those 123 countries, 33 with a population of 1 billion were "rich" while 90 with a population of 2 billion were "poor." Although all the delegates were shuttled between the Palais des Nations and the restaurants in the old city by black Mercedes limousines, the conference sessions were cast as a drama of "global collective bargaining" between rich and poor, and rightly so.[70]

The 1963 Declaration of the 75 Developing Countries signaled the success of Prebisch's efforts to solidify the tri-continental coalition. Yugoslavia had undertaken to organize the group in New York well beforehand, but this was seen as similar to the consultations that the industrial countries carried out in the OECD. That the coalition would act in the conference as a large and powerful caucus (operating as the Group of 77 developing countries, known as the G77) came as a rather unpleasant surprise to the developed countries. The group proceeded at the start of the conference by presenting jointly only resolutions that had been previously agreed upon among themselves, even on issues where they had important conflicts of interest.[71] Their adoption of this tactic was therefore not determined by the overlapping of their economic interests. Rather, it demonstrated the degree of their commitment to the conceptual framework of *Towards a New Trade Policy for Development* and their resolve to make the conference an historic event.[72] This commitment gave Prebisch a commanding role in the conduct of the conference, an eminence that was indeed extraordinary and unprecedented for a UN official, however distinguished.

The conference got off to a slow start. Ball's opening speech for the U.S. was a deliberate attempt to strike a note of realism, but it came over as essentially defensive. Dell thought it was "the most disappointing speech" and "a negative blast."[73] *Newsweek* detected in it "more than a hint of paternalism."[74] Ball himself thought that the press treatment of his speech in the U.S. had "on balance, been satisfactory" apart from "a captious and ignorant editorial in *The Washington Post.*"[75] By contrast, Edward Heath, the president of the British Board of Trade, sounded a much more positive note:

> Together we face the intolerable problem of poverty in the world. . . . We are determined to find ways in which trade and growth can help to end it. . . . This conference is the greatest collective effort that mankind has yet made for this purpose. It must be made to succeed. What is required for this is firmness of will and generosity of spirit. . . . The United Kingdom is firmly committed to the objectives of the conference.[76]

Britain and the EEC countries, as Ball had feared, demonstrated a greater willingness than the U.S. to reach accommodations with the developing countries.

The division of work followed the divisions of the Prebisch report, organizing tasks under five committees: the First Committee on international commodity problems, the Second Committee on manufactures and semi-manufactures, the Third Committee on the improvements of invisible trade (including international compensatory financing), the Fourth Committee on international arrangements for international trade expansion, and the Fifth Committee on expansion of international trade and its significance for economic development and implementation of regional groupings. These committees were cumbersome, and the work soon had to be delegated to smaller working groups. This was because the tactic of joint agreed-upon resolutions, however disconcerting to the developed countries, soon showed its limitation: it was futile to outvote repeatedly those countries from which concessions were sought if they subsequently remained unwilling to grant those concessions. Prebisch therefore steered the G77 to modify its tactics and adopt a more conciliatory approach toward the industrial countries. Conciliation and the search for compromise had its own cost, however, and a month into the negotiations Dell was reported as being aware of "a feeling within the Secretariat that the conference at the moment lacked a sense of direction."[77] In the conference hall, the industrial countries constantly made the charge that the developing countries should do more to help their own development but "took a fairly thorough beating" each time they tried to divert attention from international to domestic policy issues by this tactic.[78] The proceedings of the conference ground on slowly but soon got bogged down.[79] Drift was succeeded by deadlock in the First, Second, and Fifth Committees, relieved only by American-inspired progress on aid in the Third Committee.[80] According to Edward Heath, Ball "tired of the constant haggling that went on and gradually dropped out of the arguments." Heath later claimed that he himself had played a crucial role in breaking the diplomatic deadlock by intervening decisively with the Algerian delegation.[81]

Be that as it may, by the time the conference came to a close, agreement had been reached on hardly any of the specific proposals in the Prebisch report. The final act of the conference consisted of a series of declarations of agreed-upon principles in those areas where wording could be agreed upon, recommendations for action could be remitted to international organizations and governments (as appropriate), and programs of work could be formulated on further studies to be made on trade problems.[82] Many of these recommendations were voted on rather than adopted without a vote. It is true that consciousness of the interdependence of trade and development issues had been raised. It was also the case that the unity of the G77 had thrown the industrial countries into division and disarray and increased their willingness to support piecemeal reforms of existing international arrangements. Nevertheless, Prebisch admitted, when asked later, that "nothing important" was achieved in terms of world economic policy by the first UNCTAD meeting.[83] In his postconference report to U Thant, he dwelt on three other and more indirect claims of achievement. First, he claimed that there had been recognition, expressed or implied, of the need for great changes in international economic cooperation policy. Second, he claimed that forms of common action had emerged among developing countries that would give them greater influence over the formulation of such policies in future. Third, he pointed to the establishment of new machinery within the UN to apply such policies in the field of trade and development.[84] Even this last, which was certainly the most concrete achievement of the 1964 conference (later to be known as UNCTAD I), had to be kept vague and ambiguous. The wording of the final act does not clarify whether UNCTAD was merely an interim step on the way to setting up an ITO or intended to be a permanent fixture.[85]

Prebisch and the Politics of Economic Ideas

Raúl Prebisch was appointed as secretary-general of the new continuing institution of UNCTAD. Latin American governments lobbied heavily for him. The British had some misgivings about him. Although they recognized Prebisch's intellectual suitability for the post, they were doubtful about his impartiality and would have preferred L. K. Jha of India, then governor of the Reserve Bank of India. However, they could not get the Indian government to agree to his candidature once a Latin American, commanding strong support, was already in the field. In the event, neither the British nor the Americans opposed the appointment of Prebisch.[86]

Gamani Corea later recalled Prebisch at this moment:

> I still have a vivid recollection of Dr. Prebisch at UNCTAD I marching along the corridors of the Palais des Nations insisting that there should not only be a new and permanent institution in the form of UNCTAD but that its secretariat should be "intellectually independent." He used this phrase on many occasions because he did not see the secretariat of the new institution as a passive agency concerning itself essentially with the logistics of meetings and with servicing negotiations in an abstract way. He wished instead for an activist body which provided leadership and made its contributions through its studies, its analyses and its thoughts.[87]

Prebisch asked Sidney Dell, who had done so much to build up the conceptual framework that united the G77, to join him as UNCTAD's research director. Dell had already agreed to succeed Lurié as director of the Industry Division of DESA in New York, and he did not find it an easy choice to make: he doubted that much further progress could be made in international trade policy, but, on the other hand, the staff of the Industry Division was "weak and intensely demoralized, and I would have to do virtually everything myself." He reflected:

> Trade is big and exciting at the moment, though more in terms of politics than economics. Prebisch is also a more exciting man to work for than De Seynes, and his heart is at least in the right place even when his thinking is muddled. But he is very disorderly and frustrating in many ways, and I should be constantly under pressure to sacrifice my family life in the interests of the "cause."[88]

Kaldor was quite clear that Dell should stay with Prebisch and trade policy and advised him so. He thought that the Industry Division in New York would be no different from the industry divisions at ECE and at ECLA that he recalled as going nowhere. He was more optimistic about what might be done in the trade policy field, though that depended on the results of the U.S. and

British elections.[89] Dell still hesitated, complaining that Prebisch did not keep him informed of his discussions with the Americans and suspecting that he (Dell) was regarded as "a bit too pro-underdeveloped at a time when he [Prebisch] is seeking the goodwill of the Americans." He remained quite uneasy, confessing to being "very uncomfortable with Prebisch these days."[90] Eventually, however, he accepted Kaldor's advice and threw in his lot with Prebisch and UNCTAD.

The discomfort of Dell with Prebisch, just after they had worked so closely together to animate the trade concerns of the developing countries and embody them in a new institution, is significant. At UNCTAD I, Prebisch had shown how well he could use ideas for political purposes and develop a politics of economic ideas that could override wide differences of economic interest. Nevertheless, Dell clearly wondered about the future of this politics of ideas: Would it now shift its trajectory toward greater compromise with the views of the U.S., and if not, would it implode as it attempted to do the impossible?

The 1964 conference had wrought few changes in international policy and established few solutions to the problems of international trade. Its achievement was to create another international public institution for the further discussion and negotiation of the problems that had not been solved. This institution would be peculiar in that it formally embodied the division between developing and developed countries. What sort of research would an organization so constituted do? Could it be objective, in the old League of Nations sense, or impartial, as the British desired? Did it not have its own built-in institutional objectives—what Dell referred to as "the cause"—and thus its own doctrine to preach? What could "intellectually independent" research, which Prebisch wanted UNCTAD to produce, mean in this context? Of whom or what was the UNCTAD research to be intellectually independent? Was independence sought from the governments of the industrial countries, from the rest of the UN, or from the North American academic establishment? Whichever it was, it was not so clear that it would or could also be independence from the conceptual framework on which UNCTAD itself was founded. Prebisch's researchers would have to be committed and militant in the interests of the developing countries. Only by constantly drawing attention to problems, finding solutions, and advocating them to governments could UNCTAD become an instrument of change, and if UNCTAD were not to be an instrument of change it would, in Prebisch's view, be nothing.[91] Yet once organizations start to preach a doctrine, they face the danger that they will subvert their own capacity for independent research. How then would UNCTAD fare in this regard as it pursued the developing countries' demand for a new international economic order?

9

UNCTAD under Raúl Prebisch: Success or Failure?

- **"An Economic Doctrine for the Developing Countries"**
- **UNCTAD's Early Organizational Difficulties**
- **The Secretariat: Impartial But Not Neutral**
- **Interpreting Past International Commodity Regulation**
- **Shaping a Commodities Policy**
- **Supplementary Finance and International Monetary Reform**
- **Tariff Preferences for Industrial Exports: The Moment of Triumph**
- **The New Delhi Conference: 1968 and After**

"An Economic Doctrine for the Developing Countries"

Writing in 1965, Philippe de Seynes, the elegant Frenchman who was undersecretary for economic and social affairs at the UN, claimed that "an economic doctrine for the developing countries is gradually evolving." It was not analytically unified, he noted, nor was it purely scientific in motivation.

> As always in the history of ideas, it is compounded of many different, and often disparate, fragments: the findings of an imposing mass of statistical and analytical studies, bold simplifications and extrapolations, as well as emotions, aspirations, and frustrations.

This "special ideology" was, he thought, a "prime prerequisite" for the developing countries to pursue successfully their economic objectives, while the establishment of UNCTAD to him represented "decisive progress" in that quest.[1] Yet it is possible to argue the opposite case. The distillation of a doctrine and an ideology from the intellectual stirrings of the previous fifteen years and its installation as the creed of an institution may have marked not the start but the ending of a period of progress. After that, previous ideas became solidified and few new ones succeeded them. With the benefit of hindsight, Prebisch's biographer Edgar Dosman and Prebisch's personal assistant the late David Pollock have claimed that the UNCTAD years were, for Prebisch, sterile in theoretical terms. He was, they argued, conscious of the intellectual vacuum in his work at UNCTAD.[2]

This was not obvious at the time to many in UNCTAD who worked with Prebisch, its first secretary-general. For them, the years 1964–1968 represented the high point of their UN careers. Paul Berthoud (former deputy secretary-general of UNCTAD) was Prebisch's special advisor at this time, and he later recalled:

> The most outstanding case [in the UN] of that motivation, and of a sense that we were together trying to build something, was UNCTAD. There is no question that in the 1960s, the spirit which motivated the group that worked at that attempt at changing the world was a sense of devotion which was very enhancing of the quality of relationships, and the quality of the work itself. . . . In UNCTAD, you had a collective sense of mission which I found more articulate there than I have at any other place in all of my career.[3]

Just as he had done in ECLA, Prebisch put his very considerable personal qualities into service to build up a genuine team effort within the organization, an effort that was centered on fulfilling UNCTAD's mission. His style of work gave the impression to his close aides of the greatest professional versatility. To some, he seemed to be able to be simultaneously a thinker, an administrator, a policy formulator, and a tireless proselytizer for his, and now also UNCTAD's, vision of a more equitable world.[4]

However, the more than a million miles that Prebisch, always an inveterate traveler, covered while championing "the cause" brought him rather few successes in terms of immediate impact on policy. At the end of his stewardship, he certainly did have several trophies of this kind to show—on international reserve creation, industrial tariff preferences, and the International Sugar Agreement of 1968. Yet they were small in relation to the G77's demands and the expectations that had been raised at UNCTAD I. He explained this wryly in terms of the ever-present motives for inertia: "When the [economic] weather is good, the imperative need for a long-range policy to help the peripheral countries is not felt. And when the weather is bad . . . well, it is not the right time for formulating such a policy."[5]

This explanation tends to place responsibility for inaction on the industrial countries, but were there other reasons besides the near-tautology of lack of political will in the West? Why was UNCTAD unable to catalyze the larger political-economic changes that it sought, despite Prebisch's obvious leadership skills? Was he perhaps handicapped also by the inertia of the G77? Was UNCTAD not the right kind of organization to advance the G77 agenda? Or was the agenda itself afflicted by internal contradictions?

This chapter will examine the contradictions of "an economic doctrine for the developing countries" as they evolved while UNCTAD was under Prebisch's leadership. They arose in part from the institutional setup that Prebisch had chosen as the instrument of his mission and in part from the policy objectives that were its core. We look first at the early difficulties of the new organization and then consider the complicated position of the secretariat as it tried to be impartial but not neutral with regard to the demands of the developing countries. Then we turn to the core policy objectives that UNCTAD pursued. UNCTAD engaged with many issues, including shipping, economic cooperation between developing countries, and technology transfer.[6] All the same, the three central policy objectives of the organization, and the core of its economic doctrine, were commodity policy, supplementary finance, and industrial trade preferences for developing countries. These were the three policy areas that Prebisch repeatedly identified in his speeches as being interdependent. In particular, Prebisch asserted the unity of the UNCTAD program for commodities and supplementary finance:

> In the end, commodity agreements, the operations of the Fund [i.e., the IMF] and supplementary financial measures are complementary forms of operation, and the total volume of resources that the developing world needs to set its economy in order from the external point of view does not depend on any particular policy but on the magnitude of the fluctuation whose effects have to be corrected or countered.[7]

On commodities, this chapter will consider what economic specialists of the time thought about the technical difficulties inherent in setting up international commodity agreements (ICAs). The span of views will be illustrated from the record of the 1963 Bellagio conference and James Meade's proposal for price-compensation agreements. The professional pessimism about prospects of success in this field will be contrasted with the strategy for commodity policy followed by Prebisch as secretary-general, which by the time of UNCTAD II was to call for an "integrated commodity policy" to be embodied in a "general agreement on commodity arrangements." We will follow the rise and fall of the proposal, which the UK and Sweden had backed at UNCTAD I and the World Bank later put into draft form, for a supplementary-finance scheme. After a hopeful beginning, culminating in general agreement by April 1966, the impetus behind the scheme simply faded away. Much of the explanation for this lay in the erosion of solidarity within the G77 and the effect this had on the attitudes of the industrial countries.

Also in the area of international finance, the international gold-exchange system adopted at Bretton Woods came under strain in the 1960s, and UNCTAD hoped to enable the developing countries to influence the shape of anticipated reforms of the international monetary system. The chapter will explain the different ways in which the UN's concern to moderate commodity-price instability led it also to advocate plans for international monetary reform of a more or less ambitious character. While the radical idea of an international commodity-reserve currency made no progress, other ideas had somewhat greater impact on the trend of international policy. UNCTAD called for developing countries to have a voice in the creation of additional liquidity, which developed into the proposal for an "SDR link"—the allocation of extra international liquidity in a manner that provided additional financial assistance to developing countries.

It was on industrial trade preferences for developing countries that Prebisch scored his big political success. The incorporation of Part IV into the GATT articles in 1965 was a move by the developed countries to recognize and repair the deficiencies of the existing GATT rules that had been exposed by the Haberler report.[8] In particular, the new provisions in Part IV stated that developed countries did not expect reciprocity from developing countries in future trade negotiations. However, this was largely a rhetorical gesture by the industrial countries, because they did not recognize Part IV as containing contractual obligations. More was needed than a nonbinding agreement to waive reciprocity, and Prebisch proceeded to secure it. He won unanimous agreement at UNCTAD II on the early establishment of a mutually acceptable system of generalized, nonreciprocal, and nondiscriminatory preferences. The principle that countries could depart from most-favored-nation treatment for the exports of developing countries was finally embodied in the GATT "enabling clause" of 1979.[9] This was a real achievement to the credit of Prebisch.

UNCTAD's Early Organizational Difficulties

UNCTAD became a permanent organ of the UN General Assembly on 30 December 1964 (under General Assembly resolution 1995 [XIX]).[10] Its permanent secretariat began work the next month, and a year later it was decided to locate its permanent headquarters at Geneva and a liaison office in New York.[11] To direct the conference when it was not in session, resolution 1995 (XIX) established a Trade and Development Board of fifty-five members elected by the conference from among its membership.[12] This machinery failed to run smoothly, and the UNCTAD secretariat began to worry about its shortcomings. The meetings schedule was excessively heavy, and things became even worse as working parties and expert groups began to multiply. The level of representation that governments were prepared to provide quickly began to fall.[13] In January 1966, Prebisch complained about "the proliferation of the Board's meetings" and warned: "We are reaching the point where it will be physically impossible to service so many meetings."[14] In November 1966, he expostulated: "I find the same concern.... Yet despite this general conviction ... the number of meetings continues to increase." By this point, almost 60 percent of UNCTAD's budget was spent on meetings.[15] Some of this public wringing of hands may have been intended to bolster UNCTAD's image with the developed countries, but the proliferation was real enough.[16] Prebisch alone seemed able to maintain his powers of concentration through long and tedious meetings in which a succession of low-level diplomats read poorly prepared statements.[17]

Part of the explanation for the emerging diplomatic congestion was the adoption of the group system of negotiating that had been foreshadowed by the G77's caucusing at UNCTAD I. Within UNCTAD, countries joined groups: Group A, the developing countries; Group B, the industrial countries; and Group D, the state trading countries.[18] Countries first negotiated common group platforms and then the groups negotiated with each other.[19] The Swiss ambassador, when chairing the Trade and Development Board, characterized voting by groups as the "polarizing ritual of group negotiating leading to the decay of the collective debate."[20] Even though the G77 had already opted to present a united front, and the Group D countries were in any event primed to follow the policy lead of the Soviet Union, the adoption of group voting constantly reinforced the atmosphere of confrontation between rich and poor states and militated against the evolution of cross-linkages or new groupings with new agendas. It also was immensely time consuming. Some "broker states," such as the Nordic countries, were active in trying to resolve disagreements.[21]

By 1972, Branislav Gosovic, who had spoken to many of the key participants, painted an alarming picture of the practical problems the organization faced. It had proved politically impossible to appoint a deputy secretary-general (a post to which Prebisch had originally intended for the intense, chain-smoking Wladek Malinowski, who became instead director of the Division for Invisibles). The situation was made less manageable by the absence of a deputy and by Prebisch's own frequent missions in New York and at ECLA—where he remained director of the Latin American Institute for Economic and Social Planning (ILPES)—and by his unwillingness to delegate authority. Insistent on being informed of all developments, he found himself overloaded with work and without clearly established priorities.[22]

Nevertheless, he stood out, in Western eyes at least, as almost the sole dynamic figure. One British Board of Trade official complained haughtily: "It is, of course, one of the real weaknesses of UNCTAD that there is virtually no-one but Prebisch of any significant calibre in the Secretariat; one becomes almost grateful for Malinowski."[23] Recruitment was based on technical specialization, and if it was hard enough to find appropriate specialists, it was doubly so given the decision also to apply geographical quotas to recruitment. For example, it was virtually impossible to find shipping and insurance experts in developing countries to staff Malinowski's division. During its somewhat disorganized and hectic initial period, therefore, the secretariat had to rely extensively on the services of consultants. Thus, an important issue in the intellectual history of the organization was the way in which the consultants related to the UNCTAD mission and what intellectual input they brought. Jacob Mosak's view of consultants was clear enough. He did not want to hire any consultants who would advise in their own names; he wanted a consultant to act "purely as a supplier of a paper which the Secretariat would (as he sees it) be free to change at will."[24] Not surprisingly, there was some resistance from economists of the caliber of Nicholas Kaldor and J. K. Galbraith to their work being used in this fashion. Nevertheless, a highly instrumental approach to consultancy was maintained in UNCTAD.[25] This helped to close off one potential source of intellectual renewal.

Notwithstanding all these problems, one major benefit for the dissemination of UNCTAD's message arose from the way the organization had been structured. Against the wishes of many developing countries, UNCTAD had not been constituted as a specialized agency of the UN. It remained a unit within the UN Secretariat. This direct link to the General Assembly through the reports of the UN Secretary-General provided an excellent mechanism to raise the profile of the interdependence of trade, finance, and development. Ironically, it would have been much more difficult to mainstream this issue if specialized agency status had been agreed upon instead. This was a prime political advantage that Prebisch instinctively grasped.[26] At the same time, it raised the stakes. Failure, as well as success, would henceforth be highly visible and the Secretary-General of UNCTAD would be very exposed to the course of events.

The Secretariat: Impartial But Not Neutral

In a more multipolar arena, the question of bureaucratic neutrality might have lain reasonably dormant, but the existence of fixed groups and the ritual dance of polarization soon brought to the very forefront a question: Whose side is the secretariat on? How did the idea of the UNCTAD mission square with the traditional view of an objective international civil service? The industrial countries were suspicious that the two did not square and could not be squared. Seizing on the idea that UNCTAD was the guardian of "an eco-nomic doctrine for developing countries," one U.S. commentator went so far as to describe the body of UNCTAD officials as a "sectariat."[27] He argued that the concept of international officials working objectively in the interest of all member countries had been replaced by a concept of official advocacy on behalf of a particular group of countries.[28] The establishment of UNCTAD went beyond that of having a group on defiant bureaucrats in the UN: it was nothing less than the attempt to institutionalize defiant bureaucracy.

Even if the possibility of a truly "objective" international bureaucracy in the Weberian mold was a Western myth, it was certainly the case (as was seen in the last chapter) that Prebisch envisaged UNCTAD not as "a passive agency" but as "an activist body," "an instrument of change," and "a fighting institu-tion."[29] According to Gosovic, he gladly confessed his "bias" for development and insisted that "one could not be impartial when he saw a child beaten by an older man."[30] However, Prebisch also publicly sought to justify the secre-tariat by insisting that it was possible for it to be at the same time committed and impartial. He was once accused at a press conference of using the secre-tariat to assist the developing-country group. He replied:

> By definition of my mandate, I am looking for arrangements which will favor the position of the developing countries. This is what the mandate of UNCTAD is about. Now, I have to be impartial towards all parties in the United Nations community, and we are striving to be impartial at all times. But as for neutral-ity, we are not more neutral to development than WHO [World Health Orga-nization] is neutral to malaria.[31]

The stance that it was possible for officials to be both impartial and nonneutral was difficult for them to maintain. They were expected to be policy advocates (on behalf of developing countries) one day, then on the next to administer a forum in which no argument was granted a more favorable treat-ment than any other. The most critical area of difficulty was research. When research was being commissioned or produced, how were nonneutrality and impartiality supposed to be combined? The potential for confusion of roles in the secretariat was increased because the industrial countries themselves behaved in an inconsistent way on the matter. They both resented the exist-ence of a "sectariat" and pressed UNCTAD officials to give the developing countries disproportionate support. In 1965, for example, representatives of the U.S., the UK, the IMF, and the IBRD indicated to Sidney Dell their great disappointment at the level of developing-country representation at UNCTAD meetings. A representative of the OECD then suggested that the secretariat should help the developing-country delegations in preparing their positions.

Dell (who might well have felt perplexed at this juncture) responded that it had been severely criticized by Western delegations for having done exactly that at the Geneva conference: "[I]t was a matter for careful judgment as to where one drew the line between legitimate assistance to delegations in working out their own policies, and actions which would amount to taking sides in a controversy."[32]

Nevertheless, certain forms of positive discrimination by the secretariat in favor of the developing-country group did become institutionalized. The most visible was that in advance of each session of the conference, the secretariat would organize and service a preparatory meeting and a conference for the G77 countries in which they could negotiate their group platform. The argument for doing so was that the Group B countries made their preparations in Paris with the assistance of the OECD secretariat and the Group D countries did so in Moscow with the Council for Mutual Economic Cooperation (COMECON) secretariat, but the developing countries had no equivalent source of help. The developing countries argued that without help from the UNCTAD secretariat, they would experience "an unequal dialogue."[33] So on these occasions, the secretariat helped the G77 to prepare its case.

The attempt to remain nonneutral but impartial was based on a logical muddle. Prebisch's comparison of UNCTAD's situation with that of the WHO's commitment to the eradication of malaria was flawed. UNCTAD received from the General Assembly a series of specific mandates, not one blanket mandate to promote "development." Even if it had had a mandate to promote "development," the economic doctrine of the developing countries was that their interests were in conflict with the interests of industrial countries. Therefore, there could scarcely exist a well-defined common interest of "development," similar to disease eradication, which UNCTAD could have implemented impartially. Sidney Dell later defended the attempt with various arguments—that it was consistent with U Thant's view of the UN Charter and that it was in the developed countries' own interests that developing countries should be helped to articulate theirs. He also acknowledged that the dual role was a difficult and delicate one that risked damaging the UNCTAD secretariat's credibility.[34]

In operating the secretariat's dual role, research posed a particular problem. How far should the obvious difficulties in the path of policies to support developing countries' interests be revealed? How far should they be obscured from view, lest their acknowledgment should damage UNCTAD's mission? Once the secretariat had become politically engaged, how could it any longer refrain from believing, and acting on, its own politically opportune analyses and assessments? In no policy area was this danger more threatening than in the highly analytically complex field of commodities.

Interpreting Past International Commodity Regulation

The strongest influences on UNCTAD's commodity policy were not technical analyses of the economics of commodity regulation but nuggets of apparently practical wisdom from the past. They derived from internally accepted interpretations of two key historical episodes. The first was the operation of international regulation schemes for trade in sugar, wheat, rubber, tin, and tea during the 1930s. The second was the inclusion of a chapter on international commodity agreements in the abortive Havana Charter of 1947–1948. Proponents of international commodity regulation used the schemes of the 1930s to argue that it must be possible to devise appropriate forms of intervention in commodity markets, despite all the technical objections of economists. They took Chapter VI of the Havana Charter as de facto international recognition of the legitimacy of new schemes of regulation. In both respects, these interpretations were controversial.

Of the five major commodity-regulation schemes of the 1930s, two—for sugar and wheat—were failures. The other three—for tea, rubber, and tin—were indeed effective. Their success, however, depended heavily on the particular circumstance that the bulk of their production was concentrated within the boundaries of the British, Dutch, and French colonial empires, as indeed was much of their consumption. Their negotiation was a deal done between two or three sets of colonial masters in the interests of their overseas investors—and certainly not in the interests of the small-scale indigenous producers of the colonies.[35] By 1964, these conditions no longer applied. European colonialism was swiftly passing from the scene and with it went the ability to override conflicts of producer and consumer interests. This had transformed the politics of international commodity regulation by 1964. From then on, newly independent countries were in effect seeking to resurrect a colonial device in order to protect their interests in a postcolonial world.

The commodities chapter of the Havana Charter had clearly indicated the direction in which the postcolonial world would move. Far from being a general endorsement of the principle of international commodity regulation, it was an attempt to confine it as tightly as possible by setting up extremely stringent criteria for its legitimate use. What the charter legitimized were "international commodity agreements" (ICAs). ICAs had to be treaties between producing and consuming countries, there had to be prior agreement between them that an "emergency" existed that could not be corrected by market forces, producers and consumers had to have equal representation in the mechanisms of control, and any given ICA should last for only five years in the first instance. Compliance with these conditions would have outlawed most of the previous schemes of international commodity regulation. Even with all these limitations, however, the permitted derogation from free trade was too much for some U.S. business organizations to stomach, and in the face of divided business opinion the U.S. administration did not attempt to ratify the charter.[36]

In March 1947, ECOSOC had established the Interim Coordinating Committee for International Commodity Arrangements (ICCICA), whose function was to monitor the work of individual commodity-study groups and make recommendations on the calling of UN commodity conferences. Following on from the study on *Relative Prices* (1949), the DEA produced an extensive statistical study of the fluctuations in the export prices of primary commodities in developing countries.[37] Then in 1954, ECOSOC set up the Commission on International Commodity Trade (CICT) with a remit to examine measures to limit commodity-price fluctuation and, after 1958, the effects of terms of trade movements on developing countries. The CICT noted in 1961 that the terms of trade of primary commodity producers had declined to their lowest level since 1950 and began to study both measures for short-term compensatory finance and remedies for long-term terms-of-trade declines.[38]

These concerns went wider than the UN. Independent academic studies confirmed the terms-of-trade decline of primary commodities in the 1950s.[39] As touched upon earlier, in 1957, GATT commissioned a report from a group of four economists headed by Gottfried Haberler. It concluded that since the end of 1955, commodity prices had declined overall by 5 percent, while industrial prices had risen by 6 percent. The loss of income this caused the primary commodity–producing countries probably exceeded the total amount of foreign economic aid that they were receiving. The report's main theme was the need to stabilize the earnings of the raw material–producing countries for the products they were exporting and to open markets so that they could sell more of these products.[40] It specifically advocated the provision of funds for buffer-stock schemes to moderate price fluctuations for commodities (although it is significant that it conceded that "there are real practical difficulties in this field").[41] In many respects (and rather surprisingly, given Haberler's criticism of the Prebisch-Singer thesis the following year), the report's recommendations prefigured key themes of Prebisch's report to UNCTAD in 1964. Nevertheless, it was one of many such reports at that time, and its influence is disputed.[42] Yet the fact that the new Part IV of the GATT entered into force as early as June 1966 suggests that the report was influential in driving forward the developed countries' attempts to maintain the relevance of GATT.

The criteria in Chapter VI of the ITO Charter, which was aborted in the end, would have raised major new obstacles to the setting up of more ICAs.

Not surprisingly, negotiations for an ICA were successful for only one additional commodity in the entire period between the signing of the Havana Charter and the start of UNCTAD in 1964. It was for coffee, and the role of the United States was crucial. In the 1950s, the U.S. had resolutely opposed an international coffee agreement.[43] In 1958, the U.S. decided "as an exception to policy" to agree to discuss an international coffee agreement if this issue were raised by other countries.[44] The International Coffee Agreement of 1963 came about only because the U.S. saw it "as a way of improving our relations with a number of key Latin American countries (particularly Brazil, Colombia and Central America)" and as an instrument of foreign policy complementary to the Alliance for Progress.[45] This goal was urgent enough to override its longstanding aversion to such interventionist schemes. Nevertheless, the coffee agreement quickly ran into disagreements between producers and consumers on the level and distribution of export quotas.[46]

At Bellagio in 1963, a handpicked group of economists met to suggest policies for UNCTAD I. They explored the practical difficulties of interventions in the international commodities markets. The participants hardly formed a representative sample of economic opinion, because their presence there indicated some prior sympathy with the aspirations of the developing countries for more development-friendly forms of trade and finance. What is striking about their discussion of commodity-market intervention schemes is the considerable skepticism that was expressed about any scheme that tried to increase prices above the market trend. Some felt that price support by export restrictions would be harmful because they would encourage higher production by those outside the scheme and the development of synthetics and other substitutes. Others, while not opposed to price support in principle, emphasized the practical difficulties. They noted the example of the new International Coffee Agreement but saw that it depended on the cooperation of major consuming countries (the U.S. in the case of coffee), something that was rarely forthcoming. If consumers would cooperate, the best solution to the problem of making commodities more remunerative would be to charge an import levy, the revenue from which would be returned to low-income primary commodity–producing countries. Enthusiasm for expanding the number of ICAs that raised commodity prices was wholly absent, while it was acknowledged that the political prerequisites for price-stabilization schemes were almost always lacking.[47]

In his contribution to the debate surrounding UNCTAD I, James Meade proposed the interesting idea of price-compensation agreements, essentially to separate the efficiency function of prices from their income-distribution consequences. All transactions would take place at world market prices, but falling commodity prices would trigger compensation payments from the consuming countries while rising commodity prices would trigger payments from the producing countries. The size of the payments could be set out on a sliding scale. This was a simplification of a device used in the pre–Second World War wheat agreements.[48] Meade pointed out the difficulties of buffer-stock schemes. The capital cost, and thus the financing cost, of buffer stocks increased with the storage requirements of the commodity and would be un-economic for many. They could not be used to raise the price above market levels (after the initial purchase of the stock). Even to reduce price fluctua-tions they required that their managers had "sufficient foresight and inde-pendence of action" to do so. A permanent difficulty of managing buffer stocks is to understand the trend of prices and refrain from operations inconsistent with that trend—especially when the trend is downward.[49]

The tenor of opinion among these broadly sympathetic economists was thus that intervention to try to maintain commodity prices above market level was ill advised. In the long term, it was likely to be unsustainable, and in any case it was politically inconsistent with the goal of gaining greater access to the markets of the industrial countries. If the problem was price fluctuation and not price support, it was better to compensate countries for price declines rather than undertake schemes to suppress them. Finally, the problems of com-modity trade went beyond price fluctuations, since supplies could fluctuate too, and it was the combination of price and quantity that determined income. After UNCTAD I, Kaldor reflected: "[C]ommodity price-stabilization by means of individual commodity agreements figured high on the agenda as one of the principal objectives, yet the lengthy discussions on the subject did not suc-ceed in producing any fresh idea as to how such agreements could be more effectively promoted."[50]

Shaping a Commodities Policy

Prebisch's initial views about commodity schemes were not doctrinaire, and he accepted that for many commodities, international agreements would be out of the question for one reason or another. Yet he wanted something to be done, and he began to galvanize interest in the issue, the tenor of his think-ing being that

> the whole commodity area needs re-examination, on a commodity-by-commodity basis, and fresh minds ought to be applied to see whether the pes-simism that has so often been expressed by the commodity technicians in the past is really justified in every case.[51]

His drive to make some progress was stimulated by events. After the Geneva conference in 1964, dispute continued about whether UNCTAD should be a forum of international negotiation. The industrial countries continued to maintain their position that UNCTAD was a deliberative body only and that all trade negotiation must take place in GATT. They saw UNCTAD as a body for a general exchange of views on commercial policies conducive to development, but they were not willing to accept it as a source of legal obligations.[52] When in 1965, following Recommendation A.V.1 of UNCTAD I, ECOSOC transferred to UNCTAD all its responsibilities for the negotiation of commodity agreements so that the ICCICA and the CICT were absorbed by the new organization, this triggered the industrial countries' decision in the OECD to drop their objection to UNCTAD as a negotiating forum.[53] When UNCTAD acquired this enhanced status in the area of commodity agreements, the secretariat had a stronger incentive to develop a strategy on the commodity issue.

In terms of the objectives of commodity agreements, the secretariat blended the aims of price stabilization and price support rather than keeping them rigorously apart. Alfred Maizels, the senior commodities economist, defined the underlying aims of UNCTAD policy as:

> to create those conditions in world commodity markets which would facilitate and promote the rate of economic development in the developing countries. *First,* there is the immediate, or short-term, necessity of achieving a reasonable degree of stability in the main commodity markets and, where possible and appropriate, of achieving that stability at a reasonably remunerative price for the producing countries. *Second,* the longer-term objective of expanding the volume of commodity exports from developing countries without, at the same time, hindering their diversification and modernization, or the growth of their processing and manufacturing industries.[54]

The notion of reasonably remunerative prices was one that would dog commodity negotiators for many years as they struggled to define it for the purpose of international agreements.

Prebisch's early inclination to follow a commodity-by-commodity approach was not the only possibility. The Geneva conference had adopted a recommendation in favor of developing an internationally agreed-upon general statement of principles of commodity policy. This idea was revived and reinforced by an initiative of Richard Kahn, who in early October 1965 offered to prepare a first draft of a general agreement on the principles of commodity trade.[55] This offer was accepted. However, the practical difficulties of getting agreement on principles for the commodities trade were illustrated at the first meeting of the Commodities Sub-Committee of the Trade and Development Board in July 1966. The industrial countries, led by the U.S. and the UK, who were supported by Sweden and West Germany, voiced their opposition to price support by disputing the use of the phrase "remunerative prices." They "repeatedly stressed the difficulties of attaining a practical definition of *remunerative prices*" unless it were taken to be the long-term equilibrium price. They also argued that the concept of "import purchasing power" should not be a determinant of international pricing policy because it confused international action on commodities with action that was the responsibility of countries. Furthermore, they refused to countenance any direct policy link associated with changes in the terms of trade. Finally, they stressed that each commodity was a unique case in itself, and hence no valid negotiable principles should be accepted for commodity trade overall.[56]

As the discussion of principles of commodity trade was dogged by disputed definitions that reflected larger policy differences, the pursuit of a commodity-by-commodity approach also ran into difficulties. Prebisch reported to Secretary-General U Thant in June 1966 that the sugar conference stood adjourned since September 1965, frustrated by superpower conflict over the fate of Cuban sugar. Meanwhile, the recently resumed cocoa conference was considering a draft, "the complexity [of which] arises partly from the desire to cope with all possible situations and in particular, to avoid the difficulties that have arisen in the coffee agreement."[57] Prebisch was "deeply distressed" by the collapse of the cocoa conference, given his belief that it was "sound from the point of view of economics and finance."[58] The failure to achieve an agreement was a serious setback, since cocoa was not the commodity that gave rise to the most difficult negotiating problems. The stumbling blocks were threefold. One was the minimum price; the U.S. was holding out for the lowest option. Another was whether or not the buffer stock would buy directly from the producers. A final difficulty was the question of how to finance the buffer stock when neither the U.S. nor the World Bank would provide funds.[59]

At the end of October 1966, a meeting was held to frame a policy on buffer stocks for the looming second UNCTAD conference. As well as Prebisch and Maizels, Pollock and Krishnamurti attended, along with representatives of the World Bank and the UN Food and Agriculture Organization (FAO). This meeting decided to separate price-stabilizing and price-raising objectives as much as possible, to use the buffer-stock method for the former, and to reserve other methods (such as production controls) for the latter. In terms of the tactics of public presentation, the meeting concluded that the paper for the conference should have an overall tone that was "as conservative as possible," stressing the aim of price stabilization in order to appeal to the interests of the consumers. At the same time, the conservative tone should not stand in the way of putting forward some new ideas on buffer stocks and a central fund mechanism.

Because of the need to acquire a stock, the recurrent costs of its storage and the vagaries of price movements in relation to the agreed-upon intervention prices, buffer stocks could not be expected to be necessarily self-financing and so each required some form of finance. This could be raised in various ways, including levies on producers. At this point, the idea of a central fund rather than separate financing arrangements for each commodity was not given a specific justification. However, the commodities document for UNCTAD II was outlined as follows:

> [I]n addition to examining specific market tendencies of individual commodities, [it] should also present the basic principles of a buffer stock; broad orders of financial magnitudes but no specific dollar requirement; the need to be prepared for entering into new commodity agreements; the establishment of a central fund (including its financial and operating functions); whether such a fund could form part of the IBRD supplementary financing scheme (perhaps as a separate department, since successful operation of a buffer should reduce the level of drawings on the latter scheme).[60]

Thus, by October 1966, despite the coolness of professional economic opinion, the UNCTAD secretariat had embraced the aim of price stabilization, using the method of an extended series of buffer stocks joined to the new concept of a central fund.

Supplementary Finance and International Monetary Reform

As early as 1953, a UN committee of experts had linked the issue of commodity-price stabilization with international monetary reform. An expert group of J. Goudriaan (South Africa, chair), Charles F. Carter (UK), Klaus Knorr (U.S.), Sumitro Djojohadikusumo (Indonesia), and Francisco Garcia Olano (Argentina), with Hans Singer acting as its secretary, concluded:

> If . . . governments wish to have an assurance of as much stability of price relations as is consistent with economic change and progress, . . . they must look beyond schemes relating to individual commodities and review the general structure of the world's monetary systems.[61]

They proposed a variant of a scheme that had been advocated in the 1930s and 1940s by Goudriaan, Benjamin Graham, F. A. Hayek, and others. Its method was to monetize a representative basket of commodities to serve alongside gold as a backing for an international reserve currency. In 1963, Kaldor again revived this ambitious idea with a proposal for an international currency backed by warehouse certificates of selected primary commodities (80 percent) and precious metals (20 percent). He saw this as superior to the expedients that were being adopted at the time to shore up the gold-exchange standard, as the fixed price of gold in terms of dollars was coming under increasing stress. He asked Sidney Dell for his reaction to this "gadget" in late March 1963, but Dell was highly skeptical that it would have any appeal either for the industrial countries or for individual producer countries.[62] Kaldor nevertheless wrote it up in December 1963 with Albert Hart (Columbia University) who had been thinking on similar lines, and Jan Tinbergen agreed to add his signature.[63] The document was submitted as a background paper to UNCTAD I.

Kaldor justified his persistence in terms of the desirability of schemes of international monetary reform that would provide a widely diffused benefit to the world economy that was greater than would be provided even by a geographically well-diffused set of gold discoveries. He described it as "the one method of generating [economic] expansion through 'favourable' balance of payments situations," "one that does not require anyone to get into debt as a counterpart to the creation of added reserves." Hayek's earlier enthusiasm for it had been based on the fact that it represented an improved version of the gold standard, one in which the supply of international money would no longer be distorted by the vicissitudes of gold production.[64] An improved gold standard, however, made no provision for adjustment when individual countries' wage costs ran ahead of their labor productivity, except by the deliberate creation of unemployment. Any international monetary system with that feature would soon be abandoned, Keynes had replied to Hayek at the time. Kaldor now argued that a system could be devised in which individual countries would be free to deal with adjustment needs by devaluing their currencies in relation to the international commodity-reserve currency. He remained confident of its ultimate acceptance while recognizing the impossibility that "the central banker of the main industrial countries would be prepared to give serious consideration to a plan of this kind at the present time."[65]

It was the same strong sense that a commodity-reserve currency was simply "not now within the reach of practical politics" which had led Olano to propose an alternative "mutual insurance scheme" of compensation for adverse changes in the terms of trade to his colleagues on the 1953 expert group.[66] By 1959, the UN Commission on International Commodity Trade (CICT) had begun to prod the International Monetary Fund on the adequacy of its policies to assist countries experiencing fluctuations in their export receipts. The fund had been reluctant to do anything outside its normal operations, but eventually its board was persuaded to concede the creation of a dedicated counter-fluctuation facility.[67] Following a suggestion made in 1962 by the CICT, a new IMF scheme, the Compensatory Financing Facility, was instituted in February 1963.[68] It provided for quasi-automatic, and therefore rapidly disbursing, short-term loans for countries suffering declines in export earnings.

A facility such as this had the great advantage, from the viewpoint of the individual producer country, over schemes to compensate price falls because it operated when quantities of exports fell as well as when their prices fell. Yet it did not initially prove attractive to developing countries and was little called upon in its first decade.[69]

The new facility could be faulted on two grounds. Since it did not reduce actual price fluctuations but only temporarily compensated for price downturns (if they were not offset by quantity increases), it did nothing about the problem of underinvestment and overinvestment induced by erroneous future price expectations. This pointed back to schemes such as buffer stocks that could actually moderate price cycles. More significant in political terms was the point that this assistance was short-term only. Sometimes export earnings of developing countries underwent protracted declines, disrupting their development plans: to prevent this, short-term finance was inadequate. Before UNCTAD I, this criticism had been voiced, and Prebisch wrote to the World Bank on 17 July 1963 to ascertain its attitude toward a supplementary scheme.[70] George Woods, its new president, took a favorable line at the UNCTAD I opening session. The UK and Sweden supported the idea, and the final act of the conference invited the bank to draft a scheme, for further study, to meet the longer-term needs of countries facing export shortfalls. Prebisch called this "a very important move in the right direction." He saw the commodity issue and international monetary reform as deeply intertwined in the spirit of Keynes, who "had the stabilization problem very much in mind when he put forward his world monetary scheme."[71]

The bank issued its report in December 1965.[72] It accepted the need for a steady flow of external resources in support of a country's development plan and thus for additional funds to be available in the event of an unexpected shortfall in export revenues. At the same time, the report recommended that there should be an "understanding" on initial expectations and a procedure to assess "the extent to which agreed criteria of performance were currently being fulfilled."[73] An extraordinary meeting of the UNCTAD Committee on Invisibles and Finance Related to Trade (CIFT) was called for April 1966, at which agreement in principle was reached and final details were remitted to a technical group. By July, however, Prebisch, while not contesting the principle of conditionality, was raising the question of who should undertake the performance assessment. He suggested that this was a task for an impartial group of experts, since the developing countries were unlikely to be comfortable with the idea of the creditor institutions taking the assessment role themselves.[74] Negotiations continued both with the bank and with major donors, but Prebisch never succeeded in pressing them to completion—and neither did his successors.[75]

The spring of 1966 was the high point of hope in relation to supplementary finance. During the rest of that year, the solidarity of the G77 began to unravel. There was a general feeling among the developing countries that UNCTAD was not making much progress. Moreover, there was a particular tension around high-level secretariat appointments at UNCTAD. African representatives claimed that Africans were being excluded from the director positions in the secretariat. In 1965, Prebisch thought that he had identified two adequate candidates, but U Thant ruled them out because they were from Nigeria and Ghana, two countries whose nationals were already overrepresented. Prebisch was then accused of favoring Latin American nationals.[76] In the face of a divided G77, the industrial countries were in no hurry to press on with the supplementary finance scheme.

At UNCTAD I, notwithstanding the U.S. wish to avoid any action by the conference on international monetary reform, the Third Committee passed a recommendation calling for further study of measures related to the complementary credit system of the IMF.[77] Following this recommendation, a new expert group was convened "to study the international monetary issues relating to problems of trade and development." The basic purpose of the conference recommendation was to consider how the developing countries would be affected by nascent plans of the Group of Ten (G10) industrial countries to create additional liquidity.[78] The group, chaired by Gamani Corea, included Richard Kahn, Tibor Scitovsky, Trevor Swan, Pierre Sanner (French African Bank), M. Beheiry (governor, African Development Bank), Dias Carneiro (Brazil), and Rodrigo Gomez (governor, Bank of Mexico), among others.[79] Kaldor approved the choice of experts but thought that their subject was "completely hopeless (from the point of view of getting anywhere)."[80]

Prebisch highlighted the main points for consideration in the following terms:

a) The nature of the liquidity problem of developing countries, and possible methods of dealing with it.

b) The possibility of creating a link between the solution of the world liquidity problem and the bridging of the trade gap of developing countries.

c) The possibility of payments arrangements for developing countries that might facilitate the liberalization of their trade with one another.[81]

The experts established that the developing countries did have a need for additional unconditional liquidity, not merely a need for additional aid. Prebisch campaigned on two propositions that came out of the experts' report. The first was the basic procedural issue that the G10 countries should not simply make changes in the international monetary system on their own when such changes would have consequences for others. He demanded the participation of the developing countries, together with the developed countries, in the creation of additional reserves. The second was the substance of the matter; he wanted the allocation of any new monetary reserve units to be on a universal basis and not confined to the G10. On these points, UNCTAD was actually supporting the position of the management of the IMF against that of the G10. The G10 eventually gave way in August 1966. The UNCTAD-sponsored experts' report, along with a similar one from CIAP, does seem to have had an impact in forcing the Group of Ten to retreat and to agree that the new form of liquidity (the special drawing right, or SDR) would be created through the IMF on a universal basis.[82] When the outline scheme for SDR creation was presented in September 1967, the developing-country members were able to support it. On this issue, Kaldor had been too pessimistic. That was the good news. The bad news was that the issue of SDR creation now became competitive with the earlier scheme for supplementary finance.

Tariff Preferences for Industrial Exports: The Moment of Triumph

The Haberler report of 1958 attributed the fact that developing countries' exports were growing more slowly than world trade principally to the trade policies of the industrial countries. This finding made an impact on Western government perceptions. The *New York Times* reported that "[s]ome high British officials who read the [Haberler] report and conferred with representatives of under-developed Commonwealth nations . . . have become convinced that the only solution for the problems of these nations is vastly increased exports to industrial countries. The officials believe that economic aid can never be sufficient to start them toward development."[83] Thus, despite some recommendations that were uncomfortable for the developed countries, the overall message that trade was more important than aid could be welcomed by Western powers that were ever eager to get developing countries "off the tit," in Joseph Coppock's memorable phrase.[84] When a follow-up report by the GATT secretariat confirmed that the tariff levels and structures of industrial countries were indeed adverse for the trade prospects of developing countries' industrial exports and the GATT Ministerial Council held in May 1963 could only respond with a few empty gestures, the stage was set for the issue to be taken up in UNCTAD I.[85]

There, the G77 developing countries maintained a united front in favor of temporary preferences for their industrial exports in developed-country markets. They argued for them both on infant-industry and on economies-of-scale grounds. They managed to have adopted at UNCTAD I General Principle Eight (contained in Recommendation A.1.1) that developed countries should give preferential concession to developing countries without requiring any concession in return. Prebisch, anxious to avoid the repetition of the Latin American industrialization experience in African and Asian countries, saw trade preferences as a way to do so:

> Let us build in the world a framework in which these small countries could start their process of industrialization in an outward-looking way and not in an inward-looking way as we did in Latin America, because if they repeat the same experience as in Latin America, in 30 years they will have tremendously difficult problems.[86]

He argued that developing countries should be prepared to participate in a world movement toward freer trade in two stages. First, developing countries should apply this policy between themselves by setting up customs unions, free trade areas, or other similar arrangements. Second, this policy would help prepare developing countries for the eventual reduction of their trade barriers to imports from industrialized countries. This, however, would take time: first the trade gap had to be filled through increased exports of commodities and manufactures and by increased trade between developing countries.[87]

Prebisch tried hard to animate developing countries to undertake stage one, the setting up of regional free trade arrangements among themselves, but made little progress. He realized that while developing countries failed to take any action to remove trade barriers between themselves, this weakened his case for demanding preferences from the industrial countries.[88] If actions were not forthcoming, however, he grasped at statements of intent for action. He wrote to A. M. El-Banna, secretary-general of the Council of Arab Economic Unity, in November 1966, pleading for this limited cooperation:

> In my view, if it were possible for the developing countries to announce at the Second Conference concrete action programmes for expanding trade among themselves in the framework of their choice, in which they would, for instance, state aims for negotiations among themselves that they intend to implement between the Second and Third conferences, UNCTAD's persuasive efforts directed at the public opinion in the developed countries would be greatly facilitated. Our efforts to obtain an increase in development aid would be easier if we can point to the fact that developing countries are committing themselves to collective self-help efforts that they would implement parallel to the recommendations addressed to the developed countries. For this reason the formulation of such "action programmes" could have considerable political importance in our efforts to fulfill the objectives of UNCTAD.[89]

Since increased aid clearly had to be kept on the agenda, Prebisch and his colleagues emphasized that trade was not an alternative to aid but, at least in the short term, its complement. "It is not a matter of trade versus aid or aid versus trade, but of trade *and* aid with this qualification: one to supplant the other[,] trade as a basic, permanent solution, and aid as a temporary expedient." Support for the Kennedy Round in GATT had to go hand in hand with the recognition that trade took place in a world of unequal development and that developing countries needed a special and additional reduction of trade barriers to their manufactured exports.[90]

The industrial countries were still in disarray in their response to the demand for industrial trade preferences. The British were willing to extend existing Commonwealth preferences to all developing countries, the EEC—under French influence—wanted to safeguard the existing preferences of its African associates, and the U.S. was opposed to granting preferences altogether. For a while in the mid-1960s, Prebisch was very concerned that the U.S., attempting to strengthen its alliance against Castro's Cuba, might accede to Latin American requests "for a preferential system to be exclusive to Latin American countries."[91] Such a development would have gravely damaged the solidarity of the G77, and Prebisch repeatedly spoke out against it. It is not clear how seriously the U.S. was tempted to try such a divisive maneuver.

The U.S. administration was aware, however, that it needed to end its isolation in one way or another. In April 1967, at Punta del Este, President Johnson announced that he would explore with other industrial countries the possibility of a policy of preferences in favor of the developing countries, not just Latin American countries. Work then began in the OECD to develop the principles of a Generalized System of Preferences (GSP) for exports of manufactures and semi-manufactures. Prebisch saw this as an event of "paramount importance."[92] He welcomed it as "a departure from the extremely dangerous tendency to establish vertical preferential systems in the world at the expense of multilateralism and non-discrimination." By July 1967, sufficient progress had occurred in the discussions of the UNCTAD Group on Preferences for a quiet confidence to have grown that "a specific solution may be presented to the forthcoming New Delhi Conference [UNCTAD II]."[93] As it turned out, a specific solution could not be agreed upon, but UNCTAD II did adopt resolution 21 (II), which recognized "the unanimous agreement in favour of the early establishment of a mutually acceptable system of generalized, non-reciprocal and non-discriminatory preferences." It was a remarkable achievement to have reached agreement on the principle of the GSP, and it stood out in the otherwise barren landscape of the second conference.

The New Delhi Conference: 1968 and After

The final act of UNCTAD I had provided that the second session should be held early in 1966.[94] In fact, it took place between 1 February and 29 March 1968 in New Delhi. In the four years since the initial session, the political atmosphere had changed. The industrial countries had recovered from the collective fright induced by the emergence of the Group of 77, notwithstanding the occasional burst of rhetorical grapeshot from the UNCTAD secretary-general about "inflammable materials" and "conflagration" on the periphery.[95] They had also begun to mend their initial disunity. Inside the UNCTAD secretariat, one wit suggested that "the best way for UNCTAD to ensure positive results by the Second Conference might have been for developing countries to engineer at least one revolution per month."[96] Prebisch, the extraordinary dominating presence of the first conference, now seemed more burdened with problems and lacking in verve and force. One diplomatic observer doubted that he would be the master of UNCTAD II.[97]

At the same time as the OECD countries had become more self-confident, the G77 had become more intransigent. They had never been wholly clear about the status of the decisions that emerged from the Trade and Development Board and other UNCTAD bodies and continually raised the issue of their implementation. Meanwhile, the industrial countries gave the impression that implementation had taken place while resisting closer evaluation of their actions by reference to various legal points. These tactics had produced not only frustrations in the G77 but also the beginnings of disillusionment among them with the entire UNCTAD enterprise. These feelings underlay the Algiers Charter, which they adopted on 3 November 1967 at the end of their preparatory meeting for UNCTAD II. The charter has been described as the summation of all the grievances of the countries of the South against the industrial countries.[98]

Overloaded with work, Prebisch produced his report for the second conference only at the last minute, so there was not sufficient time for governments to consider it before the meeting started.[99] The report was entitled *Towards a Global Strategy for Development*. It emphasized the need for converging changes in both developed and developing countries.[100] Unfortunately, five weeks into the conference, there were few signs of convergence, and Prebisch announced that it was "on the verge of failure." He repeated a key theme in his report: "I do not see any real possibility of accelerating the rate of growth of developing countries without fundamental reforms in their economic and social structures and attitudes and without discipline in their development planning." Prebisch concluded his intervention with a pair of rhetorical questions:

> Will UNCTAD continue to be a mechanism absorbing aspirations and pro-
> ducing frustrations? Or will it become an effective organ of the United Nations
> which not only acts as a forum for debate, but also as a practical instrument of
> action?[101]

When conference II was over, the world's press in both developed and developing countries wrote it off as a failure. Sidney Dell explained the failure in
terms of a misreading by the industrial countries of the G77's intentions:

> The last thing that the Group of 77 wanted was a confrontation; and although
> the Charter of Algiers has been presented as an over ambitious document, it
> was never intended as anything more than a starting point for discussion. The
> 77 were more than ready for accommodation if they encountered flexibility on
> the other side, and their positions froze in terms of the Charter only when they
> discovered that the position of the other side was frozen also.[102]

The debacle of UNCTAD II was in truth more than a failure of diplomacy,
a fumble between two groups minded to converge but unable to manage it.
Rather it was an early indication of the additional antagonism and multiplied
misunderstanding between North and South that were to characterize the
struggle for a New International Economic Order over the coming decade.

As early as 1960, Prebisch had been considering retiring in order to write
books.[103] Toward the end of November 1968, Prebisch suddenly decided to
resign. This was especially surprising since a short time previously he had
accepted a new contract from U Thant. His closest associates were unsure
what finally prompted him to go. Dell ruled out despair or disillusionment
because he had only just brought off a big coup, the successful negotiation of
a new International Sugar Agreement.[104] Personal factors seem to have been
important. His marriage was in difficulty, and Adelita, his wife, had not returned to Geneva after her latest trip to Santiago. His poor health also seems
to have contributed to his decision: he was suffering greatly from arthritis in
his legs and his doctors had advised that the Geneva climate was bad for him.
Professionally, his star at UNCTAD had waned in the two previous years, and
he had been criticized from many quarters. That had hurt his pride, so he
took up the offer of Felipe Herrera, president of the Inter-American Development Bank, to play a leading role once again in Latin American affairs.[105]

The fact that Prebisch had had some limited successes in advancing the
core objectives of UNCTAD's program may have helped to disguise the pre-
cariousness of the organization's future prospects. Prebisch's departure deprived the UNCTAD secretariat of the active leadership and the ability to
promote key policy objectives that had typified his time there.[106] Although
new issues and activities were later added to the UNCTAD policy portfolio,

the central strategy had already begun to solidify around three demands: an expanded set of international commodity agreements that were centrally financed, the pursuit of an SDR link to development finance, and the implementation of the GSP. By now, the secretariat had committed itself not just to an economic doctrine that defined the problems of developing countries but also to a corporate belief in the efficacy of particular schemes as solutions to those problems.

Moreover, the international scene of North-South relations was turning stormy, stirred by the U.S. huge military buildup in Vietnam. As the New Delhi conference showed, the G77 was becoming more fretful and demanding, while as yet there was no indication that the industrial countries had lost any of their willingness or ability to procrastinate in international economic negotiations. It was far from clear how far UNCTAD would be able to move ahead with its policy objectives in this new and more difficult environment. It was even less clear, now that Prebisch was gone, what the future would do to his aspiration that the UNCTAD secretariat should be "intellectually independent."

10

World Monetary Problems and the Challenge of Commodities

- **A World Turned Upside Down**
- **All Quiet on the Commodities Front**
- **Pérez-Guerrero in Pursuit of the SDR-Aid Link**
- **A Secretariat for the Group of 77?**
- **Gamani Corea Seizes the Initiative**
- **The Contradictions of UNCTAD IV**
- **The Negotiation of the Common Fund, 1976–1980**
- **Political versus Research-Based Negotiation**

A World Turned Upside Down

After 1968, the world political and economic situation began to undergo profound changes that weakened the international power and prestige of the OECD countries. Student unrest, which had started on the U.S. West coast, spread across to Europe. The Paris events of May 1968, when students momentarily allied with workers, sparked a continuing student protest movement that was partly inspired by Mao Tse-dong's Cultural Revolution in China. The new social and political radicalism among the rising generation in the West seemed to portend larger-scale changes, and it made the tasks of governments more difficult. At this time, the industrial countries were suffering from a poor quality of political leadership; their weak governments were all at sea when the traditional levers of power no longer produced their expected effects. This was the era of the sudden departure of de Gaulle, the forced resignation of the disgraced Nixon, and the maladroit Heath's provocation of his own electoral defeat at the hands of the British coal miners.

Despite the great upheaval of the Cultural Revolution, the U.S. took dramatic steps toward restoring normal diplomatic relations with China after more than twenty years of refusing to deal with its communist government.

Though hailed by some as a geopolitical masterstroke, it could not hide the fact that the U.S. was undergoing a military humiliation at the hands of a small Third World country—Vietnam. When final defeat arrived with the fall of Saigon in April 1975, it sent a message to the world that immense techno- logical superiority could not guarantee victory against a dedicated peasant army when supported by the local population. There were limits, even for a superpower.

Economically, the collapse of the Bretton Woods system marked the end of the West's "golden age" of postwar prosperity. The twin evils of unemploy- ment and inflation, in the theoretically unexpected combination of "stagflation," beset the developed-market economies and were passed on to the developing countries in the form of falling demand for their exports and higher prices for their imports The developing countries and the intellectual champions of their interests responded with a new spirit of militancy. Partly they were emboldened by the difficulties that they believed were weakening the West, partly they were moved by fears that the changing world scene could harbor new dangers for them,[1] and partly they responded to a sense that, because of all the reversals and uncertainties, the world order was losing its former legitimacy.

Onto this increasingly turbulent international scene burst another Middle East war in late 1973, followed by a dramatic increase in the price of oil. OPEC, a group of major oil-producing states, succeeded in using oil as a weapon against an oil-dependent West that had already been alarmed by warnings of rapidly depleting exhaustible resources.[2] This crisis produced major challenges to both developed and developing countries. The industrial countries faced the prospect of having to find ways to stabilize their economies after a mas- sive external shock and, in the longer term, to decrease their dependence on oil. Moreover, they also had to face a more threatening problem of finding ways to prevent other groups of commodity producers taking similar action. The developing countries were divided into those that could produce oil, which would benefit from the price rise, and those that could not, which would, like the industrial countries, also face a large external shock. The latter would need increased balance-of-payments financing while they struggled to adjust their economies, and the immediate question that they faced was how and by whom their increased indebtedness should be managed.

This chapter argues that the increased militancy of the developing coun- tries in matters of trade, finance, and development in this period was not triggered by the rise in oil prices. Although powerfully reinforced by the in- crease, such militancy had built up gradually from accumulating frustrations over the whole previous decade. Prebisch's successor at UNCTAD, Manuel

Pérez-Guerrero, found it difficult to make significant progress on facilitating new commodity agreements, so he poured much diplomatic energy into securing for developing countries industrial trade preferences and aid linked to new forms of international liquidity. The industrial countries found various ways of minimizing the benefits of these two initiatives. This further discouraged those in the G77 who were willing to work within the existing world order.

Nevertheless, the 1974 declarations of the establishment of a New International Economic Order (henceforth NIEO) were not simply the result of pressures from the growing ascendancy of militant views in developing countries. They also derived from the defensive reaction of the U.S. to the oil crisis, which was to appear to give ground to the new rhetoric. The ensuing problem was that the member states of the UN, either in the Group of 77 or in the OECD countries, had nothing of real substance to negotiate with each other in respect of a new world economic order. Into this political and intellectual vacuum charged UNCTAD's new secretary-general, Gamani Corea, who sought to transform his organization by giving it a global leadership role.

UNCTAD was to be the source of ideas that would define the NIEO as well as a negotiating forum that would help to bring those ideas to birth. Having been frustrated in the early 1970s in two of its main policy objectives, the UNCTAD secretariat turned back to its third major idea, a common framework for the management of commodity trade. Unfortunately, the politics and the economics of the proposed Integrated Programme for Commodities were not sufficiently robust to provide the substance of an NIEO. This was because the South, as well as the North, was divided on its merits and the oil producers declined to lend their leverage to achieve it. In research, activity gravitates toward those subject areas where policymakers' demand is strong and where their demand is effective—that is to say, backed by research funding. Because the OECD countries had had little interest in the management of commodity trade and because the G77 countries were unwilling to fund their own research into the topic, the research base was weak and provided a new source of dissension for countries that were in any case not strongly minded to find agreement.

Hans Singer warned in 1960 that the production of new ideas could be dangerous if the UN Secretariat tried to run too far ahead of the real possibilities of the situation and tried to advance specific proposals before member states had more or less agreed to them. Yet this is precisely what Gamani Corea did when he launched through UNCTAD a campaign for the Integrated Programme on Commodities and the Common Fund. This daring course of action made it necessary for him to close down the internal debate in UNCTAD on the benefits from commodity-price stabilization before it had really started. UNCTAD was weakened not only by external criticism but also by internal intellectual dissent spilling over into the public realm. Thus weakened, it was easily decimated by the ideological big guns of the new conservative leaders of the OECD who arrived on the international scene at the end of the 1970s.

All Quiet on the Commodities Front

The period of office of Manuel Pérez-Guerrero of Venezuela, the second secretary-general of UNCTAD, was in the end a time of frustration for the aspirations of the developing countries. Initially reluctant, Pérez-Guerrero became a candidate for the shoes of a man who he regarded as a "living legend" after being persuaded to do so by Prebisch's famed eloquence. When Prebisch presented the idea to U Thant, he replied: "All right, however present me another two candidates so that I can choose from them."[3] Neither of the other candidates, Gamani Corea (Sri Lanka) and J. Stanovnik (Yugoslavia), proved acceptable to the "controlling" powers consulted by U Thant. Stanovnik's appointment to the UNCTAD secretariat had previously caused the United States anxiety because of "his commitment to very definite views," a diplomatic reference to his communist background.[4]

The new secretary-general had a low-key, businesslike style that moved the UNCTAD secretariat away from the controversy, activism, and innovative ideas characteristic of the Prebisch years.[5] Pérez-Guerrero had begun his international career with the League of Nations (1937–1940) and had been executive secretary of the UN Technical Assistance Board.[6] He brought to UNCTAD a noncontentious concern for technical cooperation that had never been a major part of his predecessor's agenda.[7] Unsurprisingly, the Western powers started showing greater confidence in the organization.[8] They also proposed a new deal according to which developing countries would commit themselves to a quantitative target of good economic performance as a counterpart to the aid commitment assumed by developed countries. Dell reported in the spring of 1969: "The French delegation came out with this in so many words about a week ago here, and proposed that the developing countries should accept a savings target as the counterpart of the one per cent assistance target."[9]

Pérez-Guerrero made his three priorities the issues of trade preferences, commodity arrangements, and supplementary financing, thus maintaining Prebisch's agenda.[10] Lacking the broad intellectual curiosity and grasp of Prebisch, he concentrated on international diplomacy. He generally left policy issues in the hands of his heads of divisions. The commodities issue was not easily resolved by diplomacy. Some of the difficulties are illustrated by the

new secretary-general's visits to Moscow and Washington in May and November 1970. The former aimed to secure the agreement of the USSR, as the
fourth largest consumer of cocoa, to participate in a revived cocoa conference. The Soviets were less concerned with the substance of a possible agreement than with whether its terms implied any criticism of their state trading
system. Their attitude toward the new International Sugar Agreement of 1968
was also wholly political. Although it would have been sensible to try to negotiate with nonmembers, such as the EEC, who were dumping sugar in the
international market at prices inconsistent with those in the agreement, the
USSR and its allies opposed such a negotiation, apparently because it would
have implied Soviet recognition of the EEC.[11] This stance was accompanied
by protestations that "in general the USSR has always been in favor of international commodity agreements as an important instrument aimed at stabilizing commodity prices."[12]

Pérez-Guerrero gathered only grudging support for a cocoa agreement
when he sought it in Washington. The U.S. had objections of principle to
commodity agreements, thought that they distracted attention from the main
tasks of marketing and export promotion, and agreed only to "look at the
problem" in a constructive spirit. If an international cocoa agreement proved
to be a political necessity, however, the U.S. promised to cooperate in its formulation.[13] With the U.S. less than lukewarm, progress was slow. The cocoa
conference did reconvene in March 1972, but its first session was a failure. The
second session in September managed to arrive at a three-year agreement,
but the U.S. did not join it. Building on the solid groundwork done by the
FAO, UNCTAD had at last succeeded in bringing into existence one new international commodity agreement. However, it remained inoperative throughout its duration because the market price stayed above the agreed-upon ceiling
price for intervention. The cocoa example illustrates both the very lengthy
gestation of a commodity agreement and the technical difficulty of setting
relevant intervention prices.[14] In the early 1970s, primary commodity prices
were strong, and that in itself could explain the absence of strong demand for
international commodity agreements.[15]

Pérez-Guerrero was aware of the "meagre results" that were being achieved
in the commodity field.[16] He invested his diplomatic skills more heavily in the
other two issues of policy that he had chosen as priorities. The first of these
was the attempt to turn the agreement of principle at UNCTAD II to grant
industrial preferences to developing countries into reality. Some countries
remained hostile to the GSP: the Australian government was concerned about
retaining their preferred position in the UK market and considered that the

UK's offer of preferences was a gift made at the expense of commonwealth countries and, in particular, the developed ones.[17] Despite such opposition, in October 1970, arrangements for the establishment of a GSP were completed in the UNCTAD Special Committee on Preferences after intensive consultations. Among the developed-market economies, eighteen took part as preference-giving countries—Austria, Canada, Denmark, the EEC member states, Finland, Ireland, Japan, New Zealand, Norway, Sweden, Switzerland, the UK, and the U.S. During the consultations in UNCTAD, Bulgaria, Czechoslovakia, Hungary, Poland, and the USSR made a joint declaration describing the tariff and/or other commercial measures they intended to take in favor of the developing countries' exports. Concurrently with the adoption of the GSP, the prospective preference-giving countries agreed to seek as rapidly as possible the necessary legislative or other sanctions. Accordingly, in June 1971, these countries sought and obtained a waiver of their obligations under article 1 of GATT—the principle of most-favored-nation treatment—for a period of ten years.[18]

Around this time, however, the mood in Washington was "isolationist and anti-foreign," especially in Congress, according to U.S. officials.[19] At Pérez-Guerrero's Washington meetings in November 1970, Commerce Department officials were defensive about the extent of protectionist sentiment in the U.S. Congress. At the State Department, Nathaniel Samuels (deputy under secretary for economic affairs) told him that the administration would seek legislative approval of the preferences system as soon as possible, but he explained that "no decision had been taken concerning the precise manner in which the system would be submitted to Congress."[20] This prevarication was necessary because there was so little congressional support, either among free-traders or among protectionist legislators, for developing-country preferences. The U.S. was concerned about its balance-of-payments deficit, and its inability to correct it, until Nixon devalued the dollar on 15 August 1971.[21] It was not until 1976 that the U.S. was able to pass a trade act that incorporated industrial trade preferences, and even then the legislation was loaded with protectionist-inspired limitations. Exclusions related to the types of developing countries that could benefit and the product categories that could benefit (not textiles and clothing, footwear, watches, "sensitive" steel, or electronics, for example). The benefit was phased out as exports to the U.S. of the relevant item increased, on the grounds that it was then no longer "needed."[22]

The EEC scheme of 1971, to which Ireland, Denmark and the UK acceded in 1974, did not have country and product exceptions to anything like the same degree as the U.S. provisions. Nevertheless, it did incorporate import ceilings and a very complex set of administrative rules by which official discretion could reduce benefits, and as a result it may have been even less effective in stimulating developing-country exports than the U.S. scheme. As these two examples show, major industrial countries soon deprived the GSP of much of its potential effects to stimulate developing-country trade. The GSP concept had the inherent limitation that the value of any preference falls when the MFN tariff is lowered. Yet the early failure of the GSP to stimulate trade is attributable to the restrictive nature of the particular preference schemes that the industrial countries designed and introduced. This point is sometimes blurred when the GSP is evaluated. According to David Henderson:

> It might be argued that the Generalized System of Preferences (GSP) has been a concrete outcome of the north-south dialogue, a feather in UNCTAD's cap. . . . But it is also possible to view the GSP, *at any rate as it has been put into effect,* as a backward step, because of its marked discriminatory features and the limited extent of market opening that it has brought.[23]

As soon as it was realized that UNCTAD could not control how the industrial countries put their own GSP schemes into effect—and that they took the opportunity to subvert it while appearing to implement it—the locus of responsibility for the "backward step" became clear. The failure of the outcome is not a valid criticism of UNCTAD's decision to campaign for a GSP in the first place. The various GSP schemes that the developing countries were offered in the 1970s were neither general nor were they a system.[24] Prebisch's urgent plea for "progress towards non-reciprocity, non-discrimination and generalization of the GSP" before UNCTAD III was effectively ignored.[25]

Pérez-Guerrero in Pursuit of the SDR-Aid Link

The issue in which Pérez-Guerrero invested perhaps most heavily of all was the pursuit of a link between the monetary innovation of SDRs in the IMF and development finance. Prebisch had laid the groundwork well for the involvement of developing countries in both the process of, and the benefits from, international monetary reform. Now the tasks were to maintain the solidarity of the G77 behind a particular reform proposal, to insert that proposal in the various arenas in which negotiations took place, and to lobby the OECD countries to build support for it. In 1970, when donors subscribed new capital to replenish the IDA, the shift of attention to the SDR-aid link was reinforced because this move further dimmed any prospects of their also agreeing to a supplementary finance scheme.[26]

The novel aspect of the SDR was that it was the first form of "money" that had been created by an international agreement, and it was attractive to the developing countries that their need for development finance could be linked with an international negotiation rather than dealt with ad hoc in two dozen national ministries of finance.[27] The question remained of what form the link should take. Initially, two versions were up for discussion—the organic link and the nonorganic link. The former meant the direct allocation of SDRs to the IDA, which would require minor changes in the IMF Articles of Agreement, to permit multilateral agencies to hold SDRs. The latter meant the voluntary subscription by donors to the IDA of national currency equivalents of a proportion of SDRs, not the SDRs themselves. The nonorganic link faced the obvious objection that since donors would actually give their aid separately and independently of SDR allocation, any link would be contrived and artificial.[28] Attention thus focused on the organic link, and Pérez-Guerrero and Dell visited Washington, Paris, London, and Bonn to elicit support for it. Two difficulties were German sensitivity about the dominant American and British role in the World Bank and British worries about how the socialist countries would fit into the SDR allocation exercise.[29] The IMF came out in support of an organic link. Prebisch then remarked: UNCTAD "no longer runs the risk of being unorthodox, since the Vatican itself is in favour."[30]

In the U.S., although the Joint Economic Committee of Congress also supported the organic link proposal, the Nixon administration maintained its opposition. Its main objection was that the link would impair confidence in the SDR and thus should be deferred until such time as the SDR was out of its "infancy." U.S. officials also claimed that the link would result in fewer SDRs being created and that this would hamper U.S. plans to untie its aid. The negative U.S. view toward the link proposals dominated the G10 discussions. The Nixon administration wanted consideration of the link proposals to be postponed beyond 1972, when the next SDR distribution was due and when UNCTAD III was scheduled to take place. Dell and Pérez-Guerrero were not so easily persuaded and told the emissaries of the G10 that the developing countries would raise the issue of the link at the Trade and Development Board and later at UNCTAD III.[31]

In November 1971, in Lima, the G77 succeeded in organizing itself to participate in the forthcoming negotiation on international monetary reform. It set up the Group of Twenty-Four on International Monetary Affairs, representing eight countries each in Africa, Asia, and Latin America, to be its "financial arm" and a point of liaison with the IMF.[32] Its task was, among other things, to recommend coordinated policy positions for its members to follow in international bodies. The policy that the G77 eventually adopted was to press for a change in the basis of the SDR allocation so that developing countries would receive a greater proportion than they would have been entitled to by their IMF quotas and the least-developed countries would receive an even more generous share. They had the voting power to refuse to ratify any reform that did not include the link, but the potency of that threat depended on the need of the industrial countries to secure a change in the IMF Articles of Agreement for their own purposes.[33]

Would the SDR be damaged if it were linked to development finance, as the U.S. claimed? Would the link have led to a series of allocations that were excessive from a purely monetary viewpoint? Would the developing countries press for artificially low interest rates on the SDR? Pérez-Guerrero worked hard on these issues publicly, and privately in discussions with G10 central bankers, to reassure the international financial community on the first point. He told them that

> it is a fact of considerable political importance that the developing countries are on record as being in agreement that the amount of new reserve creation should be determined solely by the monetary requirements of the world economy and not by the need for development finance.[34]

There is not much evidence that the developing countries would have tried to hold the SDR interest rate down or could have done so on their own. A bigger danger of this came from the U.S. itself, which did not want the SDR eventually to replace the dollar as the principal international reserve asset because of the loss of dollar seignorage that this would cause.

The absence of strong American motivation to construct a new international monetary system to replace Bretton Woods was, indeed, a major factor in the failure of the Committee of Twenty negotiations on international monetary reform over 1972–1974.[35] The spirit of cooperation and compromise did not prevail. The Europeans were the only group to show much flexibility: they (except for the Germans) compromised by accepting the link. The developing countries themselves remained inflexible in their demands and the U.S. adamantly opposed the link. It was a straight confrontation throughout, unyielding on either side. When the industrial world gradually discovered, after May 1973, that flotation of the major currencies was a tolerable alternative to a system that was established in a multilateral agreement, further efforts to negotiate such a system faded away. With them the idea of the SDR-aid link effectively disappeared from the international agenda.[36]

A Secretariat for the Group of 77?

In many ways, the negotiations around international monetary reform in the early 1970s represented a high point in the effort to achieve an international economic system that recognized the interdependence of trade, finance, and development. The effort that was invested in agreeing on a common G77 position, sustaining internal support for it, and lobbying for it externally was impressive. In addition, the establishment of the G24 in Washington was the first major step in the institutional evolution of the G77. The collapse of the international monetary reform effort was a double blow. It diminished the significance of UNCTAD by devaluing the area of policy to which it was directed, and it pointed to the urgent need for intellectual renewal by eliminating one more of three key policy ideas that UNCTAD had inherited from the time of Prebisch.

UNCTAD III, held in Santiago de Chile in 1972, had shown few signs of renewal. The main addition had been policies directed toward transnational corporations to prevent the permanent alienation of natural resources and to initiate a code of conduct on the transfer of technology. As a result, UNCTAD became more militant on the traditional issue of commodities, agreeing in the face of the U.S. opposition to convene "intensive consultations" on a case-by-case basis. Again over U.S. opposition, it further agreed to set up a working group to draft a Charter of Economic Rights and Duties of States. This was the brainchild of President Luis Echeverría of Mexico. These moves, made against the background of the unfolding drama of President Salvador Allende's attempts at socialist transformation in Chile, opened a gulf between the U.S. and Europe, the latter being much more sympathetic to some package of compensatory policies for developing countries.[37]

Although Echeverría's charter proposal was the one major policy initiative that originated outside the UNCTAD secretariat, the G77 had no mechanism to back it up and follow it through.[38] G77 diplomats proved unable to mount the further institutional development of setting up a secretariat of its own. That it would be preferable to have a G77-dedicated secretariat rather than to continue to rely on the UNCTAD secretariat acting in a dual capacity—part servants of all its members, part advisors to the G77—had been appreciated from the early days of UNCTAD.[39] The diplomats who did the work of the G77 were hardly in a position to develop new policy ideas. Their postings to the UN were of relatively brief duration, some three or four years. Their constant attendance at official and unofficial meetings was so time-consuming that their situation simply precluded their meaningful involvement in policy work. Nor did their national capitals drive them forward by supplying them with a flow of new policy ideas. So they needed to organize their own policymaking support.[40] However, once UNCTAD had been established, the UNCTAD secretariat became almost the sole source of the substance of the G77 policy agenda. Most of the UNCTAD secretariat's ideas were adopted, though by no means all.[41]

The only serious initiative to devise a G77 secretariat was undertaken by the UNCTAD secretariat under Pérez-Guerrero. The outline for the constitutional document was drawn up around 1971, but political obstacles stood in the way. They were in part the choice of its location (in the North or the South?) and its chief executive (from which continent?), but they were mainly about its funding. The plan faced "a *prima facie* impossibility, due to the fact that governments were not prepared to put up the money to make it work."[42] The larger developing countries thought that they would have to shoulder most of the financial burden but that a G77 secretariat might be inclined to favor the viewpoint of the many more small developing countries.[43] The result of this classic collective action dilemma was that the G77 remained totally dependent on the UNCTAD secretariat to supply it with a policy agenda through the commodities crisis of the 1970s and beyond. Later, Gamani Corea recalled that

> much of the so-called agenda of the G77 was articulated by the UN secretariats rather than the G77 itself.... Whatever we put down as the course of action on any issue, whether on commodities, the Common Fund, the transfer of technology, shipping—you name it, that was taken by the G77 and made into their own platform.[44]

At Algiers in September 1973, a conference of heads of state and government of the nonaligned countries had concluded by calling on the UN Secretary-General to convene a special session of the General Assembly to study "problems related to raw materials and development." In the commodities consultations of 1973–1974 in UNCTAD, the expectations of the G77 were running high, but nothing was achieved except the raking over of the old difficulties. While the UNCTAD secretariat could do this as well as others, it was not well equipped to be an intellectual guide in more contentious territory. Before his departure, Prebisch attempted to solve the problem of lack of African directors by recruiting Bernard Chidzero of Zimbabwe to be director of the UNCTAD Commodities Division, also thus recognizing the special African interest in this issue. However, Chidzero knew nothing about commodities and had told Prebisch so.[45] The effective direction of commodities policy thus devolved to Alfred Maizels, who was a genuine specialist in the subject and Chidzero's deputy, a quiet, scholarly man.[46]

The pace of events now quickened. In October 1973, Egypt attacked Israel in an attempt to recover territory lost in 1967. After the Yom Kippur War, the OPEC countries unilaterally introduced a massive increase in oil prices. The price of oil rose from $3.02 to $5.12 per barrel on 16 October and to $11.60 in December 1973. Supply cuts and embargoes on the U.S. and the Netherlands were announced as Arab countries punished the West for its support of Israel. On 18 January 1974, France called for an international energy conference, but OPEC opposed this. On 30 January, President Houari Boumedienne of Algeria, as chairman of the Non-Aligned Movements, told the UN Secretary-General:

> [The French proposal] could be of value if, instead of being restricted to the problem of energy alone, it covered all the questions relating to all types of raw materials. Thus, in order that useful discussions may be held on development and on international economic relations and all their implications with a view to establishing a new system of relations based on equality and the common interests of all States, I have the honour to request you to initiate the appropriate procedure for the convening ... of a special session of the General Assembly.[47]

By 14 February 1974, the required majority of member states had concurred with his request.[48] Thus the General Assembly held its Sixth Special Session on Raw Materials and Development in New York between 9 April and 2 May 1974. This was the first special session to be devoted to an economic issue.

At the Sixth Special Session, many developing-country delegates pointed out that UNCTAD III had not lived up to their high hopes.[49] Moreover, alarmingly from the point of view of the developed countries, some of them coupled such expressions of disappointment with praise for OPEC's "brilliant victories in bringing about a just and more harmonious equilibrium in international economic relations," as the delegate from Guinea put it.[50] OPEC countries in turn emphasized their own status as "developing countries, which believe that their first and foremost duty is to raise the standards of living of their peoples in all spheres, in order that they may keep pace with world progress ... and make an effective contribution to international development in general."[51] Thus, during the Special Session the rise in oil prices did not fracture the unity of the developing countries, although the majority of them were oil importers. Instead, it united them even more strongly than before in search of a New International Economic Order.

The initial U.S. reaction was threatening. Henry Kissinger, Nixon's secretary of state, dealt out heavy warnings to primary-commodity producers. They would discover, he said, that they were not insulated from the impact of supply restrictions or price escalation, since a recession in the industrial countries sharply reduces demand and higher prices for raw materials accelerate the transition to alternatives.[52] Nevertheless, on 1 May 1974 the General Assembly adopted without a vote a Declaration on the Establishment of a New International Economic Order, together with a Programme of Action, in resolutions 3201 (S-VI) and 3202 (S-VI). The U.S., together with many other countries from Group B, entered a reservation stating that it strongly disapproved of some of the provisions of the Programme of Action, but it did not vote against what it called "a significant political document."[53] Houari Boumedienne, the shah of Iran, Luis Echeverría, and Manuel Pérez-Guerrero were the four people most responsible for devising and sponsoring the NIEO texts.[54] The Charter of Economic Rights and Duties of States (resolution 3281 [XXIV]) followed in December 1974, which was adopted by a vote of 120 to 6 with 10 abstentions.[55] However, the largely consensual adoption masked a problem: What could the substance of an NIEO be when its protagonists had no proposals and its antagonists were playing a defensive game?

Gamani Corea Seizes the Initiative

Just before the start of the Sixth Session, Gamani Corea took office as the new secretary-general of UNCTAD. He had been born, an only child, into a wealthy and well-connected family in Ceylon (now Sri Lanka), several of whose members had been prominent in public life.[56] Having studied economics at Cambridge and Oxford, he drifted away from his youthful socialist sympathies to liberal technocratic concerns, returning home to become a central banker, an economic planner, and a negotiator of multilateral aid.[57] Prebisch had sought out Corea's skills at the start of UNCTAD and in its early years. He had penned the first declaration of the G77 and later chaired UNCTAD expert groups on the SDR-aid link and on shipping.[58] These close connections had probably cost him the post of secretary-general at the previous vacancy created by Prebisch's departure.

Corea's personality has been a subject of debate. He struck one colleague as having "a sort of professorial, university-type personality—not professorial in the sense of being detached from people, but articulating issues more clearly."[59] However, another observer thought his leadership style was aloof, as he was not an easy man for his staff to identify with and follow. When he was profiled in *Cosmos,* the unofficial NGO-sponsored newssheet produced during UNCTAD IV in Nairobi, it reported: "He is unfailingly courteous and affable. As a friend once said, somewhat unkindly: 'He is too bloody shy to be anything else.'"[60] He certainly appeared distant in the photo portrait on the cover of his 1980 book of speeches: his pose was pensive, his eyes averted from the camera. Perhaps inevitably, his leadership style was compared adversely with that of Prebisch.[61] Although lacking the charisma of Prebisch, he was nonetheless a substantial figure for good or ill in the way that Pérez-Guerrero was not.[62]

When Corea took over at the start of the Sixth Special Session, he felt himself to be under intense pressure from the developing countries to make

UNCTAD more than a debating house. He wanted it to be a negotiating forum while retaining its image as a think tank:

> I felt, of course, that UNCTAD should at no stage lose its image of being a generator of new ideas . . . But I felt that one needed to add a new dimension at the same time that would transform UNCTAD . . . into [a forum] in which more complex, more concrete, more specific agreements could be initiated, negotiated and agreed upon.[63]

The dramatic circumstances of the Sixth Session provided the opportunity to attempt this transformation, although the UNCTAD secretariat had produced no document for the session. Corea used the plight of the non-oil-producing developing countries to call not only for immediate short-term financial assistance, which was soon provided by the oil producers, but also for a long-run solution by means of official intervention in a range of core commodity markets. As he later recalled, "from . . . the point of view of UNCTAD, there was the need to take advantage of that situation to focus attention on other [non-oil] commodities."[64] Corea seized the initiative for UNCTAD.[65] Without having been given a mandate, he presented the UNCTAD Trade and Development Board with his "Outline of an Overall Integrated Programme" in August 1974.[66] So the die was cast. UNCTAD was committed to championing the idea of creating a new official agency that would own a multicommodity stock, although most of the details of such an agency remained to be defined. Drawing on the language of UNCTAD II, the outline argued that since individual international commodity agreements were inadequate, a new international agency should apply a wider framework of principles to a larger number of core commodities and should own and manage the stocks required for commodity-price management, purchase of which should be financed from a central fund.[67]

Although this outline was a bold initiative, going well beyond the Havana Charter, it did not endorse some of the more radical features that would have appealed to developing countries. It did not aim at raising prices but referred to the ambiguous old formula that prices should be "remunerative to producers and equitable to consumers." It therefore did not endorse "indexation"—the linking of export prices of commodities to import prices of manufactures. Nor did it aim at organizing schemes to restrict supply; rather, it sought to establish a range of commodity buffer stocks, financed by the oil producers and others, that could be used to moderate price fluctuations. The size of the Common Fund was stated as $6 billion: it was to be raised by inviting investments that would earn a return, not subscriptions of grants or loans. The surpluses of the oil producers were expected to be a major source for the fund, as well as investments from industrial countries and multilateral agencies, but "UNCTAD was inclined to leave it to the developing countries as a group to persuade the oil exporters" to invest.[68]

Two factors now came into play. One was the feebleness of the Commodities Division in championing the proposal by dialoguing with the relevant experts in the developed and developing countries, by explaining its implications, and by arguing its merits. The other was the lapse of time before the G77 decided to adopt the UNCTAD outline as its own negotiating agenda. Everyone hung back for their own reasons: members of existing ICAs were worried that under a Common Fund other countries would be able to influence the regulation of their commodity; the oil producers were importers of non-oil commodities and did not want to commit to any investment before the Common Fund was better defined. In the end, the G77 made no concrete moves until early 1976, and then they moved in contradictory directions.

The reaction of the developed countries was by no means to refuse to discuss the commodity issue. What they feared was that developing countries would use salami tactics, reproducing, for commodity after commodity, the OPEC effect of price rise and supply restriction.[69] Kissinger recalled that in the wake of the oil crisis, fear of producer power was at the heart of the American approach toward the poorer non-oil-producing developing nations:

> To keep their grievances from coalescing with OPEC, we sought to create alternatives to policies of extortion. We put forward sweeping proposals for stabilizing raw material prices and enhancing food security for the world's poorest nations. Our strategy was to give the non-oil commodity producers a stake they would be jeopardizing by following in the footsteps of OPEC or supporting it.[70]

Not surprisingly, some UNCTAD old hands wondered whether the American proposals were not also trying to undercut the UN role in the North-South dialogue in view of UNCTAD's insistence on a comprehensive approach.[71] In the heated atmosphere of the time, the UK foreign secretary claimed to see the G77 as the main threat to the UN and the EEC as a bastion for its defense![72] The reasoning here presumably was that a Common Fund financed by oil surpluses would no longer be subject to Western control. The Conference of Developing Countries on Raw Materials in Dakar had stimulated this fear in February 1975 when it resolved to set up a fund for commodity-market intervention owned exclusively by the developing countries.

In order to find agreement on the substance of the NIEO, a Seventh Special Session of the General Assembly met from 1 to 16 September 1975. One observer described it as "a cliff-hanging Session, swaying from day to day between hope and despair" and when a last-minute compromise was reached wrote of "a feeling of euphoria . . . as of a world snatched from the abyss and moved irretrievably a step towards sanity."[73] The agreement on commodities was, however, a half-baked solution. While it acknowledged the need to build up buffer stocks for commodity-price stabilization schemes, it did not recognize the need for a Common Fund for financing them.

Later that autumn, President Giscard d'Estaing of France endorsed the call for a new world economic order.[74] He had convened a preliminary meeting of what became the Conference on International Economic Cooperation (CIEC) in which the U.S., the EEC, and Japan confronted four OPEC countries and three non-oil-producing developing countries. In November 1975, he called the Rambouillet Summit between France, West Germany, Italy, Japan, the UK, and the U.S., where he in effect repeated the American game plan:

> We should try to break . . . the unholy alliance between the LDCs and OPEC. This can happen, and we can achieve our results, if they know that their disruptive actions could stop discussions on commodities or that they will pay a price in terms of cooperation, or military exports. In this way we can combat our dependence with a coherent strategy.[75]

In the Summit Declaration, these six major industrialized countries pledged, inter alia, to "play our part . . . in making urgent improvements in international arrangements for the stabilization of the export earnings of developing countries and in measures to assist them in financing their deficits."[76] Again, however, the need for a Common Fund was not recognized.

The Contradictions of UNCTAD IV

When the G77 met in Manila (from 26 January to 7 February 1976) to prepare their policy platform for UNCTAD IV, it also took up an incoherent position on commodity-price stabilization. It adopted UNCTAD's Integrated Programme as its own proposals but also decided that all operations for market regulation through a Common Fund should be through the medium of individual international commodity agreements. The latter proviso was the price of Latin American support, but it was the death knell of the idea of the Common Fund as an agency that would intervene directly in commodity markets and set minimum and maximum prices for commodities. The Common Fund would now come into play vis-à-vis individual ICAs only if they were to agree to recognize it as a source of funding for their stocks. Nonetheless, President Ferdinand Marcos flamboyantly announced that the Philippines would contribute $50 million to the Common Fund. Corea took this as a hopeful sign:

The Common Fund had not been created; its design had not been determined; its capital requirements and structure had not been estimated; the need for voluntary subscriptions had never been suggested. But a solid offer of finance had now been made and the Common Fund could no longer be seen as an impractical dream.[77]

This assessment seems rather optimistic, considering all the decisions that had been taken at Manila.

UNCTAD IV opened in Nairobi on 5 May 1976. Corea's report was entitled *New Directions and New Structures for Trade and Development.* In the months and weeks beforehand, Corea had emphasized to journalists that he aimed for a comparatively short conference with fewer agenda items that would quickly lead to negotiations and consultations on specific issues. He also stressed the need "to shift UNCTAD's function from that of 'a pressure house' to that of the negotiating arm of the United Nations system in the field of trade and development."[78] In relation to the Integrated Programme on Commodities and the Common Fund, he now explicitly had to correct the widespread belief that the scheme would avoid a case-by-case approach to each commodity. After Manila, all that the Integrated Programme envisaged was "a common frame of reference for the various case-by-case approaches." Although the report also highlighted the urgency of alleviating the developing countries' debt burden, it was the commodity issue that was to dominate.[79]

Kissinger's address was the central episode of the conference's first days. He was in Africa anyway at the end of an extended tour, the key purpose of which had been to trade U.S. support for majority rule in Rhodesia and South Africa for a refusal by African leaders to allow Soviet or Cuban involvement on the continent. Even so, his decision to address UNCTAD was very striking, as no previous U.S. secretary of state had done so, nor indeed has one done so ever since. In his memoirs, he recalled: "I chose to speak on behalf of the United States in order to symbolize the political importance we attached to the need for new cooperative international arrangements."[80] However, his commodities proposals were shaped by the U.S. game plan and conflicted with UNCTAD's modified Integrated Programme. Kissinger duly paid lip service to it: "While the United States of America could not accept all of its elements, there were many parts which it was prepared to consider." He expressed willingness to study the suitability of buffer stocks on a commodity-by-commodity basis and offered to review the adequacy of IMF lending resources for poorer countries to offset short-term price fluctuations and long-term declines in commodity earnings.[81] The centerpiece of his speech, however, was a proposal to establish an International Resources Bank with a capital fund of $1 billion, "which would mobilize capital for sound resources development projects to secure direct financing and by a partial guarantee of bonds which

could be retired through delivery of a specific commodity." Its advantages, he
said, would be the encouragement of the creation of conditions for project
development consistent with internationally accepted standards of equity,
multilateral guarantees for host countries and investors, production-sharing
arrangements, the contribution of the commodity bonds to stabilization of
commodity earnings and of commodity supply and demand, and promotion
of the transfer of technology.[82]

The British welcomed Kissinger's "important contribution." The French
wondered if a new international institution was needed. The Canadians stated:
"The International Resources Bank was an interesting idea though it was too
early to comment on it." Reaction from Asian, African, and South American
representatives ranged from guarded to hostile. The day after Kissinger's
speech, the NGO newspaper *Cosmos* pronounced that "Dr. Kissinger [had]
retreated into the ever-tightening laager of free trade, piled up his ammunition, and defied those who thought differently to do their worst."[83] Perhaps
more to the point was the subsequent comment of the Cuban delegate, who
"found it strange that delegations that rejected vital aspects of proposals that
had been under study for a long period, such as the proposals for creating a
new structure for commodity trade, should try to impose a new proposal that
had not been examined and which, as everyone knew, was designed to divert
attention from the demands of the vast majority of the countries attending
the Conference."[84] Yet Corea—whom Kissinger treated with respect[85]—felt
that the American stance seemed to offer hope that the gathering in Nairobi
would have useful results.

It did not turn out like that. Although UNCTAD had hoped only to secure
agreement to do further work on the Common Fund, a more militant mood
animated the developing-country delegations. They wanted to make the setting
up of the Common Fund a precondition for negotiation on the other parts of
the commodity program. Although this was unacceptable to the industrial countries, they were divided.[86] Whereas Kissinger had tried to upstage the Common
Fund by focusing on his own proposal, the EEC countries were split on the
merits of the issue.[87] While West Germany opposed the Common Fund concept, France was more pragmatic and the Netherlands strongly supported the
Common Fund and Integrated Programme, coalescing with thirteen "like-
minded" nations (including, notably, the Scandinavians). As Corea has noted:
"[W]ith such disarray in the camp of the developed countries, the common
spokesman of Group B was not in a position to even hint, as usually happens,
that something might be possible in the course of negotiations."[88]

The G77 had its own divisions but, to some degree, these were successfully
covered over. On 17 May 1976, an NGO observer telexed back to Britain: "Another crack in 77 plastered over yesterday when India announced readiness to

contribute 25 million dollars to C. Fund following pressure from Asian LDCs. Further pledges from OPEC countries and non-OPEC countries expected this week."[89] This was part of a process by which successive delegations (nineteen in all, mainly from the developing countries but including the Norwegians[90]) announced their willingness to make voluntary contributions, although the manner of the Common Fund's financing had still not been defined. Significantly, though, the oil producers declined to play a decisive role. Corea, anxious that the difficulties around the Common Fund should not hold up talks on the other aspects of the Integrated Programme, tried to convey this message to the G77 delegates, but they absolutely refused to negotiate further.

By 27 May, UNCTAD IV had reached the point of collapse. Corea himself "passed through the melee like a general disbanding his army," though still smiling.[91] Then Dragoslav Avramovic, a senior World Bank economist on loan to UNCTAD, gave Corea a proposed compromise draft, and this averted total failure. It sought to leave all parties uncommitted but to launch a post-Nairobi process of discussion and negotiation on the Common Fund. Corea called an informal meeting of leading conference participants in his suite at the Hilton, where talks went on for more than two days, taking the conference to the latest point that was logistically possible. A deal was finally struck. The Group B countries were willing to accept the Avramovic proposal in return for an agreement by the G77 to refer the U.S. proposal of an International Resources Bank to the permanent machinery of UNCTAD for further study. The willingness of the U.S. to move to this compromise derived not from conviction of the merits of commodity-price stabilization through international action but from a strong desire to prevent a deterioration of North-South relations in the post–oil-crisis era.[92] The Nairobi conference thus passed without vote resolution 93 (IV), entitled "The Integrated Programme of Commodities." The resolution requested the secretary-general of UNCTAD to "convene a negotiation conference open to all members of UNCTAD on a Common Fund no later than March 1977."

Ambassador Herbert Walker of Jamaica, the spokesman for the G77, called resolution 93 (IV) "but a poor shadow of the real need, a far cry from the new market structures and new forms of international economic cooperation which should exist."[93] Then the anticipated quid pro quo was not delivered: none of the G77 regional groupings was willing to endorse the draft resolution that the U.S. resources-bank proposal should be referred for further study. The U.S. delegation nevertheless pressed for a roll-call vote, and subsequently it was defeated by 33 to 31 with 44 abstentions. This, understandably, soured the atmosphere at the close of the conference.

The Negotiation of the Common Fund, 1976–1980

Corea later claimed that at Nairobi the international community had passed a great milestone:

> Despite the tension that marked its adoption, the resolution on the Integrated Programme for Commodities marks a milestone in the history of international commodity policy and of UNCTAD. It signifies the acceptance by the international community of an approach to commodity policy that the developing countries and the Secretariat had been championing ever since the Second Session of UNCTAD.[94]

That judgment may be formally correct, but UNCTAD's victory was hollow. The main outcome was that a vast effort was devoted over the subsequent four years to many meetings to negotiate individual commodity agreements alongside laborious negotiations for the Common Fund. While agreement on the constitution of the fund was reached in 1980, only one new commodity agreement emerged from all the post-1976 activity, namely the International Natural Rubber Agreement of 1979. Moreover, these meager results cannot simply be attributed to U.S. obstruction. The Carter administration took the line that "we should continue to push along with price-stabilizing commodity agreements where there is some promise of success" and was prepared to contemplate an ICA for copper as well as natural rubber.[95]

Worse was to come in the 1980s, when most of the existing commodity agreements—for sugar, tin, coffee, and cocoa—collapsed or were suspended. The Common Fund thus had only one commodity for price-stabilization purposes—rubber—and two for other purposes of marketing and export diversification—jute and tropical timber. Corea later argued that the paucity of new ICAs resulted from the slow progress on the Common Fund, but the reverse is also true—that the absence of new ICAs made the Common Fund negotiations less urgent. Originally, this kind of parallel negotiation had never been intended, since the Common Fund had been designed for getting around the need to negotiate many individual agreements, an intention torpedoed by the G77 decisions in Manila before UNCTAD IV ever began. The fallback argument that finance was the only factor inhibiting the creation of many more ICAs remains unconvincing, not least because after the Common Fund was finally ratified in 1988, no spate of new ICAs emerged. As Gilbert has argued, "the tin [agreement's] collapse in 1985 . . . has undermined the willingness of producers to look for resolutions of difficulties within ICAs and has reinforced suspicions of consumer governments that these agreements were in no-one's interests."[96]

The North-South dialogue in the Conference on International Economic Cooperation (CIEC) also failed. Convened by France from 1975 to 1977, the CIEC was a mixed and much smaller group of twenty-seven developed and developing countries that conducted a North-South dialogue. It was smaller and less unwieldy than UNCTAD, but it operated through a group negotiating system of its own. It had no greater success. The developed countries wanted to focus exclusively on energy issues, while the developing countries wanted to broaden the issues to include commodities in general and other issues. By June 1977, all that CIEC had agreed upon was to increase aid, especially to oil-importing developing countries, and to accept the principle of negotiating a Common Fund for commodities.[97] The fundamental problem was one of substance.[98] The plain fact is that there was not a strong enough underlying belief among all the parties—developing as well as developed—in the need for a New International Economic Order for commodities.

In the developed world, Europe was as usual divided, while the Carter administration, though not unsympathetic, was reluctant to invest time and political capital in unrealistic schemes merely to mollify the G77. It regarded many of the G77 proposals (e.g., the regulation of all synthetics competing with natural commodities) as "extreme," and it bemoaned the G77's adoption of a political strategy that "leaves them practically no negotiating flexibility."[99] This was fair comment. Corea and company did not always keep in step with the G77, which was in any case a difficult task, since the G77 practiced solidarity in rhetoric and militant attitudes, exhausting its capacities in passing resolutions that combined cloudiness and rigidity. Nourished with very little input from their national capitals, except on commodities of direct interest to them, G77 delegations would come to these negotiations in reactive mode, assuming that either the developed countries or the UNCTAD secretariat would have prepared some scheme in advance. Unity in favor of the NIEO was a façade behind which lay many different shadings of commitment to the Common Fund. Some of the biggest oil producers, such as Saudi Arabia, did not want to complicate their relations with the industrial world, where most of their surpluses were invested and from which they wished to buy modern armaments;[100] the Latin Americans did not want to lose the control that they had established over the commodities of interest to them, such as coffee; and the Asia-Pacific-Caribbean countries feared that the level of their special arrangements with the EEC might be eroded by more global measures. As one UNCTAD insider put it: "On both sides of the market, many countries that would be affected by direct price control of one or more of the core commodities were skeptical about the possible benefits to themselves."[101]

UNCTAD tried to make the Common Fund into the flagship of the NIEO in the mistaken belief that it would be easiest to achieve some agreements with the North in this area. Gamani Corea, with Alfred Maizels in intellectual support and Bernard Chidzero, Stein Rossen, and Jan Pronk concurring, believed that exporters of grains and minerals in the North would welcome greater stability in the markets in commodities that they sold and that northern consumers of noncompeting imports of primary commodities would welcome a degree of price stability and so would investors from the North. In this belief they were encouraged by Henry Kissinger (and Charles "Chuck" Frank, who was writing his speeches at that time), who argued vigorously that there was much sense in arranging a price-stabilization deal between developing countries and potential investors that would protect both sides over the longer run. This was a sophisticated, but in the end incorrect, assessment of where North-South interests were most convergent.[102] Moreover, beyond the issue of whether price stabilization of ten core commodities was a desirable objective of both the North and the South lay the thornier problem of who was to control the chosen instruments of stabilization. It was always implausible that the industrial countries would give much ground on that, and it was not in any way surprising that it was basically their design to which the Common Fund, as it eventually emerged in the 1980s, was built.

Political versus Research-Based Negotiation

In the four years of intensive consultations and disappointing results after UNCTAD IV, accusations of intellectual failure in the UNCTAD secretariat began to enter the public domain. These were related to the fact that the original UNCTAD "Outline of an Overall Integrated Programme" of 1974 had remained vague both about the objectives of the Common Fund and about many important aspects of its methods of operation, yet it had carried a $6 billion price tag. The secretariat had clearly not undertaken adequate analytical studies before launching the proposals of the outline for the Common Fund and had decided to launch them nonetheless. It was essentially a political decision. When in 1976 UNCTAD IV endorsed the concept of a Common Fund, it gave the secretariat a negotiating timetable of only two years in which to find agreement on its constitution. In these circumstances, Corea again opted for a "political approach" to negotiation rather than a research-based approach in which the costs and benefits of alternative schemes were carefully evaluated and made transparent to all the parties to the negotiation.

The developed countries made an issue of this, no doubt from a mixture of motives—a proper concern for relevant information plus a desire for legitimate excuses for delay. They demanded a technical economic justification of

the original $6 billion price tag. How did UNCTAD know that the stocks re-
quired to stabilize the price of the ten core commodities would cost $6 billion
and not $12 billion? A young, recently recruited UNCTAD staff economist, John
Cuddy, elaborated a set of calculations. Despite their better-than-average technical quality, the developed countries used them to generate a whole raft of
further procrastinating queries. This experience with openness pushed the secretariat further back into a political mode, especially because it feared that information on the distribution of the benefits of price stabilization would
undermine the less-than-complete solidarity within the G77. Outside economists, such as Harry Johnson, as well as developed-country delegations, then
took the opportunity to savage the secretariat's analytical competence.[103]

Inside the secretariat, as individual commodity analyses were prepared,
the directorate required changes to be made to them in order to keep them
consistent with the declared negotiating figure of $6 billion. Staff economists
had to massage the assumptions on which their calculations were based until
they gave the answer that had first been thought of. This practice—which,
incidentally, also was used by UNCTAD's critics[104]—incensed some of the
younger secretariat economists, who were already disaffected by many other
frustrations of the UNCTAD working environment. One of the dissenters
published a detailed critical account of these proceedings.[105] Internal disarray
in the secretariat was thus added to external technical criticism.

The internal critics claimed that provision of specific responses to delegations' requests for information would have "facilitated the negotiating process ... [and that] relations between opposing sides and between the Secretariat
and the members of UNCTAD might have been healthier."[106] Was there an
intellectual failure within the UNCTAD secretariat that led to political failure, namely a failure to marshal enough economic analysis to persuade member countries that the Integrated Programme would be in their interests? Would
more or better-quality economic analyses have altered the state of the underlying political will to find agreement? Surely it is more likely that it would
have caused the negotiations to unravel earlier than they did or produce an
even more vestigial version of the Common Fund than it did.

Why? Fresh studies would have had to be made, probably by external consultants. These, however, could hardly have been decisive. Consultants tend to
act as the mouthpiece for the conclusions of their principals in the secretariat.[107]
Mosak's highly instrumental view of consultants has already been mentioned.[108]
More important, both the theory and the econometrics of commodity-price
stabilization schemes were still relatively undeveloped, something that was at
least partly the result of the suddenness with which high-level political attention had shifted toward them. Many theoretical aspects of the price stabiliza-

tion problem still remained to be worked out, even in the orthodox competitive theory espoused by the OECD. "How much would it cost to buy a stock capable of reducing the range of price fluctuation by x percent, and how would that affect the income of particular groups?" might sound like simple questions. They would no longer seem so even a few short years later, after the higher political salience of the commodities question had elicited new theoretical research that explored general-equilibrium outcomes, given imperfect markets for risk.[109] Moreover, while some econometric studies done outside the secretariat but using the previous standard approach found that the price stabilization of the core commodities would have been beneficial to the G77 or regional groupings thereof, it is naive to suppose that other similar ones could not have come up with results pointing in exactly the opposite direction.[110]

The developed countries' demands for impartial analysis successfully exposed the difficulties of the UNCTAD secretariat in balancing committed policy advocacy with its neutral advisory role. They claimed that the secretariat's advocacy role prevented it from retaining objectivity and meeting the same professional standards as the IMF, the World Bank, and the OECD.[111] In the next decade they were to use these charges to move the UNCTAD secretariat back in the direction of being primarily an international policy think tank that was engaged in research, policy advocacy, and technical assistance while confining negotiations to other arenas such as GATT and the international financial institutions, where their leverage was greater. The story of how this was done is the subject of the next chapter.

At least Corea was sufficiently clear-sighted to see that if he was to transform UNCTAD into a negotiating forum by having the G77 advance the secretariat's own proposals, it could not at the same time credibly act as an impartial assessor of those proposals. That would have been too much of a juggling act for the secretariat to sustain. Since a substantial gulf existed between the OECD members and the G77 members on the choice of the relevant assumptions to model commodity trade, the very idea of objectivity was highly problematic.[112] Corea's choice of a political rather than a research-based approach was no more than the logical consequence of the decision that he took in his first weeks in office. Who sows the wind reaps the whirlwind. UNCTAD could not be transformed into a powerhouse inducing nations to legislate for a new international economic order and stay as it was when it was a mere ideas factory and a talking shop. The push to take UNCTAD into the big league, which is what the Common Fund was all about, taught once again the enduring lesson that big-league organizations tend to rein in such of their own research as does not suit their own organizational purposes.

11

The Conservative Counterrevolution
of the 1980s

- **The End of the North-South Dialogue**
- **The Debt Crisis of the Developing Countries**
- **"Sensible Economic Policies": Foreign Trade and the Role of Government**
- **The IMF: The Able Coordinator of the Western Debt Strategy**
- **The World Bank: Looking for Leverage**
- **From Structural Adjustment to Poverty Reduction**
- **The Fate of UNCTAD: Demotion and Freedom to Dissent**
- **The Cold War Ends: The WTO Arrives**

The End of the North-South Dialogue

In 1977, Robert McNamara was at the height of his influence as president of the World Bank. A man of considerable vision, he thought that the international community was in some danger of losing its bearings and needed fresh ideas on the international dimension of development.[1] He approached Willy Brandt, the former chancellor of West Germany, who agreed to head an Independent Commission on International Development Issues to chart the way ahead. Brandt agreed on condition that, unlike the earlier Pearson Commission of 1969, the World Bank did not fund the work.[2] The commission was also to be independent of the UN, to which it would present its report and recommendations. The Brandt Commission had among its members three other former heads of government: Eduardo Frei, the Christian Democrat ex-president of Chile; Olof Palme, the Social Democrat ex-premier of Sweden; and Edward Heath, who had been the Conservative prime minister of the UK from 1970 to 1974. The majority of the twenty-one members, however, came from developing countries. While all members had attained eminence in public life and represented a broad ideological spectrum, the commission was handicapped because its Western members were now out of power, and some of them had paid rather little attention to world development issues when they were in power. These problems were compounded by Brandt's marked inability to steer the commission's discussions to firm conclusions.[3]

The Brandt Commission finally published its first report in February 1980.[4] It was a brave attempt to reenergize the North-South dialogue and to create a consensus in the international community on desirable future policies to support global economic development. Given Willy Brandt's previous sponsorship of *Ostpolitik,* the policy of opening up to the socialist East, it was natural that the report should place international development issues in the broader context of disarmament and the search for world peace. In doing so, it revived and repopularized the original conception that had inspired the founding of the United Nations, the idea that the promotion of just international economic relations should be a major dimension of the active pursuit of peace. Basing himself on the premise of humankind increasingly becoming a single human community, Brandt argued a moral case for the wealthy nations shouldering additional responsibilities for alleviating the poverty of the poor countries. In addition to this moral case, he argued that, from a national perspective, to do so would be a matter of self-interest for all, given the dangers of war, poverty, famine, and exhaustion of resources.

The report's recommendations did not fulfill McNamara's hope that they would contain entirely new policy ideas. Instead, they covered a range of issues familiar from the NIEO negotiations, indicating support for the positions of the South. On commodities, they endorsed the setting up of the Common Fund and called for the swift conclusion of the series of international commodity agreements envisaged at UNCTAD IV and V. On development finance, the report advocated increased transfers of resources to the South, arguing, in line with UNCTAD's framework of interdependence, that such transfers would in turn produce economic growth in the North. Institutionally, the report reverted to the idea of UN-based development finance outside the Bretton Woods institutions. Transfers, funded by "automatic" long-term bilateral aid flows and by taxes imposed on the international arms trade, would be made through a new World Development Fund, which would have a fully international membership. This was not intended to replace the Bretton Woods institutions but to be additional to them.

These proposals naturally attracted much interest and enthusiasm in the UN. Delegates to the General Assembly paid tribute to the report in more than three dozen speeches, though these tributes came mainly from representatives of the developing countries.[5] In the developed world, copies of the report sold well in the UK (68,000), where 10,000 people attended a mass lobby of Parliament when the report was being discussed.[6] Public opinion in the Netherlands was also favorable, but elsewhere there was much less interest and support, and the international financial institutions were not welcoming. Some Western critics said that, having started from an alarmist view of the dangers of inaction, the Brandt report went on to a naively optimistic view of the benefits of "global Keynesian" policies.[7] Among those haunted by the ghost of "extreme Keynesianism" were the new conservative governments of the U.S., the UK, West Germany (Chancellor Helmut Kohl of the Christian Democratic Party), and Japan (Yasuhiro Namasone of a conservative faction of the Liberal Democratic Party). They thought that the forces of inflation were already dangerously powerful and feared that pumping more liquidity into the international economy could only aggravate inflation.

Brandt recognized that publication of the report came at a time when the industrial countries were deeply anxious about the prospects of economic recession after the second oil-price shock of 1979. Brandt formally presented the report to UN Secretary-General Kurt Waldheim in New York, while Heath launched it simultaneously in London.[8] It was noted at the Venice Economic Summit of 1980, but no action was taken. However, Brandt did not want it to be discussed in a full-scale international conference.[9] He had previously discussed with Waldheim the desirability of a smaller summit meeting of twenty-two countries in the style of the Committee for International Economic Cooperation (CIEC) meeting between 1975 and 1977. The G77 was opposed to selective meetings, but President Lopez Portillo of Mexico offered to host informal, unstructured seminar-type discussions to overcome the stalemate in North-South dialogue in October 1981 at the resort of Cancún. The Austrian co-sponsors were also explicitly seeking to create "a confrontation of ideas."[10]

British prime minister Margaret Thatcher persuaded the new American president, Ronald Reagan, that they should both attend it. He was willing to do so, since the organizers had agreed that no substantive decisions would be taken and Cuba was excluded.[11] As Mrs. Thatcher later explained:

> I felt that, whatever our misgivings about the occasion, we should be present, both to argue for our positions and to forestall criticism that we were uninterested in the developing world. The whole concept of "North-South" dialogue, which the Brandt Commission had made the fashionable talk of the international community, was in my view wrong-headed.[12]

Thus, Thatcher and Reagan went through the motions of expressing concern about poverty and hunger, but the results were slight.[13] Both were determined to resist what they interpreted as "pressure . . . to place the IMF and the World Bank directly under United Nations control."[14] She argued her position with a group of heads of government who could not understand her obsession with the "integrity" (by which she meant independence from UN control) of the IMF and the World Bank—even while agreeing that IMF loan conditionality was in some cases too rigorous. She enlightened them in her usual brutal style. As she recalled: "In the end I put the point more bluntly: I said that there was no way that I was going to put British deposits into a bank which was totally run by those on overdrafts."[15]

The new conservative leaders in the West counted the Cancún summit as a great success, but not for any of the reasons that they could declare in public. First, the independence of the IMF and the World Bank had been maintained. Second, a reason that Mrs. Thatcher thought "equally valuable" was that Cancún was "the last of such gatherings."[16] Despite a follow-up report by the Brandt Commission in 1983[17] and an attempt in 1988 to launch Cancún 2,[18] the North-South dialogue was over in October 1981. Some in the UN thought that the U.S. decision to terminate the dialogue dated from 1980.[19] Certainly its demise was foreseen without any regret in the U.S. State Department in June 1981:

> The October summit could mark the end, for the foreseeable future, of serious attempts to negotiate global economic bargains between North and South. It may be the last gasp of a decade-long effort at multilateral diplomacy.[20]

The Debt Crisis of the Developing Countries

Less than a year after the Cancún summit, Mexico was back in the headlines. This time it was because the country had to suspend payments on its international debt. The Mexican moratorium of August 1982 set off a severe debt crisis in developing countries, particularly in Latin America. There followed from this a veritable counterrevolution in North-South relations. The growth rate of production in the industrial countries in the 1980s improved slightly on that of the 1970s, but the output growth in developing countries fell dramatically to virtually nothing. Over the 1980s, the economies of middle-income developing countries, and of sub-Saharan Africa, actually contracted.[21] As their economies stagnated, their policy autonomy was seriously challenged. This is because if they wanted to continue to receive aid, they were obliged to follow the policy advice that the intellectual doctrines of neoliberalism supplied.

The ending of the North-South dialogue and the subsequent economic, political, and intellectual reverses suffered by the developing countries mark the natural conclusion of the historical narrative of this book as well as the point where archival evidence has largely run out. It remains, however, to convey with broad brush strokes how the industrial countries have consolidated their victory over the last two decades and to ask what lessons can be drawn from the whole of our narrative that will guide the building of better international institutions in the future. This chapter tackles the first of these two tasks by describing the intellectual and institutional strategies the industrial countries have used to maintain the degree of control that they had reestablished over the international economic scene by 1981.

Although the seeds of the debt problem of the 1980s were sown largely during the petrodollar recycling of the 1970s, it was the pursuit of anti-inflation policies by inexperienced conservative governments that actually triggered the debt crisis of the 1980s. These governments then made the welfare of Western banks their paramount concern and adopted an ad hoc approach toward the plight of debt-distressed states. While the developing countries remained caught in the debt trap, industrial countries took the opportunity to induce them to accept a package of structural adjustment policies that their neoliberal sponsors confidently referred to as "sensible economic policies," a combination of macroeconomic stabilization with radical microeconomic liberalization. The agencies entrusted with this task were the IMF and the World Bank.

This chapter examines the origin of these "sensible economic policies," particularly trade policy and the functions of governments in economic management. Why did the intellectual tide in favor of market intervention and state control of economic activity, which had been explicit so recently in the commodities and Common Fund negotiations, begin to ebb? How did the UN lose its intellectual influence in economic matters relative to neoliberal policy preferences of the IMF and the World Bank? We argue that from the late 1960s onward, the industrial countries made substantial investments in economic research on developing countries through organizations that they controlled, such as the OECD and the World Bank, and that this research provided the intellectual backing for a neoliberal counterrevolution. Although the intellectual eclipse of UNCTAD was never quite complete, we further argue that the Uruguay Round negotiations in GATT, the collapse of the Soviet bloc, and the establishment of the World Trade Organization (WTO) combined radically to transform the trade and development scene by the end of the twentieth century.

The single most debilitating influence on the developing countries has been the debt crisis. At UNCTAD IV in Nairobi in 1976, Gamani Corea highlighted the urgency of easing the developing countries' debt burden.[22] He later recalled that "UNCTAD's lone and prophetic warnings on the emerging debt situation were ignored on all sides—by developed and developing countries alike."[23] This, however, omits one thing—the successful initiative that Corea himself took on debt relief in UNCTAD two years after Nairobi.[24] On his proposal, at the ministerial meeting of the Trade and Development Board in March 1978, the developed countries committed themselves to undertake debt relief for the least developed countries by retroactively reducing the terms of past official aid loans. The United States did not join the effort, but other developed countries subsequently gave relief worth $6 billion.[25] Nevertheless, public warnings were certainly in order in 1976, because through the latter half of the 1970s a debt problem was growing, though it was mainly a problem of private-sector debt rather than of public-sector borrowing.

The seeds of the impending trouble had been sown after the first rise in oil prices of late 1973. The OECD countries responded by assuming that the oil shock was permanent and adjusting their economies accordingly.[26] Thus, they had little need to borrow from the OPEC surpluses placed in Western banks, and their abstention from external borrowing pushed world interest rates down. By contrast, many developing countries, particularly in Latin America, decided not to adjust but to cover the higher costs of oil by borrowing extensively from Western commercial banks at what were indeed highly advantageous rates of interest for developing countries. The collapse of the Bretton Woods system had allowed much greater volatility in the exchange rates of major currencies, and Western bank depositors wanted protection from this and from being locked into low-nominal-interest-rate loans. They successfully sought new forms of loan agreement with loans denominated in U.S. dollars and the interest terms specified with variable nominal rates. However, neither Western bankers nor developing-country borrowers understood the implications of these two changes. The banks believed that sovereign debt would be reliably repaid, while the borrowing governments did not anticipate the consequences of the arrival on the international scene of conservative Western governments dedicated to disinflation.

Mrs. Thatcher's Conservative government came to power in Britain in mid-1979, but for eighteen months it could not stop both nominal interest rates and inflation rising to double digits. By 1981, the UK was engaged on a massive fiscally induced contraction of demand. When President Reagan's Republican administration took office in early 1981, it tried to learn from what it saw as Thatcher's economic failures but ended up by creating a large structural U.S. budget deficit.[27] The U.S. government now needed to borrow a sum estimated at around 8 percent of world savings, driving up both nominal and real interest rates, so that real rates rose from negative in 1980 to 4 percent in 1982 and then stayed there—at double the average rate over 1950–1980. The rise in interest payments now applied not just to all new loans but also to all existing loans with variable-rate clauses.[28]

From August 1982, when Mexico suspended payment on its debt, new commercial lending to developing countries virtually dried up. Many developing countries were now caught in a classic debt trap. Worse still, as new money

from the commercial banks all but disappeared, nothing replaced it. Total official development finance, or "aid," did not expand to fill the gap. Although many
OECD countries did expand their aid budgets in the 1980s, other highly significant donors offset this expansion by cutting back on their aid. The aid cutters
were the OPEC countries, the UK, and—largest of all—the United States.

Nigel Lawson, UK chancellor of the exchequer 1983–1989, was centrally involved in the Western management of the debt crisis and later explained the
strategy that the industrial countries fashioned to cope with it:

> [T]he principal—although largely undeclared—objective of the Western world's
> debt strategy, ably coordinated by the IMF, was to buy time. . . . Time was needed
> not only to enable the debtor countries to put sensible economic policies in
> place but also for the Western banks to rebuild their shattered balance sheets to
> the point where they could afford to write off their bad sovereign debts. For it
> was perfectly clear that the vast bulk off these debts would never come good
> and be repaid—even though there was an understandable conspiracy of si-
> lence over admitting this unpalatable fact.[29]

The paramount concern of the West was preserving the solvency of the
commercial banks that had loaned so carelessly. Only in 1989, when the risk
to the banks was over, did the U.S. make the first serious move—the Brady
Plan—to help the debt-distressed developing countries that had borrowed so
carelessly. By then, the 1980s had become for the majority of developing countries "the lost decade."

For the developing countries, the economic policies of the Reagan and
Thatcher governments had major adverse effects. While the springing of the
debt trap was the most important, the prolonged deterioration in their terms of
trade caused by slower economic growth in industrial countries was also severe.
Politically, the international position of the developing countries was undermined. Whereas before 1982 they were able to demand vociferously a new international economic order, after 1982 their indebtedness constrained their balance
of payments and rendered them supplicants to the financial institutions of the
existing international order, the IMF, and the World Bank. Significantly, the
most affected by this reversal of economic fortune were the countries of Latin
America, whose political alliance with Asia and Africa twenty years before had
started the search for a new international trade and development regime.

"Sensible Economic Policies": Foreign Trade and the Role of Government

What were the "sensible economic policies" that the British Chancellor wanted
debt-distressed developing countries to put in place? He shared the widespread

assumption that the main obstacles impeding the economic development of developing countries were internal, not external. This perception was hardly new: it had existed right from the time of the trade and development debates in the UN in the 1940s. However, it had strengthened through the decade of the 1970s, and in the field of trade and industry it had been given a much more concrete intellectual form. The OECD was funded to produce a series of studies on trade and industry in developing countries which were influential in altering the climate of opinion.[30] The analytical key to these case studies was the measurement of effective rates of protection, a concept pioneered by Canadian and Australian trade economists in the 1950s and 1960s.[31] The notion of "effective protection" was anchored in "world prices": it is the difference in value added at domestic and world prices divided by value added at world prices. This rate is higher than the nominal rate of protection for a product—the tariff rate inscribed in the government's tariff book—to the extent that inputs required for the domestic manufacture of the product are imported at lower rates of tariff.[32] What matters, then, is not just the height of individual product tariffs; it is the whole structure of protection.[33]

These OECD studies of trade and industry thus threw new light on the extent of protection in developing countries. The effective rate of protection of some industries was at times twice as high as the nominal rate, which in many cases was already around 100 percent. The studies found examples of industries with negative value added: their imported inputs were worth more at world prices than the manufactured product. In agriculture, by contrast, protection was often negative, since tariffs were levied on its inputs while imports of the product were let in tariff-free. These results suggested that governments were exploiting agriculture, not just neglecting it, and that they were doing so in order to build up industries that could not compete internationally. That the use of protection by developing countries was excessive and distorting was already widely believed, including by Prebisch, as we have previously seen.[34] These OECD studies provided a startlingly clear picture of the extent of the excess, bringing the problem into much sharper focus.

When balance-of-payments crises became too severe, many developing-country governments resorted to imposing quantitative restrictions on imports (QRs), which could be used to maintain an overvalued exchange rate, depressing exports and restricting economies of scale in industry. An artificially strong exchange rate also cheapened imports, encouraged excessively capital-intensive technology, and thus limited job creation in industry. Nonetheless, industry was highly profitable because of the high rates of effective protection. The combination of high profits and low employment skewed the distribution of income toward the rich. Discrimination against exports caused underinvestment in agriculture, while cheaper imports did little for a sector that had low import requirements. For all these reasons, the use of QRs was singled out as a major obstacle to the rational management of the economy, causing slow growth and income inequality.

This bleak picture did not, however, immediately translate into a prescription for trade liberalization. The static gains from dismantling QRs were unlikely to be large, so change had to be motivated by research on dynamic gains. Another multivolume study sponsored by the U.S. National Bureau of Economic Research found that while reducing QRs did increase exports, and therefore growth (because exports are part of the gross national product), no increase was discernible in the elasticity of output with respect to exports.[35] While the definitive case for trade liberalization remained to be established, these trade studies of the 1970s played a significant part in changing the perspective on the nature of the link between trade and development and in defining "sensible" policies.[36]

World prices were now adopted to anchor detailed microeconomic analyses of government policy, which had been neglected in the earlier macroeconomic theories. The lesson was that the developing economy should no longer be modeled as if it were closed to foreign trade when the degree of closure was a policy choice and that it should no longer be assumed that foreign aid would fill any balance-of-payments gap, however it was caused. Responsibility for the good management of foreign trade was thus pushed back to developing-country governments. This was reasonable, in the sense that many were evidently not making the best use of the trading opportunities they faced. At the same time, however, it must be emphasized that the use of world prices as the anchor of economic calculation distracted attention from the fact that world prices were by no stretch of the imagination ideal scarcity prices. They reflected all the restraints on free trade that the industrial countries were imposing for their own protectionist purposes, such as agricultural subsidies and textile-import quotas. In other words, the world prices that were to provide the new measuring rod of economic rationality in developing countries still incorporated all the distortions that would need to be removed in any future negotiations for an international order of true freedom of trade.

More generally, the 1970s had witnessed a groundswell of negative views of the economic performance of the state, not least in developing countries. The growing negativity about the state came from all parts of the ideological compass and was by no means the monopoly of the political right. The close relation between economic advisors and the government machine, and accumulating experience of the way it worked in practice, may explain the spreading disappointment of the hope of a rational and benevolent state.[37] Whereas errors of economic policy might once have been attributed to ignorance and honest mistakes, the closer view may have suggested the possibility of more sinister motives. Analysts began to explain the failure of development policies in terms not just of the conflict between economic development and governments' other public objectives but also of conflict between the goals of development and the state's hidden agenda. The idea of the state's hidden agenda prompted a series of explorations of what lay below the political surface, generating a variety of political economy analyses of the nature of the state.

Resurgent neo-Marxism following the political turbulence in the West of the late 1960s had related the hidden agenda of the state to the interests of the capitalist class and then examined class formations in developing countries and their links with the bourgeoisie of the industrialized world. Another popular but non-Marxist formulation was that the state was dominated by an urban coalition, unified by its location but cutting across class lines, whose collective interest was the exploitation of the rural hinterland. Its policies systematically discriminated against agriculture in a way that was both inefficient and inequitable, a discrimination that was operated by maintaining an artificially high exchange rate and a state monopoly of agricultural exports. In this view, anti-agriculture policies were sustained by a political system of urban bias.[38] Accordingly, progress could be made only by weakening the power of urban elites. This required a thorough reversal of political and administrative culture and priorities and a widespread willingness to "put the last first."[39]

Once conservative governments were installed in the UK, the U.S., West Germany, and Japan, the political economy that became most acceptable in international political circles highlighted the collusion between the state in developing countries and rent-seeking domestic interest groups. The crucial link, made some years previously, was that between the syndrome of the overvalued exchange rate and the practice of administrative allocation of import licenses under a QR regime. In combination, these phenomena were said to spawn "rent-seeking activities" that were unproductive and corrupting.[40] Using this analysis as a prime exhibit, a general case was made that government failure was worse than market failure, thus challenging the original justification for the expansion of government beyond its night watchman role and into the role of development entrepreneur.[41]

The IMF: The Able Coordinator of the Western Debt Strategy

The collapse of the Bretton Woods system of fixed parities was the end of the fund's role as lender of last resort for the central banks of the OECD countries.[42] The second amendment to the IMF Articles of Agreement in 1978 allowed all forms of national exchange-rate mechanisms except pegging to gold. Many of the larger economies chose to float their currency; for example, the

U.S., the UK, Japan, and those in the EEC. Many of the smaller economies chose to peg their exchange rate to other currencies or baskets of currencies. The role of the IMF was thus reduced to one of surveillance and reporting on the exchange-rate arrangements chosen by its members, plus advocating "principles of guidance" without any real power of enforcement. The IMF, as an international organization, looked increasingly for new clients in the developing countries, thereby casting around for a new role for itself.

Under the gold-exchange standard (1944–1971), the IMF had little interest in the developing countries. Many had never been properly integrated into that system at all, apart from certain Latin American countries (Peru, Paraguay) where the IMF had pioneered policy conditionality.[43] From the early 1960s onward, largely under pressure from the UN, the IMF did develop some additional "banking" facilities relevant to the needs of developing countries, characterized by concessional interest rates compared with commercial sources of finance. The Compensatory Financing Facility (CCF), established in 1963, made limited credit available to countries experiencing a temporary fall in their trend export revenues. The tight limits that made it unattractive to developing countries were liberalized in 1975, reflecting concerns of UNCTAD.[44] This increased its usage until 1985, when tight policy conditionality was imposed on users.[45] The IMF even created a Buffer Stock Facility in 1969 after UNCTAD II, but eligibility was narrowly defined and this was barely used at all.[46] More significant was the Extended Fund Facility (EFF) of 1974, which provided medium-term finance beyond the limits of normal lending to support agreed-upon stabilization programs requiring structural adjustments. The EFF was backed up in 1976 and 1977 by a new trust fund to provide balance-of-payments loans on highly concessional terms to low-income countries and a new supplementary facility to assist countries that might otherwise be liable to debt default, subject to adoption of policies to restore the external position of the borrowing country.

As the developing countries became the IMF's sole clients, a new gulf opened up between them and the industrial countries, whose entrenched voting power still directed the IMF. The organization changed its nature from being an institution of collective action by the developed countries to being their instrument to discipline others and to induce them to adopt "sensible economic policies." The Mexican debt crisis of 1982 was thus a turning point in the history of the IMF and of the World Bank. The Reagan administration recruited these international financial institutions to be its managers for the Western debt strategy of buying time, while the commercial banks wrote off their bad sovereign debts.

The capital available to both was increased. As for the IMF, building on the EFF, its new longer-term lending facilities were created to channel credit to indebted developing countries. The Structural Adjustment Facility (SAF) was set up in 1986, followed by the Extended Structural Adjustment Facility (ESAF) in 1987. SAF/ESAF loans were provided as loans to low-income countries suffering protracted balance-of-payments problems. While interest was very low at 0.5 percent and repayment was made in $5^{1}/_{2}$ to 10 years, policy conditionality was strong. These facilities allowed the IMF to adopt a mediating role between debtors and creditors. IMF stabilization programs were intended to restore macroeconomic balance in the countries that adopted them so that they would be able to pay their debt-service obligations (rescheduled if necessary) to their creditors in an orderly manner. Participation in an IMF program was therefore expected to be a "seal of approval" that would encourage private creditors to roll over existing loans and supply new loans to the debtors. Thus, IMF money was also expected to "leverage" or "catalyze" private flows.

In the event, matters did not work out quite so well. On the one hand, the stabilization programs did not always have the intended effect of rendering the borrowing country creditworthy. They frequently broke down before completion. Between 1979 and 1993, 53 percent of 305 IMF programs were uncompleted—for a variety of different reasons, but often for reasons connected with inadequate financing.[47] Estimates of the impact of IMF programs showed that they improved the current account and the overall balance of payments and slowed inflation but that there was also a short-term reduction in growth rate. On the other hand, the IMF seal of approval was not effective in catalyzing new private lending. The overall balance of payments rarely improved by more than the improvement on the current account, as would have happened if there had been a positive catalytic effect on private and other aid inflows. Although private markets (and aid donors) valued a government's commitment to sound economic policies, they might doubt that the fund would prescribe the best policies or that fund conditionality would ensure that prescribed policies were pursued. They might also judge that amount of IMF financing to be inadequate.[48] After the fall of the Berlin Wall in 1989 and the collapse of the Soviet Union, the IMF, along with the World Bank, had to absorb many new members. Nevertheless, the transition countries did not displace developing countries as the main users of IMF funds, as the European Bank for Reconstruction and Development became a principal source for the transition states.

The World Bank: Looking for Leverage

The World Bank was the IMF's junior partner as coordinator of the West's debt strategy. For its first thirty years, the bank provided both project finance

and technical assistance in formulating and executing projects. Bank participation in these projects almost certainly raised their quality and their economic returns, but doubts about project finance began to surface in the 1960s.
If the borrowing government had undertaken the project that the bank financed even in the absence of the loan, then the loan would have effectively
financed some other project—the one that would not otherwise have been
undertaken and whose rate of return might be much less satisfactory than
that of the ostensibly bank-financed project. An early protagonist of this argument, that funds are fungible, was Hans Singer, then at UN Research Institute for Social Development (UNRISD).[49] Although fungibility need not
concern a development bank aiming to recover its loans, it should worry a
multilateral aid agency funded by public capital, as the bank became after the
establishment of the IDA. The objective of a development agency is to promote the sound development of the borrower's economy and to ensure that
projects are part of a development plan precisely because funds are fungible,
as Singer pointed out.

Singer further argued: "Even if there is no substitution of resources between projects . . . the efficiency of [the funded project] would still depend on
the soundness of the recipient's total investment programme."[50] Here is another example of how the UN "wild men" could influence the bank. In the
1970s, the World Bank came to accept this insight, believing that the success
of their individual loan projects, measured by their *ex post* rates of return,
was reduced because of the deterioration in the broader economic environment in which they had to operate (rising oil prices, high inflation, inflexible
exchange rates, import restrictions, and so on). In 1979, at UNCTAD V in
Manila, the World Bank announced that it would initiate a new type of lending, called program lending, which was intended as a way to handle this problem. The loan "vehicle" was not a physical project but a program of policy
changes. Previously regarded as unsound—Eugene Black liked to call them
"fuzzy loans"—program loans were now justified on the grounds that if successful they would render themselves redundant in future. The new types of
loans (structural- and sector-adjustment lending) provided rapidly disbursing foreign exchange on condition that the borrowing government undertook economic policy changes. This form of lending rose by the mid-1980s to
be one-third of the bank's new lending, the other two-thirds remaining as
project finance.

Program lending with policy conditions attached was the instrument that
the bank brought to the task of co-managing the 1980s debt crisis with the
fund. After A. W. Clausen and Anne Krueger replaced Robert McNamara and
Hollis Chenery as president and chief of research respectively, the World Bank

used loan conditionality to try to induce developing countries' governments to adopt what it regarded as "sensible economic policies."[51] No longer were they to be educated about how to select their industrial investments by means of shadow prices. They now had to divest themselves of state-owned industries and to liberalize actual prices comprehensively—in goods markets, labor markets, financial markets, capital markets, and foreign trade markets. They were encouraged to concentrate their efforts on law and order, education, and health. This view became codified in what was called the Washington Consensus on economic policy for developing countries, a set of precepts to which all sensible economists, according to John Williamson, could be expected to agree. Although intended modestly as a set of minimum aims, they were taken as the neoliberals' standard policy prescriptions, with the implication that "one size fits all."[52]

"Reduce poverty" was not one of the ten precepts of the Washington Consensus. Yet it would be a mistake, if one wants to understand the persuasive force of this consensus, to ignore the way in which it justified shrinking of the state in order to improve the distribution of income. The claim was that a smaller state would be good for growth and growth would be good for poverty reduction. Also, since poverty is more severe in rural areas and since state economic regulations and organizations disadvantaged agriculturists and privileged industrialists, a smaller state would tend to reduce inequality in the distribution of income and wealth. The manifesto of the counterrevolution in development was not simply about greater efficiency: it contained a promise of poverty reduction through growth and greater equity as well.[53]

The search for success stories about this new model of development led champions of the free-price mechanism to celebrate the newly industrializing countries of Asia as examples of the fast growth and good income distribution resulting from economic liberalization. Closer inspection revealed considerable evidence of remaining government intervention in trade, industry, and finance, but the neoliberals brushed it aside with the assertion that the different interventions cancelled each other out or that they were counterproductive and that growth would have been even faster without them.[54] This claim is controversial. Despite intercountry differences, the East Asian growth story is about government and business coordination to secure high investment, high saving, reinvestment, and rapid growth of competitive exports in a joint strategy of national development.[55] In the 1980s, however, the World Bank used spectacular Asian growth to confer credibility on the Washington Consensus on liberal development policies.

The bank launched itself into economy-wide policy issues just as the IMF moved heavily into medium-term adjustment lending through SAF and ESAF.

These moves brought the two institutions into potential collision. Various coordination problems arose from their overlap of functions, notably the incident in 1988 when the bank (under U.S. pressure) made a loan to Argentina, while the IMF refused its support. An IMF–World Bank "concordat" (1989) established effective (though not formal) cross-conditionality of these institutions' loans. Bank adjustment lending became conditional on a preexisting IMF program, and a statement of economic policy for the borrowing country had to be agreed to by both institutions. In usual practice, apart from one country government representative on the drafting team, they jointly drafted the Policy Framework Paper (later "Poverty Reduction Strategy Paper"), and the country government would then agree to sign it.

Conditionality or no conditionality, the bank has to rely on its power to persuade on issues of development policy. Hence, the bank has invested heavily in an intellectual infrastructure and will no doubt continue to do so. A start on this had been made in the mid-1960s under George Woods, when staff members of the bank's Economics Department expanded sixfold in five years. However, by the end of the 1980s, the bank employed no less than 800 economists and had a research budget of $25 million a year, resources that dwarf those of any university department.[56] Although the production of publishable research is only one of the functions of its research department, the bank has continued to conduct what is almost certainly the largest single publication program on development issues in the world. It is the source of a host of monographs and a multitude of working papers. The bank's influential flagship report, the annual *World Development Report*, inaugurated in 1978, has been credibly claimed as the most widely read document in development economics. In the 1980s, the bank began to publish more research through two new house journals, *The World Bank Economic Review* and *The World Bank Research Observer*. The bank has also become a major provider of statistical data, including regular published series such as the *World Debt Tables* and data from household and firm surveys. Complementing its publications are its other methods of disseminating its views on development. Since 1955, the bank's Economic Development Institute has maintained an in-house training facility for developing-country economics professionals, many of whom have returned to work at the bank.

As noted in the introduction, the bank's justification for undertaking in-house research and dissemination—rather than outsourcing these functions—is that this procedure gives it better control over the topics of research and makes it more likely that the results will be used in its operations. Yet there are good reasons to expect that the in-house research of a well-managed international organization will be trimmed to meet the top management's desire to promulgate a particular perspective. From the early 1980s, this desire has strengthened in the bank, as it was felt to be important to avoid sowing any doubts in client countries about how "sensible" the West's approach to the debt crisis, and the liberalizing content of policy conditionality, really were. Greater pressure for doctrinal conformity caused mixed reactions in the bank, and key figures on the research staff disagreed on the merits of research being subordinated to the operational requirements of structural adjustment:

> The early 1980s was full of the excitement of structural adjustment, but it was not here that the research side of the Bank led the way. A switch of interest towards markets and prices was welcomed by many. However, some spoke of a decline in the research atmosphere, of a degree of intolerance and of a requirement to tow [sic] the party line. Others saw a rescue from intellectual tiredness and dead-ends.[57]

Since 1980, the pressure of operational needs has had the inevitable effect of dampening in-house intellectual creativity and boosting research that serves the bank's current persuasive purposes. Attempts to evaluate the quality of the bank's research and publication activities have noted that their extensive influence on policymakers and educators has been matched by the modest extent of their intellectual innovation. Even World Bank insiders do not claim to have played a major role in the economics profession, and many are frustrated by the lack of a good atmosphere for serious research. Some of them do, however, claim to have "produced more high quality research than other UN agencies."[58] This claim may seem plausible, but the more interesting question is how the comparison would look on the basis of the equality of the endowment of research resources.

A particular example of research being conformable to management objectives is the World Bank's research on the debt crisis. Compared with the academic literature of the day,[59] World Bank researchers made more optimistic predictions in 1981 about the future availability of private capital flows to already-indebted developing countries. In this, they supported the view of the president at the time, Robert McNamara, that the debt problem was manageable and would not obstruct economic growth. Moreover, as the debt crisis worsened, the bank fell well behind academic opinion on the need for debt relief. The bank's chief economist, Stanley Fischer, candidly acknowledged the reasons for this:

> It was clear to the participants in this [World Bank] conference at the beginning of 1989, as it had been clear to many much earlier, that growth in the debtor countries would not return without debt relief. But the official agencies operate on the basis of an agreed upon strategy, and none of them could openly confront

the existing strategy without having an alternative to put in place. And to propose such an alternative would have required agreement among the major share-
holders of the institutions. So long as the United States was not willing to move,
the IFI's [international financial institutions] were not free to speak.[60]

From Structural Adjustment to Poverty Reduction

After 1980, the industrial countries increasingly backed away from the economic activities of the UN while devising new functions for more malleable
instruments such as the IMF and the World Bank. In the wake of the Latin
American debt crisis, the G7 industrialized countries used these financial institutions to engineer the "structural adjustment" of the economies of developing countries. For countries whose balance-of-payments gap could no longer
be filled by expanding aid grants, adjustment meant reducing aggregate demand to equal aggregate supply, plus whatever amount sustainable borrowing could finance. A simple reduction in absorption would, however, typically
create an imbalance between the supply of and demand for nontraded goods
so that contraction of demand would have to be accompanied by currency
devaluation. Contraction was not the end of the story: after successful macroeconomic stabilization, supply-side measures were intended to promote the
resumption of growth. The removal of price distortions and the shrinkage of
the public sector were intended to provide the impulse to resumed growth.

Stabilization was relatively less controversial because often there was no
feasible alternative: the only choice was between a planned and a chaotic contraction. Interest thus centered on measuring the size and duration of negative growth, plus how the different genders and socioeconomic groups were
affected.[61] More controversial were the effects of liberalization. Research trying to show that trade liberalization increased the rate of economic growth
was dogged by the difficulty of applying an unambiguous measure of trade
liberalization. The best measure is the reduction in effective rates of protection, but they are extremely laborious to calculate, although theoretically preferable. Other measures are normally used, but they can be misleading in
various ways. The World Bank has expended large sums on researching the
topic of trade liberalization by various alternative methods and has produced
some massive tomes.[62] Critics, however, have found them to be both inconclusive and tendentious.[63]

The case for financial liberalization rested on work done in the 1970s on
financial repression.[64] Although the use of low interest-rate ceilings on formal-
sector lending could be criticized as an open door for the political allocation
of loans in a context of excess demand, the expectation of rapid growth after

their removal relied on some strong assumptions, including that of coexistence of traditional and modern technology within agriculture. Moreover, institutional aspects of changing from a rationed to a free market in credit, especially the (previously superfluous) issue of bankers' ability to judge and manage risk, were neglected. One of the most prescient aphorisms of this period was Carlos Diaz-Alejandro's remark: "Goodbye financial repression, hello financial crisis"—the overture to many analyses of the Southern Cone in 1982–1983, Mexico in 1994, and the Asian crisis in 1997–1998.

Structural adjustment was a very large policy package, since it was composed of stabilization, liberalization, and privatization, and since each of these sub-categories of the package consisted of many different specific actions that, for success, should be pursued in a co-coordinated program. Development economics has not been particularly well equipped to resolve the practical issue of the sequencing of this large package of policies, and, as later evaluations showed, sequencing errors have been one of the factors that blunted the effectiveness of reform programs.[65]

The main UN riposte to the prevailing policies of structural adjustment came from UNICEF in 1987. Under the irresistible title of *Adjustment with a Human Face,* the UNICEF authors pointed to statistics that showed deteriorations in various measures of child and adult welfare since structural adjustment reforms had started, although they did not claim that the reforms had caused the deteriorations. They accepted that adjustment was necessary but argued that reforms should be carried out more gradually in a way that would consolidate their political support. They said that issues of social welfare needed to be given higher priority and that targeted remedial measures should be integrated into the overall design of the reforms. International measures were not absent from the team's recommendations. For example, they included proposals to extend the IMF's Compensatory Finance Facility and to revive the idea of an SDR-aid link.[66] The ideas in *Adjustment with a Human Face* were well publicized and undoubtedly influenced the public mood to be more critical of reform programs that neglected welfare concerns.

From the more limited economic perspective, the verdict on the structural adjustment of the 1980s was that it delivered much less than its advocates had claimed for it. Exports and overall growth grew slightly as a result, while the share of investment to GDP declined somewhat.[67] Excessive confidence was invested not only in the reforms themselves but also in the bank's ability to persuade countries to undertake them. Apparently a powerful lever over countries in need of finance, loan conditionality in fact turned out to give the bank rather little leverage. This can be explained in terms of the bank's conflict of objectives and the high costs involved in supervising the performance of borrowers.[68]

By the end of the 1980s, the very considerable effort expended on structural adjustment seemed to have distracted attention from other central issues of development, in particular from poverty reduction. The willingness to let poverty reduction wait upon increased growth eroded as the growth record of structural adjustment policies was shown to be unimpressive. Greater credence was given to the idea that growth itself depended on poverty reduction. It was argued (once again) that better health and education services for the poor would permit the formation of socially desirable human capital that would not otherwise take place and would thus make the economy more productive. These claims could be rationalized by reference to new theories of growth that installed human capital accumulation as the engine of growth.[69]

The World Bank acknowledged the new interest in poverty reduction in its *World Development Report 1990*, which stressed the need to ensure that growth was labor intensive and that basic social services were effective. The program of structural adjustment was by no means abandoned, but it now had to be pursued with a much greater concern for its effects on the level and intensity of poverty. The UN did its best both to lead and to reinforce the shift of emphasis back to the concern with poverty that was evident in the 1990s. In 1990, the UNDP began its *Human Development Report* series, featuring a novel but statistically controversial index of human development. Its purpose was to give more prominence to indicators of human well-being such as life expectancy and literacy in measures of development and to counter the widespread obsession with international-league tables of the size and growth of per capita GNP. At the turn of the century, the UNDP was seeking to embed the idea of human development in the discourse of universal human rights.

The Fate of UNCTAD: Demotion and Freedom to Dissent

As the conservative counterrevolution gathered pace, UNCTAD did not simply shut up shop but continued, in the way that bureaucracies normally do, to move into new areas of activity. This was a way of justifying its budgets and building a series of support constituencies. This process had already begun in the 1970s. An early example was its work on merchant shipping and the integration of developing countries into the system of liner conferences.[70] After 1970, the transfer of technology became an issue of concern and discussion, leading on in the 1980s to attempts to negotiate an international code of conduct on the subject. Projects of economic cooperation among developing countries were taken up as a theme in UNCTAD as well as special issues affecting the least-developed countries.[71] In the 1980s, proliferation of activities became even more pronounced, encompassing support for the economic aspects of national liberation movements in Zimbabwe, Namibia, South Africa, and Palestine.[72]

The results of this proliferation of activity were varied. It contributed to a loss of coherence and focus in the organization as a whole as the number of small units engaged in marginal and unrelated work multiplied. This fragmentation was aggravated by the growing practice of taking on technical assistance work as a sub-contractor to other international public agencies. On the other side of the account, in some of these new niche activities, the UNCTAD secretariat was able to develop special skills and deliver public goods that were genuinely valuable. By the 1990s, one of UNCTAD's sternest critics recognized its achievements in several important areas: the provision of information on statistics of international trade and data on private foreign investment and specialized technical assistance in debt-management procedures and carbon-emissions trading.[73] These real achievements, however, depended essentially on the commitment and energy of outstanding individuals in the secretariat rather than on any focused organizational drive or dynamic.[74]

UNCTAD has also maintained some high-quality publications that regularly analyze the world economic conjuncture and its impact on trade, finance, and development. The annual *Trade and Development Report* series is preeminent in that respect. It is the main UN source of regular analysis of the international economy that stands apart from the platitudes of the neoliberal consensus. Moreover, each year it selects for extensive treatment a special theme, such as international income distribution, industrialization strategies, or world financial architecture, and these sections are often vehicles for valuable research on the chosen subject.[75] Unlike the World Bank, however, the UNCTAD secretariat publishes several flagship reports. The much smaller agency puts out no less than three flagship reports, the others being *World Investment Report* and *The Least Developed Countries Report.* In consequence, the resources devoted to the *Trade and Development Report* are only one-fifth or less of those that the World Bank devotes to its *World Development Report,* and its print run is correspondingly smaller.[76] The UNCTAD management's control of the content of its three flagship publications is light, as is evident from the contradictory positions the different reports sometimes take on issues such as the benefits of foreign direct investment. The managerial attitude of "let a hundred flowers bloom" is in marked contrast to insistence on strong editorial control that accompanied what we have called the political approach adopted under Gamani Corea during the Common Fund negotiations of the late 1970s.

It is easier now for UNCTAD's managers to take a relatively relaxed and liberal attitude toward research publication because, in the broader scheme

of things, the establishment of the WTO after the Uruguay Round radically
changed UNCTAD's position among the international trade institutions. In
the presence of the WTO, it no longer made sense to have two international
bodies where trade issues were negotiated. The Brandt report itself had already suggested the integration of GATT and UNCTAD. The disempowerment
of UNCTAD as a North-South negotiating forum started at UNCTAD VIII in
Cartagena (1992) and was completed at UNCTAD IX at Midrand, South Africa (1996).[77] After 1996, UNCTAD ceased to be a negotiating forum for world
trade issues, and in line with this it reduced the scale of its intergovernmental
machinery and consolidated its divisional structure:

> 25 separate work programmes and sub-programmes were replaced by one
> programme consisting of five sub-programmes; the number of intergovernmental
> bodies was halved; the number of meetings cut to a third of what it was in 1992;
> the number of divisions in the secretariat was reduced from nine to five.[78]

Thus, Gamani Corea's ambition for the organization was formally laid to rest.
Since then its role has been ancillary to the WTO, providing a place where
trade and development issues can be discussed and where advice and technical assistance can be offered to developing countries preparing for trade negotiations in the WTO. This reduction in function and downsizing implied
greater interagency cooperation between UNCTAD and the WTO, building
on previous GATT/UNCTAD cooperation, such as their joint International
Trade Commission to help developing countries to promote their exports. As
secretary-general, Rubens Ricupero, himself a former trade negotiator for
Brazil, has been successful in adapting UNCTAD to this more modest role
and thereby gaining the goodwill of OECD governments. By UNCTAD X in
Bangkok (2000), UNCTAD no longer faced what had been a real threat to its
continued existence.

The Cold War Ends: The WTO Arrives

We have argued that the economic ideas associated with the early days of the
UN and with the radical economists who served the organization during its
first quarter-century gradually lost their power to persuade policymakers. The
establishment of UNCTAD in 1964 is a convenient point to mark a transition in
the practice of industrial countries as regards research on development-policy
problems. Broadly speaking, up to that point, they were willing to join research efforts within the ambit of the UN. After that, they preferred to fund
such research within those international organizations over which they, but
not the developing countries, exercised control. We have shown how research

output on development issues from agencies such as the OECD and the World Bank subsequently grew in volume and began to displace the received ideas and policies. The G77 has made no similar investment—indeed it has made hardly any investment at all—in development-policy research, and this neglect left them vulnerable both in the Common Fund negotiations and subsequently. When conservative governments came to power in the West and then the debt crisis decisively swung the balance of political power away from the developing countries, much of the ammunition for a neoliberal counterrevolution on trade policy and the role of the public sector more generally was already to hand.

The collapse of state socialist regimes in Eastern Europe in autumn 1989 and the subsequent disappearance of the Soviet Union marked a further phase. It consolidated the neoliberal counterrevolution of the 1980s. The awkward fact of a bloc of countries committed to a completely different method of international trade, state trading, simply disappeared. The argument used to justify the setting up of UNCTAD, that GATT could not become a truly global trade institution, fell by the wayside. At the same time, the GATT Uruguay Round was already breaking new ground for international trade agreements, going well beyond the traditional industrial tariff-reduction exercises. Plans for a multilateral (later, world) trade organization that would integrate the results of these new types of trade agreement were first discussed informally just before the collapse of the Eastern Europe dominoes and were then formally proposed by Canada and negotiated between 1990 and 1993.[79]

The arrival of the WTO was important not only because it had the potential to become a global organization. In addition to incorporating and superseding the GATT, the WTO also extended multilateral rule-making into large new areas of trade policy where no such rules had existed before. The nature of these rules was also changed, in that they were given precedence over preexisting domestic legislation and made more enforceable internationally through the WTO dispute settlement mechanism. The WTO provided the completion of the "third pillar" of the world economic system, a modern replacement for the abortive ITO of 1947–1948. The construction of the WTO was the first major institutional change related to international trade since the birth of UNCTAD, and it marked a watershed in the history of international economic relations. It must provide the perspective for our consideration, in the final chapter, of the lessons for the future that are to be drawn from our account of UN thinking on trade, finance, and development.

12

What Lessons for the Future?

- **The Contest for Global Economic Control**
- **An Economic Security Council?**
- **What Should Be Done to Reform the IMF?**
- **What Should Be Done to Reform the World Bank?**
- **WTO Rules: OK?**
- **WTO Rules, Industrial Subsidies, and Development**
- **Greater Developing-Country Participation in WTO Rule-Making**
- **Can International Organizations Be Creative Intellectual Actors?**

The Contest for Global Economic Control

Member governments support the UN for a variety of very different motives. It is a point that one writer emphasized in the following way:

> It is recorded that a traveller in France once came upon a wayside hotel named "The Immaculate Conception and Commercial." This is a very apt name for the house in which the world lives and might appropriately be hung up as an inn-sign outside the Headquarters of the United Nations. Human motives, whether expressed individually or collectively, are just such a mixture of the lofty and the base, the sacred and the profane, the sublime and the ridiculous. It is to this complexity that we have to address ourselves, and within the walls of this house we have to live and work.[1]

In seeking to draw lessons for the future, as we do in this final chapter, we shall bear this advice firmly in mind. Lessons that assume that human nature harbors, or can be easily made to harbor, only lofty aspirations and noble motivation will not be very useful ones. Our zeal to escape from the mistakes and muddles of the past should not lead us to call for a general march toward utopia.

Even in the earliest years of the UN, heady idealism was diluted by a strong dose of economic and financial calculation. Radically divergent views already existed about the constitutional relationship of the Bretton Woods institutions to the rest of the UN system. As we have seen in Chapter 1, both Harry Dexter White and Treasury secretary Henry Morgenthau were "determined that the United Nations was never going to tell the World Bank or the International Monetary Fund what to do."[2] The British firmly supported the Americans on this point, and in 1947 the Anglo-American position was entrenched in letters of agreement exchanged between ECOSOC and the IMF and the World Bank. Nevertheless, other countries had taken a different stance and were willing to see the IMF and the bank subordinated to some form of UN control.[3] The claim made by many developing countries that the Bretton Woods institutions should be part of a UN-based system of world government, although overridden in 1947, continued to compete with the established fact that they operated as independent executive agencies whose actions could be influenced only through their own contribution-weighted systems of governance. This conflict smoldered on, and it animated much of the history with which our volume has been concerned.

As UN membership began to change rapidly in size and composition with the grants of colonial independence of the 1960s, different groups of UN members increasingly vied for control of the organization. Developed countries tussled with developing countries about nothing less momentous than the appropriate forms of global economic governance, and the phases of the struggle were played out in the diplomacy of the North-South dialogue. The developing countries had lost this conflict by 1981, and indeed it is difficult to imagine how they could ever have won it. While it continued, it undermined the possibility that the UNCTAD secretariat could act successfully as a global think tank on trade and development, since they were also advisors to one of the parties to the contest. It would thus be misleadingly narrow to claim that the gradual eclipse suffered by the UNCTAD secretariat's view of the links between trade, finance, and development was simply the product of differential rates of investment in development-policy research between the North and the South. That is because the decisions about how much to invest in such research, and who should do it, were determined as part of the larger contest.

The campaign for SUNFED in the 1950s, discussed in Chapter 7, was a crucial moment of the struggle. Its protagonists aimed not only at setting up a soft-loan agency for developing countries; they also wanted to create a new financial executive agency under UN control. In the first aim it succeeded, but in the latter aim it failed. This failure came about not because the campaign could not muster the votes to outvote its opponents but because its supporters recognized the need to compromise with the countries that would be expected to subscribe the necessary funds. It is a fact of international life that aid donors prefer to operate through international agencies where they have superior control. Even those who deplore this fact recognize it.[4] The compromise that emerged over SUNFED might therefore have served as a model for future cooperation between the main economic institutions of the UN and the Bretton Woods institutions. In this compromise, new policy proposals could be presented and negotiated in the UN and, when agreed upon in principle, implemented through the independent executive agencies.

Yet that was not the route that some of the developing countries wanted to take. When the trade and development issue flared up in the early 1960s, the Bretton Woods institutions did make some attempts to accommodate, by institutional innovation, developing-country concerns on issues such as fluctuating commodity prices and trade preferences. However, the developing countries sought the establishment of a new UN institution. Following the lead of Prebisch and Malinowski, they rejected the option of setting up a think tank with a mission to fashion new policy proposals on trade and development (see Chapter 8). That would have been in the spirit of the SUNFED compromise, which was to secure improvements within the existing international order.[5] Unsurprisingly, the basic lesson of the SUNFED episode was repeated at UNCTAD I. Despite the developing countries' greater voting power, Prebisch had to come to a compromise with the U.S. and its allies: although a new UN organization was eventually agreed upon, it was an anomalous add-on to the existing institutional structure. After the NIEO declaration, Gamani Corea reopened the issue of UN control when pressed by leaders of the G77 to try to turn UNCTAD into a forum for trade negotiations. Once again, however, the mere weight of numbers did not bring ultimate success. The Brandt report recommended a World Development Fund with broadly based control, but at Cancún the Reagan-Thatcher axis successfully maintained the "integrity" of the IMF and the World Bank. When economic conditions of the 1980s weakened most developing countries and undermined G77 solidarity, the industrial countries took the opportunity to strengthen GATT (turning it into the WTO); that this would be at the expense of UNCTAD was clearly foreseen.

Ann Zammit, a delegate at UNCTAD III, clearly expressed the paradox of the Group of 77 and UNCTAD thirty years ago:

> The developing world pressed for [UNCTAD] to be set up within the UN system, believing or hoping that their numerical preponderance organized in a bloc system would enable them to exert a powerful influence on the policies of the developed world. Yet in questions of trade and development sheer weight

of numbers cannot force the rich countries to share what they have already secured or make them change a system that benefits them only too well.[6]

However, the developing countries were very unwilling to draw from this prolonged and repeated experience the lesson that the power of the UN does not lie in its capacity to pass resolutions by majority votes. Their reluctance to do so has drawn some harsh criticism. The whole North-South dialogue has been called "little more than a laborious twenty-five-year-long exploration of an intellectual and diplomatic blind alley."[7] One surely has to concede that there is some truth in this charge, at least in terms of developing countries' obstinate perseverance in a strategy that repeatedly failed.

An Economic Security Council?

The key to understanding this persistent conflict lies in the strengths and weaknesses of the UN voting principle of one country, one vote. This principle certainly has advantages. In particular, it safeguards the interests of relatively small countries by giving them their own voice in international decision making. This form of protection has become ever more important over the last sixty years as the number of small countries in the world system has grown (about half of the member countries of the UN now have a total population of 2 million or less). However, the variance of the populations of member countries has also grown, with the consequence that the principle of one country, one vote now conflicts more acutely than ever with the principle of one person, one vote, a principle that most would regard as more truly democratic.[8]

Another point must be made. The principle of one country, one vote pays no attention to whether the country casting the vote is democratic in its internal governance. Should a hundred small and undemocratic countries be able to frustrate the will of ninety-nine larger democratic countries? Would not most people be likely to judge that outcome anti-democratic? In the 1970s, in the days of the campaign for an NIEO, many countries in the Group of 77 were not internally democratic—not to mention the totalitarian regimes of the Group D countries (the Soviet bloc). Fortunately, the trend since then has been toward more democratic forms of government so that the disparity between developed and developing in that respect has now been markedly reduced. Even if had entirely disappeared, however, the first objection to relying exclusively on the principle of one country, one vote would remain a powerful one.

Since, because of size differences and governance differences between member countries, UN majority voting is and will continue to be inconclusive, some other means are necessary to arrive at binding global decisions. One way out of the impasse is to consider whether the UN voting system could be modified in a manner that would make it acceptable to all countries as a method of global collective decision making. On the occasion of the 50th anniversary of the UN, a new Economic and Social Security Council was proposed with this in mind. The idea was to replace ECOSOC with a new council that would vote by a system halfway between the UN (one country, one vote) and the Bretton Woods (contribution-weighted) models of voting. It would be a small representative body of thirty-plus countries, both developed and developing, reminiscent of the size of the CIEC. Its decisions would require a simple majority of both industrial and developing nations, but no single country would be able to exercise a veto on double majority decisions.[9] This idea has received only modest support since then.[10] A major disadvantage was that it would require changes to the charters of all the UN agencies, and this could hardly have been achieved without prolonged negotiations. Behind the legal and diplomatic difficulties lay a more intractable political one. None of the more powerful countries are "sufficiently alarmed by present problems to want major reforms" of the UN constitution.[11] It may also be true that many developing countries are wary about allowing issues that affect their sovereignty to be decided by a council on which they do not sit. So UN reform in the 1990s has largely concentrated on administrative reorganization, reduction of bureaus and budgets, and the elimination of moribund intergovernmental committees. These may have brought increases in efficiency, but they have not affected the structural mechanisms of global control.

In economic and social affairs, the world continues to be governed by a twin-track system. The UN General Assembly provides a world forum where economic ideas, interests, and policy proposals are presented, discussed, and negotiated. Its authority is, and can continue to be, a moral authority based on the fact that very large numbers of people in the world believe that it is an organization that stands for peace, justice, equality, development, and human rights—in short, for all those values that people believe will ensure the survival of humanity. This widespread and growing belief was one of the most notable and heartening features of the Iraq crisis of 2002–2003. Even great powers that say they want to ignore the organization or that override its decisions find themselves trying to make use of it in a variety of ways. Surely the most obvious lesson for the future is that every effort must be made by all members of the UN to ensure that this moral capital is not dissipated. Once the process of UN discussion and negotiation produces agreements, however, their implementation is delegated to executive agencies in which the countries that will foot most of the subsequent bills place their confidence. In matters of trade, finance, and development, that implies bodies such as the World Bank and the IMF, which have weighted vote systems, or the WTO, which, despite having a one country, one vote system, chooses to seek consensus rather than deciding matters by voting.

To make this twin-track system work tolerably, small countries need to be flexible in recognizing the greater responsibilities undertaken, and contributions made by, the larger countries. For their part, large countries need to be flexible in recognizing and catering to the needs of the smaller countries as well as to their own. The developing countries in the 1990s have adopted a partnership-based rather than a confrontational approach to trade, finance, and development. This change of attitude has to be reciprocated by the G8 countries if the twin-track global decision process is to remain a feasible way of settling the emerging international issues of the twenty-first century. *Faute de mieux* we must live with this twin-track global governance in which discussion and implementation are the responsibility of different world organizations. It would not make sense to recommend living with it, however, unless the degree of mutual flexibility necessary to make such machinery workable is forthcoming. All constitutional machinery works badly when it is abused, so restraint and prudent forbearance are indispensable elements in the statecraft of all UN member countries. That is why accusations of bad faith and double standards are such a serious matter and are so damaging to international intercourse.

Recommending living with a twin-track decision system certainly does not imply that the functioning of the international executive agencies leaves nothing more to be desired. On the contrary, setting aside the utopian prospect of the UN replacing them must inevitably bring into sharper focus the question of how they can be improved. As Sidney Dell put it shortly before his death: "there is no international agency that is dealing systematically with global questions of consistency and inconsistency" in matters of economic policy, and the triumvirate of the IMF, the World Bank, and GATT/WTO as they function at present is not up to this task.[12] How to reform this triumvirate is the issue to which we turn in the remainder of this chapter. We begin by considering reforms of the international financial institutions, the IMF and the World Bank, before posing the question of how the WTO could be made to function better.

What Should Be Done to Reform the IMF?

Over the last twenty years, the IMF has become increasingly dysfunctional. Although its resources have been allowed to decline as a proportion of world trade, the number of fund programs in developing countries has steadily increased. Meanwhile, the conditionality in these programs has expanded greatly in scope, going well beyond the traditional fields of monetary and fiscal policy and issues related to the exchange system. As the number of conditions, particularly structural conditions attached to loans, increased during the 1980s and 1990s, the rate of member countries' compliance with fund-supported programs has declined to below 30 percent in the 1990s, when compliance was defined as actions that permitted the disbursement of over 75 percent of the loan. This low rate of program compliance made it difficult to argue that these high levels of conditionality secured the repayment of loans and ensured the revolving nature of fund resources. Moreover, as compliance declined, the credibility of fund programs eroded and their catalytic character in relation to private financial flows became increasingly doubtful, a fact that again has implications for the size of IMF resources.

These trends point to the need for an expansion of the size of IMF resources, but under the existing IMF Articles of Agreement, this change would require an 85 percent majority vote. The U.S. is thus the only country that is in a position to veto this expansion. The U.S. policy of "graduating" countries from public to private funds dominates the international agenda in this area. However, this policy stance has been challenged by the arrival of a new type of financial crisis associated with financial globalization and volatile private capital flows. These new crises call for much larger amounts of support than the traditional crisis resulting from trade or current-account imbalances. The outbreak of the financial crisis in Thailand in July 1997 took the IMF unawares and led to dramatic falls in the exchange rates of Asian countries, losses of income and employment, and increases in poverty. There was an indirect effect in Africa as the preexisting recovery of primary commodity prices was reversed. This was the worst global recession since 1945. Although it hardly touched the U.S. or European economies, their governments were obliged to put together large rescue packages for the affected Asian countries.

In the aftermath of these events, the IMF came under strong criticism from different quarters. Some critics claimed that the IMF should have been aware of, and warned about, the fragility of the economies of East Asia; also that it should have been able to prevent the crisis from happening. Others charged that its remedies, especially its insistence on higher interest rates, were counterproductive and amounted to deflating the economy in the face of GDP contraction.[13] Finally, both these sorts of critics saw moral hazard in the fact that the financial costs of the crisis were borne wholly by the public taxpayers of developing countries, while the Western bankers who had made unwise loans were reimbursed in full.

The IMF's defense against the accusation that the conditions of its lending to the Asian crisis countries were misconceived was that in a short-term crisis, the resources at its disposal are fixed and they cannot fully substitute for the private outflow (and indeed should not, given the moral hazard). Thus, private capital outflow has to be balanced by loss of foreign exchange reserves, by a depreciation of the exchange rate, or, failing these, interest-rate rises to make the adjustment via loss of output and/or to reverse the outflow of private capital. Practically, it appeals to the outcome from the IMF conditions, pointing to the speed of recovery of the countries, such as South Korea, that complied with them most fully compared with the slowness of recovery of those, such as Indonesia, that resisted most. Critics maintain that looser monetary and fiscal policy, combined with rapid corporate restructuring, would have restored confidence and reversed the capital outflow with less damage to the real economy.

Hopes of an effective early warning system for financial crises are fanciful and likely to be disappointed, because financial crises are the products of complex nonlinear causes. Government policy preferences, investors' expectations, and herd behavior all enter the equation alongside measurable economic quantities such as the assets and liabilities of the banking system, the balance-of-payments deficit, and the size of the foreign exchange reserves. Moreover, the fund's surveillance faces problems to the extent that countries deliberately hold back publication of information that might reveal fragility. The IMF has since promulgated new standards and guidelines for disclosure and transparency of information, but there is a clear danger here of loading responsibility for countering financial instability onto the capital-receiving countries and saddling them, through further increases in conditionality, with inappropriate and costly financial standards. In any case, limited disclosure is not the whole story. Much vital macroeconomic and financial information that should have rung alarm bells was actually in the public domain in July 1997. What is needed is to improve the systems of information evaluation, both by the International Monetary Fund and the World Bank and by the financial markets.

It is time to move beyond the tactics of crisis prevention to a more fundamental diagnosis. We have chronicled, in Chapter 10, the failure to negotiate an exchange-rate system to replace that of Bretton Woods. This failure has permitted what is the great defect of the current system of floating exchange rates, the large and frequent misalignment of the three key global currencies—the dollar, the euro, and the yen. There are no rules of macroeconomic policy, such as apply to trade, that discipline the policies that produce great fluctuations and gyrations of global currencies. The solution, which has been advocated for twenty years, is to specify exchange-rate targets for these currencies and find instruments to move them toward the specified targets. The U.S. and the rest of the G8 countries are still very reluctant to contemplate this and have intervened only in the most extreme of disorderly markets.

Their reluctance stems from the facts of global inequality. They have large economies with a moderate exposure to international trade and financial facilities to lay off foreign currency risks. By contrast, misalignments of key currencies inflict major instability on the economies of developing countries. The financial systems of developing countries are relatively small and often fragile. Poor credit evaluation and poor control of banks' foreign currency exposure are typical aspects of fragility. These weaknesses become much more dangerous after they liberalize their capital accounts, as the IMF has persistently advocated. When foreign capital inflows, induced by relative interest rates in combination with foreign investors' expectations of exchange-rate movements, are large in relation to the size of the developing country's financial system, substantial damage can be inflicted by their sudden exit. This is the new danger that developing countries face in a more financially integrated world, and it is doubtful if any exchange-rate system that they choose— whether free-floating or hard-peg—can guarantee stability as long as the rates of key currencies fluctuate as greatly as they do.[14] The international community will have to return to this issue; as a first step, the IMF's surveillance of key currency countries needs to be redirected to achieve greater policy coherence between them.

IMF insiders have argued that its resources should be increased but with the aim that it should eventually become a global lender of last resort.[15] A lender of last resort must lend in unlimited amounts and with no conditions apart from a penalty interest rate. Even if the IMF were put in the position to do this, it could create moral hazard, encouraging imprudent lending in foreign currencies and/or imprudent borrowing by public agencies in developing countries. What is needed is an alternative approach that accepts that crises cannot always be prevented but seeks to manage their damaging consequences better. We can sketch out a three-pronged approach to reform that has much to recommend it.

First, the IMF would in future provide adequate international liquidity on appropriate conditions to support necessary macroeconomic and exchange-rate adjustment. The issue of new allocations of SDRs is a costless and efficient method to create extra liquidity. Second, a new procedure would manage international bankruptcies when they do occur so that the country is protected against the worst consequences of insolvency until its creditworthiness is restored. A scheme of orderly debt workouts, an international equivalent to domestic bankruptcy proceedings, would have to involve (a) an automatic debt standstill or moratorium; (b) access to working capital on a preferred-creditor basis; and (c) financial and managerial reorganization to restore viability and then pay off pre-standstill creditors on an equal basis. There are many detailed issues of legality, timing, and the prevention of abuse that are involved in deciding how such a scheme could be effectively brought into force for cross-border transactions, but its principle is sound.

The third prong would be advance provision for private-sector burden-sharing in the event of a bankruptcy to reduce moral hazard and inequity between the private and public sectors. It is in this policy area where least progress has been made in building an international consensus. The U.S. in particular argues that any form of private-sector burden-sharing will kill off foreign investors' interest in emerging markets. However, a scheme is now under consideration that would require debt contracts to include a clause providing in advance for collective-action agreements in the event of debt crises. The adoption of such clauses would render debt crises much more manageable. To the extent that the volume of private flows to developing countries was reduced as a result, this loss would be balanced by a reduction of the costs of financial instability.[16]

What Should Be Done to Reform the World Bank?

The World Bank began to get into political difficulties in the U.S. in the middle of the 1980s, when several U.S. environmental NGOs attacked bank-financed projects in Brazil for encouraging environmental damage. They claimed that the bank's procedures for making environmental impact assessments of its projects were inadequate. The bank gave in under pressure from the U.S. Congress and Treasury and set up an Environment Department in 1987. Then in 1992, an independent review charged that the bank had breached its own guidelines for the conditions on which the people displaced by the Narmada dams in India were to be resettled. In the course of these controversies, the U.S. NGOs demonstrated their ability to harass the bank by means of well-organized lobbying of the U.S. Congress.[17] The bank has put in place new measures of accountability, including an independent inspection panel to make public reports on contentious cases. The ironies of this are that the NGOs themselves are, for the most part, not publicly accountable and that the bank has become more accountable to U.S. politicians rather than to the politicians of its client countries.[18]

The power of NGOs to move the U.S. Congress brought about a more widespread change of political stance at the bank. Since 1996, when James Wolfensohn became president, the bank has been proactively reaching out to its NGO critics and shaping its policies to reflect their concerns. Wolfensohn has pursued this political approach both in his public rhetoric and in a managerial style that places him at odds with the bureaucratic culture of the institution. He has tried to ward off some of the NGO criticism of the bank by promoting his brain-child, the Comprehensive Development Framework (CDF), a matrix for coordinating all the development activities of a country. Being the guardian of the CDF allows the bank to adopt a central position in the development process, to provide a diverse range of services (loans, technical assistance, advice) to the entire development community, and to identify itself as a development partner and facilitator instead of as a bunch of arrogant bankers. Furthermore, bank lending has been increasingly diversified to support a new development agenda that would find favor with the U.S. NGOs—gender equality, participation, civil society, good governance, and environmental conservation.[19]

The bank has long suffered from multiple conflicting objectives—sound banking, promoting development, and policy advocacy are just three of them. In this context, a populist approach of coopting all the potential NGO critics of the bank has its own dangers. Despite the adoption of poverty reduction as the bank's paramount goal, it is leading to a loss of overall focus in strategic priorities. The bank is also failing to exploit fully the functions in which it has a genuine comparative advantage, and, by extending the responsibilities of its staff members into areas where they have relatively little competence, it is confusing and demoralizing them. The bank may well also be alienating the governments of developing countries, on whom it must rely as customers for its loans.

Given these distorting pressures on bank priorities, there is a case for reviving the proposal of an organic aid-SDR link. The idea of the link, discussed in Chapter 10, fell into abeyance in the 1980s because of U.S. reluctance to move forward with further creation of SDRs. Since then a further distribution of SDRs was agreed to in 1997. Yet it was not linked to the funding of multilateral aid agencies, although they remain strapped for cash to pursue internationally agreed-upon debt-reduction initiatives for highly indebted developing countries. Apart from the provision of necessary additional resources, funding of the World Bank by this route would do much to counter-act the current tendency to make it a hostage of NGO fashions and the whims of the U.S. Congress and Treasury Department.

A direct link between SDR creation and aid would be simple to operate. The bank and other multilateral development agencies would have accounts with the IMF, into which the newly created SDRs would be paid. They would lend in the normal way, and when the loan recipient made purchases with the loan, the exporters from whom they purchased would be paid in SDRs out of the loan agency's IMF account. No doubt the old argument that this would be inflationary would then be heard again, but the scale of SDR creation remains very small (0.3 percent) relative to the GDP of the developed countries, and their anti-inflation policies are unlikely to be changed because of anything on this scale.[20]

This new source of funding should be negotiated in return for a number of changes in the bank's lending practices. The need for the bank to continue project lending to middle-income developing countries (on IBRD terms) has been questioned on the grounds that private flows can do the job instead. Between 1970 and 1995, private flows to developing countries increased fortyfold while IBRD flows increased threefold in nominal terms, so the original post-1945 justification of this type of lending, in terms of imperfect private capital markets, is now much weaker.[21] However, private finance flows are quite concentrated geographically on about a dozen countries and they also tend to flow in pro-cyclically, so that they are there when they are least needed and absent when they would be most useful. Nevertheless, it would make sense to let the regional development banks complement private flows to the middle-income developing countries and to focus World Bank lending to low-income developing countries.[22]

It would also be necessary to look again at internal plans to reshape the bank's program lending. The policy conditions of these loans have big implications for low-income developing countries' politics and sovereignty, as explained in Chapter 11. Bank economists are now saying that these conditions have been ineffective as a means of changing the borrowers' economic and social policies, which are determined by broad political economy factors rather than by any action that the bank can take. This is true to a degree, but it is being used to argue that it would be better to lend to countries where policies are judged to be already conducive to growth and poverty reduction and where they are not conducive, not to lend.[23] Although this is described as the phasing out of conditionality, in logic it is the introduction of a new and stricter form of conditionality; the difference is that it would operate *ex ante* rather than *ex post*.

WTO Rules: OK?

The new World Trade Organization, which swallowed up the former GATT, now goes much beyond it in scope and ambition. The overall aim has broadened, from nondiscrimination and the reduction of trade barriers to the adoption of policies in support of open markets generally. New agreements cover trade in agricultural goods, sanitary and phytosanitary (plant hygiene) standards, textiles and clothing, technical barriers to trade, trade-related investment measures, trade in services, intellectual property rights, and the removal of various nontariff barriers. The WTO is potentially much more intrusive on national policies because it is now making rules across this substantial new agenda,

rules that override the preexisting national laws of members. The WTO requires countries to change existing domestic laws that conflict with the obligations of WTO membership, and a new Trade Policy Review Mechanism requires
members to give regular public accounts of the state of their compliance with
their obligations. The WTO has also strengthened its Dispute Settlement Mechanism (DSM).[24] These five institutional innovations, taken together, have two
general effects. They make considerable inroads on what were matters of domestic governance before the coming into force of the Uruguay Round agreements, and they further "judicialize" the process of trade cooperation.

Raúl Prebisch maintained that the attempt to elaborate a system of trade
rules was backward looking and that what the world needed was an agreed-
on set of policies to support the developing world (see Chapter 8). The emergence of the WTO was clearly a major defeat for that viewpoint. Yet it is widely
believed that the changes to the world trade system inaugurated by the WTO
are desirable in the interests of the developing countries because they create a
stronger umbrella to shelter them from the arbitrary trade practices of large
and powerful developed countries. It will be argued here that this general
judgment needs to be qualified and that the appropriate question for the future is not one of rules versus policies but of how policies can better support
a system of trade rules. The first task, then, is to show that WTO rules are not
sufficient to regulate trade in a world of substantial economic inequality, and
the second task is to explain how policies can support the working of a rule-
based trade system in the presence of gross inequalities.

A major question for any rule-based system is whether the rules (whatever
they are) are enforced fairly. Most would agree that the WTO handles trade
disputes much better than GATT did. The WTO restored and strengthened
the original GATT dispute-settlement process by making it more automatic
and introducing specific time limits on procedures. Requests for panels on
alleged violations are approved more automatically, as are the panel reports,
the appellate body reports, and the authorizations of retaliation. Instead of
requiring a positive consensus in order to proceed, they now need a negative
consensus to fail to proceed.[25] These changes have allowed about 160 cases to
be handled during the first five years of the WTO, roughly three times the
previous level. Developing countries have been involved in more cases, about
25 percent of the new total.[26] This has been taken as a sign that the DSM is
working well, including for the benefit of the developing countries.

Where then is there any lack of justice for developing countries? Unfortunately, it is still true that for them, serious deficiencies remain at every stage
of the WTO dispute-settlement process, from inception through judgment
and granting remedy to enforcement. These deficiencies arise from the interaction of the standard features of a legal process—its cost, absorption of time,

and uncertainty of outcome—with the incompleteness of international legal machinery and the great inequalities of wealth and power that currently exist between nations. Given the substantial cost of bringing a WTO case, in terms of legal and diplomatic person time, poor countries are deterred disproportionately from embarking on a dispute. Only governments can bring cases to the DSM, and poor governments will be disproportionately deterred from doing so by the prospect of antagonizing more powerful countries, on which they depend in many matters not connected with trade, such as defense or foreign aid. By convention, no compensation is paid by the loser for a violation, after a process that can still take over two years to complete, a fact that bears more heavily on poor states than on rich ones. If a country does not take measures to comply with its WTO obligations, there is no centralized sanction. The only sanction is retaliation. Since all economic sanctions are costly to the initiator, the ability of a poor country to sanction a rich one is much less than the reverse.[27] Thus, even if we assume an identical propensity to violate WTO rules between developed and developing countries and perfect formal justice in the panels in reaching their judgments on cases, developing countries will win fewer cases than they lose and will be less able to be sure of remedy in those that they do win.[28]

Obviously, differences in outcome that arise because of the different economic strength of the two parties cannot be remedied directly. Nevertheless, it ought to be possible to tilt the system in ways that counteract its acknowledged biases. In domestic litigation, legal aid is used to give the poor better access to costly justice; the injured party is awarded its costs by the court and centrally organized sanctions prevent the injured party from having to bear all the costs of punishing the violator. In the international sphere, these are three areas where, by analogy, progress could be made, given sufficient imagination and willingness to cooperate. An improved DSM in the WTO is still capable of further improvements in the interests of the developing countries.

Although in the WTO the formal justice of the institution has improved (and can be improved further), formal justice is not the only consideration. Formal justice can be at odds with substantive justice.[29] In the WTO, judicial improvement has coincided with the adoption of certain rules that, it seems to us, do embody substantive injustice because they carry serious implications for the possibility of economic convergence.

WTO Rules, Industrial Subsidies, and Development

The rules of the WTO, like those of its predecessor GATT, reflect the ambivalent attitude of the U.S. and some parts of Europe to free trade.[30] This ambivalence, characterized as "embedded liberalism," inspired a distinctly different set of international trade rules from ones that promoted free trade plain and simple. Its basis is open multilateralism, derived from the norms of nondiscrimination and reciprocity. While it inclines to free trade by facilitating multilateral and reciprocal tariff reductions, it also provides for "contingent protection"—that is to say, opportunities for individual countries to renege on tariff concessions under prespecified conditions to avoid injury to domestic industries adversely affected by tariff reduction.[31] Its "fairness" requires sharing both the benefits of any other country's tariff reductions *and* the burdens of any other country's "need" to reimpose tariffs to safeguard its domestic industry against so-called dumping.

Because anti-dumping actions are costly to contest, developed countries have long since found that the contingent protection provisions have a harassment value.[32] They used them to secure so-called "voluntary export restraints" on textile exports from developing countries.[33] Developing countries accepted this breach of nondiscrimination as part of a larger implicit bargain, in which their balance-of-payments deficits—worsened by trade restrictions—were met by offsetting flows of official financing from OECD country donors, or, in more familiar terms, by foreign aid. However, as Chapter 11 indicated, this bargain collapsed in the 1980s in the wake of the debt crisis and the policies of Reagan, Kohl, and Thatcher, and something had to be put in its place.

The Uruguay Round introduced new rules on the use of countervailing duties.[34] In an attempt at legal clarification, contingent protection is now permitted in the face of some subsidies but not others. Three kinds of subsidies, to research and development, to disadvantaged regions, and to the costs of complying with environmental regulations, if available to all firms or industries regardless of their status as exporters, are now not actionable with countervailing duties. All others remain actionable insofar as they inflict "material injury." If subsidies are "specific"—to an exporting enterprise or industry or to an exporting group of enterprises or industries—they can be countervailed if they cause material injury. The criterion of "material injury," already low, was further diluted.[35] Participation in this subsidies code, which developing countries could decline to join under the Tokyo Round rules, is now mandatory on all WTO members, although some have fixed transition periods before full compliance.

The effect of this is to outlaw the sorts of industrial subsidies that have been used successfully in the past to accelerate the growth and development of poor countries. It has been said that the Asian miracle of the period 1965–1995 could never occur again under present WTO rules. The phenomenal growth of the Asian tiger economies depended on selective departures from pure free trade regimes. Contrary to the opinion of the neoliberal consensus, the Asian "miracle" demonstrated that an intelligent long-term development strategy—based on interventionist departures from free trade that are genuinely selective and temporary—can be made to work. Indeed, if the right conditions can be created, it can be made to work spectacularly well.[36] What is not so clear, however, is that the annexes to the WTO agreement of 1994 absolutely prohibit *all* the instruments of such a strategy. Despite the clear outlawing of specific subsidies, there are still some unplugged gaps that an imaginative and ingenious developmental state might want to try to exploit for its purposes.[37] Much will depend on how the DSM works in practice.[38]

It is up to the legal technocrats at the WTO how activist they decide to be, since legal activism is something that the WTO rules clearly permit. If they become bolder, the interpretation of the annexes will increasingly prohibit all protection of infant industries in developing countries. This will slam the door on a vital means of economic catching up, which at least some poor countries are capable of using, and so serve to solidify the existing unequal worldwide distribution of wealth and income. Claiming that the WTO rules on subsidies are substantively unjust requires clarity about what resemblances and differences between nations are relevant to the treatment of like cases alike and different cases differently. In the spirit of Prebisch, we believe that the existing inequalities of economic and political power between developed and developing countries do constitute a relevant difference for the purpose of deciding the substantive justice of these rules. If there is to be any derogation at all from free trade, it should be in favor of the economically weak rather than the economically strong.

If in the end both global justice and global order depend on the possibility of removing existing gross economic inequalities by the successful development of the developing countries, both goals will be ill served by quasi-judicial attempts in the WTO to block off the most promising (for some countries) fast track to development. There is a compelling case for developing countries to be given exceptional treatment on "specific" industrial subsidies for infant industry purposes, with one proviso. Such subsidies must always be selective, temporary, and performance related. That is the only way for developing countries to avoid repeating the errors of their previous international trade policies.

Greater Developing-Country Participation in WTO Rule-Making

The WTO arrangements cannot be unjust, it is said, since every nation voluntarily agreed to them when joining the WTO, and voluntary agreement to an act implies that the gain and the loss from it are at least equivalent. In weighing this rebuttal, one must bear in mind the evolution of the community of nations. For all the talk of the demise of the nation-state, they have in fact been multiplying fast. The members of the UN in 1945 were 51: now there are 190. Moreover, as a result of that quadrupling, the disparities between the strongest nations and the weakest nations have also multiplied. Yet new states necessarily emerge onto a stage where the international action is already well advanced. They do not face a moral or legal tabula rasa on which they can, jointly with others, inscribe a new compact. In a dynamic international setting, a new WTO member has to put up with whatever it cannot negotiate away. If it is economically and political weak, it may have accepted nontrade inducements to abide by the existing trade rules.

Formally, all WTO members are equal. Unlike the IMF and the World Bank, the WTO does not have an unequal voting structure in which rich countries control a share of the vote that is much greater than their numbers in the world community. Thus, poor countries, which form a majority of the members, could in principle outvote the rich countries. All the experience recounted in this volume, however, indicates that to do so would be a futile move. The WTO, like GATT before it, avoids taking decisions by voting. Instead, it "finds consensus" in an informal procedure which the director-general conducts. His discussions with selected members go on until the director-general thinks he has found a basis for consensus, which he brings for approval to the WTO Council plenary session. At this stage, member countries decide that a consensus exists, or not, as the case may be. Many small developing countries are effectively marginalized by this procedure.

The informal consensus-finding procedure allows the economic inequalities that exist between members to come into play. There are two main sources of inequality; differential access to information about which agreements will benefit one's country and differential power to influence the outcome of the informal negotiation. Since the inauguration of the WTO in 1995, the problem of evaluating trade offers has been aggravated by the broadening of the trade agenda. The effects on a country of a round of mutual tariff reductions are basically calculable—albeit by economists using general equilibrium models. The effect of a change of standards, by which a country's export products may suddenly be deemed substandard, is very much harder to calculate, to understand, and to negotiate. The problem of access to information boils down to a simple economic question: Can the developing country afford to maintain an embassy in Geneva? If it cannot, it is unlikely that it will be able to follow the trade negotiations, let alone take part in them.[39] This points to the need to assist countries whose resources are inadequate. What international help is available to assist it to acquire and process trade-related information?

There has been very little. The regular WTO budget provided $741,000 in 1998 for technical assistance and training, about $7,000 for each developing-country member.[40] Of aid donors' total expenditure on technical assistance, only about 2 percent is trade related.

There is a clear need to do more to counter the information bias against developing countries in future trade negotiations; the efforts of the UNCTAD secretariat to do so should be strongly reinforced. These efforts should be concerned with the provision of high-quality information, not only about actual trade and financial flows but also about tariffs and nontariff barriers to trade and regulatory and other obstacles to cross-border flows of investment. There is much about the process of trade and investment liberalization and its economic effects that is not properly understood and that cannot be successfully researched without the collection and dissemination of better data.[41]

An institutional role of custodian of the interests of developing countries is still recognized as legitimate by the international community, even after the demise of the North-South dialogue. It, too, belongs with UNCTAD, but its exercise remains surrounded with problems and dilemmas. In a less-confrontational era, the secretariat has to judge its advocacy more carefully. It cannot simply respond to the wishes of developing countries, yet it must not hold back from criticizing developed-country policies that hurt poorer countries just because the developed countries might be thereby offended. For example, there would seem to be a good case for sharper advocacy by the UNCTAD secretariat of the need for trade and investment liberalization of key sectors of the OECD economies, especially agriculture.[42] Such decisions, however, need to be taken on the basis of objective considerations and not in response to group pressure. The secretariat will better protect its judgments from criticism by member governments if it can maintain the highest professional standards in its work. Data analysis and general advocacy can then feed into advisory work and technical-assistance projects on trade and investment for individual developing countries, but this cannot be supplied on demand; access should be given on transparent criteria for the allocation of scarce resources.

Even when a country has discovered where its interest lies, it may not be able to achieve its goals because of lack of negotiating influence.[43] A country's influence or power in informal trade negotiations depends on the extent of its trade. In a negotiation based around tariff reduction, bargaining power depends not only on how far you are willing to cut your tariff but also on the size of the trade flows to which the proffered tariff cut will apply. Small tariff cuts on big trade flows are worth much more as bargaining chips than big cuts on small flows. This is very frustrating for countries with small trade sectors, but it is not *unjust* unless a country's trade sector is being deliberately kept small by others' denial of market access.[44] This is true of some countries, but the external trade of others, notably in Africa, is constrained by unresolved difficulties of supply rather than by lack of access to markets. They cannot be helped by these kinds of trade negotiations, however they are arranged. They need other remedies, including financial aid and technical assistance.

The current political reality is that the U.S. (and to a lesser degree the EU) exercises preponderant influence on trade issues and that U.S. and European trade behavior is driven by the disparate interests of two groups of great business corporations, which are united only in their willingness to donate money to the major U.S. and European political parties. One group of such corporations, the exporters, want developing countries to liberalize and provide them with more markets, while the other group that is selling into domestic markets wants to block out foreign competition. For both their sakes, the U.S. and European governments would like to have it both ways. The ideal of embedded liberalism, when constrained by national producer interests, generates the practice of asymmetric liberalism.[45]

There is apprehension that anything that threatens U.S. and European dominance will be counterproductive. Some think that the more stringent rules and their increased formalization in the WTO will tilt the U.S. domestic political balance further in favor of protection.[46] That is valid up to a point, although it is easy to overstate the WTO's power to curb contingent protection.[47] Others argue in the same vein that further efforts to broaden the institutions of international governance would run the risk of undermining the support for it that exists in the U.S. and other industrial countries.[48] The retreat of the second Bush administration from multilateral arrangements in international affairs gives some credence to these fears. Yet in looking to the future, one should stand at some distance from the tribulations of the day and anticipate the emergence of an increasingly multipolar world.

In the long run, neither the developed nor the developing countries should be contemplating a retreat into protectionism but rather the reverse. At the highest level of generality, it is not free trade but its absence that they should beware of. The negotiation of further trade liberalization on a multilateral and nondiscriminatory basis must continue. Specifically, the promises made to developing countries during the Uruguay Round must be fulfilled so that they may gain confidence in further WTO negotiations. Then the failure of the Uruguay Round to eliminate administered protection in a wide range of intermediate industries must be rectified. The heavy protection of developed countries' agricultural sectors must be reduced. Tariffs on industrial goods of special export interest to developing countries must also be reduced.

At the same time, the idea of "special and differential treatment" of developing countries, which was added to GATT and survives in different forms in the annexes to the WTO Agreements, needs to be revisited, simplified, and given greater precision.[49] The present position, where "special and differential treatment" consists of an arbitrary deadline for full compliance with WTO obligations, unenforceable promises of technical assistance for transitional difficulties, and a wish to confine "special and differential treatment" to the forty-eight least-developed countries is highly unsatisfactory. It is true that for many years after 1955, developing countries were allowed to protect particular industries and to plead balance-of-payments reasons for adding to quantitative restrictions on trade.[50] The tragedy was that, in general, they did not use this exemption to carry out effective development strategies. They tended to protect chronically uncompetitive industries and did not implement timebound programs of selective protection to create competitive industries with the capability to export. The few, but hugely significant, exceptions to this—particularly, after 1965, the East Asian economic tigers—are the very countries that have begun successfully to converge on a Western standard of living.

The lesson here is that ultimately it is in every nation's interest that late developers succeed in catching up, because that is the only route to a world of less poverty and conflict. If their path is blocked "for legal reasons," the legitimacy of the present hegemonic ideal of embedded liberalism can only erode further, and then world trading arrangements are bound to become more disorderly. The Doha Round of WTO negotiations has the opportunity to establish the special and differential treatment of developing countries' trade on a more equitable basis than at present, although progress is as yet glacial.[51] If this could be done, the way would be opened to the eventual achievement of true freedom of trade in the twenty-first century, free trade in a world of economic equals—rather than what disfigures the world trade scene now, partly free trade between the enormously wealthy and the pitifully impoverished.

Can International Organizations Be Creative Intellectual Actors?

This volume has traced the decline of the UN as the vibrant center of thinking on issues of trade, finance, and development, and the rise—particularly after 1980—of a neoliberal consensus on these issues, orchestrated by the World Bank. It has also argued, in Chapter 2 and elsewhere, that in international organizations the degree of creative thinking—as opposed to the synthesizing and recycling of existing ideas—is inversely related to the ability of their top management to exercise strong editorial control over the research process for the purpose of preaching a doctrine that they think promotes the aims of the organization. The question for the future is whether international organizations can again be intellectually creative and if so, how this might be achieved.

In this context, it is intriguing that there should now be talk of the World Bank transforming itself into a "university of development." The proposal is that the bank would in future specialize in educational activities that can be justified as public goods and subsidize their provision with income from its subscribed capital and accumulated reserves. Lending selectively to safe borrowers would continue, but it would cease to be the bank's major function. This is a fairly astonishing proposal, given the past history of research and other types of intellectual work at the bank and seems to be problematic in various ways. Its practical success would depend in the first instance on the political feasibility of introducing greater selectivity into bank lending, an issue that remains underexplored. Second, success would depend on the extent to which the bank's research and publication activities could continue in the same way if its lending were indeed scaled back and reoriented. Finally, it would depend on whether the bank was willing to give up preaching a particular doctrine of development.

All the signs are that the bank continues to be vulnerable to pressure from the U.S. Treasury Department to defend neoliberal doctrines of economic development. Consider the case of Joseph Stiglitz, who was appointed chief economist of the bank in early 1997. He wanted to broaden the original Washington Consensus of ten policy thrusts (fiscal and exchange-rate reform, trade and financial liberalization, privatization, and deregulation, among others), by adding improved financial-sector regulation, competition policy, and technology-transfer policies. He also suggested multiplying the objectives of development policy by adding a sustainable environment, democratization, and a more egalitarian distribution.[52] He did not then question the idea that it was the bank's job to promote a consensus of some kind on development policy; he merely wanted to move away from a narrow version of neoliberalism. He also began an internal campaign against the deflationary policies recommended by the IMF during the Asian financial crisis.

The U.S. Treasury Department under Laurence Summers was unhappy with Stiglitz's intellectual ambitions and made his departure from the bank a condition of U.S. support for James Wolfensohn's second term as president. Stiglitz resigned in November 1999. Further U.S. pressure, this time to change the draft of the *World Development Report 2001*, led to the resignation of the report's independent editor-in-chief, Ravi Kanbur, in the following year.[53] After leaving the bank, Stiglitz moved from modifying the Washington Consensus to rejecting the bank's drive to promulgate a development formula as such:

Opposition to globalisation in many parts of the world is not to globalisation per se . . . but to the particular set of doctrines, the Washington Consensus policies that the international financial institutions have imposed. *And it is not just opposition to the policies themselves, but to the notion that there is a single set of policies that is right.* This notion flies in the face of both economics, which emphasizes the notion of trade-offs, and of ordinary common sense.[54]

Stiglitz's sudden conversion suggests that while in the bank, he was constrained to agree that the role of the bank is to provide the developing world with "the single set of policies that is right," an idea that he condemned as flying in the face of common sense as soon as he left. It seems that even "rebels within" cannot escape from the institutional imperative to preach a doctrine and that the U.S. will act to reinforce this imperative when it thinks it is necessary. In these circumstances, plans for the World Bank to become a "knowledge bank"—and what is more, one whose loans would carry *ex ante* conditionality—should be firmly discouraged in any negotiation to provide it with a more secure source of multilateral funding through SDRs.

Does the UN then offer a more fertile ground for intellectual creativity in the future? The implication of the inverse relation between management editorial control and creativity is that the UN, with its lighter hand and multitude of voices, is more likely to generate interesting new ideas. The 1990s showed some evidence of this in the UNCTAD *Trade and Development Report* and the UNDP *Human Development Report.* How can the UN build on these achievements? As we have suggested, more resources are needed if voices crying in the wilderness are to be heard and made influential in the crowded spaces of politics and business. Beyond that, it is hard to know what to suggest. The idea of weakening management's editorial control over UN publications is anathema to the industrial countries, which want to go farther in exactly the opposite direction. In any case, the proposal to manufacture some administrative chaos in the hope of stimulating intellectual creativity is on a par with the plea to manufacture an economic crisis in order to trigger a process of structural adjustment.[55] Both share an irreducible element of self-contradiction.

The answer seems to be to acknowledge that it is not realistic to expect that officials of the UN Secretariat, as distinct from other parts of the UN system, will be a major generator of fresh ideas. That it did so in its earliest years, before successive layers of managerial control over research could solidify, was a happy accident, but probably not one that could be easily replicated today. The Secretariat can still be a purveyor and a disseminator of ideas that its members may be just about ready to adopt. If the UN is to make a creative contribution in future, however, it will be most likely to do so by nourishing its university-like institutions and recruiting a new generation of managers who understand how best to nurture creative work. The United Nations University was set up in 1975 but at first made little impact. In the field of trade, finance, and development, a new opportunity arose a decade later with the inauguration of WIDER, the World Institute of Development Economics Research. Its history to date has also been checkered and it has run into controversy, but its difficulties have never included struggles over publication of the results of research. Another university-like, but very small, UN organization is the UN Research Institute for Social Development (UNRISD), which has a good record as an innovative think tank on development issues.

There are three reasons why quasi-university public research institutes such as WIDER and UNRISD hold out a credible hope for sustaining a creative intellectual spark in UN economic and social work. Their mission is to conduct applied research, to undertake policy advocacy, and to strengthen capacity in the area of sustainable growth. This involves no conflict with other objectives of the organization because there are no other objectives. Although they have a research staff, these tasks are also carried out by visiting scholars and by a worldwide network of collaborators. The diversity of research modes dilutes the problems of motivation that bedevil organizations that rely only on a full-time permanent research staff. Finally, governments contribute funding to the individual research projects that they wish to support. This element of voluntary sponsorship introduces multiple accountabilities, and it reduces the scope for any single country—however wealthy and powerful—to exercise an overbearing financial leverage on the entire intellectual direction of the organization. For all these reasons, it is still possible to believe that international organizations can be creative intellectual actors and that there will be more intellectual history of the United Nations to be written in the future.

Appendix: List of Archival Sources

Online Resources and Electronic Databases

UN Intellectual History Project: http://www.unhistory.org
J. M. Keynes/Roy Harrod correspondence:
http://www.e.u-tokyo.ac.jp/Exhibition/keynes/contents/index.htm.
Declassified Documents Reference System (DDRS), Farmington Hills,
    Michigan, Gale Group, 2004.

Papers of Organizations and Governments

League of Nations Archive, Geneva
UN Archive, New York
UNCTAD Archive, Geneva
GATT Archive, World Trade Organization, Geneva

U.S. National Archives & Records Administration, College Park, Maryland
    Record Group 43, International Trade Files
    Record Group 59, Office Files of the Assistant Secretaries of State for
    United Nations Affairs, Lot File 58D33
    Record Group 59, Office of Inter-American Regional Economic Affairs
    Record Group 59, Records of Under-Secretary George Ball 1961–66

Public Record Office, Kew, London
    Foreign Office files FO 475/3 and FO 371
    Board of Trade files BT 241

Papers of Individuals

Ernest Bevin Papers, Churchill College, Cambridge
Roy Blough Papers, Harry S. Truman Library, Independence, Missouri
R. H. Brand Papers, Bodleian Library, Oxford
R. W. B. Clarke Papers, Churchill College, Cambridge
Edmund Dell Papers, Bodleian Library, Oxford

Sidney Dell Papers, Bodleian Library, Oxford
Judith Hart Papers, National Museum of Labour History, Manchester
Nicholas Kaldor Papers, King's College, Cambridge
Alexander Loveday Papers, Nuffield College, Oxford
Philip Noel-Baker Papers, Churchill College, Cambridge
David Owen Papers, Columbia University Library
Raúl Prebisch Papers, courtesy of Sra. Adela Prebisch
Dennis Robertson Papers, Trinity College, Cambridge
Austin Robinson Papers, Churchill College, Cambridge
Hans Singer Papers, courtesy of Hans Singer
United Nations Career Records Project Papers, Bodleian Library, Oxford

Notes

Foreword

1. The Bretton Woods institutions, in this respect, are far ahead. The World Bank published two massive histories—one on the occasion of its 25th anniversary and the other (two volumes and more than 2,000 pages) on its 50th. The International Monetary Fund (IMF) has an in-house historian who ensures the capture of its place in history with regular publications.

2. Louis Emmerij, Richard Jolly, and Thomas G. Weiss, *Ahead of the Curve? UN Ideas and Global Challenges* (Bloomington: Indiana University Press, 2001), xi.

Introduction

1. U Thant, *View from the UN* (Newton Abbott: David and Charles, 1977), 34–35.

2. As Ernest Bevin put it in 1942: "We have to find an economic basis for collective security if individual nations and peoples are to recognise that they have a stake in maintaining it." Bevin to Anthony Eden, 8 December 1942, Ernest Bevin Papers 3/2, Churchill College, Cambridge.

3. John Pincus, *Trade, Aid, and Development: The Rich and Poor Nations* (New York: McGraw-Hill, 1967), 76–78, 126–134; Harry G. Johnson, *Economic Policies towards Less Developed Countries* (London: George Allen and Unwin Ltd., 1967), 48–52.

4. The UN's predecessor, the League of Nations, had followed the unanimity rule in decision making.

5. Javed Ansari, *The Political Economy of International Economic Organization* (Boulder, Colo.: Lynne Rienner, 1986), 140.

6. Also known, from its Spanish acronym, as CEPAL.

7. See Michael Edwards, *Future Positive: International Co-operation in the 21st Century* (London: Earthscan, 1999), 180.

8. Lyn Squire, "Why the World Bank Should Be Involved in Development Research," in *The World Bank: Structure and Policies,* ed. Christopher L. Gilbert and David Vines (Cambridge: Cambridge University Press, 2000), 108–133.

9. Lloyd I. Rudolph and Suzanne H. Rudolph, "Authority and Power in Bureaucratic and Patrimonial Administration: A Revisionist Interpretation of Weber on Bureaucracy," *World Politics* 38, no. 2 (1979): 207.

10. Weber believed that the specific nature of bureaucracy "develops the more perfectly the more bureaucracy is 'dehumanised,' the more completely it succeeds in

Notes to pages 8–14

eliminating from official business love, hatred, and all purely personal, irrational, and emotional elements that escape calculation." Max Weber in *From Max Weber: Essays in Sociology,* ed., trans., and with an introduction by H. H. Girth and C. Wright Mills (New York: Oxford University Press, 1946), 216.

11. Rudolph and Rudolph, "Authority and Power in Bureaucratic and Patrimonial Administration," 209.

12. Ansari, *The Political Economy of International Economic Organization,* 143–144.

13. In defining the criteria of the "good researcher," we do not suggest that bad researchers, who fail to meet these criteria, cannot be found in academia as well as elsewhere. Our point is that good researchers face an additional hazard in the bureaucratic context.

14. In its early years, the World Bank's most distinguished economist was Paul Rosenstein-Rodan, who contributed one of the seminal works of the new sub-discipline of development economics in 1943: "Problems of Industrialisation in Eastern and South-Eastern Europe," *Economic Journal* (June–September 1943). His sojourn at the bank between 1947 and 1954 was a contentious and unhappy one, and after many conflicts with the management, he left for academic life at MIT.

15. Jan Tinbergen, *The Design of Development* (Baltimore: Johns Hopkins Press for IBRD, 1958). His account of the publication delay and the reasons for it are given in Jan R. Magnus and Mary S. Morgan, "The ET Interview: Professor J. Tinbergen," *Econometric Theory* 3, no. 1 (1987): 134–135.

16. See John Williamson, "What Washington Means by Policy Reform" in *Latin American Adjustment: How Much Has Happened?* ed. John Williamson (Washington, D.C.: Institute for International Economics, 1990).

17. For a detailed case study of such vetting at the World Bank, see Robert Wade, "Japan, the World Bank and the Art of Paradigm Maintenance: *The East Asian Miracle* in Political Perspective," *New Left Review,* no. 217 (May–June 1996): 3–36.

18. It was slow to adopt the techniques of discounted cash flow and shadow-pricing in project appraisal, the bank's historians, E. S. Mason and R. E. Asher. *The World Bank since Bretton Woods* (Washington, D.C.: Brookings Institution, 1973), 257.

19. M. Gavin and Dani Rodrik, "The World Bank in Historical Perspective," *American Economic Review* 85, no. 2 (May 1995): 329–334. See also Nicolas Stern and Francisco Ferreira, "The World Bank as an 'Intellectual Actor,'" in *The World Bank: Its First Half Century,* ed. Devesh Kapur, John P. Lewis, and Richard Webb, vol. 2, *Perspectives* (Washington, D.C.: Brookings Institution, 1997), 523–610.

20. Henry J. Bruton, "A Reconsideration of Import Substitution," *Journal of Economic Literature* XXXVI (June 1998): 905.

21. Alfred E. Eckes Jr., *Revisiting U.S. Trade Policy: Decisions in Perspective* (Athens: Ohio University Press, 2000), 28–29.

22. Mark Bevir, *The Logic of the History of Ideas* (Cambridge: Cambridge University Press, 1999), 139–142.

23. See, for example, Richard J. Evans, *In Defence of History* (London: Granta Books, 1997), 85, for an expression of the narrow view of intellectual history.

24. Putting it so is designed to indicate again that our aim is to write intellectual history, not the history of economic analysis, which traces the lines of descent of modern pieces of economic analysis or provides a rational reconstruction of past economists' works in modern form. On the distinction between intellectual history and the history of economic analysis, see A. M. C. Waterman, "A Reappraisal of 'Malthus the Economist' 1933–97," *History of Political Economy* 30, no. 2 (1998): 303–304.

25. Eric Hobsbawm, *The Age of Empire 1875–1914* (London: Abacus, 1994), 4–5; Ulric Neisser, "John Dean's Memory: A Case Study," in *The Pleasures of Psychology,* ed. David Coleman and David Heller (New York: Mentor Books, 1986), 69–83; Sidney Dell to Jonathan Rosenhead, 10 October 1983, Sidney Dell Papers, MSS Eng c.5860, Bodleian Library, Oxford; Oral History Interview of Gerald K. Helleiner, 4–5 December 2000, 108–109, in the Oral History Collection of the United Nations Intellectual History Project, The Graduate Center, The City University of New York.

26. For edited extracts from the Oral History Collection of the United Nations Intellectual History Program, see Thomas G. Weiss, Tatiana Carayannis, Louis Emmerij, and Richard Jolly, eds., *UN Ideas: Voices from the Trenches and Turrets* (Bloomington: Indiana University Press, forthcoming).

1. The UN Trade and Development Debates of the 1940s

1. John Morton Blum, *The Price of Vision: The Diary of Henry A. Wallace 1942–1946* (Boston: Houghton Mifflin Company, 1973), 85–86 (entry for 3 June 1942).

2. For a discussion of the concepts of order and justice in the global economy and the problems of reconciling them, see John Toye, "Order and Justice in the International Trade System," in *Order and Justice in International Relations,* ed. Rosemary Foot, John Lewis Gaddis, and Andrew Hurrell (Oxford: Oxford University Press, 2003), 103–124.

3. See, for example, press release dated 15 December 1944 of a speech by Leo Pasvolsky on the Dumbarton Oaks proposals, FO 475/3, U131/12/70, Public Record Office (henceforward PRO), London.

4. Geoffrey L. Goodwin, *Britain and the United Nations* (London: Oxford University Press, 1957), 278; Cristobal Kay, *Latin American Theories of Development and Underdevelopment* (London: Routledge, 1989), 5.

5. James N. Miller, "The Pursuit of a Talking Shop: Political Origins of American Multilateralism, 1934–1945," paper presented at the 25th annual meeting of the Eastern Economics Association, Boston, Mass., 12 March 1999.

6. Text of broadcast by Stettinius, 28 May 1945, FO 475/3, U4416/12/70, PRO. Similarly, see Sumner Welles, *The World of the Four Freedoms* (New York: Columbia University Press, 1943), 20; and Blum, *The Price of Vision,* 149 (entry for 18 December 1942).

7. Cordell Hull, *The Memoirs of Cordell Hull: Volume One* (London: Hodder and Stoughton, 1948), 81–82. For Hull's 1925 remark, see U.S. Senate Committee on Finance, Hearings on International Trade Organization (80) S821-O-A, 41.

8. Wilson's address to Congress, 8 January 1918, cited in Thomas A. Bailey, *Woodrow Wilson and the Lost Peace* (New York: Quadrangle Books, 1963), 333.

9. John Maynard Keynes, *The Collected Writings of John Maynard Keynes,* 30 vols. (London: Macmillan for the Royal Economic Society, 1973–1989), 2: xix, xxiii, 50, 142–143, 168.

10. Henry A. Wallace, *The Century of the Common Man,* cited in Georg Schild, *Bretton Woods and Dumbarton Oaks: American Economic and Political Postwar Planning in the Summer of 1944* (London: Macmillan, 1995), 16.

11. Clark M. Eichelberger, *Organizing for Peace: A Personal History of the United Nations* (New York: Harper Row, 1977), 18–20; see also Clair Wilcox, *A Charter for World Trade* (New York: Macmillan, 1949), 5–9.

12. See, for example, *Foreign Relations of the United States* (henceforward *FRUS*), 1943, I: 765; and Ernest Bevin to Anthony Eden, 8 December 1942, Bevin Papers 3/2, Churchill College, Cambridge.

13. The function of the ILO was to raise "the common standard of the conditions of life, so that those nations which lead the world on social reform may not be placed at an undue disadvantage by those which compete with them by the exploitation of their labour. . . . If international markets are necessary for prosperity, international labour legislation is a vital element in world recovery." James T. Shotwell, "Introduction" to *The Origins of the International Labour Organization* (New York: Columbia University Press, 1934), 1: xix.

14. Evan Luard, *A History of the United Nations,* vol. 1, *The Years of Western Domination, 1945–1955* (London: Macmillan, 1982), 13–14.

15. However, there were disagreements within the U.S. government about the precise role the UN should play. Leroy Stinebower, a State Department economist and later U.S. representative to the United Nations Economic and Social Council, recalled of wartime discussions (presumably referring to his immediate colleagues): "[I]t was fairly clear in our own minds that we expected the specialized agencies to be operative in their own fields, but much more highly coordinated by the United Nations than was ever achieved." He also claimed that the Department of Agriculture was "always determined that the United Nations was not going to do anything other than receive reports and try to see that the agencies were working together" and that the Treasury Department was wary of excessive UN control over the specialized agencies. Leroy Stinebower Oral History, 9 June 1974, 29–30, Harry S. Truman Library, Independence, Missouri.

16. *FRUS*, 1942, I: 25–26; see also the British government white paper *Atlantic Charter August 16, 1941,* Cmd. 6321 (London: HMSO, 1941).

17. David Stafford, *Roosevelt and Churchill: Men of Secrets* (London: Little, Brown and Company, 1999), 207.

18. D. E. Moggridge, *Maynard Keynes: An Economist's Biography* (London: Routledge, 1992), 668.

19. *Proposals for an International Clearing Union,* Cmd. 6437 (London: HMSO, 1943).

20. Moggridge, *Maynard Keynes,* 679–680.

21. Keynes, *Collected Writings,* 11: 456–470.

22. Ibid., 27: 136.

23. Ibid., 199.

24. Moggridge, *Maynard Keynes,* 730.

25. H. W. Singer, "The Terms of Trade Controversy and the Evolution of Soft Financing: Early Years in the UN," in *Pioneers in Development,* ed. Gerald M. Meier and Dudley Seers (Oxford: Oxford University Press, 1984), 279–280.

26. For an assessment of the evidence that White was a Soviet agent, see James M. Boughton, "The Case against Harry Dexter White: Still Not Proven," *History of Political Economy* 33 (2001): 219–239.

27. John Morton Blum, ed., *From the Morgenthau Diaries: Years of War 1941–1945* (Boston: Houghton Mifflin Company, 1967), 230–231.

28. Stinebower Oral History, 29–30.

29. Robert Skidelsky, *John Maynard Keynes,* vol. 3, *Fighting for Britain 1937–1946* (London: Macmillan, 2000), 344, 340.

30. Gerald M. Meier, "The Formative Period," in Meier and Seers, eds., *Pioneers in Development,* 9–10.

31. Susan Howson and D. E. Moggridge, eds., *The Collected Papers of James Meade,* 4 vols. (London: Unwin Hyman, 1988–1990), 3: 27–35.

32. For Meade's views on the industrialization of "backward" areas, see James Meade to Lionel Robbins, "Mr. Harrod's Paper: 'Foreign Lending, Industrialisation and the Clearing Union,'" 24 August 1942, in the online collection of J. M. Keynes/Roy Harrod correspondence, to be found at http://www.e.u-tokyo.ac.jp/Exhibition/keynes/ contents/index.htm.

33. The words were those of Stettinius, who would become Hull's successor. Thomas M. Campbell, *Masquerade Peace: America's UN Policy, 1944–1945* (Tallahassee: Florida State University Press, 1973), 14.

34. L. S. Pressnell, *External Economic Policy since the War,* vol. I, *The Post-War Financial Settlement* (London: HMSO, 1986), 118–119, 129.

35. *FRUS,* 1944, II: 8–9.

36. Some within the U.S. government had, however, favored a different arrangement. Leroy Stinebower recalled: "[T]here were those of us who wanted . . . an economic council and a social council; not an economic and social council. We had what proves to be a well-founded fear that social objectives and well-meaning objectives would always override any hardheaded economic assessment of the consequences." Stinebower Oral History, 39–40.

37. Campbell, *Masquerade Peace,* 35; Walter R. Sharp, *The United Nations Economic and Social Council* (New York: Columbia University Press, 1969), 2.

38. *FRUS,* 1944, I: 735–736.

39. Ibid., 735; Fred L. Israel, ed., *The War Diary of Breckinridge Long: Selections from the Years 1939–1944* (Lincoln: University of Nebraska Press, 1966), 370 (entry for 18 August 1944); Schild, *Bretton Woods and Dumbarton Oaks,* 71.

40. *FRUS,* 1944, I: 732.

41. Thomas M. Campbell and George C. Herring, eds., *The Diaries of Edward R. Stettinius, Jr., 1943–1946* (New York: New Viewpoints, 1975), 232 (entry for 1 February 1945).

42. Leland M. Goodrich, Edvard Hambro, and Anne Patricia Simons, *Charter of the United Nations: Commentary and Documents,* 3rd ed. (New York: Columbia University Press, 1969), 665, 672.

43. Ibid., 687.

44. Vandenberg was an isolationist turned (cautious) internationalist who, as chairman of the Senate Foreign Relations Committee, became one of the architects of President Truman's bipartisan foreign policy. *FRUS,* 1945, I: 850–857; Stephen E. Ambrose and Douglas G. Brinkley, *Rise to Globalism: American Foreign Policy since 1938,* 8th ed. (Harmondsworth: Penguin, 1997), 80.

45. Sharp, *The United Nations Economic and Social Council,* 3.

46. One exception was Keynes, who was an early advocate of soft financing, as the American embassy in London reported in January 1944: "Keynes pointed out that the United States Treasury proposal for a United Nations bank of reconstruction and development aims at 'sound' international investment and this soundness applies to the financial prospects of the investments. Therefore, international investment in projects that raise productivity but fail to bring financial returns might not come within its operations even though many projects that fail even to produce sufficient direct financial returns to service the loans are of the greatest benefit. Keynes, of course, appreciates the political difficulties of setting up an international investment body without stressing financial 'soundness' as a fundamental principle. . . . Keynes stressed the importance of international loans that can be used by borrowers to obtain con- sumption goods to sustain workers engaged on capital projects. In some of the Asiatic countries external aid is needed for this purpose rather than for the import of capital goods." But the political obstacles to such an approach remained insuperable, and the bank was committed to the principle of sound finance. *FRUS,* 1944, II: 3–4.

47. Joseph D. Coppock Oral History, 29 July 1974, 37, Harry S. Truman Library. As well as being an advisor to the State Department on international trade policy from 1945 to 1953, Coppock was a member of the U.S. delegation to the UN Economic and Social Council (from 1946 to 1952).

48. *Documents on Canadian External Relations* (henceforward *CANEX*), Vol. 11, 1944–1945, Part II, 78.

49. H. W. Arndt, *Economic Development: The History of an Idea* (Chicago: University of Chicago Press, 1987), 22–29.

50. Alec Nove, *An Economic History of the U.S.S.R. 1917–1991* (Harmondsworth: Penguin, 1992), 126–127.

51. Gabriele Kohler, "The Early Developers: The Economic Research of the League of Nations and Its Influence on Development Economics," in *Zur kontinentalen Geschichte des okonomischen Denkens (History of Continental Economic Thought),* ed. Jorg Glomobowski, Anna Gronert, and Henk W. Plasmeijer (Marburg: Metropolis Verlag, 1998), 283–306.

52. Harry G. Johnson has argued that the influence of these and other émigré economists lent a strongly nationalistic slant to subsequent discussions of development policy: "While fundamentally concerned with policies for developing the Balkan states

on the German model, the central concepts were presented as universals and later proved equally congenial to the psychological attitudes of the new nations in the relations with the developed countries and in their conception of their development problems." These economists, he suggests, were also responsible for the strong emphasis on the need for industrialization and for protectionist policies in order to achieve it. Harry G. Johnson, ed., *Economic Nationalism in Old and New States* (Chicago: University of Chicago Press, 1967), 131–132.

53. The novel, which was completed in May 1914 and published the following year, is set in the Malay Archipelago. A plan, which subsequently fails, to exploit coal deposits in the region briefly generates fears among locally based independent European traders that they will be driven out of business by the advent of steamers. One (unidentified) character observes: "That's what they call development—and be hanged to it!" Joseph Conrad, *Victory: An Island Tale* (New York: Penguin, 1994), 34.

54. Arndt, *Economic Development*, 36.

55. Ibid., 36–38, 16.

56. Raymond Williams, *Keywords* (London: Fontana Press, 1976), 103.

57. Arndt, *Economic Development*, 46.

58. Eugene Staley, *World Economic Development: Effects on Advanced Industrial Countries*, 2nd ed. (Montreal: International Labour Office, 1945), 2, 5, 22, 97–104, 59–60.

59. However, Wilfred Benson, a former member of the ILO secretariat, was probably the first (in 1942) to use the term "underdeveloped areas" in the sense that it was used after the war. See Arndt, *Economic Development*, 47.

60. *CANEX*, Vol. 12, 1946, 891.

61. *ECOSOC minutes I*, Annex 1a (draft resolution E/4), 1946, 124–126.

62. *CANEX*, Vol. 12, 1946, 886.

63. *ECOSOC minutes I*, 11 February 1946, 64.

64. For the Australian initiative and the U.S. response, see W. J. Hudson and Wendy Way, eds., *Documents on Australian Foreign Policy 1937–49*, vol. VIII, *1945* (Canberra: Australian Government Publishing Service, 1989), esp. 58–59, 28–29, and 90–91.

65. Lleras Restrepo was a lawyer, economist, and former finance minister who had attended the Bretton Woods conference and who later (1966–1970) became his country's president. He divided the opinion of the U.S. diplomats who came into contact with him: some found him "an astute politician, [an] able negotiator, and very helpful," whereas others found him "uncooperative and obstructive." See the State Department's biographical report on him in the International Trade Files (henceforward ITF), Record Group (henceforward RG) 43, Box 145, U.S. National Archives & Records Administration (henceforward NARA), College Park, Maryland.

66. *ECOSOC minutes I*, 11 February 1946, 73–76.

67. Annex 1b (proposed amendment E/5), *ECOSOC minutes I*, 1946, 127; *ECOSOC minutes I*, 12 February 1946, 78–79; *ECOSOC minutes I*, 13 February 1946, 83.

68. *ECOSOC minutes II*, 5 June 1946, 59–60, 63–64. It may also be noted that Noel-Baker's boss, Ernest Bevin, had in 1945 (prior to his appointment as foreign secretary) welcomed the industrialization, specifically, of India: "I am glad they are going to

industrialise on a state basis." As Noel-Baker's predicament showed, the British Labour government's ideological commitment to such dirigiste state planning, in the colonies as well as at home, sat uncomfortably with its commitment to the liberalization of international trade. Text of speech by the Right Hon. Ernest Bevin at the Blackpool Conference of the Labour Party on 23rd May 1945, FO 475/3, PRO.

69. But if Anglo-U.S. policy was thus to some extent based on political expediency, even before the full outbreak of the Cold War, Soviet policy was merely posturing. In the years before Stalin's death in 1953, the repeated dogmatic insistence that heavy industry was the only possible basis of economic development was not matched by any concrete contribution to UN programs of technical assistance. Alvin Z. Rubinstein, "Soviet Policy toward Under-Developed Areas in the Economic and Social Council," *International Organization* 9 (1955): 232–243.

70. Stinebower Oral History, 49–51.

71. *FRUS,* 1946, I: 1355–1356.

72. *CANEX,* Vol. 14, 1948, 900–901.

73. *Proposals for Consideration by an International Conference on Trade and Employment,* Cmd. 6709 (London: HMSO, 6 December 1945).

74. Clair Wilcox, defending the proposed charter to Congress on behalf of the U.S. administration in March 1947, denied that there was anything in it that would lead to free trade: "I do not think that any of the nations participating in the framing of this, or the Government of the United States, believes that free trade is practicable or obtainable or I should say desirable." Such was the congressional hostility to the ITO that Wilcox also had to deny that it would lead to a planned economy. Of course, the only way that these disparate criticisms could be squared was by the suggestion that communists in the government were promoting free trade in order to undermine the United States. Republican congressman Daniel Reed argued, ingeniously, that this was indeed the case. U.S. Senate, Committee on Finance, Hearings on International Trade Organization: (80)S821-O-A, 80, 101; Thomas W. Zeiler, *Free Trade, Free World: The Advent of GATT* (Chapel Hill: University of North Carolina Press, 1999), 167.

75. *FRUS,* 1946, I: 1361; *CANEX,* Vol. 14, 1948, 900.

76. Preparatory Committee 6th Plenary Session (E/PC/T/32), 26 November 1946, Philip Noel-Baker Papers 4/753, Churchill College, Cambridge. Clair Wilcox later suggested that India was "influenced less by the substance of the *Proposals* advanced by the United States than by the fact that the United Kingdom had accorded them its formal support." Be that as it may, the Indians' later warmer attitude, in the face of concessions to their stated point of view, suggests that they were prepared to be open minded. Clair Wilcox, *A Charter for World Trade* (New York: Macmillan, 1949), 31.

77. *CANEX,* Vol. 14, 1948, 900; see also Richard N. Gardner, *Sterling-Dollar Diplomacy in Current Perspective: The Origins and the Prospects of Our International Economic Order* (New York: Columbia University Press, 1980), 271–280.

78. See John M. Leddy Oral History 15 June 1973, 64–65, Harry S. Truman Library.

79. *FRUS,* 1946, I: 1361; *Report of the First Session of the Preparatory Committee of the United Nations Conference on Trade and Employment* (London: United Nations, 1946)

(henceforward *Preparatory Committee I*), 5; see also Gardner, *Sterling-Dollar Diplomacy in Current Perspective,* 280–284.

80. *FRUS,* 1946, I: 1361.

81. *Preparatory Committee I,* 27–28; see also William Adams Brown, *The U.S. and the Restoration of World Trade* (Washington, D.C.: Brookings Institution, 1950), 289–291.

82. U.S. Senate Committee on Finance, Hearings on International Trade Organization, (80) S821-O-A, 5–6, 20 March 1947.

83. Preparatory Committee 6th Plenary Session.

84. Zeiler, *Free Trade, Free World,* 72.

85. "British Commonwealth Talks: Draft Minutes of the 7th meeting of the General Subjects Committee" (TN[P][BC][GSC][47]7th), 6 May 1947, Austin Robinson Papers, ROBN 6/6/1, Churchill College, Cambridge.

86. For some very brief biographical details, see telegram from Colombo to the State Department, 15 October 1947, ITF, RG 43, Box 145, NARA.

87. That is, G. C. S. was the son of the brother of Gamani's paternal grandfather; loosely, his "uncle." Tom Weiss, interview with Gamani Corea, February 2000; John Toye, conversation with Gamani Corea, February 2000.

88. G. C. S. Corea, "Note on Some Aspects of the Draft Charter" (TN[C][47]2), 15 April 1947, Austin Robinson Papers, ROBN 6/6/1.

89. "British Commonwealth Talks 14th Meeting" (TN[P][BC][GSC][47]14th), 13 May 1947, Austin Robinson Papers, ROBN 6/6/1.

90. For a recent review of the historical basis for the charge of hypocrisy, see Ha-Joon Chang, *Kicking Away the Ladder: Development Strategy in Historical Perspective* (London: Anthem Press, 2002).

91. Michael Yaffey, "Friedrich List and the Causes of Irish Hunger," in *A World Without Famine? New Approaches to Aid and Development,* ed. Helen O'Neill and John Toye (London: Macmillan, 1998), 84–106; Henry W. Spiegel, "Alexander Hamilton," in *The New Palgrave: A Dictionary of Economics,* ed. John Eatwell, Murray Milgate, and Peter Newman (London: Macmillan, 1987), 3: 587.

92. Calvin Colton, *Public Economy for the United States* (New York: A. S. Barnes, 1853), cited in Judith Goldstein, *Ideas, Interests and American Trade Policy* (Ithaca: Cornell University Press, 1993), 37n.

93. "British Commonwealth Talks 14th Meeting" (TN[P][BC][GSC][47]14th), 13 May 1947, Austin Robinson Papers, ROBN 6/6/1.

94. For an account of the tariff talks, see Richard Toye, "The Attlee Government, the Imperial Preference System, and the Creation of the GATT," *English Historical Review* 118, no. 478 (September 2003): 912–939.

95. *CANEX,* Vol. 14, 1948, 901.

96. Records of Geneva Discussions, E/PC/T/A/PV/3: 3rd meeting of Commission A, 28 May 1947, 3–4, 10, GATT Archive, World Trade Organization, Geneva.

97. Ibid.; E/PC/T/PV.2/6: Verbatim Report, 6th Meeting, 23 August 1947, 29, GATT Archive.

98. *FRUS,* 1947, I: 965.

99. Gardner, *Sterling-Dollar Diplomacy,* 367.

100. Wilcox, *A Charter for World Trade,* 48, 32.

101. It may be noted that in January 1949 one U.S. State Department official (Howard H. Tewksbury, chief of the Division of River Plate Affairs) conceded that the "the whole E[uropean] R[ecovery] P[rogram] is in a very real sense discriminatory against Latin America. While an attempt is made to confine this discrimination within the bounds of necessity and to balance it with programs assisting Latin America, some discrimination is inherent and unavoidable." *CANEX,* Vol. 14, 1948, 902; *FRUS,* 1949, II: 480.

102. Records of Havana Conference, E/Conf.2/23: Heads of Delegations: Summary Record of Meeting, 24 December 1947, 6, GATT Archive.

103. M. Pangestu, "Special and Differential Treatment in the Millennium: Special for Whom, and How Different?" *The World Economy* 23, no. 9 (2000): 1285–1289. See also John Toye, "Order and Justice in the International Trade System"; and T. N. Srinivasan, *Developing Countries and the Multilateral Trading System: From the GATT to the Uruguay Round and the Future* (Oxford: Westview Press, 1998), 21.

104. In view of his later criticisms of the Havana Charter and his previous role as a public servant in Argentina, it should be noted that Raúl Prebisch was not a member of the Argentine delegation, having been out of favor with the Perón government and excluded from office since 1943. *FRUS,* 1948, I: 831; Stephen R. Niblo, *War, Diplomacy, and Development: The United States and Mexico, 1938–1954* (Wilmington, Del.: Scholarly Resources, 1995), 210; Mateo Magariños, *Diálogos con Raúl Prebisch* (Mexico: Banco Nacional De Comercio Exterior/Fondo de Cultura Económica, 1991), 124.

105. Records of Havana Conference, E/Conf.2/SR.7: Summary Record of Seventh Plenary Meeting, 29 November 1947, 4, GATT Archive.

106. *Report of the Second Session of the Preparatory Committee of the United Nations Conference on Trade and Employment* (Geneva: United Nations, 1947), 42–45; Wilcox, *A Charter for World Trade,* 58–59.

107. U.S. Senate Committee on Finance, Hearings on International Trade Organization, (80) S821-O-A, 31 March 1947, 475 (Testimony of William Taylor Phillips, acting chief, International Resources Division, Department of State).

108. Records of Havana Conference, Press release ITO/86: Address by G. C. S. Corea, 1 December 1947, 3–4, GATT Archive.

109. *CANEX,* Vol. 14, 1948, 904.

110. *United Nations Conference on Trade and Employment,* Cmd. 7375 (London: HMSO, April 1948), 56.

111. *Proceedings of the United Nations Conference on Trade and Development: Geneva, 23 March–16 June 1964,* Vol. II, *Policy Statements* (New York: United Nations, 1964), 18. (Henceforward *UNCTAD I.*)

112. Gardner, *Sterling-Dollar Diplomacy,* 367–368.

113. See Richard Toye, "Developing Multilateralism: The Havana Charter and the Fight for the International Trade Organization, 1947–1948," *International History Review* XXV (June 2003): 282–305.

114. Gardner, *Sterling-Dollar Diplomacy,* 366–368.

115. *Minutes of U.S. Delegation Meeting,* 28 February 1948, ITF, RG 43, Box 148, NARA.

116. "International Trade Organisation Charter: Minutes," 25 February 1948, FO 371/ 68883, PRO.

117. Zeiler, *Free Trade, Free World,* 148.

118. Jacob Viner, "Conflicts of Principle in Drafting a Trade Charter," *Foreign Affairs* 25 (1947): 612–628.

119. Singer, "Early Years in the UN," 281.

120. Gardner, *Sterling-Dollar Diplomacy,* 371–380; Zeiler, *Free Trade, Free World,* 147–164.

121. Srinivasan, *Developing Countries and the Multilateral Trading System,* 3.

122. The Havana Charter was a proposed charter for an international trade organization that was negotiated in 1947–1948 but never came into operation.

123. *UNCTAD I,* II: 17–19.

124. Ibid.

125. Ibid., 18–19.

126. Ibid., 17–19.

127. As an example of a more radical approach, it is interesting to take the statement of Ernesto "Che" Guevara Serna, minister of industry of Cuba, who was also at the first UNCTAD conference. He argued of the Havana Conference that "the intention was to create a world order that suited the competitive interests of the imperialist Powers. . . . At that Conference, and at the previous meeting at Bretton Woods, a number of international bodies were set up whose activities have been harmful to the interests of the dependent countries of the world. And even though the United States of America did not ratify the Havana Charter because it considered it too 'daring,' the various international credit and financial bodies and the General Agreement on Tariffs and Trade—the tangible outcome of those two meetings—have proved to be effective weapons for defending its interests and, what is more, weapons for attacking our countries." Ibid., 162.

128. Ibid., 76.

129. Records of Havana Conference, E/Conf.2/23 Heads of Delegations: Summary Record of Meeting, 24 December 1947, 4, GATT Archive.

2. The UN Recruits Economists

1. For a more extended summary of the structure of the United Nations, see Peter R. Baehr and Leon Gordenker, *The United Nations at the End of the 1990s,* 3rd ed. (New York: St. Martin's Press, 1999), 20–45.

2. Alexander Loveday, *Reflections on International Administration* (Oxford: Clarendon Press, 1956), 294.

3. Ibid., 99–101.

4. Oral History Interview of Janez Stanovnik, 7–8 January 2001, 73–74, in the Oral History Collection of the United Nations Intellectual History Project, The Graduate Center, The City University of New York.

5. Loveday, *Reflections on International Administration*, 309.

6. R. W. B. Clarke diary, 12 March 1946, R. W. B. Clarke Papers, 25, Churchill College, Cambridge.

7. Comment by Yves Berthelot: "Surely the most interesting examples of UN creativity in the last decades have been those where editorial control has *not* been exercised: e.g. the World Employment Programme, the Human Development Report, and even UNICEF's work on adjustment. In contrast, where editorial control has been strict, the result has been uninteresting and has often failed—for example, the World Cultural Report after Mayo and his men got their hands on it." UNIHP publication series peer-review meetings at the Dag Hammarskjöld Foundation, Uppsala, Sweden, 13–14 June 2002.

8. Lloyd I. Rudolph and Suzanne H. Rudolph, "Authority and Power in Bureaucratic and Patrimonial Administration: A Revisionist Interpretation of Weber on Bureaucracy," *World Politics* 38, no. 2 (1979): 226–227.

9. "The enormous growth in international activity since the last war has necessitated a great increase in the demand for research workers. The total number of persons employed by international organisations, however, would seem to have grown during this period out of all proportion to either the increase in the available data or the increase in the output or the quality of the documents produced." Loveday, *Reflections on International Administration*, 311. This remark does not apply only to economists, but it certainly includes them.

10. It is the practice in the UN not to reduce the grade of its officials, but officials can be assigned to tasks appropriate to a lesser grade than the one they hold.

11. "Economic Trends," *Annual Review of United Nations Affairs* (1960–1961): 97–98.

12. Roger E. Backhouse, *The Penguin History of Economics* (London: Penguin Books, 2002), 289.

13. F. M. Scherer, "The Emigration of German-Speaking Economists after 1933," *Journal of Economic Literature* XXXVIII, no. 3 (September 2000): 614–626.

14. This and the preceding paragraph draws on Joseph L. Love, "Economic Ideas in Latin America, c. 1914–45," mimeo, Economics Department, University of Illinois, Urbana.

15. In the UN system, recruitment of intellectuals can happen in three main ways. One is to recruit them as permanent employees, the officials of an international civil service. Another is to hire them as staff members for a specific project on a temporary fixed-term contract. The third is to hire people as consultants. There is some interchange between these different forms of service: consultants or temporary staff can be recruited as permanent officials and former officials can be brought back as consultants or temporary staff. This was the case with Raúl Prebisch and Nicholas Kaldor.

16. Nicholas Kaldor, "Personal Recollections of Michal Kalecki," in *Kalecki's Relevance Today*, ed. Mario Sebastiani (Basingstoke: Macmillan, 1989), 3–4. Kalecki's voice also affected Donald MacDougall, who recalled a spell working for the UN at Lake Success in 1948 in a converted arms factory: "[O]ne disadvantage was that the small offices in which we worked were separated by thin metal partitions, so that conversa-

tion in surrounding offices could be distracting, especially as one of my neighbours was Michal Kalecki, the brilliant Polish economist, the rasping nature of whose voice was aggravated rather than softened by the partition between us." Donald MacDougall, *Don and Mandarin: Memoirs of an Economist* (London: John Murray, 1987), 80.

17. Malcolm C. Sawyer, *The Economics of Michal Kalecki* (Basingstoke: Macmillan, 1985), 5.

18. John Kenneth Galbraith, *A Life in Our Times: Memoirs* (London: Corgi Books, 1983).

19. Kaldor, "Personal Recollections of Michal Kalecki," 9.

20. Jerzy Osiatynski, ed., *Collected Works of Michal Kalecki* (Oxford: Oxford University Press, 1997), VII: 552–553 and 592–593.

21. These papers are in Osiatynski, *Collected Works of Michal Kalecki,* VII: 1–271.

22. On Kalecki's priority over Keynes, see J. Robinson, "Michal Kalecki: A Neglected Prophet," *New York Review of Books,* 4 March 1976, 28–30; E. Eshag, *Fiscal and Monetary Policies and Problems in Developing Countries* (Cambridge: Cambridge University Press, 1983), 34; S. Chapple, "Did Kalecki Get There First? The Race for the General Theory," *History of Political Economy* 23, no. 2 (Summer 1991): 243–261; and Osiatynski, *Collected Works of Michal Kalecki,* I: 463–467. However, in 1946 this priority was not widely appreciated, even in his native Poland.

23. See A. Robinson, "John Maynard Keynes 1883–1946," *Economic Journal* LVII (March 1947): 42.

24. Celso Furtado, *La Fantaisie Organisée. Le Developpment est-il encore possible?* (Paris: Publisud, 1987), 53.

25. Anthony P. Thirlwall, *Nicholas Kaldor* (Brighton: Wheatsheaf Books, 1987), 104–105.

26. Nicholas Kaldor, *Essays on Value and Distribution* (London: Duckworth, 1980), xxi, n. 2.

27. See letters of Myrdal to Owen, 19 February 1948, 12 April 1948, and 2 October 1949, David Owen Papers, Box 1, Columbia University Library, New York.

28. Shahen Abrahamian, "A Man for All Nations: Sidney Dell (1918–1990)," in *Poverty, Prosperity and the World Economy,* ed. Gerry Helleiner, Shahen Abrahamian, Edmar Bacha, Roger Lawrence, and Pedro Malan (Basingstoke: Macmillan, 1995), 3.

29. Walter Schellenberg, *Invasion 1940: The Nazi Invasion Plan for Britain* (London: St. Ermin's Press, 2000), 242.

30. "I was not very happy. . . . I went—though I really didn't want to go. For me that was a step down and I was quite looking forward to settling down in Glasgow." Oral History Interview of Hans Singer, 13 October 1995, 67, in the Oral History Collection of the United Nations Intellectual History Project, The Graduate Center, The City University of New York.

31. For further detail on Singer's life before joining the UN, see D. John Shaw, *Sir Hans Singer: The Life and Work of a Development Economist* (Basingstoke: Palgrave Macmillan, 2002), 3–36.

32. For details of the planned content of this book, see Ed Dosman, "Markets and the State: Theory and Practice in the Evolution of the 'Prebisch Manifesto,'" *CEPAL Review* 75 (December 2001): 87–102.

33. Joseph L. Love, "Economic Ideas and Ideologies in Latin America since 1930," in *The Cambridge History of Latin America,* ed. Leslie Bethell (Cambridge: Cambridge University Press, 1994), IV: 414 (henceforward *Cambridge History*); Mateo Magariños, *Diálogos con Raúl Prebisch* (Mexico: Banco Nacional de Comercio Exterior/Fondo de Cultura Económica, 1991), 127–128.

34. Magariños, *Diálogos con Raúl Prebisch,* 128–129.

35. Aldo Ferrer, "The Early Teachings of Raúl Prebisch," *CEPAL Review* 42 (1990): 27–33.

36. Raúl Prebisch to E. Castillo, 23 November 1948, Prebisch Papers, private collection of Sra. Adela Prebisch.

37. This episode is examined in detail in Dosman, "Markets and the State."

38. J. Marquez to Prebisch, 23 January 1948; Prebisch to E. Bernstein, 17 December 1948; and M. L. Parsons to Prebisch, 11 March 1949, all in Prebisch Papers. James Boughton, currently in-house historian of the IMF, passed on to us this comment from Jacques Polak: "I have absolutely no recollection of any such offer, but it would not be wholly out of character for Bernstein to make it without discussing it with me (a mere division chief at the time)."

39. Prebisch to Eugenio Castillo, 23 November 1948; and Francisco Coire to Prebisch, 24 December 1948, Prebisch Papers.

40. Prebisch to Castillo, 10 January 1949, Prebisch Papers.

41. Sidney Dell, "Raul Prebisch: His Contemporary Relevance," *Development and South-South Cooperation* II, no. 3 (1986): 14–15.

42. Raúl Prebisch, "Joint Responsibilities for Latin American Progress," *Foreign Affairs* 39, no. 4 (July 1961): 3.

43. Love, "Economic Ideas in Latin America, c. 1914–45," 16.

44. James Currie to H. M. Phillips, 8 July 1948, FO 371/69021A, PRO.

45. Furtado, *La Fantaisie Organisée,* 41–56.

46. Love, "Economic Ideas in Latin America, c. 1914–45," 11.

47. Jesus Silva Herzog, "A Manera de Introducción," in *La Economía Cubana en los primeros anos de la revolución y Otros Ensayos,* ed. Juan F. Noyola (Mexico City: Siglio Veintiuno Editores, 1978), 9–23. Noyola's resignation letter is at 10–12.

48. Arndt, "The Origins of Structuralism," 157, n. 28.

49. Oral History Interview of Janez Stanovnik, 7–8 January 2001, 58.

50. Gilpin, "London—PEP," Chapter 9 in his memoir, United Nations Career Records Project Papers, MSS Eng c.4674, f. 11, Bodleian Library, Oxford.

51. See correspondence in David Owen Papers, Box 9, Columbia University Library.

52. Loveday, *Reflections on International Administration,* 49.

53. Ibid., 69.

54. The UK civil service did, however, permit fixed-term secondment to the UN, and this gave security to those who worked there on a short-term temporary basis. This was not a particularly attractive option, in that those who returned could reenter only at the same grade at which they had left.

3. Michal Kalecki, the *World Economic Report,* and McCarthyism

1. Cited in Dean Acheson, *Present at the Creation: My Years in the State Department* (New York: W.W. Norton & Company, 1969), 222.

2. This phenomenon did not develop to its full extent for some years, however: see Chapter 7.

3. See Eric Hobsbawm, *Age of Extremes: The Short Twentieth Century, 1914–1991* (London: Michael Joseph, 1994), 229.

4. An example is the dispute over the Austrian peace settlement.

5. For several months during 1950, the Soviets withdrew from the Security Council and other UN bodies to protest the failure to transfer China's seat on the Security Council to the new communist government.

6. Robert G. Wesson, "The United Nations in the World Outlook of the Soviet Union and the United States," in *Soviet and American Policies in the United Nations: A Twenty-Five Year Perspective,* ed. Alvin Z. Rubinstein and George Ginsburgs (New York: New York University Press, 1971), 6–10.

7. Andrew Boyd, *United Nations: Piety, Myth and Truth,* rev. ed. (Harmondsworth: Penguin Books, 1964), 9.

8. The story of the IMF's successful resistance to the ambitions of ECOSOC is told in J. Keith Horsefield, *The International Monetary Fund, 1945–1965: Twenty Years of International Monetary Cooperation* (Washington, D.C.: International Monetary Fund, 1969), I: 124, 145–147. The agreement between the UN and the IMF of 15 November 1947 specifying the latter as both a specialized agency of the UN and an independent international organization is in ibid., III: 215–218. The same story is told of the IBRD in Devesh Kapur, John P. Lewis, and Richard Webb, *The World Bank: Its First Half Century,* vol. 1, *History* (Washington, D.C.: Brookings Institution Press, 1997), 1168.

9. W. Arthur Lewis, "The Economic and Social Council," in *The United Nations: The First Ten Years,* ed. B. A. Wortley (Manchester: Manchester University Press, 1957), 44–45.

10. Antony Gilpin, who served in the DEA from 1952 to 1957, initially in the regional commissions section, recalled: "The Assistant (later Under-)-Secretary-General for Economic and Social Affairs, during most of the time I worked in the Section, was Philippe de Seynes, a debonair Frenchman with the high rank in France of 'Inspecteur de Finance.' I soon learnt that there was constant tension between him and Wladek [Malinowski, head of the regional commissions section], partly on temperamental grounds, but primarily because he reckoned that the executive secretaries of the regional commissions—Gunnar Myrdal (Economic Commission for Europe), Raúl Prebisch (Economic Commission for Latin America) and P. S. Lokanathan (Economic Commission for Asia and the Far East)—although of equal rank, should be subordinate to him, in the same way as in principle the commissions were subordinate to ECOSOC. Gunnar and Raúl in particular were such outstanding personalities, and ECOSOC such a tame organ of the UN, that Philippe must have realized that what might have been the

position on paper could hardly be that in practice." Antony Gilpin, unpublished memoirs, "Chapter 15: New York," United Nations Career Records Project Papers, MSS Eng.c.4675, ff. 323–324, Bodleian Library, Oxford.

11. See Coire to Prebisch, 24 December 1948, Prebisch Papers, private collection of Sra. Adela Prebisch.

12. Correspondence between David Owen and Will Clayton, August–September 1946, ITF, RG 43, Lot File 57D 284, Box 118, NARA, cited in Theodore Charles Stallone, "The Political Economy of William L. Clayton" (Ph.D. diss., Columbia University, 1997), 282n.

13. Oral History Interview of Hans Singer by Richard Jolly and John Shaw, 20, 21, and 26 August 1997, 26–27, in the Oral History Collection of the United Nations Intellectual History Project, The Graduate Center, The City University of New York.

14. Kalecki was appointed as a special advisor to the director with the rank of assistant director in the Division for Economic Stability and Development of the DEA. Kalecki headed the economic stability section, the other two sections being Foreign Trade and Economic Development. See Osiatynski, *Collected Works of Michal Kalecki,* VII: 553.

15. United Nations, Department for Economic Affairs, *Economic Report: Salient Features of the World Economic Situation 1945–1948* (New York: Lake Success, 1948).

16. Ibid., 3, 243–257.

17. This decision cannot be construed as an attack on Kalecki himself, who in any case wrote only Part I, Chapter 2, "Inflationary and Deflationary Developments" (Osiatynski, *Collected Works of Michal Kalecki,* VII: 563). Rather, it was an example of Austin Robinson's frequent attempts to use his considerable influence constructively to bring forward new and better ideas. See A. Cairncross, *Austin Robinson: The Life of an Economic Adviser* (Basingstoke: Macmillan, 1993), 111, 166.

18. Austin Robinson, "Five Economic Surveys," *Economic Journal,* LIX (December 1949): 629–638.

19. For Condliffe and Meade, see de Marchi, "League of Nations Economists and the Ideal of Peaceful Change in the Thirties," *History of Political Economy* 23, Annual Supplement (1991): 151; and Susan Howson, "James Meade," *Economic Journal* 110, no. 461 (2000): F122–F145. Meade wrote the surveys for 1937–1938 and 1938–1939 himself, as did Kaldor for the ECE surveys of 1947 and 1948. See Anthony P. Thirlwall, *Nicholas Kaldor* (Brighton: Wheatsheaf, 1987), 104–107.

20. Alexander W. Southam was a UK Foreign Office staff member who had been recommended by the Foreign Office for the post of chief of Myrdal's Central Office in the ECE. Myrdal found that Southam "is at odds with everybody and is really not very good for the work" and pleaded with Owen to put Southam "on a mission to some undeveloped country, far away from Europe." Owen obliged, and Southam complained to the Foreign Office. The resulting estrangement between Owen and the Foreign Office lasted from April to October 1949. See letters from Myrdal to Owen, 27 and 30 March and 15 October 1949, David Owen Papers, Box 1, Columbia University Library.

21. Dell to Kaldor, 9 January 1950, Kaldor Papers, NK/3/30/55/34, King's College, Cambridge.

22. Ibid.

23. See Osiatynski, *Collected Works of Michal Kalecki,* VII: 554. Osiatynski here relies on the recollections of Stanislaw Braun in later interviews.

24. Donald MacDougall, *Don and Mandarin: Memoirs of an Economist* (London: John Murray, 1987), 80.

25. Éprime Eshag, "Kalecki's Political Economy: A Comparison with Keynes," *Oxford Bulletin of Economics and Statistics* 39, no. 1 (February 1977): 83.

26. J. Robinson, "Michal Kalecki: A Neglected Prophet," *New York Review of Books,* 4 March 1976, 30.

27. E. Lipinski, "Michal Kalecki," reprinted in *The Oxford Bulletin of Economics and Statistics* 39, no. 1 (February 1977): 74.

28. Éprime Eshag, "Introduction," *Oxford Bulletin of Economics and Statistics* 39, no. 1 (February 1977): 2.

29. "Mr Kalecki was one of the first theoretical economists working in this country to make full use of statistical data to check the validity of his theories." G. D. N. Worswick, "'Modern' Economics and Politics," *The Modern Quarterly* 1, no. 1 (December 1945): 17n.

30. J. Robinson, "Michal Kalecki: A Neglected Prophet," *New York Review of Books,* 4 March 1976, 30, emphasis added.

31. S. Dell, "Kalecki at the United Nations, 1946–54," *Oxford Bulletin of Economics and Statistics* 39, no. 1 (February 1977): 32.

32. Osiatynski, *Collected Works of Michal Kalecki,* I: 233–318 for the *Essays* and VII: 1– 209 for the wartime papers. For a summary account of Kalecki's Oxford views of the links between demand, output growth, price and profit rises, and the fall in real wages, see G. D. N. Worswick, "Kalecki at Oxford, 1940–44," *Oxford Bulletin of Economics and Statistics* 39, no. 1 (February 1977): 20–21.

33. Richard Toye, *The Labour Party and the Planned Economy, 1931–1951* (London: Royal Historical Society, 2003), 94–95.

34. This was in line with the preferred policy of the British socialists: see Richard Toye, *The Labour Party,* 112.

35. United Nations, *Food Shortages and Economic Stability and Development,* (ECOSOC E/CN.1/Sub 2/5), 22 November 1947.

36. Quoted in Osiatynski, *Collected Works of Michal Kalecki,* VII: 560.

37. United Nations, *Inflationary and Deflationary Tendencies, 1946–1948* (Lake Success, New York: UN DEA, 1969), 5–14. The citation is from paragraph 8.

38. Michal Kalecki, "El problema del financiamento del desarrollo económico," *El Trimestre Economico* 21, no. 4 (1954): 381–401.

39. Osiatynski, *Collected Works of Michal Kalecki,* V: 25.

40. Ibid., 44.

41. Kalecki has been criticized by later writers for not exploring in more detail and depth the economics of the marketed surplus of food and its response to the internal terms of trade between food and nonfood consumer goods. See E. V. K. FitzGerald, *The Macroeconomics of Development Finance: A Kaleckian Analysis of the Semi-industrial Economy* (Basingstoke: Macmillan, 1993), 123–127.

42. Osiatynski, *Collected Works of Michal Kalecki,* V: 30.

43. This episode is described by Osiatynski in ibid., VII: 555.

44. Ibid., V: 37–38.

45. Kapur, Lewis, and Webb, *The World Bank,* 1:1168.

46. "It was through this mechanism that other specialized agencies of the UN system, which would be consulted in appointing members of the council, hoped to exercise some degree of influence on Bank policy." This is the reason for allowing the council to fall into disuse; Edward S. Mason and Robert E. Asher; *The World Bank since Bretton Woods* (Washington, D.C.: The Brookings Institution, 1973), 32.

47. One biographer of Truman comments: "Truman genuinely appreciated the civil libertarian tradition, but he never came close to imposing his sentiments on key branches of his administration." Alonzo L. Hamby, *Man of the People: A Life of Harry S. Truman* (Oxford: Oxford University Press, 1995), 569. See also 427–429, 529–532, 564–568; and Ambrose and Brinkley, *Rise to Globalism,* 108–109. For the activities of the Dies Committee in 1939–1940, see Ted Morgan, *FDR: A Biography* (London: Grafton Books, 1986), 564–565.

48. For example, in April 1953, an FBI agent interviewed Herbert Feis in order to determine the political views of a colleague in the department, Leo Pasvolsky, who had been a key figure in U.S. planning for the postwar era and who was under suspicion of holding communist sympathies. Pasvolsky, Feis explained to the FBI man, could hardly have been a communist as he had figured among a group in the State Department intently focused upon reducing trade barriers and liberalizing international commercial and financial affairs. The agent was unconvinced: the "zeal and purpose" that Pasvolsky had demonstrated suggested the presence of an ulterior motive. See Jamie Miller, "Wartime Origins of Multilateralism, 1939–1945" (Ph.D. thesis, University of Cambridge, 2003), Chapter 2.

49. As Ambrose notes, "There was in McCarthyism an appeal to the inland prejudice against the eastern-seaboard establishment and the things it stood for in the popular mind.... Anti-intellectualism was always prominent in the movement." Ambrose and Brinkley, *Rise to Globalism,* 109. See also Richard Hofstadter, *Anti-Intellectualism in American Life* (New York: Knopf, 1963).

50. Boyd, *United Nations: Piety, Myth and Truth,* 33.

51. A prominent exception was the case of Alva Myrdal, director of UNESCO's Department of Social Sciences (and the wife of Gunnar Myrdal, head of the Economic Commission for Europe). In the spring of 1953, when trying to visit UN headquarters, she was denied entry to the United States unless she agreed to sign a parole agreement. Brian Urquhart, *Hammarskjold* (New York: W.W. Norton & Company, 1994), 64.

52. Hans Singer, for example, recalled that the British delegation to the UN "firmly supported me during the McCarthy years, when the popular press described me as part of a communist conspiracy, in the pocket of the Russians [and trying] to extract money from the pockets of the American taxpayer." Interview with Hans Singer by Richard Jolly and John Shaw, 20, 21, and 26 August 1997, 28. See also Margaretta Jolly, obituary of Ilse Singer, *The Guardian,* 13 March 2001; and Gilpin, unpublished memoirs,

"Chapter 15: New York," United Nations Career Records Project Papers, MSS Eng c.4675, f. 312, Bodleian Library, Oxford.

53. Acheson, *Present at the Creation,* 698.

54. *FRUS,* 1952–1954, III: 327–328; Alan Ford, "The Secretariat," in Wortley, ed., *The United Nations,* 102. See also James Barros, *Trygve Lie and the Cold War: The UN Secretary-General Pursues Peace, 1946–1953* (DeKalb: Northern Illinois University Press, 1989), 311–320.

55. Unsigned memorandum to John D. Hickerson, 31 December 1952, Office Files of the Assistant Secretaries of State for United Nations Affairs, RG 59, Lot File 58D33, Box 1, NARA.

56. Trygve Lie, *In the Cause of Peace: Seven Years in the United Nations* (New York: Macmillan, 1954), 389–390, 396–397. More people than the eighteen were affected by the controversy, however. In January 1953, the *New York Times* ("11 In U.N. Accused of Communist Ties," 2 January 1953) estimated that thirty-five people had up to that point been removed from the UN staff and that the total number touched by the affair was forty-six.

57. Sidney (and Ethel) Dell to Kaldor, 20 December 1952, Kaldor Papers, NK/3/119/ 91–93.

58. "United States Nationals in the United Nations—Governor Bowles' Letter of July 6, 1950," 24 July 1950, Office Files of the Assistant Secretaries of State for United Nations Affairs, RG 59, Lot File 58D33, Box 1, NARA.

59. Andrew W. Cordier and Wilder Foote, eds., *Public Papers of the Secretaries-General of the United Nations,* vol. I, *Trygve Lie 1946–53* (New York: Columbia University Press, 1969 [henceforward *Public Papers*]), 485–486; see also Lie, *In the Cause of Peace,* 399.

60. Cordier and Foote, *Public Papers,* I: 498.

61. It is worth noting that Ivar Rooth, the Swedish managing director of the IMF, also cooperated with the U.S. authorities and demanded the resignation of the secretary of the fund, V. Frank Coe, in November 1952, after he had pleaded the Fifth Amendment before the grand jury and refused to testify before a Senate sub-committee. See J. Keith Horsefield, *The International Monetary Fund, 1945–1965: Twenty Years of International Monetary Cooperation* (Washington, D.C.: IMF, 1969), I: 339–40. The World Bank also complied with Eisenhower's Executive Order 10422, but "there were very few casualties." The practice of loyalty screenings for U.S. employees of the bank continued until 1986. See Kapur, Lewis, and Webb, *World Bank,* 1:1173.

62. See, for example, Joseph P. Lash, *Dag Hammarskjöld* (London: Cassell, 1962), 49.

63. Urquhart, *Hammarskjold,* 63–64.

64. For Weintraub's experience in New Deal agencies, the State Department, and UNRRA, see David Weintraub to David Owen, 23 August 1946, David Owen Papers, Box 9.

65. Interview with Hans Singer by Richard Jolly and John Shaw, 20, 21, and 26 August 1997, 32.

66. "United States Nationals in the United Nations—Governor Bowles' Letter of July 6, 1950," 24 July 1950, Office Files of the Assistant Secretaries of State for United Nations Affairs, RG 59, Lot File 58D33, Box 1, NARA.

67. "United States Citizens on the United Nations Secretariat Called Before the Senate Sub-Committee," 31 October 1952, ibid.

68. Isador Lubin to John D. Hickerson, "Appointment of a Director of the Economic Section of UN," 7 April 1952; and John D. Hickerson, "Memorandum for the Files," 17 April 1952, both in Office Files of the Assistant Secretaries of State for United Nations Affairs, RG 59, Lot File 58D33, Box 3, NARA.

69. Dell to Kaldor, 15 March 1953, Kaldor Papers, NK/3/119/75–76; "11 In U.N. Accused of Communist Ties."

70. John H. Williams to Kaldor, 30 April 1953, Kaldor Papers, NK/3/119/28.

71. "United States Citizens on the United Nations Secretariat Called Before the Senate Sub-Committee," 31 October 1952, Office Files of the Assistant Secretaries of State for United Nations Affairs, RG 59, Lot File 58D33, Box 1, NARA; "11 In U.N. Accused of Communist Ties"; Thomas J. Hamilton, "Weintraub Resigns U.N. Job Under Fire," *New York Times*, 7 January 1953. In UK English, a "grass" is a snitch. A "supergrass" is an informer who names many other people as criminals to authorities.

72. According to Dell; see Dell to Kaldor, 25 March 1953, Kaldor Papers, NK/3/119/63.

73. William O. Hall, "Weintraub Case; Opal Thomas Case," 30 December 1952, Office Files of the Assistant Secretaries of State for United Nations Affairs, RG 59, Lot File 58D33, Box 1, NARA.

74. Hamilton, "Weintraub Resigns U.N. Job Under Fire."

75. Dell to Kaldor, 15 March 1953, Kaldor Papers, NK/3/119/75–76; and Kaldor to Hugh Gaitskell, 14 March 1953, Kaldor Papers, NK/3/119/57.

76. Dell to Kaldor, 21 April 1953, Kaldor Papers, NK/3/119/32–33.

77. Oral History Interview of Hans Singer, 13 October 1995, 18–19.

78. David Weintraub to Vincent Knowles, 29 June 1953, Kaldor Papers, NK3/119/16.

79. Owen to Weintraub, 17 April 1959; and Owen to J. O'Neil Lewis, 17 April 1959, David Owen Papers, Box 11.

80. Note marked "strictly confidential," unsigned and undated (probably between March and April 1953), Roy Blough Papers, Box 18, Harry S. Truman Library, Independence, Missouri.

81. Blough was a former member of President Truman's Council of Economic Advisers who owed his UN appointment to the failure to promote Weintraub in 1952. Isador Lubin to John D. Hickerson, "Appointment of a Director of the Economic Section of UN," 7 April 1952, Office Files of the Assistant Secretaries of State for United Nations Affairs, RG 59, Lot File 58D33, Box 3, NARA.

82. Caustin stated: "I would have wished to consult my colleagues, Mr. Hilgerdt and Mr. Kalecki, before presenting comments." Memorandum by H. E. Caustin to Roy Blough, 4 November 1953, Roy Blough Papers, Box 18.

83. Bulletin SG/SGB/99 of 10 March 1954. This bulletin is referred to in a memo from A. G. Katzin to all Assistant Secretaries-General and Principal Directors, 27 May 1954, Roy Blough Papers, Box 18.

84. Note on "Some Planning and Implementation Aspects of the Secretariat Reorganization," marked "strictly confidential," unsigned, 27 April 1954, Roy Blough Papers, Box 18.

85. Memorandum by A. G. Katzin to all ASGs and Principal Directors, 27 May 1954; and Blough to A. G. Katzin, 16 June 1954, Roy Blough Papers, Box 18.

86. Hammarskjöld referred to these conversations in his subsequent letter to Robertson of 1 December 1954 formally convening the committee. See Dennis Robertson Papers, B8/1, 1–2, Trinity College, Cambridge. The UN file is ECA 334/03.

87. Blough to Sune Carlson, 30 September 1954, Roy Blough Papers, Box 18.

88. Memorandum from Michal Kalecki to Dag Hammarskjöld, 1 October 1954, Roy Blough Papers, Box 18.

89. Memorandum from Blough to Hammarskjöld, 6 October 1954, Roy Blough Papers, Box 18.

90. Éprime Eshag, "Kalecki's Political Economy: A Comparison with Keynes," _Oxford Bulletin of Economics and Statistics_ 39, no. 1 (February 1977): 84.

91. Hammarskjöld did not consider Svennilson, who was a substitute for Bertil Ohlin, "in the same class as" the other three group members. Aide-memoire by Roy Blough, 4 December 1954, Roy Blough Papers, Box 19.

92. Hammarskjöld to Robertson, 1 December 1954.

93. Richard M. Bissell, Dennis Robertson, Ingvar Svennilson, and John H. Williams to Hammarskjöld, 25 January 1955, Dennis Robertson Papers, B8/1, 3–6.

94. "No-one here seriously believes that the downgrading of Kalecki's post was a _bona fide_ economy measure. . . . The Secretary General himself, when he sent for Kalecki recently to say goodbye to him, had sufficient respect for his intelligence not to pretend that the issue was one of economy." Dell to Kaldor, 2 December 1954, Kaldor Papers, NK/3/30/64/160–162.

95. Eshag, "Kalecki's Political Economy," 84.

96. Ibid. Braun also made the same point; see Osiatynski, _Collected Works of Michal Kalecki,_ VII: 557.

97. Kaldor to Dell, 22 April 1955, Kaldor Papers, NK/3/30/64/131. As the Secretary-General put it diplomatically when Myrdal was leaving the UN: "[T]he [economic] scientist may sometimes feel a little unhappy because everyone who has this kind of academic background, whether it is Mr. Myrdal or Mr. Hammarskjold, of course likes to think in his own way." See Urquhart, _Hammarskjold,_ 371.

98. Paul Mizen, Don Moggridge, and John Presley, "The Papers of Dennis Robertson: The Discovery of Unexpected Riches," _History of Political Economy_ 29, no. 4 (Winter 1997): 584. There is a vague mention of "plans I told you about and which might give me a new chance of collaborating with you" in Hammarskjöld to Robertson, 12 June 1958, Dennis Robertson Papers, C20/10, but it is implausible that this could be a reference to the reform of the _WER._

99. Dell to Kaldor, 2 December 1954, Kaldor Papers, NK/3/30/64/160–162.

100. Dell to Kaldor, 11 October 1955, Kaldor Papers, NK/3/30/64/126–127.

101. Kalecki's fate in the reorganization was shared by Folke Hilgerdt, whose post was also deemed surplus to departmental needs, but the blow was less harsh for him because he was due to retire in October 1955. See memorandum by Blough to A. Katzin, 16 June 1954, Roy Blough Papers, Box 18.

102. Dell to Kaldor, 2 December 1954, Kaldor Papers, NK/3/30/64/160–162.

103. Peter Kihss, "Five Americans in U.N. Balk at Queries on Communist Tie," *New York Times*, 14 October 1952.

104. "11 In U.N. Accused of Communist Ties."

105. For a personal testimony on McCarthyism in the UN, see Eshag, "Kalecki's Political Economy," 83.

106. The Eisenhower administration was extremely sensitive about communist China and the UN. When handing over the presidency to Kennedy, Ike told him that he would support him completely in foreign policy except if he permitted communist China to enter the UN. W. W. Rostow, *Diffusion of Power: An Essay in Recent History* (New York: Macmillan, 1972), 116.

107. "Defectors among Iron Curtain Delegations to the United Nations and among Iron Curtain Nationals on the Secretariat," n.d., Office Files of the Assistant Secretaries of State for United Nations Affairs, RG 59, Lot File 58D33, Box 3, NARA.

108. This is demonstrated by the following conversation reported by W. O. Hall of the State Department:

> The SYG UN told me yesterday that Dell had somehow learned of U.S. concern about his continued employment in the Secretariat. He said indications were that someone in the UN Secretariat, probably Blough, or some State Department source had been the leak. In the light of this development, he felt he could not transfer Dell to Geneva without extensive damage to Dell's reputation and many staff difficulties. He asked me:
>
> a. If I had any hint as to the source of information to Dell.
>
> b. If the U.S. would be too disturbed if Dell remained at Headquarters.
>
> I indicated that the Dell case had been discussed by USUN only with SYGs Lie and Hammarskjold, and with Blough and Price, and that I had no knowledge of the leak.
>
> In view of the Department's earlier expressed desire that Dell remain in New York in preference to transfer to ECE, I indicated the U.S. had no objection to his retention at Headquarters.

Memorandum of conversation between William O. Hall and Hammarskjöld, "Proposed UN Personnel Changes—Mr. Sidney Dell," 23 June 1954, Office Files of the Assistant Secretaries of State for United Nations Affairs, RG 59, Lot File 58D33, Box 4, NARA.

4. From Full Employment to Economic Development

1. L. M. Goodrich, "From League of Nations to United Nations," *International Organization* 1, no. 1 (February 1947): 21.

2. See reference to the work of the Bruce Committee in Chapter 1.

3. See N. de Marchi (with the cooperation of Peter Dohlman), "League of Nations Economists and the Ideal of Peaceful Change in the Decade of the Thirties," *History of Political Economy* 23, Annual Supplement (1993): 143–178.

4. For example, G. Haberler, *Prosperity and Depression* (Geneva: League of Nations, 1937) or 3rd ed. (London: George Allen and Unwin, 1964); J. Tinbergen, *Statistical Testing of Business Cycle Theories,* 2 vols. (Geneva: League of Nations, 1938–1939).

5. Paul Mizen, Don Moggridge, and John Presley, "The Papers of Dennis Robertson: The Discovery of Unexpected Riches," *History of Political Economy* 29, no. 4 (Winter 1997): 575–576. In his biography *Understanding Dennis Robertson: The Man and His Work* (Cheltenham: Edward Elgar, 2000), Gordon Fletcher does not mention Robertson's connection with the League and later with the UN (see Chapter 3), but he does explore very fully the nature of Robertson's professional and personal conservatism.

6. Dennis Robertson to Alexander Loveday, 14 June 1939, League of Nations archive, Geneva.

7. Tinbergen later recalled that Loveday "sent me to England to discuss my work with [Henderson and Robertson]; interestingly enough, not with Keynes." Jan R. Magnus and Mary Morgan, "The ET Interview: Professor Jan Tinbergen," *Econometric Theory* 3, no. 1 (1987): 125.

8. John Maynard Keynes, *The Collected Writings of John Maynard Keynes,* 30 vols. (London: Macmillan for the Royal Economic Society, 1973–1989), XIV: 285–320. For a review of this controversy, see Robert Leeson, "'The Ghosts I Called I Can't Get Rid of Now': The Keynes-Tinbergen-Friedman-Phillips Critique of Keynesian Macroeconomics," *History of Political Economy* 30, no. 1 (Spring 1998): 51–94.

9. Erin E. Jacobssen, *A Life for Sound Money: Per Jacobssen: His Biography* (Oxford: Clarendon Press, 1979), 167. The original Swedish edition of Myrdal's book was published in German translation as *Warnung vor Friedensoptimismus* (Zurich: Europa Verlag, 1945).

10. "Developments in the United States, Western Europe and Japan were covered in some detail in twenty-six pages; the 'primary producing countries' (Australia, Canada, New Zealand, Argentina, Brazil, Chile, Hungary, Rumania, Yugoslavia) rated one paragraph and a table; the Balkans, the Dutch East Indies, one sentence each; South America one paragraph; all the rest, including all of Asia (except Japan), Africa, and the USSR, were completely ignored." H. W. Arndt, *Economic Development: The History of an Idea* (Chicago: University of Chicago Press), 33.

11. This change was also influenced, of course, by the preferences of the respective member governments. See Alexander Loveday, *Reflections on International Administration* (Oxford: Clarendon Press), 295.

12. Haberler, *Prosperity and Depression,* v.

13. Alvin Hansen, "Economic Progress and Declining Population Growth," *American Economic Review* XXIX, no. 1 (March 1939): 4, 12–13.

14. This is what he advised the Full Employment Act Hearings in 1945, according to Robert Leeson; see "The Political Economy of the Inflation-Unemployment Trade-Off," *History of Political Economy* 29, no. 1 (Spring 1997): 136–137.

15. Paul Samuelson, *Economics: An Introductory Analysis* (New York: McGraw-Hill Book Company, 1948), 435.

16. "Since the early 1950s . . . I urged that Keynesian policies were not enough and that labour, business and government would have to come to an agreement on a wage and price policy that would reconcile a high and steady rate of growth with price stability, or even decline." W. W. Rostow, *Diffusion of Power: An Essay in Recent History* (New York: Macmillan, 1972), 121.

17. Michal Kalecki, "The Political Aspects of Full Employment," *The Political Quarterly* 14, no. 4 (July 1943): 322–331. Reprinted in Jerzy Osiatynski, *Collected Works of Michal Kalecki* (Oxford: Oxford University Press, 1997), I: 347–356.

18. W. Arthur Lewis, "The Economic and Social Council," in *The United Nations: The First Ten Years,* ed. B. A. Wortley (Manchester: Manchester University Press, 1957), 39.

19. Susan Howson and Donald Moggridge, eds., *The Collected Papers of James Meade,* vol. IV, *The Cabinet Office Diary, 1944–46* (London: Unwin Hyman, 1990), 106 (entry for 8 July 1945).

20. See UN document E/CN.1/sub.2/SR.45, 10-5, quoted in Sidney Dell, "Kalecki at the United Nations, 1946–54," *Oxford Bulletin of Economics and Statistics* 39, no. 1 (February 1977): 26, n. 5; and UN DEA, *Recent Developments in the World Economic Situation* (Lake Success, New York: UN DEA, October 1949), Appendix C, 47–48.

21. On the position of the Attlee government on international economic issues, see Richard Toye, *The Labour Party and the Planned Economy, 1931–1951* (London: Royal Historical Society, 2003), Chapter 7.

22. ECOSOC resolution 221 E (IX), 11 August 1949. The British government had taken the initiative that led to this report: see Alec Cairncross, ed., *The Robert Hall Diaries 1947–1953* (London: Unwin Hyman, 1989), 289, n. 11.

23. David Owen cabled Kaldor on 23 September 1949 to come to New York by 16 October; Kaldor Papers, NK1/13/49, King's College, Cambridge.

24. For a recent evaluation of the report, see Louis Emmerij, Richard Jolly, and Thomas G. Weiss, *Ahead of the Curve?* (Bloomington: Indiana University Press, 2001), 29–31.

25. Anthony P. Thirlwall, *Nicholas Kaldor* (Brighton: Wheatsheaf Books, 1987), 108. Kaldor acknowledged the assistance of Sidney Dell in the drafting; see Kaldor to H. Kidd, 15 July 1961, Kaldor Papers, NK/3/30/64/73–74.

26. UN, *National and International Measures for Full Employment: Report by a Group of Experts Appointed by the Secretary-General* (Lake Success, N.Y.: UN DEA, 1949), paragraph 102.

27. Ibid., paragraph 6, page 7.

28. Ibid., paragraph 20, pages 11–12.

29. The Fifth Committee of the General Assembly is responsible for all administrative and budgetary matters.

30. Kaldor to Dell, 21 February 1950, Kaldor Papers, NK/3/30/55/28–29.

31. S. Abrahamian, "A Man for All Nations: Sidney Dell (1918–1990)," in *Poverty, Prosperity, and the World Economy: Essays in Memory of Sidney Dell,* ed. G. Helleiner et al. (Basingstoke: Macmillan, 1995), 28, n. 3.

32. Dell to Kaldor, 21 January 1950, Kaldor Papers, NK/3/30/55/32–33.

33. Dell to Kaldor, 20 February 1950, Kaldor Papers, NK/3/30/55/26.

34. Kaldor to Dell, 24 January 1950, Kaldor Papers, NK/3/30/55/30–31.

35. Entry for 31 January 1950, in Cairncross, *The Robert Hall Diaries,* 1:104.

36. Ibid.

37. Entry for 29 June 1950, ibid., 1:120.

38. Entry for 13 July 1950, ibid., 1:123. For the political context of the proposed Full Employment Bill, see Richard Toye, *The Labour Party and the Planned Economy,* 234–235.

39. J. Keith Horsefield, *The International Monetary Fund, 1945–1965: Twenty Years of International Monetary Cooperation* (Washington, D.C.: International Monetary Fund, 1969), 1:287–288.

40. Thirlwall, *Nicholas Kaldor,* 109.

41. *ECOSOC Records,* Eleventh Session, 385th Meeting, 12 July 1950, paragraphs 41 to 64, pages 78–80. The World Bank did not set a target for its lending until the presidency of Robert McNamara some twenty years later.

42. *ECOSOC Records,* Eleventh Session, 390th Meeting, 17 July 1950, 113–118.

43. Ibid., paragraph 24, 115.

44. Ibid., paragraph 27, 116.

45. Ibid., paragraphs 12 and 48, 118.

46. Ibid., paragraphs 110–114, 125.

47. See note 5 of Chapter 3 on the Russian boycott.

48. Philip M. Williams, *The Diary of Hugh Gaitskell, 1945–1956* (London: Jonathan Cape, 1983), 193–194 (entry for 11 August 1950).

49. Jacob Viner, "Full Employment at Whatever Cost," *Quarterly Journal of Economics* LXIV (August 1950): 384–407.

50. Viner, "Full Employment at Whatever Cost," 407.

51. He particularly disliked the idea (derived from Kalecki) that rising prices in one sector should not be countered by measures of general deflation. Viner saw this as evidence of the experts' covert preference for an overheated economy with inflationary pressure suppressed by means of extensive economic controls.

52. This was also a concern of the executive directors of the fund, who "foresaw great difficulty in determining with any promptitude the amount which a surplus country ought to contribute, and the amount to which a deficit country would be entitled." See Horsefield, *The International Monetary Fund, 1945–1965,* 1:288.

53. Viner, "Full Employment at Whatever Cost," 401.

54. Walt W. Rostow, "The United Nations' Report on Full Employment," *Economic Journal* LX, no. 238 (June 1950): 349–350.

55. "But the plan is directed largely to the United States"; Viner, "Full Employment," 405.

56. Rostow, "The United Nations' Report on Full Employment," 345. See also 326, where Rostow describes the proposals as owing much to "a contemplation of the sort of domestic and international measures which would have avoided the debacle after 1929."

57. Dell to Kaldor n.d. (but post-June 1950), Kaldor Papers, NK/3/30/55/21–23.

58. Kaldor to Arthur Smithies, 31 October 1950, Kaldor Papers, NK/7/33/8. Thomas Balogh concurred with this view in "The International Aspect," in *The British Economy 1945–1950,* ed. G. D. N. Worswick and P. H. Ady (Oxford: Clarendon Press, 1952), 509.

59. Dell, "Kalecki at the United Nations," 27. The details of Kalecki's efforts to follow up on country full-employment policies are set out by Osiatynski, *Collected Works of Michal Kalecki,* VII: 570–572.

60. This expert group consisted of James W. Angell (U.S.), G. D. A. MacDougall (UK), Hla Myint (Burma), Javier Marquez (Mexico), and Trevor W. Swan (Australia). UN, *National and International Measures for Full Employment.*

61. UN DEA, *Measures for International Economic Stability: Report by a Group of Experts Appointed by the Secretary-General* (New York: UN DEA, 1951).

62. ECOSOC resolution 427 (XIV), 10 July 1952.

63. Referring to Trygve Lie's request for "alternative practical ways" of reducing the international impact of recessions, Donald MacDougall later commented: "I think we did this rather well, with realistic suggestions for action by Governments, the IMF and the World Bank." Donald MacDougall, *Don and Mandarin: Memoirs of an Economist* (London: John Murray, 1987), 80.

64. IMF, "Adequacy of Monetary Reserves," *IMF Staff Papers,* III, *1953–54*: 181–227, reproduced in Horsefield, *The International Monetary Fund, 1945–1965,* II: 343.

65. This point was not lost on the UK politicians who had read this UN report. See, for example, Aneurin Bevan, *In Place of Fear* (London: William Heinemann, 1952), 163.

66. Per Jacobssen diary entry for 4 October 1954, quoted by Jacobssen, *A Life for Sound Money,* 254.

67. "The Veritas Foundation sought to extirpate Keynesian thought from Harvard and to prevent the adoption and use of Samuelson's textbook throughout the United States." J. K. Galbraith, *A History of Economics* (London: H. Hamilton, 1987), 240.

68. Viner, "Full Employment at Whatever Cost," 386.

69. Henry C. Wallich, "United Nations Report on Full Employment," *American Economic Review* 40, no. 3 (June 1950): 878.

70. The forerunner of this style of critical attack on the *General Theory* had been Hubert Henderson's theory of "transfer unemployment" in "Mr. Keynes's Theories," a paper first delivered in Cambridge in May 1936 and published in Hubert Douglas Henderson, *The Inter-War Years and Other Papers* (Oxford: Clarendon Press, 1955), 161–177. In the UK between 1945 and 1949, some government economists argued in favor of medium-term plans for specific industries as a supplement to management of aggregate demand. These included Austin Robinson, Richard Kahn, and Brian Reddaway, all at the Board of Trade, plus Treasury official R. W. B. ("Otto") Clarke. They opposed James Meade at the Cabinet Office, who was prepared to rely for policy purposes mainly on calculating the annual "inflationary gap." See Richard Toye, *The Labour Party and the Planned Economy,* Chapter 8. It is worth noting that while in Britain Keynesian policies faced objections to aggregation from the political left, in the U.S. essentially the same argument against aggregative methods was made from the political right.

71. UN, *Full Employment*, paragraph 183, 87. See also Sidney Dell, "Kalecki at the United Nations," 26.

72. Charles P. Kindleberger, "Economists in International Organizations," *International Organization* 9, no. 3 (August 1955): 338–352.

73. Ibid.

74. "I don't think we can expect much from *him*," Keynes had told Bertil Ohlin. See Brian Urquhart, *Hammarskjold* (New York: W.W. Norton & Company, 1994), 368n.

75. Bjorn Hanssen, "Dag Hammarskjöld, (1905–1961)," in *The New Palgrave. A Dictionary of Economics,* ed. John Eatwell, Murray Milgate, and Peter Newman (London: Macmillan, 1987), 2: 590.

76. Per Jacobssen diary entry for 21 January 1943, quoted in Jacobssen, *A Life for Sound Money,* 166.

77. Urquhart, *Hammarskjold,* 370–371.

78. "It appears to be generally agreed that asking you to do anything would infuriate the Americans." Dell to Kaldor, n.d. (but post-June 1950), Kaldor Papers, NK/3/30/55/21–23.

79. Kaldor to Dell, 22 April 1955, Kaldor Papers, NK/3/30/64/133–135.

80. Dell to Kaldor, 25 April 1955, Kaldor Papers, NK/3/30/64/131.

81. Oral History Interview of Janez Stanovnik, 7–8 January 2001, 21, in the Oral History Collection of the United Nations Intellectual History Project, The Graduate Center, The City University of New York.

82. SG/430, July 12 1955, quoted in Urquhart, *Hammarskjold,* 373.

83. SG/493, July 16 1956, quoted in ibid., 373.

84. UN, *Yearbook of the United Nations 1950* (New York: UN Department of Public Information, 1951), 468.

85. *ECOSOC Records,* Eleventh Session, 390th Meeting, 17 July 1950, 125.

86. Kenneth Dadzie, "The United Nations and the Problem of Economic Development," in *United Nations, Divided World: The UN's Roles in International Relations,* ed. Adam Roberts and Benedict Kingsbury (Oxford: Clarendon Press, 1988), 140.

87. UN, *Measures for the Economic Development of Under-Developed Countries* (New York: UN DEA, 1951).

88. Ibid., 28. See also Arndt, *Economic Development,* 62–63.

89. Hans Singer, "La creation de la CNUCED," *Revue Tiers-Monde,* XXXV, no. 139 (Juillet–Septembre 1994): 492.

90. Arthur Lewis, "Economic Development with Unlimited Supplies of Labour," *The Manchester School of Economic Studies* XXII (1954): 139–191.

91. Arndt, *Economic Development,* 62.

92. The UN had begun its Technical Assistance Programme in 1948, before Point 4 in Truman's inaugural speech of January 1949. The Soviet Union, which originally refused to cooperate with the Technical Assistance Programme, subsequently agreed to contribute to it. See Edmund H. Kellogg, *The 7th General Assembly "Nationalization" Resolution: A Case Study in United Nations Economic Affairs* (New York: Woodrow Wilson Foundation, 1955), 4–5.

93. W. Arthur Lewis, *Economic Survey, 1919–1939* (London: Allen and Unwin, 1949), 175.

94. Peter T. Bauer, "Lewis' *Theory of Economic Growth:* A Review Article," *American Economic Review* XLVI, no. 4 (September 1956): 635.

95. See, for example, the speech of Mr. Ali (Pakistan) on behalf of the Asian underdeveloped countries. "At the moment, agricultural labour was under-employed. The introduction of mechanical methods of farming would still further reduce the demand. The result might be that a very large proportion of the rural population might become superfluous. . . . [T]hey would have to be absorbed into industries." *ECOSOC Records,* 10th Session, 367th Meeting, 28 February 1950, 172, paragraph 71.

96. Gerald M. Meier, "The Formative Period" in Meier and Seers, eds., *Pioneers in Development,* 18.

97. S. Herbert Frankel, "United Nations Primer for Development," in S. Herbert Frankel, *The Economic Impact on Under-Developed Societies* (Oxford: Basil Blackwell, 1953), 82–110.

98. See his *Principles of Economic Planning* (London: Allen and Unwin, 1949).

99. Dadzie, "The United Nations and the Problem of Economic Development," 141.

100. Wallich, "United Nations Report on Full Employment," 882.

101. Sidney Dell, "Relations between the United Nations and the Bretton Woods Institutions," paper presented at the North-South Roundtable on the Future of the UN, Uppsala, Sweden, 6–8 September 1989, 31.

102. "The [UN] organization was thus forced to occupy itself with matters on which there was more of a consensus, 'development' being one of the most important of these"; Gilbert Rist, *The History of Development from Western Origins to Global Faith* (London: Zed Books, 1997), 81.

103. See Bauer, "Lewis' *Theory of Economic Growth,*" 634–635.

104. Dell, "Relations between the United Nations and the Bretton Woods Institutions," 31.

5. The Early Terms-of-Trade Controversy

1. S. E. Ambrose, *Rise to Globalism: American Foreign Policy since 1938,* 7th rev. ed. (New York: Penguin, 1993), 101.

2. The whole of colonial Africa continued to be dealt with by the UN Trusteeship Office under Ralph Bunche. This was quite separate from the UN Economics Department, whose work on terms of trade is discussed in this chapter.

3. Oral History Interview of Hans Singer, 11 October 1995, 18, in the Oral History Collection of the United Nations Intellectual History Project, The Graduate Center, The City University of New York.

4. H. W. Singer with D. Sapsford and P. Sarkar, "The Prebisch-Singer Terms of Trade Controversy Revisited," in *Growth, Development, and Trade: Selected Essays of Hans W. Singer,* ed. H. W. Singer (Cheltenham: Edward Elgar, 1998), 141.

5. H. Bloch and D. Sapsford, "Prebisch and Singer Effects on the Terms of Trade between Primary Producers and Manufacturers," in *Development Economics and Policy,* ed. D. Sapsford and J. Chen (London: Macmillan, 1998), 35–62.

6. For an extended discussion, see John Toye, *Keynes on Population* (Oxford: Oxford University Press, 2000), Chapter 1. When criticizing the views of Prebisch and Singer, Jacob Viner and Gottfried Haberler both made reference to this doctrine, though without themselves endorsing it. Jacob Viner, *International Trade and Economic Development* (Oxford: Oxford University Press, 1952), 114; Gottfried Haberler, *International Trade and Economic Development* (San Francisco: International Center for Economic Growth, 1988), 39–40.

7. Joseph L. Love, "Raúl Prebisch and the Origins of the Doctrine of Unequal Exchange," *Latin American Research Review* 15, no. 3 (1980): 45–72.

8. Cristobal Kay, *Latin American Theories of Development and Underdevelopment* (London: Routledge, 1989), 32. Singer recalled, "My discovery that Prebisch thought along lines that were so congenial to me came after I had drafted my paper." This suggests a belief that Prebisch *had* arrived at both the secular-decline thesis and an economic explanation of it independently. John Toye and Richard Toye, interview with Singer, 12 May 2000.

9. Cited in Joseph L. Love, "A New Look at the International Intellectual Environment of the Thirties and Forties," unpublished paper, 1991, 2. Copy in Hans Singer Papers, private collection of Hans Singer.

10. A. P. Whitaker, ed., *Inter-American Affairs 1944* (New York: Columbia University Press, 1945), 143.

11. See, for example, R. C. Simonsen, *Brazil's Industrial Evolution* (São Paulo: Escola Livre de Sociologia E Política, 1939), 15.

12. Central European thinkers had advocated state-led industrialization in the 1920s on the grounds of unequal exchange between groups of nations at the center and the periphery of the world economy. This idea, particularly as used by Werner Sombart, was introduced to Latin America by Ernest Friedrich Wagermann in his *Evolución y ritmo de la economía mundial* (Barcelona: Editorial Labor, 1933). See E. V. K. FitzGerald, "ECLA and the Formation of Latin American Economic Doctrine," in *Latin America in the 1940s: War and Postwar Transitions,* ed. D. Rock (Berkeley: University of California Press, 1994), 94–95.

13. C. P. Kindleberger, "Planning for Foreign Investment," *American Economic Review: Papers and Proceedings* 33, no. 1, Supplement (March 1943): 349.

14. C. P. Kindleberger, *The Life of an Economist: An Autobiography* (Oxford: Basil Blackwell, 1991), 142.

15. C. P. Kindleberger, "International Monetary Stabilization," in *Postwar Economic Problems,* ed. S. E. Harris (London: McGraw-Hill Book Company, 1943), 375–395. See discussion in Joseph L. Love, "Economic Ideas and Ideologies in Latin America since 1930," in Bethell, ed., *Cambridge History,* VI: 421 and n. 84.

16. See, for example, F. H. Cardoso, *Les Idées à Leur Place* (Paris: Éditions A. M. Métailié, 1984), 23; and Celso Furtado, *La Fantaisie Organisée. Le développement est-il encore possible?* (Paris: Publisud, 1987), 101. This view is also to be found in Love, "Raúl Prebisch and the Origins of the Doctrine of Unequal Exchange," 63 (which was endorsed by Kay, *Latin American Theories of Development and Underdevelopment,* 5); and in Love, "Economic Ideas and Ideologies in Latin America," 422.

17. Paul Samuelson, "International Trade and the Equalisation of Factor Prices," *The Economic Journal* 58, no. 230 (June 1948): 183–184. Emphasis added.

18. Raúl Prebisch to Eugenio Castillo, 10 January 1949, Prebisch Papers, private collection of Sra. Adela Prebisch.

19. Rosemary Thorp, *Progress, Poverty and Exclusion: An Economic History of Latin America in the 20th Century* (Baltimore: Johns Hopkins University Press, 1998), 105, Table 4.1.

20. Raúl Prebisch, "La inflación escolástica y la moneda Argentina," *Revista de Economía Argentina* 17, no. 193 (July 1934): 11–12; and 17, no. 194 (August 1934): 60. This article is reprinted in Raúl Prebisch, *Obras 1919–1948*, 3 vols. (Buenos Aires: Fundación Raúl Prebisch, 1991), 2: 337–350. The citation is from 341.

21. Mateo Magariños, *Diálogos con Raúl Prebisch* (Mexico: Banco Nacional de Commercio Exterior/Fondo de Cultura Económica, 1991), 63–64.

22. He believed that "the normal oscillation in the economic life of an agrarian country can be supported by the monetary system, if that system is in good condition." Prebisch, *Obras 1919–1948*, 2: 566.

23. Margariños, *Diálogos con Raúl Prebisch*, 100. In March 1933, *The Times* (London) published four articles by Keynes, which, expanded by an introductory and concluding chapter, was published in pamphlet form as "The Means to Prosperity." The slightly enlarged American edition is in John Maynard Keynes, *The Collected Writings of John Maynard Keynes*, 30 volumes (London: Macmillan for the Royal Economic Society, 1973–1989), 9: 335–366.

24. "Prebisch's main concern was the international propagation of the business cycle," according to Furtado (quoted in Kay, *Latin American Theories of Development and Underdevelopment*, 9). See also W. C. Mitchell, *Business Cycles* (New York: National Bureau of Economic Research, 1927); Joseph Schumpeter, *Business Cycles: A Theoretical, Historical, and Statistical Analysis of the Capitalist Process* (London: McGraw-Hill Book Company, 1939).

25. In 1980, Prebisch did not recollect Sombart's earlier use of these terms; Love, "Raúl Prebisch and the Origins of the Doctrine of Unequal Exchange," 63. However, FitzGerald thinks that it is "most unlikely" that Prebisch "was unaware of the origins of the contemporary center-periphery concept"; "ECLA and the Formation of Latin American Economic Doctrine," 95.

26. Raúl Prebisch, "Introducción al curso de Economía Política," *Revista de Ciencias Económicas* 33 (1945): 529.

27. Raúl Prebisch, "Responsabilidad de los Paises de la Periferia," in Banco de México, *Memoria: Primera Reunion de Técnicos Sobre Problemas de Banca Central del Continente Americano* (Mexico City: Banco de México, S.A., 1946), 163–164.

28. Raúl Prebisch, "Dictamen del Dr. Raúl Prebisch acerca de los anteproyectos sobre Banco Central y bancos," *Revista de Hacienda* 13, no. 28 (1948): 161.

29. Raúl Prebisch to Eugenio Gudin, 20 December 1948, original in Spanish, Prebisch Papers.

30. Raúl Prebisch to Eugenio Castillo, 23 November 1948, original in Spanish, Prebisch Papers.

31. Love, "Raúl Prebisch and the Origins of the Doctrine of Unequal Exchange," 57, 65; Love, "Economic Ideas and Ideologies in Latin America," 417–418.

32. Raúl Prebisch, *Apuntes de Economía Política (Dinámica Económica): Clases Dictadas en el Curso Universitario de 1948* (Buenos Aires: Faculty of Economic Sciences, University of Buenos Aires, 1948), 87–98.

33. H. W. Singer, "The Terms of Trade Controversy and the Evolution of Soft Financing: Early Years in the UN," in *Pioneers in Development,* ed. G. M. Meier and Dudley Seers (Washington, D.C.: The World Bank, 1984), 280.

34. Cited in United Nations, *Post War Price Relations in Trade between Under-developed and Industrialized Countries* (Lake Success, N.Y.: UN Department of Economic Affairs, 1949), 1.

35. League of Nations, *Industrialization and Foreign Trade* (N.p., League of Nations Series II, Economic and Financial 1945.II.A.10), 154–167, 116–121.

36. Comment by Hans Singer on Edgar J. Dosman and David H. Pollock, "Raúl Prebisch, 1901–1971: The Continuing Quest," unpublished paper, 1991, 9. Copy in Hans Singer Papers.

37. United Nations, *Post War Price Relations in Trade between Under-developed and Industrialized Countries.* It should be noted that this is available in the United Nations Office Geneva Library in Geneva, but not in the Dag Hammarskjöld Library at the United Nations in New York.

38. United Nations, *Relative Prices of Exports and Imports of Under-Developed Countries* (Lake Success, N.Y.: UN Department of Economic Affairs, 1949), 7; John Toye and Richard Toye, interview with Hans Singer, 12 May 2000.

39. United Nations, *Relative Prices of Exports and Imports,* 23.

40. Ibid., 16, 127, 126.

41. "I thought if you look at foreign trade from the point of view of the poor countries, exporters of primary products, what does it look like? And it appears an unequal system that is weighted against them." Oral History Interview of Hans Singer, 11 October 1995, 33 in the Oral History Collection of the United Nations Intellectual History Project, The Graduate Center, The City University of New York.

42. H. W. Singer, "Economic Progress in Underdeveloped Countries," *Social Research: An International Quarterly of Political and Social Science* 16, no. 1 (March 1949): 2–3. We are most grateful to John Shaw for drawing this document to our attention.

43. "The Economic Commission for Latin America . . . shall arrange for such surveys, investigations and studies to be made of economic and technical problems [of the region] as it may deem proper and participate in the same." Proposal addressed to the Secretary-General by the Delegation of Chile (ECOSOC document E/468), *ECOSOC Official Records,* 2nd Year, 5th Session, 12 July 1947, 391.

44. "Resolution of the First Session of ECLA" (E/CN.12/71), 24 June 1948.

45. Celso Furtado tells the story of how as a new recruit to ECLA, he was urged by the executive secretary, Martínez Cabañas, to bring to Santiago as many documents on Brazil as possible for the purpose of strengthening the survey: *La fantaisie organisée,* 54–56.

46. L. A. Shapiro to H. W. Singer, 5 January 1949, RAG-2/43, UN Archive, New York.

47. Ibid.

48. J. Ahumada and A. Nataf, "Terms of Trade in Latin American Countries," *IMF Staff Papers* 1, no. 1 (1950): 123–135.

49. United Nations, *Economic Survey of Latin America 1948* (Lake Success, N.Y.: UN Department of Economic Affairs, 1949), xix, 216–220.

50. Castillo to Prebisch, 16 February 1949, Prebisch Papers.

51. Letter from Gustavo Martínez Cabañas to Prebisch, 5 March 1949, original in Spanish; Francisco Coire to Prebisch, 8 April 1949, Prebisch Papers.

52. Martínez Cabañas to Prebisch, 5 March 1949, original in Spanish, Prebisch Papers.

53. Telegram from Castillo to Prebisch, 9 March 1949, Prebisch Papers.

54. "1. Wholesale prices indices of the United Kingdom from 1873 to 1947, divided, if possible, into indices of manufactured products and raw materials. 2. Price indices for exports and for imports for the United Kingdom and for the United States for the same period. 3. United States national income from 1910 to 1929." Castillo to Shapiro, 1 April 1949, UN Archive, New York.

55. *Economic Survey of Latin America 1949* (New York: UN DEA, 1951).

56. Castillo to Coire, 1 April 1949, RAG-2/43, UN Archive, New York.

57. This first draft does not appear to have survived among the manuscript papers and correspondence currently in the possession of Sra. Prebisch, although these have not been fully catalogued.

58. Furtado, *La fantaisie organisée,* 64–66.

59. Castillo to Shapiro, 1 April 1949 and Shapiro's reply, 27 April 1949, RAG-2/43, UN Archive, New York.

60. John Spraos, "The Statistical Debate on the Net Barter Terms of Trade between Primary Commodities and Manufactures," *The Economic Journal* 90, no. 357 (March 1980): 107 and n. 2; Table 1 and notes, 111–112.

61. United Nations, *Economic Survey of Latin America 1948* (Lake Success, N.Y.: UN Department of Economic Affairs, 1949), 247, n. 1; Coire to Prebisch, 8 April 1949, Prebisch Papers.

62. Raúl Prebisch, *The Economic Development of Latin America and Its Principal Problems* (Lake Success, N.Y.: United Nations, 1950), 8–10, 1, 16.

63. Love, "Raúl Prebisch and the Origins of the Doctrine of Unequal Exchange," 45–72.

64. "It is an interesting fact, perhaps not widely known because of the anonymity of UN staff publications, that the principal author [of *Post-War Trends* and *Relative Prices*] was Hans Singer who became the second twin in the 'Prebisch-Singer thesis' through a subsequent signed article" (Spraos, "The Statistical Debate on the Net Barter Terms of Trade," 107, n. 3).

65. See, for example, the efforts of Jerzy Osiatynski to identify the UN writings of Michal Kalecki, in *Collected Works of Michal Kalecki,* ed. Jerzy Osiatynski (Oxford: Oxford University Press, 1990–1997), 7: 552–575.

66. *Report to the Economic and Employment Commission on the Third Session of the Sub-Commission held from 21 March to 11 April 1949* (E/CN.1/65), 12 April 1949, 12.

67. "As you know, first the secretariat published, on their own responsibility, a study on the long-term trends in terms of trade between developed and developing countries. This was bitterly attacked by the industrial countries, because they considered that this was outrageous that the secretariat on its own responsibility, not being asked for that, produced a statistical document like this which gave a very clear evidence that there was a long-term fall in commodity terms of trade." Oral History Interview of Janez Stanovnik, 7–8 January 2001, 48, in the Oral History Collection of the United Nations Intellectual History Project, The Graduate Center, The City University of New York.

68. Prebisch, *The Economic Development of Latin America*, 10, n. 3, 1.

69. Magariños, *Diálogos con Raúl Prebisch*, 130.

70. Martínez Cabañas to Trygve Lie, 9 October 1949, letter of transmittal printed in Prebisch, *The Economic Development of Latin America*, p. v.

71. H. E. Caustin to A. D. K. Owen, 12 October 1949, UN Archive, DAG-17, Box 33; see also Magariños, *Diálogos con Raúl Prebisch*, 129.

72. Furtado, *La fantaisie organisée*, 80.

73. Its first incarnation was in Spanish as UN document E/CN.12/89, dated 14 May 1949. It appeared in *El Trimestre Economico* 16, no. 63 (July–September 1949): 347–431. At the instance of Furtado, it was published in Portuguese in the *Revista Brasileira de Economia* in October 1949. It was republished in Spanish in Santiago in April 1950 and again in English later in 1950 in Lake Success, N.Y., as UN document E/CN.12/89, Rev.1. Its subsequent publication history until 1986 is to be found in United Nations, *Raúl Prebisch: Un Aporte al Estudio de su Pensiamento* (Santiago de Chile: CEPAL, 1987), 52.

74. H. W. Singer, "The Influence of Schumpeter and Keynes on the Development of a Development Economist," in *Zur deutschsprachigen wirtschaftswissenschaftlichen Emigration nach 1933*, ed. H. Hagemann (Marburg: Metropolis-Verlag, 1997), 141.

75. Prebisch, *The Economic Development of Latin America*, 12–13. The dislocation to relative prices caused by monopolistic tendencies in the labor and manufactures markets of Europe had been the theme of Gustav Cassels's 1927 League of Nations study *Recent Monopolistic Tendencies in Industry and Trade*; Love, "A New Look at the International Intellectual Environment of the Thirties and Forties," 2.

76. Prebisch, *The Economic Development of Latin America*, 13–14.

77. The basic idea of a structural difference between countries where increased efficiency of production leads to higher incomes and those where it leads to falling product prices was already in Singer's March 1949 publication, "Economic Progress in Underdeveloped Countries," 2–3.

78. H. W. Singer, "The Distribution of Gains between Investing and Borrowing Countries," *American Economic Review* XL, no. 2 (May 1950); in H. W. Singer, ed., *The Strategy of International Development: Essays in the Economics of Backwardness* (London: Macmillan, 1975), 43–57.

79. Ibid., 49–51.

80. Cardoso, *Les Idées à Leur Place*, 27, 29–30; Furtado, *La fantaisie organisée*, 66–67.

81. Raúl Prebisch, "Commercial Policy in Under-Developed Countries," *American Economic Review* XLIX, no. 2 (May 1959): 251–273. For commentary, see M. J. Flanders,

"Prebisch on Protectionism: An Evaluation," *The Economic Journal* 74, no. 294 (June 1964): 305–326; and E. V. K. FitzGerald, "ECLA and the Theory of Import Substituting Industrialization in Latin America," in *An Economic History of Latin America*, vol. 3, *Industrialization and the State in Latin America: The Postwar Years*, ed. E. Cardenas, J. A. Ocampo, and R. Thorp (London: Macmillan, 2000), 61–69. As FitzGerald indicates, there are two stages in Prebisch's explanation of terms-of-trade decline. The first was based on a neo-Ricardian model of price formation at the center and technical progress; the 1959 version, the second stage, had no functional distribution or technical progress, just certain nonstandard characteristics of exogenous demand.

82. Oral History Interview of Victor Urquidi, 18–19 June 2000, 83, in the Oral History Collection the United Nations Intellectual History Project, The Graduate Center, The City University of New York.

83. Kay, *Latin American Theories of Development and Underdevelopment*, 8.

84. Prebisch, *The Economic Development of Latin America*, 7, n. 1. See also Furtado, *La fantaisie organisée*, 66.

85. Viner was wrong to attribute to "the technical staff of the United Nations" the view that "the exchange by [underdeveloped] countries of primary products for the manufactures of developed countries, while especially profitable for the latter, is *positively injurious* to the former"; Jacob Viner, *International Trade and Economic Development* (Oxford: Oxford University Press, 1952), 43, emphasis added.

86. Viner nevertheless felt obliged to assert the opposite; ibid., 112.

87. Ibid., 113–114.

88. Ibid.

89. United Nations, *Relative Prices of Exports and Imports*, Appendix A, 133–134.

90. Ibid., 126; Prebisch, *The Economic Development of Latin America*, 10, n. 3.

91. Furtado, *La fantaisie organisée*, 154.

92. "Statement on Terms of Trade by Robert E. Asher, at the Fifth Session of ECLA," April 1953, ECLAC Library, Santiago de Chile.

93. P. T. Ellsworth, "The Terms of Trade between Primary Producing and Industrial Countries," *Inter-American Economic Affairs* 10, no. 1 (Summer 1956): 48.

94. Ibid., 51.

95. Ibid., 57, citing Carl Major Wright, "Convertibility and Triangular Trade as Safeguards against Economic Depression," *The Economic Journal* 65, no. 259 (September 1955): 425–426.

96. Ellsworth, "The Terms of Trade between Primary Producing and Industrial Countries," 64–65.

97. The paper was presented at the Detroit meeting of the Econometric Society in September 1956. An abstract was published as T. Morgan, "The Long-Run Terms of Trade between Agriculture and Manufacturing," *Econometrica* 25, no. 2 (April 1957): 360.

98. G. M. Meier, "International Trade and International Inequality," *Oxford Economic Papers* 10, no. 3 (October 1958): 277–289.

99. Ibid., 288.

100. Haberler, *International Trade and Economic Development*, 36.

101. Ibid., 40.

102. H. W. Singer, *The Strategy of International Development: Essays in the Economics of Backwardness* (London: Macmillan, 1975), 15–16.

103. H. W. Singer with D. Sapsford and P. Sarkar, "The Prebisch-Singer Terms of Trade Controversy Revisited," in *Growth, Development, and Trade: Selected Essays of Hans W. Singer,* ed. H. W. Singer (Cheltenham: Edward Elgar, 1998), 141.

104. *GAOR,* 16th Session, Second Committee, 720th Meeting, 11 October 1961, 22–24.

6. ECLA, Industrialization, and Inflation

1. *GAOR,* 16th Session, Plenary Meetings, 1013th Meeting, 25 September 1961, 58.

2. Sebastian Edwards, "Openness, Trade Liberalization and Growth in Developing Countries," *Journal of Economic Literature* 21 (September 1993): 1358–1359. There is also much gross misrepresentation of Prebisch, for example by the economist John Kay, who claimed, wholly mistakenly, that Prebisch "developed dependency theory." See *The Financial Times,* 16 January 2002.

3. Mateo Magariños, *Diálogos con Raúl Prebisch* (Mexico: Banco Nacional De Comercio Exterior/Fondo de Cultura Económica, 1991), 129.

4. Magariños, *Diálogos con Raúl Prebisch,* 136.

5. Hernán Santa Cruz, "The Creation of the United Nations and ECLAC," *CEPAL Review* 57 (December 1995): 17–33.

6. *ECOSOC minutes,* 1 August 1947, 131–133.

7. Cuba "pointed out that the development of Latin America had long been hindered by colonial Powers. . . . After the era of colonization, he added, other Powers had continued the exploitation." In addition, Bolivia, El Salvador, and Uruguay supported the proposal, although these countries were not members of ECOSOC. Ibid., 131–139, 145–154.

8. Ibid., 138.

9. *CANEX,* Vol. 13, 1947, 741. Arnold C. Smith later became first secretary-general of the Commonwealth.

10. Ibid., 740.

11. W. R. Malinowski, "Centralization and Decentralization in the United Nations Economic and Social Activities," *International Organization* 16 (1962): 521–541.

12. Hernán Santa Cruz, "The Creation of the United Nations and ECLAC," *CEPAL Review* 57 (December 1995): 17–33.

13. Ibid.; *ECOSOC minutes,* 25 February 1949, 261–263.

14. Stinebower Oral History, 9 June 1974, 65–66, Harry S. Truman Library, Independence, Missouri.

15. In "ECLA and the Theory of Import Substituting Industrialization in Latin America," in *An Economic History of Latin America,* vol. 3, *Industrialization and the State in Latin America: The Postwar Years,* ed. E. Cardenas, J. A. Ocampo, and R. Thorp (Basingstoke: Macmillan, 2000), 61, E. V. K. FitzGerald argues that "as an institution the ECLA logically adopted a specifically *regional* viewpoint . . . [and] this meant that

regional coordination of import substitution was taken for granted, and thus the limitations on plant scale imposed by country size could be overcome by local market integration."

16. *Report of the Ad Hoc Committee on Proposed Economic Commission for Latin America* (E/630/Add.1), 29 January 1968, 46–47, 29, 9–16; Santa Cruz, "The Creation of the United Nations and ECLAC," 17–33.

17. *Statement by the Chairman of the Peruvian Delegation, Mr. Juvenal Monge* (ECLA document E/CN.12/20), 9 June 1948, 4; *Speech delivered by Sr. Alberto Baltra Cortés, Chilean Minister of Economy and Commerce* (ECLA document E/CN.12/17), 7 June 1948, 2–3.

18. *Speech delivered by Mr. Julio Alvarado* (ECLA document E/CN.12/29), 11 June 1948, 10–11. Emphasis in original.

19. *Speech delivered by Sr. Alberto Baltra Cortés* (ECLA document E/CN.12/17), 7 June 1948, 7.

20. *Statement by the Chairman of the Peruvian Delegation*, 8; *Speech delivered by Mr. Julio Alvarado*, 12.

21. *Statement by the Chairman of the Peruvian Delegation*, 7–8; *Speech by the Representative of Brazil, Doctor Octavio Bulhoes* (ECLA document E/CN.12/30), 11 June 1948, 4–5.

22. *Statement by the Chairman of the Peruvian Delegation*, 4.

23. "The actual results of the Session were summed up by the leader of the U.S. delegation as 'satisfactory having regard to the great potentiality which existed throughout for pressing embarrassing or impracticable resolutions'. This also sums up the UK delegation's view." Hugh Jones, summary note on "1st Session of the Economic Commission for Latin America," 1 July 1948, FO 371/69021A, PRO.

24. See *FRUS*, 1948, IX: 74.

25. Joseph L. Love, "Economic Ideas and Ideologies in Latin America since 1930," in Bethell, ed., *Cambridge History*, VI: 413.

26. The Mexican foreign minister's "reference to the desirability of the industrialization of the American Republics evoked very considerable applause. In the latter connection he said that it was vital for the Americas to do more than produce raw materials and live in a state of semi-colonialism." *FRUS*, 1945, IX: 123.

27. Magariños, *Diálogos con Raúl Prebisch*, 147.

28. Robert R. Kaufman, "How Societies Change Developmental Models or Keep Them: Reflections on the Latin American Experience in the 1930s and the Postwar World," in *Manufacturing Miracles: Paths of Industrialization in Latin America and East Asia*, ed. Gary Geretti and Donald L. Wyman (Princeton, N.J.: Princeton University Press, 1990), 110.

29. Love, "Economic Ideas and Ideologies in Latin America," in Bethell, ed., *Cambridge History*, VI: 396.

30. Gabriel Palma, "From an Export-Led to an Import-Substituting Economy: Chile 1914–39," in *Latin America in the 1930s: The Role of the Periphery in World Crisis*, ed. Rosemary Thorp (London: Macmillan, 1984), 50–80.

31. Victor Bulmer-Thomas, "The Latin American Economies, 1929–1939," in Bethell, ed., *Cambridge History,* VI: 75–80.

32. O. Rodrigez, *La Teoria del subdesarrollo de la Cepal,* Siglo XXI (Mexico: Fondo de Cultura Económica, 1980).

33. Edwin Williamson, *The Penguin History of Latin America* (London: Penguin Books, 1992), 315.

34. Bulmer-Thomas, "The Latin American Economies," in Bethell, ed., *Cambridge History,* VI: 83, 88, 90–92, 101–102.

35. For India, see, for example, Sir M. Visvesvaraya, *Planned Economy for India* (Bangalore: Bangalore Press, 1934), 220–222 and 256–257.

36. The Taylorist technocratic vision was, however, also an important influence on the Soviet planners themselves. See Charles S. Maier, "Between Taylorism and Technocracy: European Ideologies and the Vision of Industrial Productivity in the 1920s," *Journal of Contemporary History* 5 (1970): 27–61.

37. Barbara Weinstein, "The Industrialists, the State, and the Issues of Worker Training and Social Services in Brazil, 1930–50," *Hispanic American Historical Review* 70 (1990): 379–404.

38. P. T. Ellsworth, *Chile: An Economy in Transition* (New York: Macmillan, 1945), 131–133.

39. As Getúlio Vargas, the country's president, put it in 1939, he could not accept the idea of his country remaining a "semi-colonial" economy. Swift industrial expansion, he believed, was the means to overcome this. Stanley E. Hilton, "The Armed Forces and Industrialists in Modern Brazil: The Drive for Military Autonomy (1889–1954)," *Hispanic American Historical Review* 62, no. 4 (1982): 629–673; Love, "Economic Ideas and Ideologies in Latin America," in Bethell, ed., *Cambridge History,* VI: 401.

40. William S. Stokes, "Economic Anti-Americanism in Latin America," *Inter-American Economic Affairs* XI, no. 3 (Winter 1957): 3–22.

41. *FRUS,* 1945, IX: 97. The Chapultepec conference established the Inter-American Economic and Social Council (IA-ECOSOC).

42. Magariños, *Diálogos con Raúl Prebisch,* 147–150.

43. United Nations, *Economic Survey of Latin America 1948* (New York: UN DEA, 1949), 183–184.

44. Rosemary Thorp, "The Latin American Economies in the 1940s," in *Latin America in the 1940s: War and Postwar Transitions,* ed. David Rock (London: University of California Press, 1994), 53.

45. See M. Antonieta P. Leopoldi, "Industrial Associations and Politics in Contemporary Brazil: The Associations of Industrialists, Economic Policy-Making and the State with Special Reference to the Period 1930–61" (D.Phil. thesis, University of Oxford, 1984), 137–138; and E. V. K. Fitzgerald, "ECLA and the Formation of Latin American Economic Doctrine," in Rock, ed., *Latin America in the 1940s,* 93–94.

46. Leopoldi, "Industrial Associations and Politics in Contemporary Brazil," 138.

47. UN Sub-Commission on Economic Development, *Report to the Economic and Employment Commission on the Second Session of the Sub-Commission* (E/CN.1/61), 1 July 1948, 3.

48. In Chapter 5, note 81.

49. See FitzGerald, "ECLA and the Theory of Import Substituting Industrialization," 61–69, for his formal reconstruction of the logic of the 1959 article.

50. Williamson, *The Penguin History of Latin America,* 333–334.

51. Love, "Economic Ideas and Ideologies in Latin America," in Bethell, ed., *Cambridge History,* VI: 429–431.

52. Kathryn Sikkink, "The Influence of Raúl Prebisch on Economic Policy-Making in Argentina, 1950–1962," *American Research Review* 23 (1988): 91–114.

53. Love, "Economic Ideas and Ideologies in Latin America," in Bethell, ed., *Cambridge History,* VI: 401–402.

54. League of Nations, *Industrialization and Foreign Trade* (Geneva: League of Nations, 1945), 35–38.

55. See, for example, N. S. Buchanan, "Deliberate Industrialisation for Higher Incomes," *Economic Journal* 56 (1946): 533–553.

56. See, for example, United Nations, *Economic Survey of Asia and the Far East 1948* (New York: UN DEA, 1949), 94.

57. United Nations, *The Economic Development of Latin America and Its Principal Problems* (New York: UN DEA, 1950), 1–16; quotation is from page 16.

58. Magariños, *Diálogos con Raúl Prebisch,* 148.

59. Raúl Prebisch, "Five Stages in My Thinking on Development," in *Pioneers in Development,* ed. Gerald M. Meier and Dudley Seers (Oxford: Oxford University Press for the World Bank, 1984), 177.

60. David Pollock, Daniel Kerner, and Joseph L. Love, "Raúl Prebisch on ECLAC's Achievements and Deficiencies: An Unpublished Interview," *CEPAL Review* 75 (December 2001): 11.

61. Magariños, *Diálogos con Raúl Prebisch,* 131–133.

62. Pollock, Kerner, and Love, "Raúl Prebisch on ECLAC's Achievements and Deficiencies," 12.

63. See Bela Balassa, *The Process of Industrial Development and Alternative Development Strategies,* Essays in International Finance No. 141 (Princeton, N.J.: Princeton University, 1980), 7–13.

64. Furtado, *La fantaisie organisée,* 64–65, 57–58.

65. League of Nations, *Industrialization and Foreign Trade,* Series II. Economic and Financial 1945.II.A.10 (n.p.: League of Nations, 1945).

66. Ibid., 61–63.

67. United Nations, *Economic Survey of Latin America 1948* (New York: UN DEA, 1949), 51–54.

68. United Nations, *The Economic Development of Latin America and Its Principal Problems,* 5.

69. Ibid., 6.

70. Furtado, *La fantaisie organisée,* 87.

71. United Nations, *Economic Survey of Latin America 1949* (New York: DEA, 1951), 26–34, 9.

72. United Nations, *Economic Survey of Latin America 1949*, 18.

73. *Statement Made by Raúl Prebisch* (ECLA document E/CN.12.AC.8/1), 7 June 1950, 3–4.

74. See Furtado, *La fantaisie organisée*, 107.

75. *Statement Made by Raúl Prebisch*, 7–8; United Nations, *Economic Survey of Latin America 1949*, 85.

76. *Statement Made by Raúl Prebisch*, 8.

77. Furtado, *La fantaisie organisée*, 84.

78. *Statement by the Acting Representative of the United States, Christian M. Ravndal* (ECLA document E/CN.12/AC.8/1), 12 June 1950, 3.

79. Magariños, *Diálogos con Raúl Prebisch*, 142; Furtado, *La fantaisie organisée*, 123–128; David H. Pollock, "Raúl Prebisch versus the U.S. Government: Changing Perceptions over Time," *Canadian Journal of Development Studies* IX, no. 1 (1988): 121–129; David H. Pollock, "Some Changes in United States Attitudes towards CEPAL over the Past 30 Years," *CEPAL Review* 6 (1978): 57–80.

80. Foreign Office UN (Economic and Social) Dept. to UK Permanent Delegation to the UN, 25 July 1950, CO852/1278/5, PRO.

81. Magariños, *Diálogos con Raúl Prebisch*, 138–141; Furtado, *La fantaisie organisée*, 94; *Progress Report Made by the Executive Secretary to the Fourth Session* (EC/CN.12/220), 29 May 1951. See also Pollock, Kerner, and Love, "Raúl Prebisch on ECLAC's Achievements and Deficiencies," 13–14.

82. See Alfonso Santa Cruz to W. R. Malinowski, 28 August 1951, UN Archive, DAG-17, Box 32.

83. *FRUS*, 1951, II: 1074.

84. UNCTAD, *Raúl Prebisch: Thinker and Builder: Proceedings of the Tribute and Symposium Organized in Honour of Raúl Prebisch, Geneva, 2–3 July 1986* (New York: United Nations, 1989), 31.

85. Furtado, notably, felt that Prebisch's designation "peripheral" did not adequately describe the economy of his native Brazil. This, he felt, should properly be described as "colonial," which would allow the question to be reintroduced into its historical setting; he applied this analysis to the cyclical relationship between Brazil's textile industry and its primary-export sector. Furtado, *La fantaisie organisée*, 74–77.

86. Balassa, *The Process of Industrial Development*, 6–7.

87. Magariños, *Diálogos con Raúl Prebisch*, 149–150.

88. *Progress Report Made by the Executive Secretary to the Fourth Session* (EC/CN.12/220), 29 May 1951.

89. "Oral Statement by the Executive Secretary on 11 February 1952," in ECLA, *Fourth Annual Report to the Economic and Social Council for the Period 17 June 1951 to 14 February 1952* (E/CN.12/AC.16/15), 21 March 1952, 26.

90. Ibid.

91. Pollock, Kerner, and Love, "Raúl Prebisch on ECLAC's Achievements and Deficiencies," 14–15.

92. Prebisch to Roy Blough, 8 May 1953, UN Archive, RAG-2, Box 43/2.

93. "Statement by Dr. Raúl Prebisch to the Fifth Session," 10 April 1953, in ECLA, *Annual Report to the Economic and Social Council for the Period 15 February 1952 to 25 April 1953* (E/CN.12/324), 13 May 1953, 45.

94. Pollock, Kerner, and Love, "Raúl Prebisch on ECLAC's Achievements and Deficiencies," 15.

95. Furtado, *La fantaisie organisée*, 142–144.

96. *FRUS*, 1952–1954, IV: 306.

97. Furtado, *La fantaisie organisée*, 105.

98. "Statement made by Raúl Prebisch," 3.

99. United Nations, *Economic Survey of Latin America 1949*, 11.

100. Carolyn Craven, "A Transformation Problem: Monetarism to Structuralism in the Economic Commission for Latin America," *History of Political Economy* 26, no. 1 (1994): 1–19. We concur with much of Craven's argument, as expressed in this and in the following section.

101. United Nations, *Economic Survey of Latin America 1949*, 387.

102. United Nations, *Economic Survey of Latin America 1953* (UN: DEA, April 1954), 71.

103. United Nations, *Economic Survey of Latin America 1954* (UN: DEA, July 1954), 28–29.

104. United Nations, *Economic Survey of Latin America 1953*, 69.

105. United Nations, *Economic Survey of Latin America 1953*, 84.

106. Henri Aujac, "Inflation as the Consequence of the Behaviour of Social Groups: A Working Hypothesis," *International Economic Papers* 4, no. 1 (1954): 109–123.

107. Carolyn Craven does not speculate on the reasons for the sudden transformation of the previous monetarist approach to inflation, but one may ask whether it was linked to Prebisch's preoccupations with the Argentine economy in 1955 and the seizing of an opportunity by the younger generation of ECLA economists. "A Transformation Problem: Monetarism to Structuralism in the Economic Commission for Latin America," *History of Political Economy* 26, no. 1 (1996): 1–19.

108. Juan Noyola, "El Desarollo Economico y la Inflacion en Mejico y Otros Paises Latinamericanos," *Investigacion Economica* 16, no. 3 (1956): 604.

109. Osvaldo Sunkel, "La inflacion chilena: un enfoque heterodoxo," *El Trimestre Economico* 25, no. 4 (1958): 110.

110. It did so even in the *World Economic Survey*, the 1956 issue of which also had a structuralist view of inflation. *World Economic Survey 1956* (New York: UN Department of Economic and Social Affairs, 1957), 8.

111. Nicholas Kaldor, "Economic Problems of Chile," *El Trimestre Economico* (April–June 1959): 235 and 274–277.

112. Hollis Chenery, "Development Policies and Programmes," *Economic Bulletin for Latin America* 3, no. 1 (1958): 51–77.

113. Heinz W. Arndt, "The Origins of Structuralism," *World Development* 13, no. 2 (1985): 151–159. For the role of Kalecki in relation to structuralism, see also Éprime Eshag, *Fiscal and Monetary Policies and Problems in Developing Countries* (Cambridge: Cambridge University Press, 1983), 216–227.

114. J. Gabriel Palma and Mario Marcel, "Kaldor on the 'Discreet Charm' of the Chilean Bourgeoisie," *Cambridge Journal of Economics* 13, no. 1 (1989): 245–272.

115. *UNCTAD I,* II: 14.

116. Ibid., 14–15.

117. "Statement of Mr. R. Prebisch before Economic Commission for Africa Conference in Lagos," February 1967, UNCTAD Archive, Geneva.

118. See Ian Little, Tibor Scitovsky, and Maurice Scott, *Trade and Industry in Developing Countries* (Oxford: Oxford University Press for the OECD, 1970); and Bela Balassa, *The Structure of Protection in Developing Countries* (Baltimore: Johns Hopkins University Press, 1971).

119. Henry J. Bruton, "A Reconsideration of Import Substitution," *Journal of Economic Literature* XXXVI (June 1998): 917 and n. 33.

120. Prebisch to Joseph Grunwald, 28 September 1965, UNCTAD Archive.

121. *UNCTAD I,* II: 15.

122. UNCTAD, *Raúl Prebisch,* 50.

123. Simon G. Hanson, "Case Study in Futility: United Nations Economic Commission for Latin America," *Inter-American Economic Affairs* 2, no. 2 (Autumn 1948): 81–99.

124. Sikkink, "The Influence of Raúl Prebisch on Economic Policy-Making in Argentina, 1950–1962," *American Research Review* 23 (1988): 91–114.

125. Ibid.

126. "Statement of Mr. R. Prebisch before Economic Commission for Africa Conference in Lagos."

127. "First Draft of the Outline for the Economic Survey of Latin America, 1949," 22 August 1949, 3, UN Archive, DAG-17, Box 33. Internal evidence identifies Prebisch as the author.

128. Louis N. Swenson to Philippe de Seynes, 30 November 1955, UN Archive, RAG-2/43–44.

7. Competitive Coexistence and the Politics of Modernization

1. Louis Emmerij, Richard Jolly, and Thomas G. Weiss, *Ahead of the Curve? UN Ideas and Global Challenges* (Bloomington: Indiana University Press, 2001), 59, Table 2.1.

2. Alonzo L. Hamby, *Man of the People: A Life of Harry S. Truman* (Oxford: Oxford University Press, 1995), 509. Joseph D. Coppock, an official involved in the design of the Point 4 program, recalled: "Many of us saw that if the U.S. is going to provide aid, you only perpetuate a balance-of-payments deficit for other countries which the U.S. would be expected to fill. We would be the suckers. How were you going to get the adjustment process back to a more normal situation? What would be a sensible transition policy?" Technical assistance "was something you could do, and it was in keeping with the American missionary tradition." Joseph D. Coppock Oral History, 90, 97, Truman Library, Independence, Missouri.

3. Hamby, *Man of the People,* 510.

4. Coppock Oral History, 112–113.

5. The People's Republic of China, moving away from a dependent relationship with the USSR, used the Bandung conference to put itself at the head of the nonaligned nations, along with Yugoslavia and India.

6. Robert G. Wesson, "The United Nations in the World Outlook of the Soviet Union and of the United States," in *Soviet and American Policies in the United Nations: A Twenty-Five-Year Perspective*, ed. Alvin Z. Rubinstein and George Ginsburgs (New York: New York University Press, 1971), 11–13; Emmerij, Jolly, and Weiss, *Ahead of the Curve*, 43.

7. Roy Blough, "Economic Activities," *Annual Review of United Nations Affairs* (1953): 97.

8. Alvin Z. Rubinstein, *The Soviets in International Organizations: Changing Policy toward Developing Countries, 1953–1963* (Princeton, N.J.: Princeton University Press, 1964), 15, 17, 154–155, 171.

9. Ibid., 32–89. Quotations at 60, 51.

10. John Foster Dulles to C. D. Jackson, 24 August 1954, quoted in W. W. Rostow, *Eisenhower, Kennedy, and Foreign Aid* (Austin: University of Texas Press, 1985), 104.

11. "Then in the autumn of [1957], the Soviets, as a result of a much more purposeful use of a much less productive economy, surged ahead of us in space. The questioning and anxiety that followed the first Sputnik made me certain that I would be heard"; J. K. Galbraith, *The Affluent Society* (London: Pelican, 1962). Galbraith's thesis of private affluence coexisting with public squalor had a clear message for those concerned about U.S. national security; see 211, 282.

12. In response, U.S. support for the creation of the Inter-American Development Bank (IADB) was announced in July 1958.

13. Adlai Stevenson complained: "Congress generously supports our defense effort, but every year we have to fight the battle of trade and aid, as if the Russian economic offensive was something temporary and less dangerous or permanent than the military threat." Adlai E. Stevenson, *Friends and Enemies: What I Learned in Russia* (London: Rupert Hart-Davis, 1958), xvi.

14. The Kennedy-Cooper resolution was a bipartisan initiative in the U.S. Senate stating: "The Congress recognizes the importance of the economic development of the Republic of India to its people, to democratic values and institutions, and to peace and stability in the world. Consequently, it is the sense of the Congress that it is in the interest of the United States to join with other nations in providing support of the type, magnitude, and duration, adequate to assist India to complete successfully its current program of economic development." See Rostow, *Eisenhower, Kennedy, and Foreign Aid*, 4.

15. Christopher Matthews, *Kennedy and Nixon: The Rivalry That Shaped Postwar America* (New York: Simon & Schuster, 1996), 136.

16. Stephen G. Rabe, *The Most Dangerous Area in the World: John F. Kennedy Confronts Communist Revolution in Latin America* (Chapel Hill: University of North Carolina Press, 1999), 14–15, 196.

17. D. John Shaw, *The UN World Food Programme and the Development of Food Aid* (Basingstoke: Palgrave, 2001), 12–14.

18. See ibid., 6–9. McGovern's initiative did not quite equal Hernán Santa Cruz's act of audacity in proposing the establishment of ECLA. He did at least ensure that he had Kennedy's support for the World Food Programme, even though before leaving Washington he had not discussed with him any proposals at all.

19. For biographical detail on Rostow, see his obituary in *The Guardian,* 17 February 2003; and Kimber Charles Pearce, *Rostow, Kennedy, and the Rhetoric of Foreign Aid* (East Lansing: Michigan State University Press, 2001), 11–27. The term "enlightened anti-communism" refers to attempts to create conditions in which people do not choose to become communists.

20. Walt W. Rostow, *The Diffusion of Power: An Essay in Recent History* (New York: Macmillan, 1972), 11.

21. "[It] is true that, as Nicky is not trusted by [the British government], they do not have anybody of Rostow's type in on the policy-making of the Commission." Gunnar Myrdal to David Owen, 14 February 1948, David Owen Papers, Box 1, Columbia University Library, New York. Rostow later claimed that the UNECE helped Tito to secure access to Ruhr coal supplies in 1948, frustrating Stalin's attempts to gain an economic stranglehold over Yugoslavia. Rostow, *The Diffusion of Power,* 16.

22. Myrdal to Owen, 21 March 1948, David Owen Papers, Box 1.

23. See letters of Myrdal to Owen, 8, 12, and 15 October and 18 December 1949, David Owen Papers, Box 1. See also excerpt from a personal letter from W. W. Rostow to Myrdal, 9 November 1949, David Owen Papers, Box 4.

24. Pearce, *Rostow, Kennedy, and the Rhetoric of Foreign Aid,* 14.

25. Office memorandum from N. A. Pelcovits to Mr. Burgin, 20 December 1956, Office of Inter-American Regional Economic Affairs, RG 59, Box 8, NARA.

26. Rostow, *Diffusion of Power,* 88.

27. Nick Cullather, "Development? It's History," *Diplomatic History* 24, no. 4 (2000): 652.

28. Outlining the contents of a planned ECE report on development and trade, Rostow wrote: "I do not know what the data show concerning the relative price movements of agricultural and industrial products. If, in fact, the argument could be couched in the language of terms of trade, and the need to make them more favourable to industrialized areas, so much the better." Memorandum from Rostow to Hal B. Lary, 9 June 1948, David Owen Papers, Box 4.

29. "As an economic historian, Rostow shared with other modernization theorists a general style of theory building that can be characterized as deductivist and taxonomi-cal"; Pearce, *Rostow, Kennedy, and the Rhetoric of Foreign Aid,* 4.

30. Ibid., 12, quoting Lester Tanzer, ed., *The Kennedy Circle* (Washington, D.C.: Luce, 1961), 41.

31. Walt W. Rostow, *The Process of Economic Growth* (Oxford: Clarendon Press, 1953), v–viii and 9.

32. Walt W. Rostow, "The Take-Off into Self-sustained Growth," *Economic Journal* LXVI, no. 261 (March 1956): 48.

33. Ibid., 31, n. 1.

34. "Scholars such as Gabriel A. Almond, Lincoln Gordon, John J. Johnson, Seymour Martin Lipset, Max F. Millikan, Lucian Pye, Walt Rostow, and Kalman Silvert . . . posited a universal, quantitatively measurable movement of all societies from a 'traditional' situation toward a single ideal form or 'modern' organization"; Rabe, *The Most Dangerous Area,* 25. The term "modernization" had been used in the eighteenth century of buildings

and spelling, but by the twentieth century became used of institutions and industry "to indicate something unquestionably favourable or desirable." See Raymond Williams, *Keywords: A Vocabulary of Culture and Society* (London: Fontana Press, 1976), 208–209.

35. See, for example, Simon Kuznets, "Long Term Trends in Capital Formation Proportion," *Economic Development and Cultural Change* IX, no. 4, pt. II (July 1961): 3–56.

36. Simon Kuznets, "Notes on the Take-Off," in *The Economics of Take-off into Sustained Growth*, ed. W. W. Rostow (London: Macmillan, 1963), 27.

37. Kuznets, "Notes on the Take-Off," 43.

38. Albert Fishlow, "Empty Economic Stages?" *Economic Journal* LXXV, no. 297 (1965): 115.

39. Rostow was a leading member of the "Charles River School of action intellectuals," a designation of Arthur M. Schlesinger Jr. in *A Thousand Days: John F. Kennedy in the White House* (Boston: Houghton Mifflin, 1965), 588–589.

40. Rostow, *The Diffusion of Power*, xvii.

41. The characterization is that of David Halberstam, *The Brightest and the Best* (New York: Random House, 1972), 43.

42. Rabe, *The Most Dangerous Area*, 27, 128, 179.

43. Walt W. Rostow, *View from the Seventh Floor* (New York: Harper & Row, 1964), 22.

44. Cullather writes that "under the influence of Walt Whitman Rostow and Lucian Pye, developmentese became the Kennedy administration's court vernacular"; "Development? It's History," 641.

45. Rostow, *View from the Seventh Floor*, 13, 85, 123–124.

46. V. K. R. V. Rao, "Suggestions for the Creation of a New International Agency for Financing Basic Economic Development," in *Methods of Financing Economic Development in Under-Developed Countries* (New York: United Nations, 1949), Annex 1, 129–132.

47. See Chapter 4 of this volume for further discussion of this report.

48. H. W. Singer, "The Terms of Trade Controversy and the Evolution of Soft Financing: Early Years in the UN," in *Pioneers in Development*, ed. Gerald M. Meier and Dudley Seers (Oxford: Oxford University Press, 1984), 297–303. SUNFED's principal supporters were India (V. K. R. V. Rao), Chile (Hernán Santa Cruz), and Yugoslavia (Leo Mates and Janez Stanovnik).

49. A. Widener, "UN Economics," *U. S. A.: An American Bulletin of Fact and Opinion* III, no. 2 (27 July 1956). We are grateful to John Shaw for drawing our attention to this and the following reference.

50. Philippe de Seynes, "Economic Development Fund: UN Official Explains Origins and Aims of the Proposal" (New York) *Herald Tribune*, 1 August 1956.

51. Singer to Owen, 26 September 1956, David Owen Papers, Box 8.

52. Owen to C. V. Narasimhan, 19 February 1957, David Owen Papers, Box 8.

53. Rubinstein, *The Soviets in International Organizations*, 32, 92–102.

54. Mahdi Elmandjra, *The United Nations System: An Analysis* (London: Faber & Faber, 1973), 64–65.

55. John G. Hadwen and Johan Kaufman, *How United Nations Decisions Are Made* (New York: Oceana Publications, 1962), 111–112.

56. GA resolution 1240 (XIII), 14 October 1958, Article 1, quoted in Elmandjra, *The United Nations System,* 65.

57. Devesh Kapur, John P. Lewis, and Richard Webb, *The World Bank: Its First Half Century* (Washington, D.C.: Brookings Institution Press, 1997), 1: 155.

58. Ibid., 1121, n. 2.

59. H. W. Singer, "Significant Recent Trends in the Economic Work of the United Nations," *Annual Review of United Nations Affairs* (1960–1961): 69.

60. H. W. Singer, "Stages of Development and Pre-investment Activities," mimeo., n.d. but probably early 1961, David Owen Papers, Box 24.

61. H. W. Singer, "Significant Recent Trends in the Economic Work of the United Nations," 69.

62. Oral History Interview of Hans Singer, 20, 21, and 26 August 1997, 37, in the Oral History Collection of the United Nations Intellectual History Project, The Graduate Center, The City University of New York.

63. Singer, "The Terms of Trade Controversy and the Evolution of Soft Financing," 298–302.

64. The origin of the Alliance for Progress was a proposal by President Kubitschek of Brazil, in the wake of Nixon's disastrous tour of Latin America, for "Operation Pan-america," which was essentially a resurrection of the idea of a Marshall Plan for Latin America. See W. W. Rostow, *The Diffusion of Power,* 99. See also Edwin McCammon Martin, *Kennedy and Latin America* (Lanham, Md.: University Press of America, 1994), 9–16.

65. Rabe, *The Most Dangerous Area,* 10.

66. Martin, *Kennedy and Latin America,* 53. In this, Kennedy was following an Eisenhower precedent: the U.S. had joined an international coffee price-stabilization agreement in September 1958; see W. W. Rostow, *Eisenhower, Kennedy, and Foreign Aid* (Austin: University of Texas Press, 1985), 145.

67. Rostow, *View from the Seventh Floor,* 13.

68. Ibid., 161.

69. Beatrice Bishop Berle and Travis Beale Jacobs, eds., *Navigating the Rapids 1918–1971: From the Papers of Adolf A. Berle* (New York: Harcourt Brace Jovanovich, 1973), 721 (entry for 10 December 1960).

70. Pollock, Kerner, and Love, "Raúl Prebisch on ECLAC's Achievements and Deficiencies," 18.

71. He also told Berle that ECLA contemplated a closed common market for Latin America. Berle noted: "I asked whether the United States might come in on it—opening its own markets now to Latin American manufacture against their commitment to reduce their tariffs on our manufactured goods over a period of X years. This brought him up standing (he is alleged to be anti-American) and he thought it would be wonderful. He made the point that the United States must stop making out that its entire policy is to increase a field for investing its capital." In Berle and Jacobs, *Navigating the Rapids,* 721 (entry for 10 December 1960).

72. Love, "Economic Ideas and Ideologies in Latin America," in Bethell, *Cambridge History,* VI: 427. See also Raúl Prebisch, "Economic Aspects of the Alliance," in *The*

Alliance for Progress: Problems and Perspectives, ed. John C. Dreier (Baltimore: Johns Hopkins Press, 1962), 24–65.

73. "What is the negative part? That Richard Goodwin [assistant under secretary of state for inter-American affairs 1961–1962] without consulting us gave this document the name 'Alliance for Progress.'" See Pollock, Kerner, and Love, "Raúl Prebisch on ECLAC's Achievements and Deficiencies," 18.

74. Pearce, *Rostow, Kennedy, and the Rhetoric of Foreign Aid,* 27.

75. Pollock, Kerner, and Love, "Raúl Prebisch on ECLAC's Achievements and Deficiencies," 19.

76. Rostow, *The Diffusion of Power,* 216–217, 424–425.

77. I. J. M. Sutherland, minute, 21 January 1964, BT 241/1348, PRO; but see also Pollock, Kerner, and Love, "Raúl Prebisch on ECLAC's Achievements and Deficiencies," 18–19. President Johnson appointed Walt Rostow as the U.S. representative on this committee in 1964: see Pearce, *Rostow, Kennedy, and the Rhetoric of Foreign Aid,* 27.

78. Rosemary Thorp, *Progress, Poverty and Exclusion: An Economic History of Latin America in the 20th Century* (Washington, D.C.: Johns Hopkins University Press for the Inter-American Development Bank, 1998), 145–149.

79. Memorandum from Rostow to Kennedy, 2 March 1961, reprinted in Rostow, *The Diffusion of Power,* 647, n. 3. See also Rabe, *The Most Dangerous Area,* 27.

80. *Public Papers of the Presidents of the United States: John F. Kennedy, Containing the Public Messages, Speeches and Statements of the President, January 20 to December 31, 1961* (Washington, D.C.: U.S. Government Printing Office, 1962), 205.

81. *FRUS,* 1961–1963, IX: 406–408.

82. Ibid., 413–414.

83. Ibid., 415.

84. *General Assembly minutes,* 16th Session, Second Committee, 718th Meeting, 6 October 1961, 12.

85. Klutznick's statement is reproduced in the Department of State *Bulletin* (4 December 1961): 939–947.

86. *FRUS,* 1961–1963, IX: 423–424.

87. Oral History Interview of Hans Singer, 20, 21, and 26 August 1997, 13.

88. Ibid., 14–15.

89. Ibid., 13.

90. Branislav Gosovic, *UNCTAD: Conflict and Compromise: The Third World's Quest for an Equitable World Economic Order through the United Nations* (Leiden: A. W. Sijthoff, 1972), 24 and n. 67. See also Oral History Interview of Hans Singer, 20, 21, and 26 August 1997.

91. David Owen, "A Decade for Development," *Annual Review of United Nations Affairs* (1961–1962): 101.

92. H. W. Singer, "Significant Recent Trends in the Economic Work of the United Nations," *Annual Review of United Nations Affairs* (1960–1961): 73.

93. Eisenhower was quite clear about preferring more foreign aid to more defense spending to keep India out of the Soviet orbit. See his robust exposition of this point to Senator Styles Bridges, quoted in Rostow, *Eisenhower, Kennedy, and Foreign Aid,* 321–323.

94. See Anna Bezanson, "Early Use of the Term Industrial Revolution," *Quarterly Journal of Economics* 36 (February 1922): 343–349.

95. Kuznets, "Notes on the Take-Off," 28.

96. The term "pragmatic illusions" is borrowed from Bruce Miroff, *Pragmatic Illusions: The Presidential Politics of John F. Kennedy* (New York: McKay, 1976).

97. Singer, "The Terms of Trade Controversy and the Evolution of Soft Financing," 299.

98. "Walt viewed our Vietnam involvement, the conduct of our operations, and the prospects for achieving our political and military objectives very optimistically. Optimistic by nature, he tended to be skeptical of any report that failed to indicate we were making progress. Years later [March 1991] he continued to assert that America's decision to intervene in Vietnam, and the way we prosecuted the war, had proved beneficial to our nation and the region." Robert S. McNamara with Brian Van De Mark, *In Retrospect: The Tragedy and Lessons of Vietnam* (New York: Times Books, 1995), 235–236.

99. W. W. Rostow, *Theories of Economic Growth from David Hume to the Present* (New York: Oxford University Press, 1990), 413–414.

100. Kapur, Lewis, and Webb, *The World Bank*, I: 1126.

101. Rostow, *Theories of Economic Growth from David Hume to the Present*, 413–414.

102. At the time of writing, the U.S. is prosecuting a "war on terrorism," the conduct of which is governed by the principle, articulated by Donald Rumsfeld, President George W. Bush's secretary of defense, in the autumn of 2001, that "the mission determines the coalition: the coalition does not determine the mission." If one disregards its takeoff into self-sustaining rhetoric, much the same could be said of the foreign policy of John F. Kennedy.

8. The Birth of UNCTAD

1. *UNCTAD I*, I: 66–68.

2. *Statement delivered by the Secretary-General of the United Nations Conference on Trade and Development at the One Thousand Three Hundred and Twentieth Plenary Meeting of the Economic and Social Council on 16 July 1964*, ECOSOC minutes, 16 July 1966, 35–36.

3. Diego Cordovez, "The Making of UNCTAD: Institutional Background and Legislative History," *Journal of World Trade Law* I (1967): 243–244.

4. Charles L. Robertson, "The Creation of UNCTAD," in *International Organisations: World Politics*, ed. Robert W. Cox. Studies in Economic and Social Agencies (London: Macmillan, 1969), 263.

5. *GAOR*, 16th Session, 720th Meeting, Meeting of the Second Committee, Speech of M. Lavrichenko, 11 October 1961, 26.

6. Alvin Z. Rubinstein, *The Soviets in International Organizations: Changing Policy toward Developing Countries, 1953–1963* (Princeton, N.J.: Princeton University Press, 1964), 170–171.

7. For an account of how Commonwealth preferences survived, despite the extreme hostility of the U.S. at the time of the negotiation of GATT, see Richard Toye, "The Attlee Government, the Imperial Preference System and the Creation of the GATT," *English Historical Review* 118 (September 2003): 912–939.

8. George W. Ball, Memorandum to the President, 23 October 1961, Records of Under-Secretary George Ball 1961–66, RG 59, Lot 74D272, Box 20, NARA.

9. Robertson, "The Creation of UNCTAD," 263.

10. Ibid., 266.

11. Branislav Gosovic, *UNCTAD: Conflict and Compromise: The Third World's Quest for an Equitable World Economic Order through the United Nations* (Leiden: A. W. Sijthoff, 1972), 17, n. 44.

12. United Nations, *The History of UNCTAD 1964–1984* (New York: United Nations, 1985), 10.

13. *FRUS*, 1961–1963, IX: 445–447.

14. United Nations, *The History of UNCTAD*, 10.

15. *FRUS*, 1961–1963, IX: 445–447.

16. Robertson, "The Creation of UNCTAD," 268.

17. Dell to Kaldor, 24 October 1962, Kaldor Papers, NK/3/30/64/66, King's College, Cambridge.

18. United Nations, *The History of UNCTAD*, 10.

19. Mateo Magariños, *Diálogos con Raúl Prebisch* (Mexico: Banco Nacional De Comercio Exterior/Fondo de Cultura Económica, 1991), 153–155; Edgar J. Dosman and David H. Pollock, "Hasta la UNCTAD y de regreso: divulgando el evangelio, 1964–1968," in *Prebisch y Furtado: El estructuralismo latinoamericano,* ed. Jorge Lora and Carlos Mallorquin (Mexico: Benemérita Universidad Autónoma de Puebla, Instituto de Ciencias Sociales y Humanidades, 1999), 202–203.

20. On de Seynes's aspirations for DESA and their frustration by the appointment of Prebisch, see Robertson, "The Creation of UNCTAD," 265, 267, and 270.

21. Magariños, *Diálogos con Raúl Prebisch*, 153–156.

22. Dell to Lawrence S. Finkelstein, 9 November 1962, Sidney Dell Papers, MSS Eng c.5860, ff. 480–484, Bodleian Library, Oxford.

23. Finkelstein to Dell, 13 November 1962, Sidney Dell Papers, MSS Eng c.5860, ff. 486.

24. Dell to Richard Kahn, 23 November 1962, Sidney Dell Papers, MSS Eng c.5860, ff. 487–488.

25. Dell to Kahn, 23 November 1962 and 3 December 1962, Sidney Dell Papers, MSS Eng c.5860, ff. 488 and 491.

26. Dell to Richard Ruggles, 18 January 1963, Sidney Dell Papers, MSS Eng c.5860, ff. 492.

27. Dell to Andrew Shonfield, 8 March 1963, Sidney Dell Papers, MSS Eng c.5861, ff. 52–54.

28. Dell suggested a list of possible members of the informal group. They were R. Campos (Brazil); J. Ahumada (Chile); V. Urquidi (Mexico); I. G. Patel (India); S. Lombardini (Italy); R. Frisch (Norway); M. Kalecki (Poland); R. Kahn, R. Harrod, N. Kaldor, or J. Meade (UK); and R. Ruggles, R. Triffin, or R. Vernon (U.S.). Dell to Andrew Shonfield, 8 March 1963.

29. The economic experts were Josef Bognar (Hungary), Albert G. Hart (U.S.), Nicholas Kaldor (UK), Charles P. Kindleberger (U.S.), Irving B. Kravis (U.S.), Alexander Lamfalussy (Belgium), Alfred Maizels (UK), H. M. A. Onitiri (Nigeria), I. G. Patel and

K. N. Raj (India), V. S. Safronchuk (USSR), Osvaldo Sunkel (Chile), Shigeto Tsuru (Japan), Pierre Uri (France), and Victor Urquidi (Mexico).

30. Royal Institute of International Affairs, *New Directions for World Trade: Proceedings of a Chatham House Conference, Bellagio, 16–24 September 1963* (London: The Institute, 1963), 7–22.

31. Ibid., 3, 11.

32. Dell to Ruggles, 18 October 1963, Sidney Dell Papers, MSS Eng c. 5860, ff. 502.

33. Dell to Prebisch, 22 March 1963, Sidney Dell Papers, MSS Eng c.5860, ff. 312.

34. Dell to Shonfield, 14 June 1963, Sidney Dell Papers, MSS Eng c.5861, ff. 91.

35. Nicholas Kaldor, "Introduction," in *Essays on Economic Policy II,* ed. Nicholas Kaldor (London: Duckworth, 1980), xvii, n. 1.

36. Unwin to F. C. Mason, 22 October 1963, BT 241/1348, PRO.

37. Oral History Interview of Gamani Corea, 1 February 2000, 16–17, in the Oral History Collection of the United Nations Intellectual History Project, The Graduate Center, The City University of New York.

38. "Statement by Dr Raúl Prebisch, Secretary-General of the United Nations Conference on Trade and Development, at an Informal Meeting of Members of the Second Committee," n.d. but probably late 1963, Sidney Dell Papers, MSS Eng c.5860, ff. 408–419.

39. In the debate on the timing of the conference, "the U.S. delegate said that no-one in Washington would lose an hour's sleep if the Conference never took place at all." See Sidney Dell to Kahn, 3 December 1962, Sidney Dell Papers, MSS Eng c.5860, ff. 491.

40. Robertson, "The Creation of UNCTAD," 269.

41. "Statement by Dr Raúl Prebisch," ff. 410.

42. "There is no prospect of a violent irruption of manufactured goods from the developing countries into the developed countries." Ibid., ff. 413.

43. Ibid., 414–415.

44. Oral History Interview of Janez Stanovnik, 7–8 January 2001, 54, in the Oral History Collection of the United Nations Intellectual History Project, The Graduate Center, The City University of New York.

45. See Raúl Prebisch, "Two Decades After," in *UNCTAD and the North-South Dialogue: The First Twenty Years—Essays in Memory of W. R. Malinowski,* ed. Michael Zammit Cutajar (Oxford: Pergamon, 1985), 3.

46. See Sidney Dell, "The Origins of UNCTAD," in ibid., 26–28. We are grateful to Mr. R. Krishnamurti, who was executive assistant to the UNCTAD I Committee on Institutional Questions, for pointing out to us this and the previous reference.

47. Oral History Interview of Janez Stanovnik, 7–8 January 2001, 55.

48. Edgar J. Dosman and David H. Pollock, "Hasta la UNCTAD y de regreso: divulgando el evangelio, 1964–1968," in *Prebisch y Furtado: El estructuralismo latino-americano,* ed. Jorge Lora and Carlos Mallorquin (Mexico: Benemérita Universidad Autónoma de Puebla, Instituto de Ciencias Sociales y Humanidades, 1999), 206.

49. Robertson, "The Creation of UNCTAD," 268–269.

50. George W. Ball, Memorandum to the President, 29 October 1963, Records of Under-Secretary George Ball 1961–66, RG 59, Lot 74D272, Box 32, NARA. Although this memorandum is marked "not sent," it gives an insight into Ball's concerns about the conference.

51. "Memorandum of Conversation: UN Conference on Trade and Development," November 1963, The Secretary's and the Undersecretary's Memoranda of Conversations, 1953–64, RG 59, Lot 65D330, Box 28, NARA.

52. Reproduced in *FRUS, 1961–1963,* IX: 622–627. All quotations in this section, unless otherwise identified, are from this document.

53. Gregory A. Fossedal, *Our Finest Hour: Will Clayton, the Marshall Plan and the Triumph of Democracy* (Stanford, Calif.: Hoover Institution Press, 1993), 272–279.

54. Rubinstein, *Soviets in International Organizations,* 170.

55. I. J. M. Sutherland, minute, 21 January 1964, BT 241/1348, PRO.

56. R. M. Allott, "Dr. Prebisch," 21 January 1964, BT 241/1348, PRO.

57. *UNCTAD I,* II: 4.

58. New York (UK Mission to UN) to Foreign Office, 29 January 1964, BT 241/1348, PRO.

59. Ball stated: "If . . . the EEC extended preferential arrangements to additional African countries, then perhaps the U.S. should consider acting similarly towards Latin America." See memorandum of conversation between George Ball, Robert Roosa, Walter Heller, Christian Herter, and EEC Delegation on 5 March 1964, Records of Under-Secretary George Ball 1961–66, RG 59, Lot 65 D330, Box 28, NARA.

60. Minute by J. R. S. Guinness, 14 February 1964, BT 241/1348, PRO.

61. Magariños, *Diálogos con Raúl Prebisch,* 156.

62. Oral History Interview of Janez Stanovnik, 7–8 January 2001, 55–56.

63. "North v. South and East v. West," *Financial Times,* 17 February 1964.

64. "Politique commerciale et Développement de 'tiers monde,'" *Le Monde,* 23 March 1964, 1.

65. According to George Ball, France had "given the appearance of sympathy to Dr. Prebisch's ideas—although with no intention of adopting them." Memorandum to the President, 30 March 1964, Records of Under-Secretary George Ball 1961–66, RG 59, Lot 74 D272, Box 31, NARA.

66. Magariños, *Diálogos con Raúl Prebisch,* 156.

67. All quotations in this and the previous paragraph are from "Interdepartmental Group on the United Nations Conference on Trade and Development: The Prebisch Report (Note by the Board of Trade)," UNC(64)34 Revise, 20 March 1964, BT 241/1348, PRO.

68. Memorandum from George Ball to McGeorge Bundy, 3 March 1964, Records of Under-Secretary George Ball 1961–66, RG 59, Lot 74 D272, Box 31, NARA.

69. For the record, the original 121 decreased to 120 when two countries merged in the course of the conference.

70. "In Geneva: Global Collective Bargaining," *Newsweek,* 6 April 1964, 25.

71. Harry G. Johnson, *Economic Policies towards Less Developed Countries* (London: George Allen and Unwin, 1967), 34.

72. Robertson, "The Creation of UNCTAD," 272.

73. Minute by J. R. S. Guinness, 1 April 1964, BT 241/1348, PRO.

74. "In Geneva: Global Collective Bargaining," 28.

75. Memorandum for the President from George W. Ball, 30 March 1964, Records of Under-Secretary George Ball 1961–66, RG 59, Lot 74 D272, Box 31, NARA.

76. Speech of 6 April 1964, quoted in Edward Heath, *The Course of My Life: My Autobiography* (London: Hodder and Stoughton, 1998), 602.

77. Minute by J. R. S. Guinness, 28 April 1964, BT 241/1348, PRO.

78. Robertson, "The Creation of UNCTAD," 273.

79. For a more detailed account, see Kamal M. Hagras, *United Nations Conference on Trade and Development: A Case Study in U. N. Diplomacy* (New York: Frederick A. Praeger, 1965).

80. J. R. S. Guinness, minute distributed to UK delegation, 7 May 1964, BT 241/1348, PRO.

81. Heath, *The Course of My Life,* 602–603.

82. *UNCTAD I,* I: 3–16.

83. "Interview," *The Banker* 117, no. 499 (September 1967): 748–754.

84. Dag—1/5.2.17/3, Office of the Secretary-General, Records of U Thant—1961–1971, UN Commission, Committees and Conferences: UNCTAD, 1. We are indebted to Professor J. Love for sending us a copy of this document from the UN Archive in New York.

85. Robertson, "The Creation of UNCTAD," 270–271.

86. L. E. Chasanovitch, "Dr Raul Prebisch," 25 June 1964, BT 241/1348, PRO.

87. United Nations, *Raúl Prebisch: Thinker and Builder* (New York: United Nations, 1989), 34–35.

88. Dell to Kaldor, 11 July 1964, Kaldor Papers, NK/3/30/64/35–39.

89. Kaldor to Dell, 17 July 1964, Kaldor Papers, NK/3/30/64/33.

90. Dell to Kaldor, 27 July 1964, Kaldor Papers, NK/3/30/64/33.

91. United Nations, *Raúl Prebisch,* 34–35.

9. UNCTAD under Raúl Prebisch

1. Philippe de Seynes, "Developing New Attitudes in International Economic Relations," in *The Quest for Peace: The Dag Hammarskjöld Memorial Lectures,* ed. Andrew W. Cordier and Wilder Foote (New York: Columbia University Press, 1965), 187–189.

2. Edgar J. Dosman and David H. Pollock, "Hasta la UNCTAD y de regreso: divulgando el evangelio, 1964–1968," in *Prebisch y Furtado: El estructuralismo latino-americano,* ed. Jorge Lora and Carlos Mallorquin (Mexico: Benemérita Universidad Autónoma de Puebla, Instituto de Ciencias Sociales y Humanidades, 1999), 225.

3. Oral History Interview of Paul Berthoud, 9–10 January 2001, 19, in the Oral History Collection of the United Nations Intellectual History Project, The Graduate Center, The City University of New York.

4. Personal communication from David H. Pollock to John Toye, 26 October 2000.

5. UN, *Proceedings of the United Nations Conference on Trade and Development.*

Second Session, New Delhi, 1 February–29 March 1968 (New York: United Nations, 1968) (henceforward *UNCTAD II*), I: 416.

6. For treatment of these issues, see UNCTAD, *The History of UNCTAD, 1964–1984* (New York: United Nations, 1985).

7. "Statement by Raúl Prebisch at the 60th Plenary Meeting of the Trade and Development Board," 26 January 1966, Speeches and Statements by Raúl Prebisch, TD/B/54, UNCTAD Archive, Geneva.

8. The Harbeler report is *Trends in International Trade* (Geneva: GATT, 1958).

9. Bhagirath Lal Das, *The World Trade Organisation: A Guide to the Framework of International Trade* (London: Zed Books, 1999), 24.

10. Branislav Gosovic, *UNCTAD: Conflict and Compromise: The Third World's Quest for an Equitable World Order through the United Nations* (Leiden: A. W. Sijthoff, 1972), 43–44.

11. *UNCTAD II*, I: 4.

12. J. A. C. Gutteridge, *The United Nations in a Changing World* (Manchester: Manchester University Press, 1969), 76.

13. Dell to Prebisch, "Suggestions for the Organization of the Work of the Trade and Development Board," 8 December 1965, Office of the Secretary-General of UNCTAD: Interoffice Memoranda 1965, UNCTAD Archive.

14. "Statement by Raúl Prebisch at the 60th Plenary Meeting of the Trade and Development Board."

15. "Statement by Prebisch at the 1078th meeting of the Second Committee," 28 November 1966, A/C.2/L.908, UNCTAD Archive.

16. As recommended in Interoffice Memorandum, C. Eckenstein to Dr. R. Prebisch, 16 August 1965, UNCTAD Archive.

17. Oral History Interview of Paul Berthoud, 9–10 January 2001, 34.

18. In the 1970s, China joined the organization but never joined any group. State trading refers to a situation when a government undertakes all, or at least a substantial part of, its foreign trade instead of leaving it to private enterprise. Group C had only one member after China was admitted to the United Nations in 1974—China (who voted with Group A at the time).

19. For Group D countries, the platform formation exercise ceased in the early 1990s.

20. Quoted in the Oral History Interview of Paul Berthoud, 9–10 January 2001, 70.

21. Charles A. Jones, *The North-South Dialogue: A Short History* (London: Frances Pinter, 1983), 29.

22. Gosovic, *UNCTAD: Conflict and Compromise*, 304–309. For a brief character sketch of Malinowski, see Antony Gilpin, unpublished memoirs, "Chapter 15: New York," UN Career Records Project Papers, MSS. Eng 4675, f. 323, Bodleian Library, Oxford.

23. S. Golt (Board of Trade) to R. W. Jackling (Foreign Office), 4 May 1967, BT 241/1350, PRO.

24. Dell to Kaldor, 16 March 1963, Kaldor Papers, NK/3/30/64/48, King's College, Cambridge.

25. Oral History Interview of Paul Berthoud, 9–10 January 2001, 92.

26. Ibid., 56–57.

27. Richard N. Gardner, "The United Nations Conference on Trade and Development," in *The Global Partnership: International Agencies and Economic Development,* ed. Richard N. Gardner and Max F. Millikan (New York: F. A. Praeger, 1968), 106.

28. Gosovic, *UNCTAD Conflict and Compromise,* 310.

29. UN, *Raúl Prebisch: Thinker and Builder* (New York: UN, 1989), 34–35.

30. Gosovic, *UNCTAD: Conflict and Compromise,* 310.

31. Oral History Interview of Paul Berthoud, 9–10 January 2001, 68.

32. Dell to Prebisch, "Board and Committee Procedures," 16 December 1965, Office of the Secretary-General of UNCTAD: Interoffice Memoranda 1965, UNCTAD Archive.

33. Oral History Interview of Paul Berthoud, 9–10 January 2001, 76.

34. Sidney Dell, "The Origins of UNCTAD," in *UNCTAD and the North-South Dialogue: The First Twenty Years—Essays in Memory of W. R. Malinowski,* ed. Michael Zammit Cutajar (Oxford: Pergamon, 1985), 28–30.

35. L. N. Rangarajan, *Commodity Conflict: The Political Economy of International Commodity Negotiations* (London: Croom Helm, 1978), 35–37.

36. John Odell and Barry Eichengreen, "The United States, the ITO and the WTO: Exit Options, Agent Slack, and Presidential Leadership," in *The WTO as an International Organization,* ed. Anne O. Krueger (Chicago: University of Chicago Press, 1998), 181–209.

37. UN, *Instability of Export Markets of Under-Developed Countries* (New York: United Nations, 1952); *Relative Prices of Exports and Imports of Under-Developed Countries* (Lake Success, N.Y.: UN DEA, 1949).

38. UN, *Everyman's United Nations: A Basic History of the Organization 1945 to 1963* (New York: United Nations, 1964), 184–189.

39. P. H. Ady, "The Terms of Trade," in *The British Economy in the Nineteen-Fifties,* ed. G. D. N. Worswick and P. H. Ady (Oxford: Clarendon Press, 1962), 160–161.

40. GATT, *Trends in International Trade: A Report by a Panel of Experts* (Geneva: GATT, 1958).

41. Edwin L. Dale Jr., "Wide Trade Shift Proposed in West," *New York Times,* 3 October 1958.

42. Oral History Interview of Paul Berthoud, 9–10 January 2001, 41.

43. Harold M. Randall (U.S. representative on IA-ECOSOC) to Don Armado C. Amador (Chairman, IA-ECOSOC), 27 April 1956, Declassified Documents Reference System (DDRS), Farmington Hills, Michigan, Gale Group, 2004.

44. *Extract from the Minutes of the Council on Foreign Economic Policy Meeting,* 20 May 1958, DDRS.

45. "The Third International Coffee Agreement: an Analysis," no date but probably December 1975, 1; DDRS.

46. Rangarajan, *Commodity Conflict,* 107–108.

47. "Summary of Discussion," in *New Directions in World Trade: Proceedings of a Chatham House Conference, Bellagio, 16–24 September 1963* (London: Oxford University Press, 1964), 216–219.

48. For a fuller discussion, see Nicholas Kaldor, "A Reconsideration of the Economics of the International Wheat Agreement," in *Essays in Economic Policy,* ed. Nicholas Kaldor (London: Duckworth, 1980), 2: 61–111.

49. James Meade, "International Commodity Agreements" in *The Collected Papers of James Meade,* ed. Susan Howson (London: Unwin Hyman, 1988), 3: 285–296.

50. Nicholas Kaldor, "Introduction," in Kaldor, ed., *Essays on Economic Policy,* 2: xvi, n. 1.

51. Sidney Dell to Edmund Dell, 11 March 1965, Sidney Dell Papers, MSS Eng c.5857, ff. 61–64, Bodleian Library, Oxford.

52. J. Stavnovik to Prebisch, "A Note on the Secretariat's Policy with Respect to Implementation of UNCTAD's Recommendations," 31 August 1965, Office of the Secretary-General of UNCTAD: Interoffice Memoranda 1965, UNCTAD Archive.

53. Oral History Interview of Paul Berthoud, 9–10 January 2001, 56–57.

54. A. Maizels to R. Prebisch, P. R. Judd, D. H. Pollock, and D. E. Feldman, "Problems of Commodity Policy," 15 September 1965, Office of the Secretary-General of UNCTAD: Interoffice Memoranda 1965, UNCTAD Archive.

55. Dell to Prebisch, "General Agreement on Commodity Trade," 14 October 1965, Office of the Secretary-General of UNCTAD: Interoffice Memoranda 1965, UNCTAD Archive.

56. D. H. Pollock to Prebisch, "Permanent Sub-Committee on Commodities (First Session)," 21 July 1966, UNCTAD Archive.

57. Prebisch to U Thant, "Recent Developments in UNCTAD," 14 June 1966, UNCTAD Archive.

58. Raúl Prebisch, unpublished talk to the World Council of Churches, July 1966, 7, UNCTAD Archive.

59. "Directors Meeting—28 June 1966," UNCTAD Archive; Prebisch to U Thant, "Recent Developments in UNCTAD," 12 August 1966, UNCTAD Archive.

60. Pollock to Prebisch and P. R. Judd, "Meetings at La Pelouse," 2 November 1966, Interoffice Memoranda Sept. 1966, UNCTAD Archive. (This November 1966 document is misfiled in the September 1966 box in the archive.)

61. UN, *Commodity Trade and Economic Development* (New York: United Nations, 1953), 82.

62. Kaldor to Dell, 23 March 1963 and Dell to Kaldor, 28 March 1963, Kaldor Papers, NK/3/30/64/52–53 and NK/3/30/64/45.

63. Tinbergen later engaged in another highly ambitious project: the attempt to launch a worldwide system of indicative economic planning through the UN Committee on Development Planning in New York. Dell to Prebisch, "First Session of the Committee for Development Planning," 26 May 1966, Office of the Secretary-General of UNCTAD: Interoffice Memoranda 1966, UNCTAD Archive.

64. F. A. Hayek, "A Commodity Reserve Currency," *Economic Journal* LIII (June–September 1943): 176–184.

65. Nicholas Kaldor, "Introduction" and "The Case for an International Commodity Reserve Currency," in Kaldor, ed., *Essays on Economic Policy,* 2: xvii–xviii, 131–177.

66. "The great virtue of the [commodity-reserve currency] scheme—automaticity—seems also to be its great defect; it may prove impossible to remedy its defect without losing its virtue"; "Note by F. G. Olano," in UN, *Commodity Trade and Economic Development,* 66. Olano amplifies his view in Appendix D, 97–102.

67. J. Keith Horsefield, *The International Monetary Fund, 1945–1965: Twenty Years of International Monetary Cooperation* (Washington, D.C.: International Monetary Fund, 1969), I: 531–536.

68. UNCTAD, *The History of UNCTAD, 1964–1984* (New York: United Nations, 1985), 78.

69. John Toye, "Supranational Compensation Schemes for Temporary Export Losses: A Critique," in *Development Economics and Policy,* ed. David Sapsford and John-Ren Chen (Basingstoke: Macmillan, 1998), 349–373.

70. Dosman and Pollock, "Hasta la UNCTAD y de regreso," 210.

71. Prebisch, speech at International Chamber of Commerce, London, October 1965, Speeches and Statements by Raúl Prebisch, UNCTAD Archive.

72. "Supplementary Financial Measures—A Study Requested by the United Nations Conference on Trade and Development," Washington, D.C., IBRD, December 1965.

73. Ibid., 4.

74. *Statement by the Secretary-General of UNCTAD at the 1434th Meeting of ECOSOC, ECOSOC minutes,* 16 July 1966, 109–110.

75. For the subsequent phases of the waning of the supplementary finance scheme, see UNCTAD, *The History of UNCTAD,* 80.

76. Dosman and Pollock, "Hasta la UNCTAD y de regreso," 213–214.

77. Oral History Interview of Gamani Corea, 1 February 2000, 26, in the Oral History Collection of the United Nations Intellectual History Project, The Graduate Center, The City University of New York.

78. See *UNCTAD I,* Annex A. IV.19.

79. Dell to Kaldor, 11 July 1965, Kaldor Papers, NK/3/30/64/24–26. See also Oral History Interview of Gamani Corea, 1 February 2000, 26.

80. Kaldor to Dell, 19 July 1965, Kaldor Papers, NK/3/30/64/23.

81. Prebisch to Kaldor, 24 June 1965, Kaldor Papers, NK/3/112/298–299.

82. Margaret Garritsen de Vries, *The International Monetary Fund, 1966–1971: The System under Stress* (Washington, D.C.: IMF, 1976), 1: 95–99, 104, 159.

83. Edwin L. Dale Jr., "Wide Trade Shift Proposed in West," *New York Times,* 3 October 1958.

84. That is, off Western aid programs. Coppock used these words in relation to the Point 4 program. Coppock Oral History, 29 July 1974, 90, Harry S. Truman Library, Independence, Missouri.

85. UNCTAD, *The History of UNCTAD*, 107–108.

86. "Statement by Prebisch to the U.S. Council of the International Chamber of Commerce (ICC)," n.d., 1965, Speeches and Statements by Raúl Prebisch, UNCTAD Archive.

87. Prebisch, speech at ICC, London, October 1965, Speeches and Statements by Raúl Prebisch, UNCTAD Archive.

88. "Statement by Prebisch to the U.S. Council of the ICC," n.d. [1965–1966], UNCTAD Archive.

89. Prebisch to A. M. El-Banna, 9 November 1966, Correspondence November and December 1966, UNCTAD Archive.

90. *Speech by Prebisch to the ICC*, London, October 1965, UNCTAD Archive. Hans Singer, as usual, pushed for something more radical, going beyond tariff preferences to the idea of negative tariffs, on the analogy of negative income tax.

91. UN document TD/B/9, cited in Sidney Dell, "UNCTAD: Retrospect and Prospect," *Annual Review of United Nations Affairs* (1964–1965): 66.

92. "Statement by Prebisch to Thomas Hamilton of the *New York Times*," 16 May 1967, UNCTAD Archive.

93. *Statement made by Prebisch at 1489th Meeting of ECOSOC, ECOSOC minutes*, 18 July 1967, 81–82.

94. See *UNCTAD II*, I: 414.

95. "Statement by Prebisch to the U.S. Council of the ICC."

96. Memorandum by Pollock, 23 September 1966, attached to Pollock to Prebisch, 26 September 1966, Interoffice Memoranda September 1966, UNCTAD Archive.

97. R. W. Jackling, "UNCTAD" (note of a discussion with Prebisch and Berthoud after dinner on 18 April 1967), 24 April 1967, BT 241/1350, PRO.

98. Gilbert Rist, *The History of Development from Western Origins to Global Faith* (London: Zed Books, 1997), 143.

99. Gosovic, *UNCTAD Conflict and Compromise*, 309, n. 12.

100. [Raúl Prebisch], "Towards a Global Strategy of Development," submitted by the Secretary-General of UNCTAD to the Conference, UNCTAD document TD/3/Rev. 1, January 1968.

101. *UNCTAD II*, I: 420–423.

102. Sidney Dell to Edmund Dell, 7 May 1968, Sidney Dell Papers, MSS Eng c. 5857, ff. 78–81.

103. Beatrice Bishop Berle and Travis Beale Jacobs, eds., *Navigating the Rapids 1918–1971: From the Papers of Adolf A. Berle* (New York: Harcourt Brace Jovanovich, 1973), 721 (entry for 10 December 1960).

104. It was a triumph because any international commodity agreement was a triumph, although this one was in fact "full of holes"; Rangarajan, *Commodity Conflict*, 216.

105. Dell to Kaldor, 23 November 1968, Kaldor Papers, NK/3/30/64/21. See also Dosman and Pollock, "Hasta la UNCTAD y de regreso," 203, 223–224.

106. Gosovic, *UNCTAD: Conflict and Compromise*, 314–315.

10. World Monetary Problems and the Challenge of Commodities

1. Some in the developing world even took the process of détente between the Soviet Union and the U.S. to be an agreement between superpowers to carve up the world between them. See "Look Out—There's a Soviet Bear About," *Cosmos,* 10 May 1976, copy in Judith Hart Papers, 8/36, National Museum of Labour History, Manchester. See also Henry Kissinger's recollection that President Julius Nyerere of Tanzania "feared great-power collusion [in Africa] as much as he feared great-power conflict." See *Years of Renewal* (London: Weidenfeld and Nicolson, 1999), 936.

2. Club of Rome, *Limits to Growth: Report to the Club of Rome* (London: Pan Books, 1972).

3. Manuel Pérez-Guerrero Oral History, Dag Hammarskjöld Library, New York, 107–108.

4. U.S. State Department, incoming telegram from Adlai Stevenson on "UNCTAD—Appointment of Stanovnik," 11 June 1965. The background to this concern is stated in an earlier airgram from Dean Rusk to selected U.S. missions dated 23 May 1965: "DEPT recognizes that UNCTAD, as part of UN, of necessity will have certain Communists in its secretariat. However, we are anxious to do whatever feasible prevent their penetrating Latin American programs." Both documents are from DDRS.

5. "Manuel [Pérez-Guerrero] was a very successful diplomat, but I don't think that Manuel was the best choice for secretary-general of UNCTAD. Gamani Corea certainly was." Oral History Interview of Janez Stanovnik, 7–8 January 2001, 67, in the Oral History Collection of the United Nations Intellectual History Project, The Graduate Center, The City University of New York.

6. Nessim Shallon, "Early Years in the United Nations (1946–1963)," in *Peace through Economic Justice: Essays in Memory of Manuel Pérez-Guerrero,* ed. Mikio Tajima (Geneva: Victor Chevalier, 1988), 1–9.

7. Oral History Interview of Paul Berthoud, 9–10 January 2001, 103, in the Oral History Collection of the United Nations Intellectual History Project, The Graduate Center, The City University of New York.

8. Gosovic, *UNCTAD: Conflict and Compromise,* 314–315.

9. Sidney Dell to Kaldor 2 May 1969, Kaldor Papers, NK/3/112/36–37, King's College, Cambridge.

10. Meeting at State Department with John W. McDonald Jr. (director, Office of International Economic and Social Affairs, Bureau of International Organization Affairs) and others. See Diego Cordovez, "Notes on Meetings Held by Mr M. Pérez-Guerrero in Washington (12–13 November 1970)," 16 November 1970, Confidential Correspondence and Memoranda, 1970, UNCTAD Archive, Geneva.

11. B. T. G. Chidzero to Pérez-Guerrero, "Commodity Matters Which Might Be Discussed in Moscow," 20 May 1970, Confidential Correspondence and Memoranda, 1970, UNCTAD Archive.

12. "Stock-Taking Report on the Official Visit of the Secretary-General of UNCTAD to the USSR, 25–29 May 1970," Confidential Correspondence and Memoranda, 1970, UNCTAD Archive.

13. Diego Cordovez, "Notes on Meetings," 16 November 1970, Confidential Correspondence and Memoranda, 1970, UNCTAD Archive.

14. L. N. Rangarajan, *Commodity Conflict: The Political Economy of International Commodity Negotiations* (London: Croom Helm, 1978), 42–43.

15. Angus Hone, "The Commodities Boom," *New Left Review* 81 (September–October 1973): 82–92.

16. "Notes on the Meeting with Prime Minister Heath on 20 Oct. 1970," Confidential Correspondence and Memoranda, 1970, UNCTAD Archive.

17. C. R. Greenhill to R. Krishnamurti, "Discussions with Officials in Canberra," 16 June 1970, Confidential Correspondence and Memoranda, 1970, UNCTAD Archive.

18. See Raúl Prebisch, "The General Preferential System against the Background of Changing Views of International Trade," presented at UNCTAD III symposium, The Hague, January 1972, Judith Hart Papers, 8/33.

19. C. R. Carlisle to Pérez-Guerrero, "Conversations with US officials," 1 September 1970, Confidential Correspondence and Memoranda, 1970, UNCTAD Archive.

20. Cordovez, "Notes on Meetings," 16 November 1970, Confidential Correspondence and Memoranda, 1970, UNCTAD Archive.

21. His justification for devaluation was: "There is no longer any need for the United States to compete with one hand tied behind her back." See B. W. E. Alford, *Britain in the World Economy since 1880* (London: Longman, 1996), 286.

22. Rolf J. Langhammer and Andre Sapir, *Economic Impact of Generalized Tariff Preferences* (Hants, UK: Aldershot, 1987), 16–19.

23. David Henderson, "International Agencies and Cross-Border Liberalization," in *The WTO as an International Organization,* ed. Anne O. Krueger (Chicago: University of Chicago Press, 1998), 111, n. 12, emphasis added.

24. "I was always annoyed at those who argued that it [the Generalized System of Preferences] should be removed and that we go back to a level playing field, because it never amounted to anything anyway. Well, the reason it never amounted to anything was because those who subsequently argued for its removal did not do what Prebisch and his people at that time thought that they ought to do. It was not a general system. It was not general, and it was not a system, as the saying used to be. But that was a remarkable achievement, nonetheless, to get through the GATT authority. That was Prebisch." Oral History Interview of Gerald K. Helleiner, 4–5 December 2000, 65, in the Oral History Collection of the United Nations Intellectual History Project, The Graduate Center, The City University of New York.

25. Raúl Prebisch, "The General Preferential System," January 1972, Judith Hart Papers, 8/33.

26. "Notes on the Meeting with Prime Minister Heath on 20 Oct. 1970," and Dell to Pérez-Guerrero, "Copenhagen Meeting on the Link," 28 September 1970, Confidential Correspondence and Memoranda, 1970, UNCTAD Archive.

27. The word "money" is put in quotation marks because SDRs are not a medium of exchange between private actors (they are only for official transactions) and because, since SDRs must be reinstated after use, they function like credit.

28. Dell to Pérez-Guerrero, "Subcommittee Hearings," 29 May 1969, Interoffice Memoranda Vol. I: 1 January–31 May 1969, UNCTAD Archive.

29. Dell to Kaldor, 20 April 1970, Kaldor Papers, NK/3/30/64/10–11.

30. Dell to Pérez-Guerrero, "The 'Link,'" 13 May 1970, Confidential Correspondence and Memoranda, 1970, UNCTAD Archive.

31. Dell to Pérez-Guerrero, "Copenhagen Meeting on the Link," 28 September 1970, Confidential Correspondence and Memoranda, 1970, UNCTAD Archive.

32. Margaret Garritsen de Vries, *The International Monetary Fund, 1966–1971: The System under Stress* (Washington, D.C.: International Monetary Fund, 1976), 1: 607, n. 20 and 617–618.

33. John Williamson, *The Failure of World Monetary Reform, 1971–74* (Sunbury-on-Thames: Thomas Nelson and Sons Ltd., 1977), 91–95.

34. Pérez-Guerrero to Participants in the Taormina Discussions, 9 March 1971, Interoffice Memoranda 1971: 1 May to 31 Aug., UNCTAD Archive.

35. The Committee of Twenty (1971–1974) was appointed to design a replacement monetary system after the collapse of the Bretton Woods system.

36. Williamson, *The Failure of World Monetary Reform*, 143–147, 173–176.

37. Remarkable evidence of this divergence is the robust exchange between Sicco Mansholt, the president of the EC Commission, who had been at UNCTAD III, and Nixon's advisor for International Economic Affairs, Peter M. Flanagan, in *FRUS, 1969–1976*, III: 228–231.

38. "Echeverría produced certain reports on so-called state sovereignty and resources. Again, the impact was nil." Oral History Interview of Janez Stanovnik, 7–8 January 2001, 88.

39. See discussion of this issue in Chapter 9 of this volume.

40. For a discussion of the reasons why a G77 secretariat was needed, see Farooq Sobhan, "A Secretariat for the Group of 77?" in *Peace through Economic Justice: Essays in Memory of Manuel Pérez-Guerrero*, ed. Mikio Tajima (Geneva: V. Chevalier, 1988), 95–106.

41. Oral History Interview of Gerald Helleiner, 4–5 December 2000, 65–66.

42. Oral History Interview of Paul Berthoud, 9–10 January 2001, 67.

43. Sobhan, "A Secretariat for the Group of 77?" 103–104.

44. Oral History Interview of Gamani Corea, 1 February 2000, 30, in the Oral History Collection of the United Nations Intellectual History Project, The Graduate Center, The City University of New York.

45. Oral History Interview of Bernard Chidzero, 11 May 2000, 40–41 and 58–59, in the Oral History Collection of the United Nations Intellectual History Project, The Graduate Center, The City University of New York.

46. His main published work at this date was Alfred Maizels, *Industrial Growth and World Trade* (Cambridge: Cambridge University Press, 1963).

47. *GAOR*, Sixth Special Session, Plenary Meetings 2208–2231, Ad Hoc Committee Meetings 3–21, 30 January 1974, Agenda Item 7, Annexes (S-VI) 7, 11–12.

48. Ibid., 12.

49. *GAOR*, Sixth Special Session, 2212th Plenary Meeting, 12 April 1974, 6.

50. *GAOR*, Sixth Special Session, 2211th Plenary Meeting, 11 April 1974, 5–6.

51. These were the comments of the delegate from Qatar. *GAOR*, 2219th Plenary Meeting, 17 April 1974, 12.

52. *GAOR*, 2214th Plenary Meeting, 15 April 1974, 5.

53. *GAOR*, 2229th Plenary Meeting, 1 May 1974, 7.

54. Gilbert Rist, *The History of Development: From Western Origins to Global Faith* (London: Zed Books, 1997), 144.

55. UNCTAD, *The History of UNCTAD, 1964–1984* (New York: United Nations, 1985), 62.

56. For example, Sir Claude Corea, whose contribution to early UN debates on trade and development was discussed in Chapter 1 of this volume.

57. Oral History Interview of Gamani Corea, 1 February 2000, 10.

58. See Chapter 8 and Oral History Interview of Gamani Corea, 1 February 2000, 25–26.

59. Oral history Interview of Bernard Chidzero, 11 May 2000, 57.

60. "Man in the Hot Seat," *Cosmos,* 5 May 1976, copy in Judith Hart Papers, 8/36.

61. "Secretariat staff who had worked under Raoul [*sic*] Prebisch . . . felt by comparison a conspicuous absence of leadership and interest from [Corea]. . . . [H]e was not a man prone to the usual corridor diplomacy that may have resolved differences: button-holing delegates, holding meetings, in smoke-filled rooms, of those delegations with contentious views and the like in order to bring about concession and compromise." Christopher P. Brown, *The Political and Social Economy of Commodity Control* (London: Macmillan, 1980), 138.

62. Oral History Interview of Gerald Helleiner, 4–5 December 2000, 67. Of Perez-Guerrero it has been written that "his partisanship on the side of [less-developed] countries became more marked as the years passed culminating with his becoming Co-Chairman with MacEachen of Canada of [CIEC] from 1975 to 1977. He was then squarely in the camp of the Group of 77. . . . P. G. the universalist had become P. G. the defender of the economically under-privileged and the sometimes virulent opponent of industrialized countries' policies in United Nations conferences." Shallon, "Early Years in the United Nations," 9.

63. Gamani Corea, *Need for Change: Towards the New International Economic Order* (Oxford: Pergamon Press, 1980), 3.

64. Oral History Interview of Gamani Corea, 1 February 2000, 44.

65. "The NIEO period was the period when the UNCTAD forces really did try to compete and did try to lead. That was . . . the product of a new mood in the developing countries and they [the UNCTAD Secretariat] responded to it. . . . I think they were always perceived as a developing country organization, whereas the Bretton Woods institutions certainly were not. So when the mood kind of altered, they took full advantage of it and probably overshot in their aspirations in responding to it and trying to lead it and direct it." Oral History Interview of Gerald Helleiner, 4–5 December 2000, 60–61.

66. UNCTAD, "Outline of an Overall Integrated Programme," TD/B 498, 8 August 1974.

67. UNCTAD, "Problems of Raw Materials and Development: Note by the Secretary-General of UNCTAD," 1974, quoted in Gamani Corea, *Taming Commodity Markets: The Integrated Programme and the Common Fund in UNCTAD* (New Delhi: Vistar, 1992), 28–29.

68. Corea, *Taming Commodity Markets*, 37. Three minor elements of the Integrated Programme for Commodities and the Common Fund were long-term multilateral contracts, improved compensatory provisions for shortfalls in export revenue, and improvements to processing, distribution, and marketing.

69. Oral History Interview of Gamani Corea, 1 February 2000, 45.

70. Kissinger, *Years of Renewal*, 677–678.

71. Edmund Dell diary (entry for 31 July 1974), Edmund Dell Papers, Bodleian Library, Oxford. A liner conference is an agreement on freight rates between shipping companies.

72. Jim Callaghan (UK Foreign Secretary) told the British Cabinet that one reason for supporting the EEC was that "[t]he seventy-seven non-aligned countries which are now banded together at the United Nations have the potential to destroy the UN and we are better able to withstand them in a regional group." Tony Benn, *Against the Tide: Diaries, 1973–1976* (London: Arrow Books, 1989), 345 (entry for 18 March 1975).

73. Gordon Evans, "A New International Economic Order," 25 September 1975, unpublished paper, Judith Hart Papers, 8/22.

74. Talk by Valéry Giscard D'Estaing at the Ecole Polytechnique on 28 October 1975, Judith Hart Papers, 8/22.

75. Kissinger, *Years of Renewal*, 678.

76. *The Rambouillet Summit Declaration*, Cmd. 6314 (London: HMSO, November 1975).

77. Corea, *Taming Commodity Markets*, 48–49.

78. "Issues of UNCTAD IV: Consultation for Journalists, Cartigny/Geneva, 27 & 28 Feb. 1976," Judith Hart Papers, 8/36. Not all journalists were convinced: on 3 May 1976, the leader column of *The Guardian* repeated the jibe that UNCTAD really stood for "Under No Circumstances Take Any Decisions."

79. "A Report of the UNCTAD IV Encounter for Journalists, 29–30 April, Nairobi, Kenya," Judith Hart Papers, 8/37.

80. Kissinger, *Years of Renewal*, 941, 953.

81. "Summary of U.S. Initiatives at the Fourth United Nations Conference on Trade and Development (UNCTAD), in Nairobi, May 6, 1976," 2, DDRS.

82. *Proceedings of the United Nations Conference on Trade and Development: Fourth Session, Nairobi, 5–31 May 1976* (New York: UN, 1977), II: 122–123. (Henceforward *UNCTAD IV*.)

83. "Some Slept, Some Wept All the Way with Dr. K"; and Iain Guest, "Dr K Prepared for War!" *Cosmos*, 7 May 1976, copy in Judith Hart Papers, 8/36.

84. *UNCTAD IV*, I: 52. A similar reaction was felt by many other delegations; see Brown, *The Social and Political Economy of Commodity Control*, 93–94.

85. Corea recalled: "We were sitting at lunch [at the Nairobi conference], he was next to me and talking; and then he made a remark which was rather complimentary to UNCTAD. I responded that I was very happy to hear him say that because most of the comments we heard on UNCTAD from the United States were rather distant or even hostile. Then he asked me, 'What makes you say that?' I said, 'I don't know. Maybe they think we are too partisan, that we are trying to mobilize forces to impose pressures on them beyond what they could do.' He said, 'No, no, no. You should not talk like that. That is your job. You do what you are doing because if you do not do it there will be no one to do it. Don't have this kind of inhibition. You go ahead.' I was very encouraged by that remark. It may have been tactful lunchtime diplomacy, but I think he meant what he said. I interpreted it to mean, don't worry about us we can look after ourselves." Oral History Interview of Gamani Corea, 1 February 2000, 32.

86. Corea, *Taming Commodity Markets*, 53.

87. Iain Guest, "Huge Rich Split," *Cosmos*, 10 May 1976, copy in Judith Hart Papers, 8/36.

88. Corea, *Taming Commodity Markets*, 55–56.

89. Maggie Burns to Vic Sutton (telex), 17 May 1976, quoting telex from Nairobi from John Tanner of the same day, Judith Hart Papers, 8/36.

90. *UNCTAD IV*, I: 52.

91. Iain Guest, "Shameful Stalling by the West!" *Cosmos*, 28 May 1976, copy in Judith Hart Papers, 8/36.

92. Corea, *Taming Commodity Markets*, 57–60.

93. *UNCTAD IV*, I: 48.

94. Corea, *Taming Commodity Markets*, 61–63; *UNCTAD IV*, I: 54.

95. Memorandum from Richard N. Cooper to Jimmy Carter, 3 July 1978, 4, DDRS.

96. See Christopher Gilbert, "International Commodity Agreements: An Obituary Notice," *World Development* 24, no. 1 (1996): 1–19.

97. Charles A. Jones, *The North-South Dialogue: A Brief History* (London: Pinter, 1983), 56–61.

98. "I am very skeptical about the contention that if we hadn't had the group system but a better negotiating mechanism, we would have achieved dramatically better results. I just don't believe that. I think that the basic nut to crack—which never was cracked—was substantive. It was a problem of political will in the negotiation, and not a problem of the form of the mechanisms which were used for negotiating." Oral History Interview of Paul Berthoud, 9–10 January 2001, 80.

99. Memorandum of Richard N. Cooper to Carter, 3 July 1978, 2, DDRS.

100. Gamani Corea, *Taming Commodity Markets*, 80–81.

101. Brown, *The Social and Political Economy of Commodity Control*, 211.

102. Oral History Interview of Gerald Helleiner, 4–5 December 2000, 60–62.

103. Harry G. Johnson, "World Inflation, the Developing Countries, and an Integrated Programme for Commodities," *Banca Nazionale del Lavoro Quarterly Review* XXXIX, no. 119 (1976): 309–335.

104. "And there was a lot of hanky-panky going on. I remember a paper on the copper market generated for the OECD, I think it was, that did not produce the answers

that they wanted. So they just hired another consultant and got the one that they did want. It was very difficult to get middle-of-the-road analysis of the critical issues at that time." Oral History Interview of Gerald Helleiner, 4–5 December 2000, 60–62.

105. See Brown, *The Political and Social Economy of Commodity Control,* especially Chapter 5, "The Role of Economic Analysis," 139–165.

106. Ibid., 150.

107. "My gut reaction is that they [hired consultants] have been systematically . . . 'an extension of orthodoxy.' They have been used [by UNCTAD] to beef up your position or the direction in which you wanted your thoughts to go." Oral History Interview of Paul Berthoud, 9–10 January 2001, 91.

108. See Chapter 8 in this volume.

109. "As our work progressed, it became increasingly clear that much of the received wisdom [on commodity-price stabilization] was incorrect, and that the standard model used in most empirical work rested on such special assumptions as to make it of very limited use"; David M. G. Newbery and Joseph E. Stiglitz, *The Theory of Commodity Price Stabilization* (Oxford: Clarendon Press, 1981), v.

110. See Jere R. Behrman, "International Commodity Agreements: An Evaluation of the UNCTAD Integrated Programme for Commodities," in *Stabilizing World Commodity Markets,* ed. F. Gerard Adams and Sonia A. Klein (Lexington, Mass.: D. C. Heath and Company, 1978), 295–321; and Jere R. Behrman and Pranee Tinakorn, "The UNCTAD Integrated Program: Earnings Stabilization through Buffer Stocks for Latin America's Commodities," in *Commodity Markets and Latin American Development: A Modeling Approach,* ed. Walter C. Labys, M. Ishaq Nadiri, and Jose Nunez Del Arco (Cambridge, Mass.: Ballinger Publishing Company, 1980), 245–274.

111. David Henderson, "International Agencies and Cross-Border Liberalization: The WTO in Context," 111.

112. Gerald K. Helleiner, "The Refsnes Seminar: Economic Theory and North-South Negotiations," *World Development* 9, no. 6 (1981): 539–555.

11. The Conservative Counterrevolution of the 1980s

1. Willy Brandt, *My Life in Politics* (London: Hamish Hamilton, 1992), 341.

2. The bulk of the funding came from the Netherlands government; ibid., 342. Other contributions came from the German party-affiliated foundations, but "finance remained a permanent problem"; Barbara Marshall, *Willy Brandt: A Political Biography* (Basingstoke: Macmillan, 1997), 114.

3. Edward Heath, *The Course of My Life: My Autobiography* (London: Hodder and Stoughton, 1998), 608–610.

4. Independent Commission on International Development Issues, *North-South: A Program for Survival* (Cambridge, Mass.: MIT Press, 1980).

5. Brandt, *My Life in Politics,* 344. Here is a comment from a member of the UNCTAD secretariat: "Of all those reports, the Brandt report is the one which I found most useful, a penetrating analysis of the system as a whole and especially of the role of

the Bretton Woods institutions"; Oral History Interview of Paul Berthoud, 9–10 January 2001, 100, in the Oral History Collection of the United Nations Intellectual History Project, The Graduate Center, The City University of New York.

6. John Campbell, *Edward Heath: A Biography* (London: Pimlico, 1994), 720.

7. P. D. Henderson, "Survival, Development and the Report of the Brandt Commission," *IDS Bulletin* 12, no. 2 (April 1981): 72–81.

8. Campbell, *Edward Heath*, 719.

9. "I was extremely sceptical about mammoth conferences, or anyway more sceptical than many of my colleagues [on the commission], who expected great things of the United Nations"; Brandt, *My Life in Politics*, 345. Algeria, however, was opposed to CIEC-style meetings and made its presence at Cancún conditional on Willy Brandt being asked to stay away.

10. U.S. State Department, "The Mexico Summit: Sign of a New Era in North-South Negotiations?" Bureau of Intelligence and Research Report 166-AR, 22 June 1981, 1–2, DDRS.

11. Ibid., 3.

12. Margaret Thatcher, *The Downing Street Years* (New York: Harper Collins, 1993), 168–169.

13. Nevertheless, it was agreed that a new energy affiliate of the World Bank would be set up.

14. Thatcher, *The Downing Street Years*, 169.

15. Ibid.

16. Ibid., 170.

17. The Brandt Commission, *Common Crisis: North-South Cooperation for World Recovery* (London: Pan Books, 1983). This was the second report of the Brand Commission. "Brandt II made even less real impact than Brandt I, and the commission disbanded"; Campbell, *Edward Heath*, 721 (quoting Heath).

18. Brandt, *My Life in Politics*, 353.

19. Oral History Interview of Paul Berthoud, 9–10 January 2001, 82.

20. U.S. State Department, "The Mexico Summit," 7–8.

21. Paul Mosley, Jane Harrigan, and John Toye, *Aid and Power: The World Bank and Policy-Based Lending*, 2nd ed. (London: Routledge, 1995), 1: 6, Table 1.2.

22. "A Report of the UNCTAD IV Encounter For Journalists, 29–30 April, Nairobi, Kenya," Judith Hart Papers, 8/37, National Museum of Labour History, Manchester.

23. Gamani Corea, *Taming Commodity Markets: The Integrated Programme and the Common Fund in UNCTAD* (New Delhi: Vistar, 1992), 52.

24. Sidney Dell, "Preface," in *Policies for Development: Essays in Honour of Gamani Corea*, ed. Sidney Dell (Basingstoke: Macmillan, 1988), xiv.

25. UNCTAD, *The History of UNCTAD, 1964–1984* (New York: United Nations, 1985), 96.

26. For example, the UK ran a substantial balance-of-payments deficit in 1974 but returned to surplus by 1977.

27. The history of this episode is well told by Reagan's first budget director, David A. Stockman in *The Triumph of Politics* (New York: Harper and Row, 1986).

28. For a more detailed exposition of the role of the Thatcher and Reagan governments in triggering the debt crisis of the 1980s, see John Toye, "Britain, the United States and the World Debt Crisis," in *The Economic Legacy 1979–1992*, ed. Jonathan Michie (London: Academic Press, 1992), 11–33.

29. Nigel Lawson, *The View From No. 11: Memoirs of a Tory Radical* (London: Bantam Press, 1992), 520.

30. The findings of the OECD studies were summarized in Ian M. D. Little, Tibor Scitovsky, and Maurice FG. Scott, *Industry and Trade in Some Developing Countries* (Oxford: Oxford University Press, 1970). The OECD work on industrial project appraisal was in I. M. D. Little and J. Mirrlees, *Project Appraisal and Planning for Developing Countries* (London: Heinemann Educational, 1974).

31. This work was consolidated in W. Max Corden, *The Theory of Protection* (Oxford: Clarendon Press, 1971).

32. If the nominal tariff on an imported car is 100 percent, and (say) the power train constitutes half the value at world prices, importing the power train tariff free as an input into domestic car assembly would create an effective rate of protection of the domestic value added in car manufacturing of 200 percent.

33. Bela Balassa, *The Structure of Protection in Developing Countries* (Baltimore: Johns Hopkins University Press, 1971).

34. Henry J. Bruton, "A Reconsideration of Import Substitution," *Journal of Economic Literature* 35 (June 1998): 917 and n. 33.

35. Jagdish N. Bhagwati and Anne O. Krueger, *Anatomy and Consequences of Exchange Control Regimes* (Cambridge, Mass.: Ballinger, 1978).

36. Roger E. Backhouse, *The Penguin History of Economics* (London: Penguin Books, 2002), 305.

37. Albert Fishlow, "Review of *Handbook of Development Economics*," *Journal of Economic Literature* XXIX (December 1991): 1728–1737.

38. The term "urban bias" is attributed to Michael Lipton, who used it in *Why the Poor Stay Poor* (London: Maurice Temple-Smith, 1977).

39. Robert Chambers, *Rural Development: Putting the Last First* (London: Longman, 1983).

40. Anne O. Krueger, "The Political Economy of the Rent-Seeking Society," *American Economic Review* 64, no. 3 (June 1974): 291–303.

41. Deepak Lal, *The Poverty of Development Economics* (London: Institute of Economic Affairs, 1983).

42. The exceptions were IMF loans to the UK and Italy in 1976.

43. See Cheryl Payer, *The Debt Trap: The International Monetary Fund and the Third World* (New York: Monthly Review Press, 1974).

44. For the technical details of how this was done, see "Proposals for Liberalizing IMF's Compensatory Financing Facility," 25 August 1975, DDRS.

45. See John Toye, "Supra-National Compensation Schemes for Temporary Export Losses: a Critique," in *Development Economics and Policy*, ed. David Sapsford and John-Ren Chen (Basingstoke: Macmillan, 1998), 349–373.

46. Christopher P. Brown, *The Political and Social Economy of Commodity Control* (London: Macmillan, 1980), 99.

47. Tony Killick, *IMF Programmes in Developing Countries: Design and Impact* (London: Routledge, 1995), 58–65.

48. Graham Bird and Diane Rowlands, "The Catalyzing Role of Policy-Based Lending by the IMF and the World Bank: Fact or Fiction?" *Journal of International Development* 12, no. 7 (2000): 951–974.

49. H. W. Singer, "External Aid: For Plans or Projects?" *Economic Journal* LXXV, no. 299 (1965): 539–545.

50. Ibid., 540.

51. Nicholas Stern with Francisco Ferreira, "The World Bank as an 'Intellectual Actor,'" *STICERD Working Paper No. 50* (London: LSE, November 1993), 17, 24.

52. John Williamson, ed., *The Political Economy of Policy Reform* (Washington, D.C.: Institute of International Economics, 1994), 11–28.

53. These issues were further explored in John Toye, *Dilemmas of Development* (Oxford: Basil Blackwell, 1993).

54. Ian M. D. Little, "An Economic Renaissance," in *Economic Growth and Structural Change in Taiwan*, ed. W. Galenson (Ithaca, N.Y.: Cornell University Press, 1979).

55. Robert H. Wade, *Governing the Market* (Princeton, N.J.: Princeton University Press, 1990); Ha-Joon Chang, *The Political Economy of Industrial Policy* (London: Macmillan, 1994); Yilmaz Akyuz, ed., "East Asian Development: New Perspectives," *Journal of Development Studies* 34, no. 6 (1998): 1–137.

56. Stern with Ferreira, "The World Bank as an 'Intellectual Actor,'" 1, 13.

57. Ibid., 87, 102.

58. Ibid., 83, n. 51.

59. See J. Eaton and M. Gersovitz, "Debt with Potential Repudiation: Theoretical and Empirical Analysis," *Review of Economic Studies* 48, no. 2 (1981): 289–309.

60. I. Diwan and I. Husain, *Dealing with the Debt Crisis* (Washington, D.C.: World Bank, 1989), v, cited in Beatriz Armendariz and Francisco Ferreira, "The World Bank and the Analysis of the International Debt Crisis," in *The New Institutional Economics and Third World Development*, ed. John Harriss, Janet Hunter, and Colin M. Lewis (London: Routledge, 1995), 215–229 at 226.

61. See M. S. Khan and M. D. Knight, *Fund-Supported Adjustment Programmes and Economic Growth*, Occasional Paper 41 (Washington, D.C.: International Monetary Fund, 1985); and Diane Elson, ed., "Gender, Adjustment and Macroeconomics," *World Development* 23, no. 11 (1995): 1825–2017.

62. For example, D. Papageorgiou, M. Michaely, and A. Choksi, *Liberalizing Foreign Trade*, 7 vols. (London: Oxford University Press, 1991).

63. David Greenaway, "Liberalising Foreign Trade through Rose-Tinted Glasses," *Economic Journal* 103, no. 416 (January 1993): 208–222.

64. Ronald I. McKinnon, *Money and Capital in Economic Development* (Washington, D.C.: Brookings Institution, 1973).

65. Paul Collier and Jan Willem Gunning, "Explaining African Economic Performance," *Journal of Economic Literature* XXXVII (1999): 64–111.

66. Giovanni Andrea Cornia, Richard Jolly, and Frances Stewart, *Adjustment with a Human Face* (Oxford: Clarendon Press, 1987).

67. Mosley, Harrigan, and Toye, *Aid and Power.*

68. Tony Killick, *Aid and the Political Economy of Policy Change* (London: Routledge, 1998). This result is consistent with the history of abortive U.S. attempts to force Britain to abandon the System of Imperial Preferences in the GATT negotiations of 1947. See Richard Toye, "The Attlee Government, the Imperial Preference System, and the Creation of the GATT," *English Historical Review* 118 (September 2003): 912–939.

69. See Maurice FG. Scott, *A New Theory of Economic Growth* (Oxford: Oxford University Press, 1989); and Robert E. Lucas, "On the Mechanics of Economic Development," *Journal of Monetary Economics* 22, no. 1 (1988): 3–42.

70. This was described as "the splendid muckraking of the Invisibles Division, under Dr Malinowski's care, [which] has exposed the murky practices and evasions of the price-fixers in international shipping." See Michael Lipton, "UNCTAD SCHMUNCTAD?" *IDS Bulletin* 5, no. 1 (1973): 30.

71. UNCTAD, *The History of UNCTAD,* 183–185.

72. Details of all these activities are to be found in UNCTAD, *The History of UNCTAD.*

73. David Henderson, "International Agencies and Cross-Border Liberalization," in *The WTO as an International Organization,* ed. Anne O. Krueger (Chicago: University of Chicago Press, 1998), 124.

74. On carbon-emissions trading, the key individual was Frank Joshua; on debt-management systems, it was Enrique Cosio-Pascal.

75. Paul Berthoud commented: "I regret in the United Nations today a loss of intellectual capacity. Well, I don't want to minimize the importance of the *Trade and Development Report,* or *The Human Development Report.* Those documents are exceedingly interesting. But they are sort of cries in the desert." See Oral History Interview of Paul Berthoud, 9–10 January 2001, 124.

76. The *Trade and Development Report* budget is around $0.7 million, while the *World Development Report* budget is $3.5–5.0 million, and the English print runs are 12,000 and 50,000 respectively. See Robert Wade, "Showdown at the World Bank," *New Left Review,* second series, no. 7 (2001): 130, n. 10.

77. "UNCTAD VIII, in Cartagena, largely stripped UNCTAD from much of its responsibilities in respect of the international dimension of development. It decided for instance to look into the question of services, but the building up of services at the national level. Negotiations on services would be left to the WTO. Then UNCTAD IX, at Midrand, completed the dismantling." Oral History Interview of Paul Berthoud, 9–10 January 2001, 119–120.

78. Rubens Ricupero, "A Parallel Case: The Evolving Role of UNCTAD," in Carlos A. Margariños, George Assaf, Sanjaya Lall, John D. Martinussen, Rubens Ricupero, and

Franco Sercovich, *Reforming the UN System: UNIDO's Need-Driven Model* (The Hague: Kluwer Law International, 2001), 141.

79. John H. Jackson, *The World Trade Organization: Constitution and Jurisprudence* (London: Pinter, 1998), 27.

12. What Lessons for the Future?

1. J. Duncan Wood, *Building the Institutions of Peace* (London: George Allen and Unwin, 1962), 4.

2. Stinebower Oral History, 9 June 1974, 29–30, Harry S. Truman Library, Independence, Missouri.

3. R. H. Brand to Wilfrid Eady, 22 April 1946, R. H. Brand Papers, Bodleian Library, Oxford.

4. According to Hans Singer, "some of us in the United Nations never had any illusions" that a soft-loan facility would be set up in the UN rather than the World Bank. H. W. Singer, "The Terms of Trade Controversy and the Evolution of Soft Financing: Early Years in the UN," in *Pioneers in Development,* ed. Gerald M. Meier and Dudley Seers (Oxford: Oxford University Press, 1984), 298 and n. 52.

5. Oral History Interview of Janez Stanovnik, 7–8 January 2001, 55, in the Oral History Collection of the United Nations Intellectual History Project, The Graduate Center, The City University of New York.

6. J. Ann Zammit, "UNCTAD III: End of an Illusion," *IDS Bulletin* 5, no. 1 (January 1974): 3.

7. David Henderson, "International Agencies and Cross-Border Liberalization," in *The WTO as an International Organization,* ed. Anne O. Krueger (Chicago: University of Chicago Press, 1998), 111.

8. Oral History Interview of Janez Stanovnik, 7–8 January 2001, 14–16.

9. Mahbub al Haq, "An Economic Security Council," *IDS Bulletin* 26, no. 4 (October 1995), 20–27.

10. Louis Emmerij, Richard Jolly, and Thomas G. Weiss, *Ahead of the Curve? UN Ideas and Global Challenges* (Bloomington: Indiana University Press, 2001), 202.

11. Frances Stewart, "The Governance and Mandates of the International Financial Institutions," *IDS Bulletin* 26, no. 4 (October 1995): 28–34.

12. Sidney Dell, "Relations between the United Nations and the Bretton Woods Institutions," paper presented at the North-South Roundtable on the Future Role of the UN, Uppsala, 6–8 September 1989, 33.

13. See, for example, Robert Wade and Frank Veneroso, "The East Asian Crash and the Wall Street-IMF Complex," *New Left Review,* no. 228 (March–April 1998): 3–23; and Joseph E. Stiglitz, *Globalization and Its Discontents* (London: Allen Lane, 2002), 43–52.

14. Yilmaz Akyuz, "Towards Reform of the International Financial Architecture: Which Way Forward?" in *Reforming the Global Financial Architecture: Issues and Proposals,* ed. Yilmaz Akyuz (London: Zed Books, 2002), 8–12.

15. Stanley Fischer, "On the Need for an International Lender of Last Resort," *Journal of Economic Perspectives* 13, no. 4 (Autumn 1999): 85–104. The Meltzer Commission went so far as to recommend that the IMF discontinue all other forms of lending.

16. Yilmaz Akyuz, "Crisis Management and Burden Sharing," in Akyuz, ed., *Reforming the Global Financial Architecture,* 117–156.

17. For an account of these episodes, see Robert Wade, "The Greening of the Bank: The Struggle over the Environment 1970–1995," in Kapur, Lewis, and Webb, eds., *The World Bank: Its First Half Century,* II: 611–734.

18. Ngaire Woods, "Order, Justice, the IMF and the World Bank," in *Order and Justice in International Relations,* ed. Rosemary Foot, John Lewis Gaddis, and Andrew Hurrell (Oxford: Oxford University Press, 2003), 100–102.

19. See Michelle Miller-Adams, *The World Bank: New Agendas in a Changing World* (London: Routledge, 1999).

20. See A. P. Thirlwall, *Growth and Development,* 7th ed. (Basingstoke: Palgrave Macmillan, 2003), 729–735.

21. A. O. Krueger, "Whither the World Bank and the IMF?" *Journal of Economic Literature* 36, no. 4 (1998): 1983–2020.

22. As recommended by the Meltzer Commission, which reported in 2000 in *Report of the International Financial Institution Advisory Commission* (chair, Allan H. Meltzer).

23. See David Dollar and J. Svensson, "What Explains the Success or Failure of Structural Adjustment Programmes?" *Economic Journal* 110, no. 466 (October 2000): 894–917; and Paul Collier, "Conditionality, Dependence and Coordination: Three Current Debates in Aid Policy," in *The World Bank: Structure and Policies,* ed. Christopher L. Gilbert and David Vines (Cambridge: Cambridge University Press, 2000), 300–312.

24. The full text of the Understanding on the Settlement of Disputes is given in John H. Jackson, *The World Trade Organization: Constitution and Jurisprudence* (London: Pinter for Royal Institute of International Affairs, 1998), 145–169.

25. B. L. Das, *The World Trade Organisation: A Guide to the Framework for International Trade* (London: Zed Books, 1999), 7; Gary P. Sampson, "The World Trade Organisation After Seattle," *The World Economy* 23, no. 9 (2000): 1097–1117.

26. B. M. Hoekman and P. C. Mavroidis, "WTO Dispute Settlement, Transparency and Surveillance," *The World Economy* 23, no. 4 (2000): 527–528.

27. Das regards this as a "serious limitation" of the dispute-settlement understanding; *The World Trade Organisation,* 397. On these four major systemic deficiencies, see Hoekman and Mavroidis, "WTO Dispute Settlement," 529–532.

28. The fact that developing countries have started to bring disputes to the dispute-settlement mechanism does not detract from this point if, as seems to be the case, these are disputes mainly with other developing countries; Jackson, *World Trade Organization,* 74.

29. Formal justice is the equal application of the existing rules of an institution in its legal or administrative processes. See Herbert L. A. Hart, *The Concept of Law* (Oxford: Clarendon Press, 1961), 156–158; and John Rawls, *A Theory of Justice* (Oxford: Oxford University Press, 1972), 58–60.

30. After 1933, "There began to crystallize . . . a conception of 'economic order' that included norms, rules and frameworks for . . . decision-making on a multinational level—this to supply the deficiency of the liberal ideal, in which the key legal, institutional and 'moral' context was simply taken for granted"; Neil de Marchi, "League of Nations Economists and the Ideal of Peaceful Change in the Thirties," *History of Political Economy* 23, Annual Supplement (1991): 144.

31. Judith Goldstein, "International Institutions and Domestic Politics: GATT, WTO and the Liberalization of International Trade," in *The WTO as an International Organization,* ed. Anne O. Krueger (Chicago: University of Chicago Press, 1998), 139, 146–149. According to John G. Ruggie, "that multilateralism and the quest for domestic stability were coupled and even conditioned by one another reflected the shared legitimacy of a set of social objectives to which the industrial world had moved, unevenly but 'as a single entity.' Therefore, the common tendency to view the postwar regimes as liberal regimes, but with lots of cheating taking place on the domestic side, fails to capture the full complexity of the embedded liberalism compromise." "International Regimes, Transactions and Change: Embedded Liberalism and the Postwar Economic Order," *International Organization* 36, no. 2 (1982): 398. Ruggie borrowed the term "embedded" from Karl Polanyi, who used it in *The Great Transformation: The Political and Economic Origins of Our Time* (1944; reprint, Boston: Beacon Press, 1957). The treatment of tariff reductions as "concessions" which must be reciprocated is a residue of mercantilist thinking.

32. "Frequent investigations, even if the complaints are finally rejected, amount to a kind of harassment of the defendants because of the uncertainty and expenses such actions create"; P. K. M. Tharakan, "Political Economy and Contingent Protection," *Economic Journal* 105, no. 433 (1995): 1551. See also H. P. Marvel and E. J. Ray, "Countervailing Duties," *Economic Journal* 105, no. 433 (1995): 1583–1584; and I. M. Destler, *American Trade Politics: System under Stress* (Washington, D.C.: Institute for International Economics, 1986).

33. "Most governments . . . [negotiated] a 'voluntary' export restraint with the presumably reluctant exporter who had been previously 'softened' by threats of emergency action under GATT (Article XIX)"; Ruggie, "International Regimes," 411. The 1962 Cotton Textiles Arrangement (later the Multi-Fiber Agreement) was a voluntary export restraint administered by GATT, although it was clearly a new form of trade discrimination. See Harry G. Johnson, *Economic Policies towards Less Developed Countries* (London: Allen and Unwin, 1967), 21–22. After nearly forty years, it still has not been fully phased out, although it is now slated to end in 2005; see Sam Laird, "Multilateral Market Access Negotiations in Goods and Services," *CREDIT Research Paper No. 00/4* (Nottingham: University of Nottingham, 2000), 4–5.

34. Although anti-dumping duties and countervailing duties are analytically and legally distinct, they are linked in practice. In most U.S. cases, they are sought jointly by the complainant industry and granted together by the U.S. ITC. This is evidence that they are being used for protection and not for their original purpose of removing trade distortions. Marvel and Ray, "Countervailing Duties," 1587–1588.

35. Robert E. Baldwin, "Imposing Multilateral Discipline on Administered Protection," in *The WTO as an International Organization,* ed. Anne O. Krueger (Chicago: University of Chicago Press, 1998), 311.

36. See Robert Wade, *Governing the Market: Economic Theory and the Role of Government in East Asian Industrialization* (Princeton, N.J.: Princeton University Press, 1990); and Ha-Joon Chang, *The Political Economy of Industrial Policy* (Basingstoke: Macmillan, 1994), 91–129.

37. Y. Akyuz, H.-J. Chang, and R. Kozul-Wright, "New Perspectives on East Asian Development," *Journal of Development Studies* 34, no. 6 (1998): 30–32.

38. Alice Amsden argues that the new WTO rules leave ample room for developing countries to pursue industrial strategies that use subsidies. See *Industrialization under New WTO Law* (Geneva: UNCTAD, 2000). This is true, but the problem is that the developmental use of subsidies requires them to be temporary, selective, and conditional on the performance of the beneficiary firm (see W. H. Kaempfer, E. Tower, and T. D. Willett, "Performance Contingent Protection," *Economics and Politics* 1, no. 3 [1989]: 272). If the selection criteria include export performance, it will be difficult to avoid the charge of giving a "specific" subsidy.

39. Sampson, "The World Trade Organisation after Seattle," 1100.

40. Ibid., n. 7.

41. L. Alan Winters, "Trade Policy as Development Policy: Building on Fifty Years Experience," in *Trade and Development: Directions for the 21st Century,* ed. John Toye (Cheltenham: Edward Elgar, 2003).

42. Hans Binswanger and Ernst Lutz, "Agricultural Trade Barriers, Trade Negotiations and the Interests of Developing Countries," in John Toye, ed., *Trade and Development.*

43. "[P]owerful countries have far more bargaining chips to use . . . to leverage less powerful countries into 'agreeing' on the preferred 'consensus decision'"; Gary P. Sampson, "The World Trade Organisation after Seattle," 1101.

44. This would breach norms of nondiscrimination and universality.

45. The idea of asymmetric liberalism is captured in the following remark of Alan Winters: "The 1980s saw increased numbers of VERs [voluntary export restraints], tighter MFA [Multi-Fiber Agreement] restrictions, and more anti-dumping actions, but this did not prevent [liberal] opinion from covering trade policy when [industrial] countries offered development policy advice." L. Alan Winters, *Trade Policy as Development Policy: Building on Fifty Years' Experience* (Geneva: UNCTAD, 2000), 5.

46. Judith Goldstein, "International Institutions and Domestic Politics: GATT, WTO and the Liberalization of International Trade," 149–151.

47. Das, *The World Trade Organisation,* 425.

48. Peter Evans, "Economic Governance Institutions for a Global Political Economy: Implications for Developing Countries," in John Toye, ed., *Trade and Development,* 301–304.

49. See the discussion of special and differential treatment in M. Pangestu, "Special and Differential Treatment in the Millennium: Special for Whom, and How Different?" *The World Economy* 23, no. 9 (2000): 1285–1302.

50. Ibid., 1285–1289.

51. Christopher Stevens, "If One Size Doesn't Fit All, What Does?" *IDS Bulletin* 34, no. 2 (2003): 1–11.

52. Joseph E. Stiglitz, "More Instruments and Broader Goals: Moving Towards the Post-Washington Consensus," in *Joseph Stiglitz and the World Bank: The Rebel Within,* ed. Ha-Joon Chang (London: Anthem Press, 2001), 17–56.

53. These two episodes are chronicled in Robert Wade, "Showdown at the World Bank," *New Left Review,* second series, no. 7 (2001), 124–137.

54. Joseph E. Stiglitz, *Globalization and Its Discontents* (London: Allen Lane, 2002), 221, emphasis added.

55. "We should ask whether the net effects of a crisis might be positive, or whether the direct costs always—or usually—outweigh the indirect benefits of permitting policy reform after the crisis has past. . . . Is it possible to conceive of a pseudo-crisis that could serve the same positive function without the costs of a real crisis? What is the least unpleasant type of crisis that seems to be able to do the trick?" John Williamson, "In Search of a Manual for Technopols," in *The Political Economy of Policy Reform,* ed. John Williamson (Washington, D.C.: Institute for International Economics, 1994), 20.

Index

Page numbers in **bold** indicate entire chapters.

Office of Price Administration, 91

Ohlin, Bertil, 52

Ohlin, Göran, 152

oil prices, 231, 240, 243–44, 250, 256, 258–59

Olano, Francisco Garcia, 220, 221

Organization for Economic Cooperation and Development (OECD): Bellagio meeting, 190; debt crises, 259–60; multilateral institutions, 4; NIEO and, 232–33; objectivity, 253; origin, 167; political negotiation, 253; price stabilization, 253; SDR-aid link, 236; staff, 52; trade research, 261; UNCTAD and, 212–13, 218, 227; WTO and, 275, 290

Organization for European Economic Cooperation (OEEC), 52, 57, 166–67

Organization of Petroleum Exporting Countries (OPEC), 231, 240, 241, 244, 245, 248, 259–60

Ostpolitik, 255

"Outline of an Overall Integrated Programme," 251

Owen, David, 55, 57, 61, 67–68, 116, 147, 168, 173, 179

Pakistan, 3, 102, 166, 177

Palestine, 273

Palma, Gabriel, 142

Palme, Olof, 254

Pan-American Union, 139

Paris Peace Conference, 20, 32

Parsons, Maurice L., 58

Pasvolsky, Leo, 318n48

Pearl Harbor, 19, 21

per capita income, 111

Pérez-Guerrero, Manuel, 12, 231–38, 240, 242, 360n62

Perón, Juan Domingo, 156

Peru, 31, 102, 139, 140

Philippines, 44, 177, 245

planning, 106, 153–54, 354n63

Polak, J. J., 88

Poland, 235

Policy Framework Paper, 268

Policy Planning Council, 171

Political and Economic Planning (PEP), 61

political parties, 294

Pollock, David, 151, 207, 219

population growth, 111–12

Post War Price Relations in Trade between Under-developed and Industrialized Countries, 118, 122, 124–25

"Post-War International Economic Policy," 26–27

poverty reduction, 268, 270–72

"Poverty Reduction Strategy Paper," 268

Prebisch, Raúl: activism, 212; Alliance for Progress, 175–76; anonymous authorship, 124–25; Bretton Woods and, 43, 62, 278; business-cycle research, 88–90; commodity prices and, 217; consulting position, 312n15; Corea and, 242; criticized, 134; dependency theory and, 335n2; developing country doctrine, 206–209; Development Decades and, 138; development economics, 109; ECLA and, 111, 135, 140–41, 144–47, 158–62; economic theory and, 19; Furtado on, 339n85; GATT and, 201; on Great Depression, 141–42; Havana conference, 310n104; as historical source, 15; on industrialization, 138–39, 141, 160; on inflation, 155–56, 157, 340n107; influence, 136, 154; on Latin America, 158–62; leadership, 360n61; modernization and, 181; monetary reform, 222, 236; neoclassical economics and, 130–31; 1940s debate, 41–43; North-South dialogue, 10–12; personality, 315n10; Prebisch-Singer thesis, 111–16; on preferential trading, 226, 358n24; on price controls, 40; on protectionism, 261; resignation, 228; role in Argentina, 58–60; terms-of-trade issues, 125–28, 129, 333–34n91; Trade and Development Board, 209–10; travels, 192, 207; UNCTAD and, 184–96, 198–99, 202–205, **206–29;** WTO and, 288

Prebisch-Singer thesis, 111–16, 120–24, 126–34

About the Authors

John Toye is a political economist who has directed research on economic development at the Universities of Wales, Sussex, and Oxford. He has also worked as a British civil servant, as the director of a private consultancy company, and as a director of the United Nations Conference on Trade and Development. His previous books include *Dilemmas of Development* (2nd ed., 1993) and *Keynes on Population* (2000) and he has published numerous academic articles.

Richard Toye is Lecturer in History at Homerton College, Cambridge. He is the author of *The Labour Party and the Planned Economy, 1931–1951* (2003) and co-author, with Jamie Miller, of *Cripps versus Clayton* (forthcoming). He is currently researching a book on David Lloyd George and Winston Churchill. He was recently elected a Fellow of the Royal Historical Society.

About the Project

The United Nations Intellectual History Project was launched in mid-1999 to fill a gaping hole in the literature about the world organization. The project is analyzing the origins and evolution of the history of ideas cultivated within the United Nations family of organizations and of their impact on wider thinking and international action. Certain aspects of the UN economic and social activities have of course been the subject of books and articles; but there is no comprehensive intellectual history of the world organization's contributions to setting the past, present, or future international agendas.

This project is examining the evolution of key ideas and concepts about international economic and social development born or nurtured under United Nations auspices. Their origins are being traced and the motivations behind them as well as their relevance, influence, and impact are being assessed against the backdrop of the socioeconomic situations of individual countries, the global economy, and major international developments. Indiana University Press will publish fourteen books about human rights and economic and social ideas central to UN activity.

The project also has conducted in-depth oral history interviews with leading contributors to crucial ideas and concepts within the UN system. Excerpts are being published in a volume entitled *UN Ideas: Voices from the Trenches and Turrets.*

For further information, the interested reader should contact:
UN Intellectual History Project
Ralph Bunche Institute for International Studies
The CUNY Graduate Center
365 Fifth Avenue, Suite 5203
New York, New York 10016-4309
212-817-1920 Tel
212-817-1565 Fax
UNHistory@gc.cuny.edu
www.unhistory.org